TRAILS OF THE FRANK CHURCH - RIVER OF NO RETURN WILDERNESS; THIRD EDITION

Low clouds hang over the Middle Fork of the Salmon River.

Trails of the Frank Church-River of No Return Wilderness

Third edition, updated and expanded

by Margaret Fuller

TRAIL GUIDE BOOKS

TRAIL GUIDE BOOKS

Published by
Trail Guide Books
P.O. Box 148
Weiser, Idaho 83672

Updated and expanded third edition

Manufactured in the United States

Edited by Doug Fuller
Maps by Jerry Painter
Cover and book design by Matt TeNgaio of Trail Guide Books

All photographs by the author unless otherwise noted

Cover photograph: Fishfin Ridge in the Bighorn Crags

Library of Congress Catalog Card Number: 88-209615
Fuller, Margaret, 1935–

ISBN 0-9911561-3-9

Foreword

When Margaret asked me to write the foreword for her third edition of Trails of the Frank Church River of No Return Wilderness I was deeply honored. Margaret's dedication to wilderness trails has inspired me for many years. Her knowledge of Frank Church Wilderness trails, acquired through decades of hiking and exploration in the remote, rugged landscapes of the Frank has always impressed me.

This is the most comprehensive collection of information on hiking trails in the Frank Church Wilderness you will find.

Margaret published the first edition of Trails of the Frank Church River of No Return Wilderness in 1987. She has explored and hiked hundreds of miles in this wild, 2.3 million acre wilderness jewel since 1974, six years before the Central Idaho Wilderness Act was signed into law in 1980. Margaret's 50 year commitment to bringing us to the beauty and vastness of Idaho's wild areas has also been her passion.

Trails of the Frank Church River of No Return Wilderness is a testimony to Margaret's advocacy for wilderness trails and dedication to keeping trails open and accessible. In spite of diminished funding and few resources available for wilderness trail maintenance, she has continued to promote the importance of keeping wilderness trails open and accessible for hikers and equestrians.

Wilderness trails further wilderness values. Trails show us the way into wilderness, where we have opportunities to find solitude and experience renewal. A trail provides an opportunity for us to see ourselves as a momentary part of the wilderness.

Trails create human connections too. Through my work with the Selway Bitterroot Frank Church Foundation I have worked side by side with dozens of volunteers to restore access along the historic Marble Creek Trail on the west side of the Frank. This 25 mile section of the Idaho Centennial Trail runs through the heart of Idaho, from the Middle Fork of the Salmon River to the sites of old Thunder Mountain mines.

The work of opening and restoring the Marble Creek Trail, as well as other trails in the Frank Church River of No Return Wilderness, has brought many people together. When we come together to open a trail we also learn and share wilderness values and feel we are part of something much bigger.

I'm grateful to Margaret for her vision and decades of commitment to wilderness trails.

One of Margaret's favorite wilderness quotes is also one of mine:-

"Climb the mountains and get their good tidings. Nature's peace will flow into you as sunshine flows into trees. The winds will blow their own freshness into you and the storms their energy, while cares will drop off like autumn leaves." - John Muir

Sally Ferguson,
Executive Director of the
Selway Bitterroot Frank Church Foundation
www.selwaybitterroot.org
January 2020

TABLE OF CONTENTS

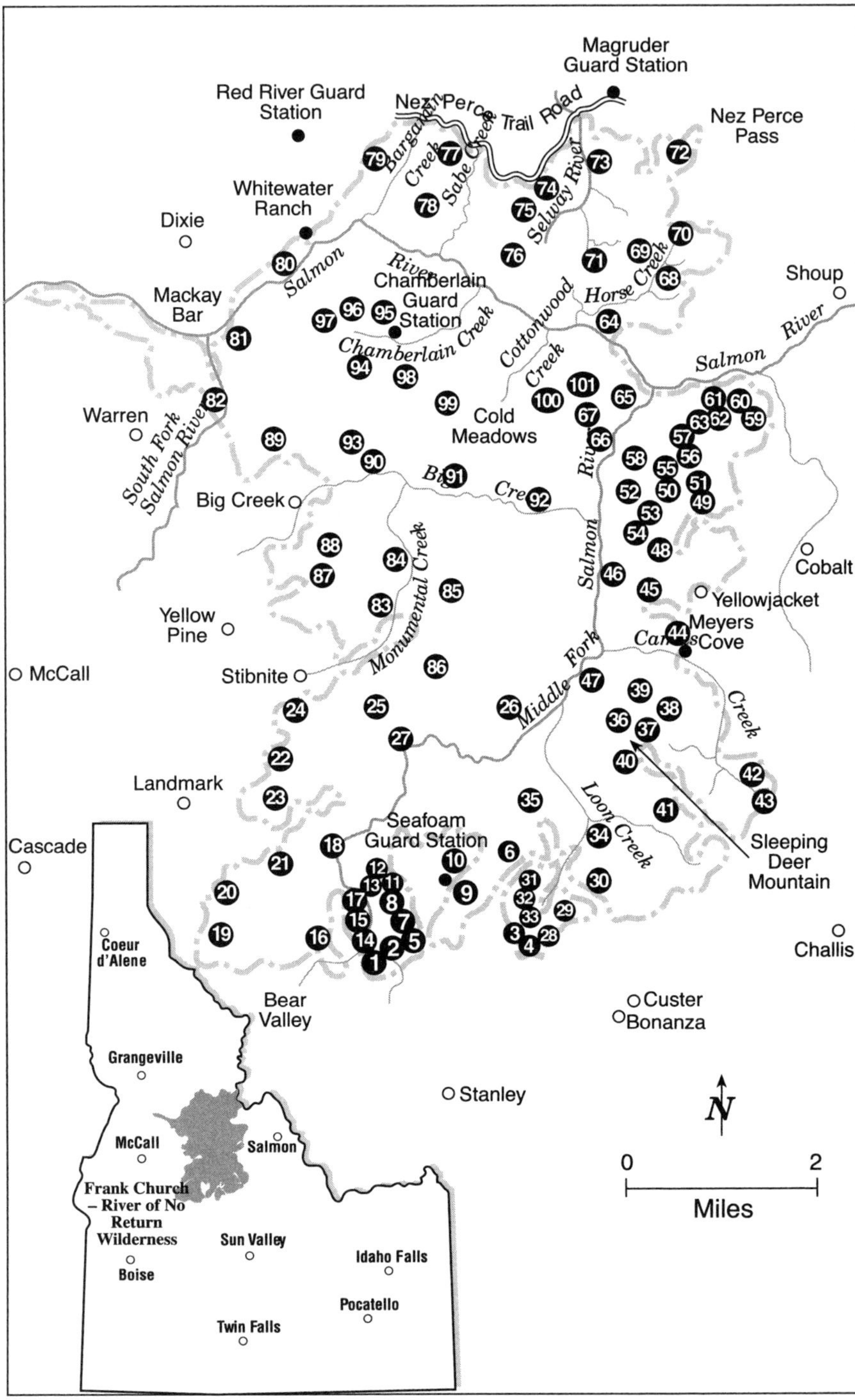
Magruder Guard Station
Red River Guard Station
Nez Perce Trail Road
Nez Perce Pass
Bargamin Creek
Sabe Creek
Selway River
Whitewater Ranch
Dixie
Salmon River
Chamberlain Guard Station
Chamberlain Creek
Cottonwood Creek
Horse Creek
Shoup
Mackay Bar
Salmon River
Warren
South Fork Salmon River
Cold Meadows
Big Creek
Cobalt
Yellowjacket
Yellow Pine
Meyers Cove
Camas Creek
McCall
Stibnite
Monumental Creek
Middle Fork Salmon River
Landmark
Loon Creek
Seafoam Guard Station
Sleeping Deer Mountain
Cascade
Challis
Bear Valley
Custer
Bonanza
Stanley
N
0
2
Miles
Coeur d'Alene
Grangeville
McCall
Salmon
Frank Church – River of No Return Wilderness
Sun Valley
Idaho Falls
Boise
Pocatello
Twin Falls

Introduction

The Salmon River and its tributaries have carved Idaho's Frank Church - River of No Return Wilderness into a maze of deep canyons and isolated peaks. From any high point a gigantic relief map of ridges extends to distant blue crags. Closer views yield gems like Fishfin Ridge, a row of triangular granite fins in the Bighorn Crags, and the more than two dozen hot springs that bubble along the rivers and creeks.

Darkening the deepest canyons, black lichen coats the pale tan granite of the Idaho batholith, relieved by splashes of chartreuse and orange lichens. The walls of the main Salmon River canyon rise 5,000 feet to summits of rose-gray rock, cutting off the northern section of the wilderness. Lined with 2,000-foot cliffs, the Middle Fork of the Salmon River wanders south from that canyon, dividing this wilderness into east and west. Where the Middle Fork joins the main Salmon, turquoise water blends into jade green. Blue and turquoise alpine lakes cluster at the heads of tributaries of the two rivers.

Ponderosa pine, Douglas fir or lodgepole pine color some canyons and ridges dark green. Others are feathered with the black and silver-gray of burned trees. Grasses and wildflowers soften outcrops and cliffs and brighten huge meadows, especially in Chamberlain Basin.

Bighorn sheep and mountain goat live on the peaks and in the canyons. Elk, deer and moose use the trails in this wilderness much more often than humans. The Salmon River and Middle Fork canyons are two of the most important wintering areas for big game in Idaho.

The steep walls and many rapids of the Salmon River Canyon led a National Geographic party in 1935 to nickname the river "The River of No Return." The Salmon River and Middle Fork canyons are the second- and third-deepest gorges in North America. Only Hells Canyon of the Snake River is deeper.

Because of the unusually large elevation differences in this wilderness (2,000 to 10,000 feet), trails climb and descend thousands of feet in only a few miles. Since many of the trails and access roads edge drop-offs, with a river or creek hundreds or thousands of feet below, travel in this wilderness is challenging, requiring both skill and patience. Many of the roads, trails and lookouts were built by the Civilian Conservation Corps (CCC) in the 1930s.

This wilderness is the largest in the continental United States. Its 2.3 million acres (3,678 square miles) contain parts of five national forests: the Bitterroot, Boise, Salmon-Challis, Nez Perce and Payette. The headquarters for the wilderness is at the Salmon-Challis Forest office, but the individual forest offices manage their sections of the wilderness, except for the Boise section, which is managed by the Salmon-Challis.

Historic ranches on private land and Forest Service ranger and guard stations receive mail and supplies by air at 24 airstrips. Within the Frank Church - River of No Return Wilderness, 37 historically significant buildings and more than 400 archeological sites have been identified. There are 54 parcels of private or state-owned land.

The Middle Fork and Main Salmon are two of the most popular places in the country for whitewater rafting and kayaking. These two rivers and the Selway, part of which is in this wilderness, are designated U.S. wild and scenic rivers. Few people hike or ride the trails, and even fewer fly into the backcountry airstrips, and most of the trailheads are served by rough dirt roads. Therefore, solitude is likely. Trout fishing here is usually excellent. The limit of six can be caught in an hour at several backcountry lakes, especially those off-trail or more than 20 miles from a trailhead. The Middle Fork and most of its tributaries are open to catch and release fishing only. To protect spawning salmon some creeks are closed to fishing part of the summer.

This guide covers only the Frank Church - River of No Return Wilderness, referred to in this book as the Frank Church Wilderness or the wilderness. All of the more than 850 miles of trail described in detail have been hiked by the author. Nearby hikes not in this wilderness are covered in Trails of Western Idaho and Trails of the Sawtooth and White Cloud Mountains by the author and Trails of Eastern Idaho by the author and Jerry Painter.

Purpose of this guide

The purpose of this guide is to give information to hikers and horseback riders about trails in the Frank Church - River of No Return Wilderness to encourage them to ride and hike there. The guide will also help rafting parties plan evening walks or side trips by trail to some of the scenic and historic spots. To help hikers avoid building new fire rings or burying cans, this book presents information on low-impact camping. To encourage respect for historical and archaeological sites, bits of history are included in the trail descriptions. To learn more about the history, read An Outline of the Cultural History of the Frank Church - River of No Return Wilderness Administered by the Payette National Forest by Peter Preston, published in 2001. Although this publication covers only part of the wilderness, it gives you an idea how complex the history of the Frank Church Wilderness is and how many people once tried to live within it.

Features in this area

WHITEWATER RAFTING

In 1805, when William Clark of the Lewis and Clark party, the first Europeans to view the Salmon River, saw Pine Creek Rapids, 15 miles below North Fork, he decided it was not navigable. The first known attempt to descend the Salmon was made in 1832. On that trip, Hudson Bay Company trapper John Work sent four men down the river in a skin canoe. On the 30th day of the trip, two of them drowned and the canoe was destroyed. The two survivors reached Walla Walla with the help of Nez Perce Indians. The first successful trips down the river were made in 1872, when John McKay floated down to placer mine and later that year when Col. W.W. DeLacy surveyed the river for the Northern Pacific Railroad.

The first documented trip down the Middle Fork of the Salmon was made in 1926 by Payette photographer and beekeeper Henry Wiedner, his son and a friend — in canoes. A second friend left the party at the beginning of the Impassable Canyon, 18 miles from the end, and hiked out 100 miles. To read about more early trips and the history of sites along the rivers, read River of No Return and The Middle Fork: A Guide by Johnny Carrey and Cort Conley.

Because more people want to float the rivers than the rivers can accommodate without sacrificing wilderness values, permits for rafters are required on the Main Salmon and Middle Fork. Permits are divided between private parties and commercial outfitters; commercial operators are allowed larger parties. The number of permits is limited and they are allocated by a computerized lottery system. Applications are accepted only between December 1 and January 31 the winter before by the Middle Fork Ranger District of the Salmon-Challis Forest for both the Middle Fork and Main Salmon. Permits are required year-round. Lottery permits are required from June 1 through September 3. Pre- and post-season launches may be requested by phone after October 1 on a first-come, first-served basis.

AIR SERVICE

A unique feature of this wilderness is its airstrips; some are open to the public and others are privately owned and open only to their owners. Air charter service is available for a reasonable fee in Cascade, McCall, Hailey, Challis, Grangeville, Salmon and Boise. In addition, Arnold Aviation in Cascade provides mail service all year, and hikers can arrange to have food sent ahead to a guard station or ranch. The rate in 2006 was a reasonable rate on the mail plane.

Pilots who are expert in mountain flying can fly in to some of the strips — but

Plane at Big Creek

many of these strips are marginal. There have been fatalities at all backcountry strips along the Middle Fork. Airstrips still on the map but not listed here are probably too dangerous . More information can be obtained from the Idaho Division of Aeronautics in Boise (address in Appendix.)

Public airstrips include Forest Service strips at Cabin Creek, Chamberlain, Cold Meadows, Indian Creek, Soldier Bar and Mahoney. State-owned strips are at Lower Loon Creek, Stonebraker Ranch, Taylor Ranch and Thomas Creek. Bernard is a Forest Service strip but is tricky. Chamberlain and Indian Creek are the least difficult. Public airstrips outside the Frank Church Wilderness that give access to it are Big Creek, Bruce Meadows and Upper Loon Creek. Avoid landing at any of the private strips.

WILDERNESS FIRE

Another unique characteristic of this wilderness is that in the last 20 years more than 60 percent of it has burned. However, don't be discouraged, for within the perimeter of most of the fires some vegetation stays green. The fires mean you can see better through the needleless and leafless trees, but some of the dead trees fall across the trails each year It is hard for the Forest Service to keep up with cutting them out, so you have to expect some downed timber. Where burned trees are close to the trail, any strong winds bring danger of falling trees. In addition, it means that the trails will not be in pre-fire condition because of the long-term need to repair damage from landslides and erosion caused by the fires.

The Frank Church Wilderness is therefore an excellent place to observe the fire cycle in forests. Because some older burns are still visible, such as the Mortar Creek Fire of 1979, you can get an idea of the recovery process, in which different species dominate burned areas in succession. Fire is a necessary part of ecosystems everywhere, and it is easy to see the need as you observe unburned lodgepole forests stacked chest high with dead, downed trees and burned forests where seedlings are getting established among a light scattering of logs. The length of the fire cycle varies with the kinds of dominant trees, from the 25-year average natural length between fires in forests of ponderosa pine to the 200- to 300-year length for lodgepole pine and even longer for coastal trees like western hemlock. The intensity of forest fires varies, so some areas within a recent burn may have no vegetation and only blackened spars left of the original trees, while others may have green as well as dead trees with grasses and shrubs showing new growth.

Most fires here are started by lightning, which is common in summer. Because the forests are mainly lodgepole whose natural fire cycle is 200 years or more, and because the area is so remote, fire suppression has had little effect on fire frequency or size. The main determinants are drought, hot weather, wind and the number of lightning strikes. Every summer there are more fires, so please call ahead.

Fires within this wilderness are allowed to burn for the good of the ecosystem if they do not leave the wilderness or threaten buildings or people. Forest Service personnel carefully monitor them to make sure they stay within certain parameters. During the fire season you should check with the forest ranger district office in charge of the area you plan to go into to learn if there are any fires that may threaten your progress. For safety stay out of areas with active burning because a small slow fire can change to a speeding inferno in hot, windy conditions. On the other hand, lightning strikes shouldn't make you nervous, for most don't start fires, and when they do it may take a few days before such a fire becomes a threat.

There have been so many fires since the second edition of this book came out in 2003 I have made no attempt to locate or name them. You should just expect to see some burned trees or logs wherever you go in this wilderness.

Wilderness Travel

DIFFICULTY OF HIKES

In this book, hikes are classified as follows:

Easy: up to 7 miles round trip, less than 1,000 feet elevation gain, no cross-country travel.

Moderate: 7-10 miles round trip, 1,000 to 2,000 feet elevation gain, little or no cross-country travel.

Strenuous: more than 10 miles round trip, more than 2,000 feet elevation gain, little or no cross-country travel or treacherous footing. Sections of trail of any length fall into this category if reaching that section requires more than one day.

Cross-country: some off-trail travel, but no major hazards or route-finding problems, may have some travel on non-system trail.

Expert: treacherous footing or route-finding problems, If any trail, it is non-system.

Elevation gain or loss: Means the number of vertical feet climbed or descended. Elevation lost is also listed as return climb because you have to climb back up it to get back to the trailhead.

ROUTE DESCRIPTIONS

Information at the start of each hike description includes round-trip or through mileage, elevation gain and loss, elevation of the highest point, topographic maps, GPS coordinates for the trailhead, hiking time and difficulty, and type of access road. Sections of trail more than one day from the trailhead have the mileage listed one way for that section. If the hike is a day hike, the time includes one hour at the destination. Unless the access road is completely four-wheel drive, trail mileage begins at the farthest point a two-wheel drive vehicle can reach. Except where the text mentions no water, trails have water available from side streams. The book begins with the hikes nearest to Boise because that is the closest population center, and except for the first sections, they are arranged counterclockwise around the perimeter of the wilderness.

Maps accompany each trail description, but where a trail along a creek is many miles long and only the first part of it is described in detail, the map may cover only the first part of the trail. The maps are drawn to the scale shown on each one, but they are not all the same scale. They are for planning purposes only; Forest Service maps are needed to find the access roads and U.S. Geological Survey topographic maps are

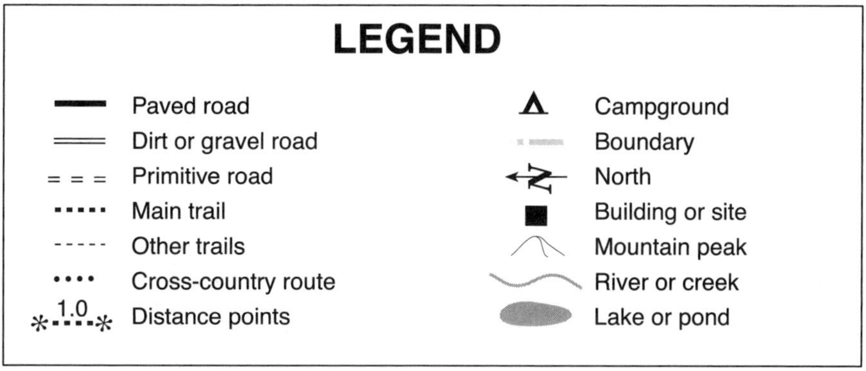

essential for following the trails. Maps published by the National Geographic are often not detailed enough.

TRAIL CONDITIONS

Trail conditions vary seasonally and by how often a trail is maintained. Maintenance occurs most often on the main trails and much less often on others. A few trails still on the maps are not maintained, and that means they have mostly disappeared. There are also some trails that are not Forest Service trails, called non-system trails.

Signs within the wilderness are being replaced gradually with ones with no mileages and only one destination in any direction. Most trails are signed, but you may find some trails without any signs even at the trailhead. Signing varies from year to year. Therefore, the hike descriptions do not say whether a trail is signed. Most roads and trails have Forest Service identification numbers but I have not included them, since their arrangement is often confusing. The best sources of information on trails and access roads are the ranger district offices, rather than the main offices of the forests. Note that Forest Service ranger stations keep office hours but guard stations do not. The districts' names, addresses and phone numbers are listed in the Appendix. In addition, some information on the forests is listed on the web sites for the forests. The roads and trails are mostly in poor shape compared to 1987 when the first edition of this book came out. Volunteers have done some maintenance but lack of funds and the many fires have left downed trees, landslides, deep ruts and ravines. You should always call the ranger district first to check the conditions.

ACCESS ROADS

In the wilderness inventory, the Forest Service classifies the unpaved access roads as suitable for sedans, high-clearance vehicles or four-wheel drive. This book follows that system, but is more cautious because the condition of unpaved roads varies with the season and maintenance. Traveling on unpaved roads when they are wet damages them and can cause a vehicle to slide off or bog down. Passenger cars should not be driven on high-clearance roads, but four-wheel drive usually isn't needed. However, condition of the roads is much worse than it was 15 years ago when the last edition of the book came out. I found a few roads impassable to my high wheelbase—four wheel drive vehicle due to two-foot deep gullies, so be sure to consult with the ranger responsible before a trip.

Road mileage given here is only approximate as odometer readings vary by a few tenths of a mile each time you drive a road in the same car. The odometers of different vehicles vary even more.

Because mud or snow can make dirt roads impassable, always ask a forest ranger about road conditions early in the season or when the weather is uncertain. A table of access road quality and opening and closing dates is in the Appendix. Be sure to carry emergency auto repair equipment, extra food, warm clothes and bedding in your vehicle, which should have a locking gas cap. It is essential to carry a wood saw and maybe an axe, too, in your car in case you find a tree has fallen across the road, which can happen any time. Roads listed as having exposure have steep drop-offs on one or both sides and may make passengers and drivers nervous.

TOPOGRAPHIC MAPS

Because several landmarks in some areas are similar, topographic maps are essential in this wilderness. They may be purchased from backpacking or office supply stores, or ordered online from the USGS Web site (address in Appendix). The maps needed for each hike are listed at the top of the hike description.

The whole wilderness has been mapped in the 71/2 minute size with a scale of 1 inch to 2,000 feet. Most have 40-foot contours, but on some the contours are 80 feet. Note that the U.S. Geological Survey omits all apostrophes in place names and the commas in elevations.

Detailed Forest Service maps of the Frank Church Wilderness, one for the south half and one for the north half of the wilderness are useful for finding and following the access roads, but the details are not as current as those on the maps of the individual forests: Salmon-Challis, Bitterroot, Nez Perce and Payette. These maps can be purchased from the Forest Service offices listed in the Appendix but are adequate only for driving the access roads, not for following the trails.

To help readers plan trips, the book contains maps in line-drawing format showing each hike. The maps also give the mileages of trail sections and the elevations of high and low points. Occasionally, where a trail along a creek is many miles long and only part of it is described in detail, the book map may not show all of it.

COMPASS USE AND CROSS-COUNTRY TRAVEL

To help you know where you are on the topographic map, you will want to orient the map with a compass at the beginning of a hike and several times during it.

To do this:

1. Turn the compass so the needle points to N on the dial.

2. Place the compass on the map, turning the map so the needle is parallel with the sides of the map and points toward the top of it.

3. Turn the map with the compass on it until the needle points to 19 degrees east of north to allow for the angle of declination here, the difference between magnetic north and true north. North on the dial is now north on the map and in your surroundings.

Hikers who have become thoroughly experienced in using map and compass on trails can safely attempt cross-country travel, but it's a good idea to begin with short, gently sloping routes in semi-open country.

Much of this wilderness has enough landmarks that a GPS unit is not essential, except in the parts that are mostly wooded hills, such as Chamberlain Basin — but an altimeter could be useful. If you rely on a GPS, be sure to take a compass and topographic map as a backup, because GPS units can fail. How to use GPS units is beyond the scope of this book.

TRAVEL WITH STOCK

Before being taken into the wilderness, horses, llamas, and pack goats/ like people, need conditioning to heavy exercise. Also, horses should have been picketed or hobbled or tied to a line strung between trees at home a few times and should have been introduced in advance to the feed. They should also have been trained to walk on trails carrying packs. These precautions apply to llamas and pack goats as well. Pack goats do well only with their owners.

A horse or llama outfitter can spot pack your gear into a base camp for a reasonable fee. This can make longer trips possible for families with young children. To obtain a list of packers, contact the Idaho Outfitters and Guides Association (address and Web site listed in Appendix).

The number of stock allowed in one party within the wilderness is limited, and in some areas fewer are allowed per party than in others. Some campsites have limits on the number of days. At some lakes only day-use is allowed for horses. Check with a ranger in advance on the current regulations for travel with stock.

When packing with llamas or goats, it is important to remember that horses are afraid of them. Someone should walk ahead so if a horse party appears, the animals can be led off the trail before the horses see them and spook. Pack goats bond with their owners and follow them, so it won't work to borrow or rent goats for packing.

Wilderness Manners

LEAVE NO TRACE CAMPING

A trashed and damaged campsite is no fun and the Forest Service uses our tax dollars to clean up after wilderness slobs, so well-mannered wilderness travelers leave no trace of their presence.

To practice leave no trace camping:

1. Carry out all unburnable trash, including foil freeze-dry food envelopes and trash left by others. Burnable items must be thoroughly burned. Remember that aluminum foil, plastic and glass will never break down into soil, and tin cans take hundreds of years to do so. In addition, trying to burn aluminum foil releases toxins into the soil that prevent plant growth. Glass and tin cans also cut people.

2. When possible, camp more than 200 feet from lakeshores and more than 200 feet from streams. Wash dishes or clean up with biodegradable soap or no soap in a pan away from the lake or stream and remember to dump the wash water at least 200 feet from the water source. If you want to swim or cool off in the lake or creek, do so only after washing and rinsing yourself.

3. Select a moderately used campsite with little or no ground cover more than 100 feet from a trail.

4. Use a backpack stove for cooking. Warming fires don't need a fire ring, unless one is already there. To prevent scarring the rock and to prevent pieces of the rock from flaking off and falling on you, never build a fire against a big rock. Before leaving a campsite, be sure your fire is cool to the touch. At an unused campsite, bury or scatter the cold ashes and charcoal. To keep from scarring the landscape, avoid building fires except in an emergency when you are above 7,000 feet, where plants and trees grow slowly,.

5. Gather only wood that is down and dead and is at some distance from camp.

6. Don't dig trenches around tents.

7. If there is no outhouse, dispose of human waste in a hole six to eight inches deep, at least 200 feet from the high water mark of rivers, streams or lakes. Fill in the hole after use and burn or pack out toilet paper.

8. Camp in small groups of fewer than 10 people.

9. Never take a shortcut between switchbacks. Doing so forms a path others will follow. Then water will run down the path and across the trail, creating a gully.

10. Leave dogs at home or be willing to clean up after them, and keep them out of the water source and away from other dogs, animals and campsites. Untended dogs often get their noses full of porcupine quills.

11. To avoid a fine and jail sentence, leave historical or archaeological objects as they are for researchers and visitors.

12. For more information on "leave no trace" camping, look under the LNT Web site (address in Appendix.).

LEAVE NO TRACE CAMPING WITH STOCK

1. Use lightweight food and equipment, so only a few animals will be needed.

2. To prevent grazing damage to high meadows, pack pellets or alfalfa cubes for feed in the high country. To prevent introducing noxious weeds, use only certified weed-free feed. This is required by state law and applies to hay, straw and compressed hay as well.

3. Picket and hobble animals 200 feet from camp or water. Picket only one and hobble the rest, or tie animals to a rope strung between two mature trees as a "high line." Avoid tying animals directly to trees, even temporarily. Water stock only where the creek crosses the trail, not at sensitive lakeshores.

4. Camp at least 200 feet off the trail.

PREVENTING THE SPREAD OF NOXIOUS WEEDS

In recent years, noxious weeds have begun to spread into the Frank Church Wilderness with increased visitor use. Noxious weeds are invasive, non-native species that spread rapidly, choking out native plants. You can obtain booklets about noxious weeds at Forest Service offices. Some of the worst offenders here are yellow star thistle and spotted knapweed.

1. If taking stock into the wilderness, use certified weed-free feed and brush animals before and after backcountry trips.

2. Check clothing and equipment for weed seeds before and after trips. If needed, sponge off or wash any suspect clothing or equipment.

3. Wash vehicles before and after each trip.

4. Avoid traveling through or camping in weed-infested areas.

5. Camp only at existing campsites and stay on established roads and trails.

6. Pull any noxious weeds you can identify and bag and pack out seed-producing parts.

AVOIDING USER CONFLICTS

Along the Middle Fork of the Salmon River, rafting parties are assigned campsites. Several large campsites are leased to outfitters under special-use permit. Hikers and horse riders may camp anywhere they wish. However, to avoid conflicts with rafters, it's a good idea to avoid camping at rafting campsites from June 15 to September 15. Rafting sites are the large sites right by the river marked on the river maps. They are often difficult to reach from the trail anyway.

Backcountry elk hunting often starts Sept. 15. Some of the large meadows, such as Cold Meadows and Chamberlain, become hunting centers for outfitters and private parties. During hunting season, to avoid being shot by mistake, wear bright-colored clothing (preferably fluorescent orange) and avoid camping or walking close to other groups.

Travelers on the narrower access roads will find far less traffic if they avoid driving in on Sunday or holiday afternoons and evenings and avoid driving out on Friday afternoons or evenings. Those going uphill have the right of way. A driver going downhill must back uphill until there is plenty of room for the other vehicle to pass. It is a good idea to use the horn on blind corners to alert oncoming traffic.

Safety

SAFETY PRECAUTIONS FOR REMOTE AREA TRAVEL

Because of the large size of the wilderness, 50 miles by 90 miles, and its remoteness, special safety precautions are needed. Whenever possible, travel with a minimum of three or four people, as help may be two or three days away. Because the weather is unpredictable and the trails steep, a trip may take longer than planned, so you need to allow one or two days' extra time and food. Always leave your itinerary and time of return with someone at home or at a ranger station, and then follow it. Following your planned itinerary can save your life and those of your companions.

Be sure to have adequate clothing and shelter for medical emergencies and for wintry conditions. Although it seldom snows in summer, it can. Consult a physician for recommended medicines. Take signaling devices such as smoke bombs or signal flares. As already mentioned, topographic maps and a compass are essential.

Before traveling any of these trails, be sure to check the elevation gain and plan accordingly. Several of these trails challenge even expert hikers because their elevation

A hiker crosses Elkhorn Creek before the bridge was built.

gains are 5,000 to 6,000 feet and the trails begin at the rivers between 2,000 and 3,000 feet where it is often 110 degrees in the summer.

TWELVE ESSENTIALS

Most hikers and horseback riders have heard of the 10 essentials, items you should always carry with you on backcountry trips, even on day hikes.

They are:

1. Extra clothes: long pants, sweater or pile or fleece jacket, insulated parka, rain jacket and pants, wool or pile hat, gloves, and wool socks (all are essential)
2. Extra food (On a weekend hike, what are you going to have for Monday's lunch?)
3. Pocketknife
4. Waterproof matches or butane lighter
5. Firestarter (jelly or stick type, or homemade paraffin cups)
6. First-aid kit, including pain prescription
7. Flashlight
8. Topographic map
9. Compass
10. Sunglasses

The author recommends two additional items:

11. Tent or tarp (tube tent or tarp for day hikers) – Nights are cold in these mountains.
12. Full water bottle and a water filter

CONDITIONING

You'll have much more fun if you are in good shape when hiking or backpacking. To make sure you are in good condition, try to exercise at least three times a week for several weeks or months before a backpacking trip. Activities such as running, bicycling, swimming, or even walking up the down escalator, should condition the heart and lungs. In addition, take short hikes on weekends. Lack of conditioning can lead to accident-causing fatigue or even a heart attack. (However, chest pains suffered in the backcountry may just be sore muscles from breathing more deeply than usual.) A regular exercise program done with care to increase the exercise gradually can overcome much back, knee or ankle trouble that might hinder hiking.

HIGH WATER

Because of their low elevation, trails along the rivers open when the high country is still under snow. As snow melts, the rivers and their tributaries rise, creating a life-threatening hazard for hikers. In years of heavy snow, the water can be 10 times the average flow. A hike taken in early May shouldn't be a problem if the trail is snow-free, but from mid-May to July 1 the water is high and dangerous.

Plan hikes along rivers and creeks in this wilderness only after the rivers have crested because a sudden spell of hot weather can cause an extreme rise in water levels. Information on the river levels can be obtained from the National Weather Service in Boise or online at the NOAA Web site (addresses in Appendix.) The Middle Fork, Big Creek, Camas Creek, Monumental Creek, Marble Creek, Horse Creek, the East Fork of Mayfield Creek, Warm Spring Creek, the South Fork of the Salmon River, Bargamin Creek, and Clear Creek trails have high-water problems.

CREEK CROSSINGS

Crossing a creek or river is a major danger in this wilderness. Before the trip, check the creek crossings on the topographic map and find out from a district ranger whether the crossings will be a problem at the time of your trip. Instead of crossing a dangerously high creek, detour to avoid that crossing. It is safer to walk across on gravel in a wide part of a stream than to cross on narrow, slippery logs or rocks. A treacherous log can be crossed more safely by scooting across in a sitting position if it lacks protruding branches.

When in doubt, wade. Keep your boots on to prevent cutting your feet; the water will numb them so much they can't feel sharp rocks. Because boots support the ankles, they are safer than river sandals or running shoes. You may wish to take off your socks to keep them dry; wet socks cause blisters. A stick will help you keep your balance. Face upstream and put the stick upstream ahead of your feet. Then walk sideways, moving only one foot or the stick at a time. Three people can cross using one another for support by making a circle facing inward and putting their hands on one another's shoulders. Once across, dump the water out of your boots, dry the insides with bandannas, and put socks and boots back on. The depth of water that can be crossed safely depends on its speed. Generally, it shouldn't be more than knee-deep. Deeper water requires mountaineering methods, equipment and training.

HYPOTHERMIA

The biggest danger in the outdoors is hypothermia, formerly known as exposure. To prevent this fatal drop in body temperature, wear warm clothes, including a hat and gloves; keep dry; eat often; and make camp in bad weather. The combination of wet clothing and wind can be fatal even at temperatures well above freezing. A full suit of rain gear is essential, including both a rain jacket and rain pants. In a down pour, even the best will leak, so underclothing should be wool, pile or have synthetic insulation. Cotton and down are useless when wet. You should carry a waterproof nylon poncho to wear over your rain suit in a drenching rain. Even the best rain gear will leak when it rains hard, and thunderstorms produce that kind of rain.

To get warm, first get out of the wind, because wind chill rapidly takes heat from the body. When someone in your party first feels uncomfortably cold, that is the time to stop, build a fire and make camp. Shivering that won't stop is the first sign of hypothermia and should never be ignored. Hot drinks help at this time, but at later stages may worsen the condition. A confused, stumbling person should be stripped and put into a warm sleeping bag with another stripped person.

To prevent getting this cold in the first place, wear long pants and carry a sweater or fleece top and an insulated jacket as well as your rain suit even on a beautiful day because weather can change rapidly here in the Northern Rockies. Take precautions to keep clothing and sleeping bags dry by carrying them in plastic garbage bags inside waterproof stuff sacks. At night, use a tent, and always put up the rain fly, because dew can dampen sleeping bags even when it doesn't rain.

HEAT HAZARDS

There are three heat-caused illnesses to watch for. The first is sunstroke, which can be fatal. Symptoms are hot, dry skin; temperature higher than 105 degrees and sometimes unconsciousness. Immerse the victim in cold water or cover with cool, wet cloths, then take him or her to a doctor as soon as possible.

Symptoms of less serious heat exhaustion are pale, moist, cool skin; a low temperature; nausea; and fainting. Have the victim drink lightly salted water and lie down until he or she feels better. If you haven't eaten recently you will be more likely to get this.

Dehydration causes thirst, slow motion, lack of appetite, dark urine, high fever and sometimes delirium. The victim should drink plenty of water. Dehydration can occur even in cold weather, with the loss of body moisture in exercise. In the cold, it makes hypothermia more likely. Hiking when hungry also makes heat exhaustion more likely.

Prevent heat problems by carrying and drinking three quarts to a gallon of water a day, resting in the shade in the hottest part of the day and wearing a hat.

EARLY SNOW

In this wilderness, it can snow any day of the year but usually doesn't during June, July, and August. In September, a snowstorm can close an access road for a few days, or even for the winter, so if traveling then, it is a good idea to leave extra food in the car. The Forest Service also recommends carrying tire chains and a shovel in your car.

Access roads likely to be closed by early snow are the Nez Perce Trail Road, the road to Crags Campground, the Sleeping Deer Road and the Beaver Creek - Loon Creek Road.

PURIFYING WATER

Water in this wilderness may have giardia, other bacteria, and even viruses, especially along the Middle Fork. Giardia, a protozoa found in animals as well as humans, causes diarrhea. The incubation period is six days to four weeks. To kill any bacteria, boil water for three to five minutes or run it through a water filter. Be sure to renew the filter unit as often as the directions say. Filters need to be able to trap various kinds of bacteria so the pores need to be less than 0.2 micron across. The best filters include iodine treatment to kill viruses as well.

The only way to be sure drinking water is safe is to filter it or boil it. In addition, remember to wash dishes and brush your teeth in boiled or filtered water.

INSECTS

Ticks are found in spring and early summer, but are usually gone by mid-July. To avoid ticks, wear tightly cuffed pants and long-sleeved shirts and inspect yourself twice a day. They usually don't start to burrow for several hours and seldom cause harm unless they burrow. In that case, consult a doctor after the trip. If insect repellent won't make it back out, a tick can be pulled out with tweezers or special tick tongs.

Another insect danger is fleas that carry bubonic plague. These are found on rodents such as chipmunks and ground squirrels, so avoid touching any. Also, don't pitch a tent near rodent burrows.

The stings of Idaho scorpions are similar to bee stings, so treat a scorpion sting as a bee sting. Be sure anyone allergic to wasp or bee stings carries medicine at all times.

The biggest problem is mosquitoes, which now carry West Nile virus, so be sure to carry insect repellent, a head net and a bug proof tent and cover up.

POISON IVY

Poison ivy grows in the main Salmon River and lower Middle Fork and South Fork canyons. You can recognize it by its shiny leaves in groups of three. To avoid its effects, change clothes and scrub with soap and cool water or a poison ivy preventive skin cleanser immediately after exposure. The preventive cleanser is more effective than soap. If possible, wash your clothes. If not, wear them when going through the poison ivy again, and save the other set of clothes to wear after bathing. Carry cortisone ointment to relieve itching if someone does get poison ivy.

BEARS

Few bears in remote areas such as this wilderness will come near people or campsites, especially since they are hunted. Almost all the bears you will see are black bears, but grizzlies may rarely be seen in remote areas Black bears have no shoulder hump like grizzlies, but they may be black, brown, blond or even have frosted-looking fur like that of grizzlies. There is a plan to reintroduce grizzlies here, but it is on hold.

To prevent bear problems, wrap food in plastic and enclose in a cloth sack, then at night or when leaving camp for a while, hang the sack in a tree 12 feet above the ground, five feet below a branch and at least five feet from the tree. (Hard-sided bear proof food containers for backpacking are available but are not necessary here.) You will want to take the additional precautions of cooking at a distance from your sleeping area and burning all food scraps, fish guts, and sanitary napkins or tampons or double-wrapping them in heavy plastic bags to carry out, and hanging them with you food. In an emergency a troublesome bear may be scared away with bear spray. Bears also don't like flashlights shone in their eyes.

SNAKES

Rattlesnakes are found along the Middle Fork, the South Fork, the Main Salmon and on the hillsides above Panther Creek as high as 7,000 feet, especially around springs. You are most likely to see snakes when it is between 80 and 90 degrees F, and when night temperatures are above freezing. If someone is bitten, try to stay calm. In many snake bites, little venom is injected, so there is no need to treat a person unless symptoms occur. If they do, apply a constricting band (not a tourniquet) and have the victim lie down. Do not use ice or the cut-and-suck method because of potential tissue and tendon damage. Get the victim to a doctor as soon as possible.

UNNECESSARY HAZARDS

Tradition emphasizes the use of axes, hunting knives and guns in the backcountry. With today's stoves and backpacking food, these things are more of a danger than a help to everyone except hunters. They also weigh a lot!

Another hazard is swimming in cold backcountry water. Unless you are an expert, avoid it or swim only in shallow water. To prevent falls in camp, use light-colored tent guy lines or mark them with bright-colored tape. To prevent falls on the trail, wear boots and use a walking stick or trekking poles.

WILDERNESS USERS' RESPONSIBILITY

Since there is unlikely to be anyone out in this wilderness to help in emergency, travelers here must take responsibility for their own safety. One way you can do this is by using common sense and not relying totally on the advice of anyone else, whether it is a friend, a Forest Service official or a guidebook writer. Another way is by learning as many wilderness skills as possible.

There is no attempt here to describe every hazard along the trails. Weather, water, snow, ice and mud change road and trail conditions, sometimes in only a few minutes. Also, individuals vary in their ability to follow poorly marked trails, drive rough access roads, and withstand steep climbs or heat and cold. When in doubt, always make camp or turn back. Also try not to get distracted from where you are putting your feet. And watch out for roots or sticks extending from the side of the trail.

FIRST AID

To prepare for a trip, you should take a course in first aid, including cardiopulmonary resuscitation, if you haven't taken one recently. You may also want to read and carry the most recent Red Cross textbook on first aid or a comparable mountaineering-oriented first aid book. If you are the one injured, your knowledge and reaction could be crucial.

The recommended method of treating injuries is in this order: breathing, bleeding, shock. If a victim is not breathing, be sure the airway is open, then give chest compressions. Then for bleeding, pressing directly on the wound is usually most effective, with a clean cloth if available. Don't move any victim unless he or she is still in danger. Instead, cover him or her with warm clothing and treat for shock.

After first aid, plan how to get the person to medical help. Send for help to evacuate someone who is seriously injured. A large party can carry out an injured person on an improvised stretcher, but this may not be practical in this wilderness because of distance. A person with a possible back or neck injury should not be moved anyway until professional help is obtained. Helicopter rescue is available, but the injured person or his family will have to pay the costs, unless they have life flight insurance. To arrange rescue, notify the nearest Forest Service office or county sheriff. The office handling the rescue in a particular area will be the sheriff of the county in which the emergency occurred even if you call for rescue with an electronic rescue device. The Frank Church Wilderness includes portions of Custer, Idaho, Lemhi and Valley counties.

EMERGENCY COMMUNICATION

Ranger stations and most private ranches in the backcountry may still have two-way radios. Some have internet. In an emergency, travelers who are able to reach a station or ranch can arrange to send a message or get help, if anyone happens to be home. Cell phones don't work in this wilderness except occasionally on a few high ridges around the periphery. Backcountry guard stations are at Lantz Bar, Indian Creek, Chamberlain and Cold Meadows, but remember that guard stations don't keep office hours. Private ranches are Taylor (University of Idaho), Root, Whitewater, Campbells Ferry, Mackay Bar, Sulphur Creek, Flying B, Loon Creek (Simplot), Middle Fork Lodge, Pistol Creek and a few ranches along the Main Salmon River. Most other ranches on the maps are no longer occupied. Guard or ranger stations at trailheads include Upper Loon Creek, Corn Creek, Big Creek, Magruder, Crags Campground and Seafoam. Others farther from the wilderness boundary, but along the access roads, are Elk Creek, Cobalt, Indianola, Red River, Dixie, Warren and South Fork.

Only a few lookouts are still staffed; and many shown on maps have been removed. Where buildings still exist, they are historic structures and should be respected as such.

Natural History

PLANTS AND ANIMALS

Five main vegetation types or plant zones typical of the Northern Rocky Mountain occur, varying with the terrain. On north- and east-facing slopes and canyons, higher-zone plants grow at lower elevations.

Along the lower Middle Fork and Main Salmon River canyons in the drier areas is a sagebrush-grass zone. Mountain mahogany, aspen, willow and cottonwood are the main trees.

The ponderosa (yellow) pine zone is found in the Middle Fork and main Salmon River canyons and in scattered locations elsewhere. Ponderosa pine is one of two of the most common trees in this wilderness. The other is Douglas fir. Quaking aspen is usually the only other tree in this zone, but there are many shrubs such as serviceberry, bitterbrush, and syringa.

In the next higher zone, the main tree is Douglas fir, with aspen, lodgepole, Rocky Mountain maple, water birch, ninebark and snowberry associated with it. Western larch, ponderosa pine and Pacific yew also grow in this zone in some places.

The cedar-hemlock forest is a zone not related to elevation but to climate. It occurs at the same elevation as the ponderosa and Douglas fir zones but north of the Salmon River. Some outposts of this forest are found south of the Salmon River in the western part of the wilderness. Western hemlock, red cedar and white pine are the major trees, with western larch and grand fir common also. White fir usually grows with the grand fir, and the two may hybridize. Grand fir is the only fir with a single, flat row of needles on each side of the twig. Deciduous trees in this zone are alder, birch, Rocky Mountain maple and bitter cherry.

The Engelmann spruce-subalpine fir zone occurs near the tops of mountains and ridges and along streams at elevations above 5,000 feet. The lodgepole pine is the most common tree in this zone. Whitebark and limber pine, which are almost identical in appearance, grow on exposed ridges. The cones of limber pine are bigger than those of whitebark (up to five inches long) and open while still on the trees. Mountain hemlock and subalpine larch are occasionally found in this zone. For example, subalpine larch is found on and near Salmon Mountain. In contrast to the smooth twigs of Western larch, subalpine larch has hairy twigs; the twigs holding the needles are swollen, like little volcanoes spewing needles. Sitka alder, aspen, bog birch and common juniper also occur.

Few peaks are above timberline, so there are only scattered bits of the highest zone, the alpine zone, with its tundra-like plants.

Beargrass is common both to the Douglas fir and spruce-fir zones. In the spruce-fir zone, grouse whortleberry usually grows under the lodgepoles. Pine grass is often the ground cover under Douglas fir. Common shrubs at lower and mid-elevations are ninebark, spirea, creeping barberry, bearberry and huckleberry.

There are several special plants in the Frank Church Wilderness. The Forest Service, Bureau of Land Management and the State of Idaho categorize rare plants in various systems and monitor how those species are doing. One of the most beautiful of the rare plants in this wilderness is the Lemhi penstemon, found in the sagebrush grassland. It is two to three feet tall and has intense cobalt blue flowers. Another is the candy stick, which has no chlorophyll. When the plant first comes up, it is brilliant white with red stripes. Later it fades to a rusty color. It gets nutrients from the mycorrhizae (threadlike soil fungi) that lodgepole pines also depend on. It is common along the coast and is disjunct in (skips to) central Idaho. The giant helleborine is a member of the orchid family found around hot and cold springs. Its flowers are greenish and purplish with purple lines. It too depends on a wild fungus that walking on will destroy, so avoid walking near these plants. Another rare plant is the cluster lady slipper, which differs from most other lady slippers in having greenish flowers.

There are 370 species of mammals and birds in the Frank Church - River of No Return Wilderness, including six endangered species: the grizzly bear (a rare visitor), the gray wolf, peregrine falcon, the northern bald eagle, the bull trout and the chinook salmon. The most common mammal is the Columbian ground squirrel and the most common bird is the robin.

Big game animals are mule and whitetail deer, elk, bighorn sheep, mountain goat, mountain lion, black bear and moose. Because no grazing is allowed in most of the area except by pack stock, elk and mule deer have an unusual advantage. Most wildernesses allow cattle and/or sheep grazing. This wilderness, with its deep canyons and many cliffs, is excellent habitat for bighorn sheep and mountain goat.

Some unusual animals and birds found here are the fisher, lynx and wolverine. Of these, the fisher is perhaps the most unusual. Closely related to weasels, it resembles a large black house cat with frosted fur. It travels through the branches of trees much of the time and can kill much larger animals.

Hikers will rarely see the Rocky Mountain wolf, but wolves have been reintroduced. You are more likely to hear a wolf than see one. Bison were still found along the upper Salmon River as late as 1880. Samuel Parker described the Indians hunting them there in 1835. The bison jump along Idaho 75 near Challis may have been used as recently as 1860.

Fish include trout, whitefish, smallmouth bass, arctic grayling, sturgeon, and the anadromous (migratory) chinook salmon and steelhead. The westslope cutthroat trout is found in the Middle Fork drainage in the summer only but may winter in the main Salmon.

The steelhead trout is the anadromous form of rainbow trout. Most steelhead spend two years in fresh water and two years in the ocean and then return to spawn in the stream where they originated. The spawning time is from March through June.

The endangered chinook salmon may migrate as much as 900 miles to spawn in the headwaters of the Salmon River. For this salmon, there are different runs at different times of the year. Chinook spend one year in fresh water and three years in the ocean. At Dagger Falls on the Middle Fork, chinook salmon used to be seen leaping from the water in their attempts to climb the falls.

The Middle Fork and its tributaries are open only to catch-and-release fishing. Please consult the annual Idaho Fish and Game Department fishing regulations booklet for more information. All bull trout, which are endangered, must be released no matter where caught. Bull trout are identified by a lack of spots on the dorsal fin.

GEOLOGY

In the Pre-Cambrian and Paleozoic eras (up to about 500 million years ago), seas and a few chains of volcanic islands covered the western states, including Idaho. The marine sediments deposited here were folded, metamorphosed and uplifted. Then in the Cretaceous period 100 million years ago, molten rock, called magma, rose beneath the sediments of what would become central Idaho, pushing them upward and then cooling underground. Later erosion and glaciation exposed this rock, now called the Idaho batholith.

Much of the rock of the mountains and canyons of the Frank Church - River of No Return Wilderness is part of this Idaho batholith. The batholith is one of the largest in the world, measuring 100 miles by 300 miles. The older rock around its edges was metamorphosed by the heat of the rising magma and folded and faulted by its pressure. As the molten rock cooled, minerals flowed out of it to form ore deposits in the surrounding older rock. The batholith itself is composed of granite and related rock.

South of the Salmon River in the central and eastern part of the wilderness, most of the exposed rocks are the Challis volcanics. They formed 50 million years ago, during the Eocene epoch, when composite volcanoes like those of the Cascades arose and began three million years of explosive volcanism. At this time, the Crags pluton (a small batholith) intruded, which when exposed and glaciated formed the Bighorn Crags. The explosive eruptions emitted thousands of cubic feet of volcanic material, followed by collapse. There are several eroded calderas in the Challis volcanics, near Twin Peaks and Thunder Mountain. The land within these calderas is now rolling upland, and the calderas have been lifted and folded, so they are difficult to recognize. Some vents such as the Lookout Mountain above Big Creek continued erupting until about 40 million years ago. Erosion within a caldera is especially noticeable along Monumental Creek where an erosion-resistant boulder has kept the soft volcanic ash from eroding away. In the nearby Thunder Mountain area, rapid erosion of the ash causes instability leading to frequent slides, such as the one in 1909 that dammed Monumental Creek, covering the town of Roosevelt with a lake. The 24 hot springs within the wilderness, concentrated in the Pistol, Loon and Indian Creek drainages of the Middle Fork, show that heat still lingers from formation of the Challis volcanics.

Rivers and glaciers have sculpted the batholith and the volcanic rock into a network of canyons and ridges. Glaciers existed only above 7,000 to 8,000 feet; their farthest advance is marked by U-shaped glacial canyons changing to the V-shaped channels cut by streams. Along the rivers and larger creeks, common features are the flat or gently rolling areas called river bars. They really are river terraces above the high-water line or alluvial fans at the mouths of the streams. The terraces were made by changes in the course of the river, and the fans by sand and gravel brought down by side creeks. In geology, bars, sometimes called point bars, are stream deposits on the inside curves of a meandering river and are usually not large enough to be labeled as bars on maps.

HISTORY

Several of the hike descriptions contain short histories of some of the settlements, mines and ranches of this wilderness. These are prefaced by the words "A little history."

In the Idaho Primitive area, now enclosed in the wilderness, there were 5,000 mining claims with a total production of $1,600,000. Most of the ore was low-grade and the veins short. Wilderness areas are no longer open to mineral entry, but some of the 20 patented claims are still active. Patented claims are those where the owner has received title to the land.

INDIANS OF THE CENTRAL IDAHO MOUNTAINS

Some experts believe that the Sheepeater Indians were a branch of the northern Shoshoni and others believe the Sheepeaters of the central Idaho mountains were a separate tribe. Since the Shoshoni named sections of their tribes by what they ate, the Tukudeka, (meaning sheepeaters) may well have been just a branch of the northern Shoshoni.

Although many Indian trails have been traced showing the Nez Perce and Northern Shoshoni traveled on both sides of the Salmon River and hunted in the mountains, the river was the boundary between the tribes, who were enemies except for brief truces when they traded each spring.

The Nez Perce belonged to the Plateau Indian culture and the Shoshoni to the Great Basin culture, so their languages were not closely related. In the Plateau culture, people formed communities of up to 100, who depended on fishing, root gathering and big game hunting. Great Basin people lived in isolated groups of fewer than 20 people and ate small animals, seeds, nuts, birds and insects. The religions of both cultures focused on vision quests for a totem spirit.

The culture of the Northern Shoshoni was much more like that of the Plateau culture and the Nez Perce than it was like that of their Shoshoni neighbors to the south: the Western Shoshoni, Bannack and Northern Paiute. The Northern Shoshoni and the Nez Perce both relied on fish, which they caught in fish traps, and they moved around during the year to hunt big game and to gather berries and camas and kous (biscuitroot) roots. Both tribes used poisoned arrows and bows made of mountain sheep horns that had been uncurled by heat. They made elaborate clothing of sewed leather resembling that of the Plains Indians. By about 1730, both tribes had obtained horses.

The Nez Perce practiced horse breeding and bred a distinctive variety of horse, the spotted Appaloosa. In winter, they usually lived in 150-foot-long pole lodges along rivers. They took daily baths in the rivers, even in winter.

The Northern Shoshoni lived in two- or three-family groups in four-pole skin tepees or conical grass or sagebrush shelters. Most had horses, but they did not do selective breeding.

The authors who have said the Sheepeaters were a separate tribe and not just a branch of Northern Shoshoni attributed the mountain sheep horn bows to them. They said they also made snowshoes out of the mountain sheep horn. Because of their tanning method (use of two animal brains per skin rather than one) their skins were superior to those of other tribes and were in demand for trade. House pit sites on Big Creek were occupied as early as A.D. 1300 by Northern Shoshoni thought to be Sheepeaters.

Because of the fame of the Sheepeaters, a war was named after them, although the group involved turned out to be of mixed tribes. The 1879 war led to the first European exploration of the Middle Fork of the Salmon River. Capt. R.F. Bernard and his troops came to the Middle Fork to search for a group of so-called Sheepeater Indians who were suspected of killing several settlers. In June 1878, Indians had killed Bill Mundy,

Jack Groseclose and Tom Healy in Long Valley when the settlers pursued the Indians to retrieve 60 stolen horses. Later that summer, settlers Dan Crooks and Boone Helm were killed in Round Valley. By the time some Chinese miners (from five to eleven of them, depending on the account) were killed on Loon Creek in February 1879, settlers were demanding the army go after the Sheepeaters. Then in April 1879, two settlers on the South Fork were killed. When Gen. Howard heard about the South Fork killings, he dispatched troops to find the murderers. Capt. Bernard and 60 cavalry left from Boise on May 31, and Lt. Henry Catley and 50 infantry started from Camp Howard at Grangeville.

Catley and his troops turned back twice because of heavy snow and then spent a month at Warrens, waiting for it to melt. Once across, they climbed to Chamberlain Basin, descended Crooked Creek on an old Indian trail into Big Creek, and continued down Big Creek where in places it was necessary to ride their horses across the faces of cliffs. In an ambush on July 29, about 2.5 miles upstream from the Taylor Ranch, two men were wounded and many men, including Catley, fell off their frightened horses. Over the protest of the second in command, W.D. Muhlenberg, Catley hadn't bothered to send any scouts ahead that morning. Also, after the ambush, Catley didn't give orders to go back and get the wounded, so First Sgt. J.F. Sullivan sent five men back to get them.

The next morning, when the troops attempted to escape onto ridges to the north, the Sheepeaters surrounded them on a grassy hill above Cabin Creek and set fire to it. The men saved themselves from the fire by setting a backfire, but were surrounded for 14 hours. When the men ran out of water, they drank from a keg of vinegar, so they named the hill "Vinegar Hill."

As soon as the moon went down that night, Catley and his troops abandoned most of their supplies and rode up the ridges to Cold Meadows. From there they retreated to the South Fork. One source said there may have been as few as 15 warriors surrounding Catley's troops.

Capt. Bernard and his men entered the Middle Fork country by way of Loon Creek, descending the Middle Fork as far as Cache Creek, but high water and deep snow on the peaks above forced them to turn back there, so they circled around to the South Fork by way of Warm Lake. Entering the country this way was easier because a toll bridge had been established across the South Fork in 1872.

On August 11, Catley's troops and eight cavalry and twenty Umatilla scouts under Lt. E.S. Farrow joined Bernard on the South Fork. Here, Bernard relieved Catley of his command and ordered him to stay with the pack train. The troops climbed over into Big Creek and descended the canyon. On August 14, A.G. Forse's cavalry of twenty-five men joined the group near Elk Summit. On August 16 or 17, Indians who were pursuing Catley's retreat, murdered James Rains at his South Fork Ranch. Catley was court-martialed in July the next year for his retreat and his conduct in the ambush, but President Hayes later set aside the verdict.

On August 20, at Soldier Bar just above Big Creek Gorge, about 15 Indians fired on Bernard's pack train, shooting Pvt. Harry Eagan in the legs. At the time of this attack, Bernard's troops and Farrow's scouts were looking for the Indians to the south. Amputation was performed, but Eagan died from loss of blood. The soldiers destroyed the 12 wickiups (brush or bark shelters built over a framework) in the Indian village at Soldier Bar, regained some of the loot taken from Catley's retreat and captured 35 horses. The Indians escaped down the Middle Fork into the cliff-walled section between Big Creek and the Main Salmon, which the soldiers named "The Impassable Canyon."

Because Bernard was out of supplies and his men were in poor condition, he and his troops went back to Loon Creek, where he asked for and received orders to return to Boise. It was no wonder: They had traveled more than 1,000 miles, and lost more than 60 horses and mules.

Lt. Farrow and the scouts returned to the South Fork for supplies and then retraced Catley's route into Chamberlain Basin. From there, Farrow pursued the Sheepeaters into the country east of Cold Meadows, above the Impassable Canyon. On the way, he discovered Black Lake. On September 17, Farrow captured two squaws, a papoose and a small boy in Papoose Gulch, a tributary of the Middle Fork. Hoping the woman could arrange a surrender of the Indians, he held the papoose hostage. When the woman left camp to try to contact her people, the baby's crying kept everyone awake most of the night. On September 20, the troops surrounded the Indians, but when they entered the camp, it was empty.

On September 25, Chief Tamanmo (War Jack) came to negotiate. War Department records show that Farrow captured 14 Indians at Big Salmon meadows September 21, and that 39 surrendered near the Middle Fork on October 1, and 12 more in Chamberlain Basin on October 6. They surrendered because they had lost most of their winter supplies. Those who surrendered were of mixed tribes, several of them refugees from the Bannack War of 1878. Only 12 were warriors, and they had only eight guns, two of which were muzzle loaders. The group was taken first to Fort Vancouver, and a year later to Fort Hall. However, a small group of the Sheepeaters stayed up in the mountains under Chief Eagle Eye until about 1900.

NATIONAL FOREST HISTORY OF CENTRAL IDAHO

In 1910, forest fires in northern Idaho as far south as Elk City took several lives. The fires were some of the worst ever in the United States. At that time the Forest Service considered grazing an important fire-control measure so they permitted overgrazing, but it didn't do them any good that summer.

In 1934, when refugees from the Dust Bowl set fires in order to get jobs as firefighters, Gov. H. Ben Ross had to declare martial law in Idaho national forests. Because of the manpower shortage in World War II, people were gathered off the streets to fight fires and checked for proper equipment as they boarded buses. Once, a woman checking equipment in Cascade realized that 13 different men had used the same pair of boots for inspection, handing the boots out the bus window to the next in line.

After World War II, firefighting became more organized. A five-man smoke jumper team was stationed in McCall in 1943. In 1947 a smoke jumper training center was established there and is still in operation. Helicopters were first used in firefighting in 1949 when one rescued an injured smoke jumper.

For fire control, the Forest Service also depends on a network of roads and trails. originally constructed by the Civilian Conservation Corps in the 1930s. When World War II broke out, one CCC crew was working on a road along the Main Salmon east from Riggins and another was working on a road west from North Fork. Because the CCC was disbanded when World War II began, the road was never completed.

HISTORY OF THE AIR SERVICE

Backcountry flying in central Idaho began in 1921 with a Forest Service airplane patrol with headquarters in Butte, Montana. In July 1928, a biplane from the Washington National Guard landed in a meadow at the Stonebraker Ranch in Chamberlain Basin, and later that year an airstrip was constructed there. However, newspaper accounts say that one of the two pilots, Nick Mamer, had been flying hunters in to Chamberlain since 1922.

Backcountry air mail and freight service became widespread in the 1930s. In November 1930, freighter George Stonebraker started delivering mail by airplane instead of dogsled to Yellow Pine, east of McCall.

The Chamberlain Basin airstrip was first used by firefighting crews in 1931. Myron McCoy, who grew up in Yellow Pine and worked for the Forest Service, especially remembers one pilot who worked on that 1931 fire. He said, "He had a little light plane. He took off and about two hours later he come walkin' back down the trail. He started up one a them cricks, and that hill just clumb faster'n he could. Had a little cut on his elbow and that was all."

The flying service begun by Stonebraker eventually was purchased by Bob Johnson, owner of a flying service in Missoula. In 1932 the Forest Service constructed airstrips at Big Creek, Soldier Bar and Bernard Creek. Johnson Flying Service began delivering mail to each backcountry ranch with an airstrip in 1950, and in 1952 the route was extended to the ranches along the main Salmon River.

According to the bill setting up this wilderness, none of its airstrips can be closed except in cases of extreme danger. Backcountry pilots in the Salmon River country have hauled everything from pianos to horses. When Bob Johnson brought in the cables for the suspension bridge at the Flying B on the Middle Fork of the Salmon, he wrapped them around the outside of the plane, which was illegal. One of the backcountry pilots, Ray Arnold, who obtained the mail contract in 1975, has been featured in the Wall Street Journal and Time.

FORMATION OF THE FRANK CHURCH - RIVER OF NO RETURN WILDERNESS

Controversy over how the mountain areas of central Idaho should be managed began as soon as the forest reserves were established in 1891 to limit certain activities in the forests. In 1931, formation of the Idaho Primitive Area was protested because of its effect on mining and logging. The controversy eventually came to a head from 1972 to 1979 in a great argument over how much wilderness should be established in the area.

A letter by Frank Church shows the typical feelings of Idahoans at the public hearings on the wilderness. "Each hearing proved both colorful and controversial, but none more so than the hearing which took place in Salmon, where one protestor, a cowboy wishing to show his displeasure and disdain, rode his horse into the hearing room, down the central aisle to where the committee sat up front and then out the side door."

By 1905 there were the Weiser, Seven Devils and Little Salmon forest reserves in Idaho, and the Bitterroot in Idaho and Montana. In 1906, Congress passed the Forest

Reserves Homestead Act, allowing the Secretary of Agriculture to grant homesteads within the forest reserves. In 1907 a bill transformed the forest reserves into national forests and provided that Congress alone had the power to create them. The first wilderness area in the United States, the Gila in New Mexico, was established in 1924, followed by establishment of the national wilderness system in 1926.

Attempts to give the central Idaho forests special protection began in 1927, when a party including Gov. H.C. Baldridge and S.C. Scribner, forest supervisor for the Payette Forest, and others, went into the Big Creek area to study it as a possible primitive area. As a result of that trip, in 1930 Baldridge and Scribner recommended a large area south of the Salmon River for a primitive area, and in 1931, Forest Service Chief R.Y. Stuart established the 1.1 million-acre Idaho Primitive Area. The Selway-Bitterroot Primitive Area north of the Salmon River was established in 1936.

In 1939, outdoor writer Ted Trueblood took his bride, Ellen, to the Idaho Primitive Area for their honeymoon and spent the entire summer and fall there. As a result, Trueblood became an advocate for designating the area wilderness.

In 1963, Secretary of Agriculture Orville Freeman announced the establishment of the Selway-Bitterroot Wilderness and the Salmon River Breaks Primitive Area, located between the Nez Perce Trail Road and the Salmon River.

The 1964 Wilderness Act required reclassification of 34 primitive areas as wilderness and the review of all roadless areas and wildlife refuges for wilderness. Use of aircraft or motorboats where already established could be continued subject to restrictions. In wilderness areas, the bill withdrew minerals from all forms of appropriation.

In 1968, Frank Church wrote and introduced the Wild and Scenic Rivers Act, which included the Middle Fork of the Salmon, and the bill passed. In 1972, when the Forest Service began reviewing the Idaho and Salmon River Breaks Primitive areas, Ted Trueblood formed the River of No Return Wilderness Council to lobby for wilderness for the entire area. In proposing a 2.2 million-acre wilderness, the council argued that there was little harvestable timber and the area contained the largest high-quality remaining river system in the country.

In 1974, President Nixon sent Congress a proposal for a 1.1 million-acre Central Idaho Wilderness. President Ford added Chamberlain Basin to Nixon's bill, but it was not enacted. In 1978, Secretary of the Interior Cecil Andrus brought President Carter to see the proposed wilderness on a Middle Fork float trip. In 1979, Church introduced Carter's 1.9 million-acre bill, the conservationists' 2.2 million-acre bill, and the timber industry's 1.3 million-acre bill.

On November 20, 1979, the Senate approved the Church-sponsored 2.2 million-acre bill. Of the Idaho delegation, only Church signed the House-Senate compromise. The final vote in Congress on July 1, 1980, added 105,600 acres to the Selway-Bitterroot Wilderness and 125 miles of the main Salmon River between Corn Creek and Long Tom Bar to the Wild and Scenic Rivers System. In 1984, the acreage was recalculated at 2.3 million acres.

The bill established a special mining area for cobalt along the west side of Panther Creek and allowed operation of the backcountry airstrips and of jet boats on the main Salmon, but not on the Middle Fork. Sen. Church said when the bill was passed: "The winners are the people of Idaho, who will have to enjoy the finest wilderness in the west, the crown jewel of the National Wilderness System."

FRANK CHURCH

Even when Frank Church knew his views would be unpopular in Idaho, he spoke out on many issues. As United States senator from Idaho from 1957 to 1980, he helped change American foreign policy, especially regarding the war in Vietnam. He led changes in laws affecting senior citizens, multinational corporations, the CIA, presidential powers, wild rivers and wilderness. Also, he served as floor manager for the Wilderness Act of 1964, and wrote the Wild and Scenic Rivers Act of 1968.

He spearheaded the formation of four Idaho wildernesses: the Sawtooth National Recreation Area and Wilderness (1972), the Hells Canyon National Recreation Area and Wilderness (1975), the Gospel Hump Wilderness (1978), and the one that now bears his name (1980).

Frank Church was known around the world for his leadership in foreign relations. In 1957, when new to the Senate, he helped Lyndon Johnson, then Senate majority leader, pass the first Civil Rights Act since Reconstruction by working for a compromise jury trial amendment. In 1959, Johnson appointed him to the Foreign Relations Committee.

In 1965, Church gave a speech on the Senate floor urging the United States to end the Vietnam War by negotiations. He was one of the first to speak against U.S. involvement in that war. After Nixon sent soldiers to Cambodia in 1971, Church co-authored the Cooper-Church Amendment, which outlawed expanding the war in Vietnam into Laos, Thailand and Cambodia. To help improve U.S. relations with Fidel Castro, Church made a controversial visit to Cuba in 1977. Because Church believed colonialism was poor foreign policy and that U.S. ownership of the Panama Canal was colonialism, he led the fight for ratification of the Panama Canal treaty in 1978. In 1979, when Sen. John Sparkman retired, Church became chairman of the Senate Foreign Relations Committee.

Another area of Frank Church's work as senator was the ethics of political power. In 1972, he became chairman of a temporary committee on multinational corporations. For three years this committee investigated abuses and covert political activity of U.S. companies in other countries. In 1973, he sponsored a law requiring financial disclosure of candidates during campaigns. In 1974, he was made chairman of the Senate Intelligence Committee, the "Church Committee," which investigated abuses of individual rights by the FBI, the CIA and the National Security Agency, and illegal activities of the CIA in other countries. The investigation led to laws prohibiting abuses and to a permanent Senate committee to oversee the CIA.

In 1971, Church became chairman of a special Senate Committee on Aging, a position he held for ten years. The committee succeeded in obtaining the capital gains exemption for those over 55 for the one-time sale of their homes and in obtaining a method of indexing Social Security benefits to the cost of living.

Frank Church first showed his political gifts at an early age. When he was in the eighth grade in Boise, he wrote the editor of the Capitol News defending the policies of Sen. Borah. His letter was so well-written the paper printed it on the front page. During high school, in the first National American Legion Oratorical contest, he won a $4,000 scholarship for a speech on the American way of life.

Also in high school, he met Bethine Clark at a student government convention. When Bethine's father, Chase Clark, was elected governor and the Clark family moved to Boise from Idaho Falls, Bethine and Frank became friends.

After high school, Church went to Stanford but soon enlisted. For his action in military intelligence in the Far East, he was awarded the Bronze Star. After World War II, he went back to Stanford, where he graduated Phi Beta Kappa. In 1947, he and Bethine were married on the steps of her family's summer cabin at Robinson Bar on the Salmon River near Stanley. (To avoid any possible conflict of interest, the ranch was sold out of the family about the time the Sawtooth National Recreation Area was formed.)

Frank Church, 1924-84
U.S. Senator 1957-80

That fall, Frank started law school at Harvard. When he developed back pains, he thought it was from the cold weather, so he transferred to Stanford Law School. At Stanford, the pains were discovered to be due to cancer. After surgery, the doctors gave him only six months to live, but one doctor believed X-ray treatments might work. The treatments and Bethine's nursing saved Frank's life, and he was able to graduate from law school in 1950.

After establishing his law practice in Boise, Church ran for the state legislature in 1952 but lost. From 1952 to 1954, he served as state president of the Young Democrats. In a five-man primary in 1956, he ran for the U.S. Senate. One of the five, Glen Taylor, was a former senator and Progressive Party vice presidential candidate. After beating Taylor by 170 votes, Church defeated Herman Welker, a supporter of Joseph McCarthy, in the general election. At 32, Church was one of the youngest men ever elected to the U.S. Senate.

In 1960, he was asked to give the keynote speech at the Democratic National Convention. In a race against Jack Hawley in 1962, Church became the first Idaho Democrat re-elected to the Senate. In 1968, Church ran against former Congressman George Hansen and was re-elected. He was re-elected again in 1974 when he opposed Bob Smith, an aide to Congressman Steve Symms.

In 1976, Church announced his candidacy for president in the old mining town of Idaho City where his grandfather had been a banker and where Sen. Borah had announced his presidential candidacy 40 years before. Church defeated Carter in the Nebraska, Oregon, Montana and Idaho primaries but withdrew in favor of Carter before the convention.

In the 1980 election, the National Conservative Political Action Committee targeted six liberal senators for defeat in the 1980 election, with Church as their main target. Exit polls televised nationally showed Church had lost to Steve Symms more than an hour before the polls in the Democratic stronghold of northern Idaho closed. The margin of defeat was less than one percent.

From 1981 to 1983, Church practiced international law in the New York law firm of

Whitman and Ransom. In January 1984, he had surgery to remove a blockage in his bile duct and then had chemotherapy for pancreatic cancer. Church died of cancer April 7, 1984, a few weeks after Congress officially changed the name of this wilderness to the Frank Church - River of No Return Wilderness. The vast sweep of high mountains and deep canyons of this wilderness are a fitting memorial to a man of his stature.

SALMON - CHALLIS NATIONAL FOREST
MIDDLE FORK DISTRICT
CAPEHORN AREA

1.

Collie Lake

Round trip: 7 miles
Elevation gain: 1,800 feet, elevation loss (return climb) 60 feet
Highest point: 8,200 feet
Topographic map: Cape Horn Lakes
GPS at trailhead: N 44 24' 4" W 115 12' 7"
At non-system trail: N 44 24' 43" W 115 10' 54.7"
Time: 6.5 hours for round trip; difficulty: moderate except that non-system trail may be hard to follow.

Access: From Stanley drive 18 miles northwest on Highway 21. Turn left (north) onto the improved dirt Seafoam Road. In 10 yards where the Seafoam Road turns right (east), keep straight ahead toward Lola Creek Campground and drive 1.5 miles to a parking area at the end of the road.

What you will see: The 400-foot cliffs of Capehorn Mountain overlook emerald green Collie Lake. Snow-filled chimneys divide the dark gray wall into three sections. Above the rest of the shore, short cliffs drop into the water from woods and talus. The trail to Collie Lake is not on any map and is a non-system trail (not a Forest Service trail), so it is not maintained.

Directions: From the transfer camp at the end of the road at 6,448 feet, hike along Marsh Creek until at 1.1 miles, a path turns left (southwest) 125 yards beyond a bridge over Collie Creek. Take this path over wooded knolls to a grassy area below black talus at 1.4 miles. After the trail edges the base of the talus, it returns to forest. At 1.6 miles it crosses a tiny stream, and at 1.8 miles reaches a gorge lined with willows.

The trail jogs to the right (west) away from the gorge, then follows it at a distance, climbing steeply. At 2.3 miles, the path threads talus 100 feet above Collie Creek, then goes over a stream and descends to Collie Creek in a marsh. After the route skirts more talus and turns right (north) up a hillside at 2.7 miles, it continues to climb the creek on the right side, with a view of the divide between Collie and Lola creeks.

When Collie Creek emerges from a ravine at 3 miles, the trail fords to the south (left) side, and follows it along a gentle wooded hillside, then goes over a rise to the lake (8,200 feet) at 3.5 miles. There are several campsites, but the one by the inlet is overused.

Collie Lake

2.

Marsh Creek to Big Hole

Round trip: 10 miles
Elevation gain: 200 feet, elevation loss (return climb) 500 feet
Highest point: 6,460 feet
Topographic map: Cape Horn Lakes
GPS at trailhead: N 44 24' 4" W 115 12' 7"
Time: 7 hours for round trip; difficulty: moderate
Access: From Stanley drive 18 miles northwest on Highway 21. Turn north onto the improved dirt Seafoam Road. In 10 yards where the Seafoam Road turns right, keep straight ahead toward Lola Creek Campground, and drive 1.5 miles to a parking area at the end of the road.

What you will see: Bear Valley Creek rushes through a narrow gorge and around an island to join Marsh Creek and begin the Middle Fork of the Salmon River. Just below this confluence is a deep emerald green pool called Big Hole, where 20-foot gray cliffs line a 100-yard-long pool downstream from a beach of golden sand.

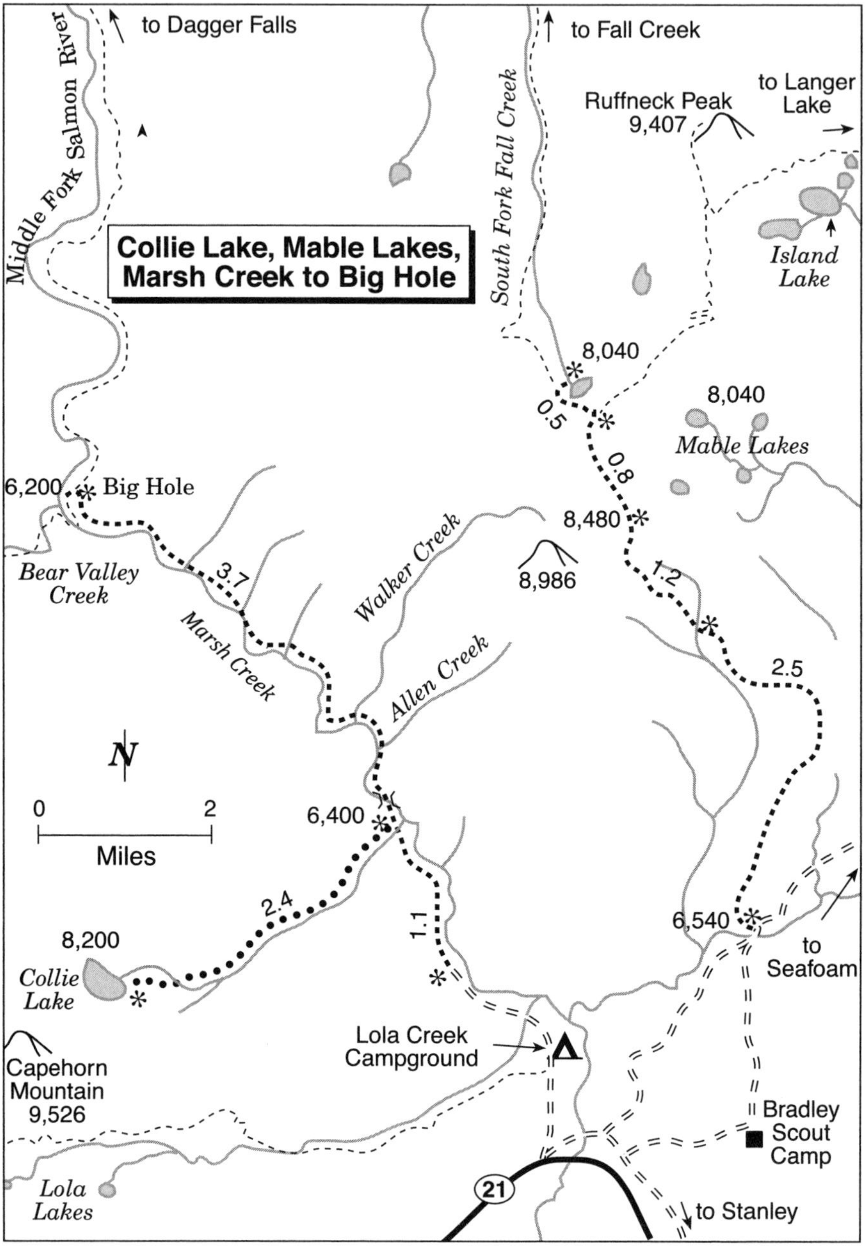

Directions: From the transfer camp at the end of the road at 6,448 feet, the Marsh Creek Trail winds through woods and talus across from cliffs to a bridge over Collie Creek at 1.1 miles. It spans Marsh Creek at 1.2 miles, then treads talus across from cliffs and towers. At 1.5 miles, the path enters lodgepoles, crossing Allen Creek at

1.7 miles and a bridge over Walker Creek at 2 miles. At 2.2 miles, the trail turns 90 degrees to the north and at 2.7 miles has been blasted into cliffs high above the creek. It continues on an open hillside, going across Dodge Creek in a ravine of alders at 3 miles and Huffman Creek at 3.5 miles. At 3.7 miles below wooded canyon walls, the trail skirts a long grass and willow flat beside the swirling, pale green creek. At 4 miles, it fords New Creek, then winds high above Marsh Creek across slabs and dynamited shelves. Just before the confluence of Marsh and Bear Valley creeks to form the Middle Fork at 4.7 miles (6,200 feet), a trail leads off up Bear Valley Creek to the left (west), but within a mile this trail fords Marsh Creek once and Bear Valley Creek twice.

From this junction, take the trail along the Middle Fork north to a second junction at 4.8 miles where paths lead west to Big Hole at 5 miles. From here the Middle Fork Trail runs north 10 miles on the east side of the river to a bridge over the Middle Fork at Dagger Falls. The Marsh Creek Trail is good for early or late season because of the low elevation, good road and bridges, and because it is above high water.

3.

Horseshoe Lake from Knapp Creek

Round trip: 18 miles
Elevation gain: 1,840 feet; elevation loss (return climb): 650 feet
Highest point: 8,640 feet
Topographic map: Langer Peak, Knapp Lakes
GPS at trailhead: N 44 24" 38.5" W 115 11' 05.8"
Time: 10 hours; difficulty: strenuous
Access: From Stanley drive 18 miles northwest on Idaho 21. Turn right (east) and drive 5 miles on gravel to .5 mile west of Cape Horn Guard Station. Turn right (northeast) and drive 3.1 miles on a dirt road to the Asher-Knapp Creek trailhead.

What you will see: Splitting the green water of Horseshoe Lake is a peninsula with an apple-green carpet of grouse whortleberry underlying lodgepoles and firs. Near the peninsula, willows cover a tiny island below a white and orange peak. The trail described here continues down Loon Creek to the Loon Creek Road. That section is covered in Loon Creek Trail to Horseshoe Lake.

Directions: From the Asher-Knapp Creek trailhead, the trail begins as an old road, now closed motor vehicles. At 1.4 miles, it crosses a side stream in a mud hole, and at 1.9 miles enters a 1-mile-long meadow. At 2.4 miles, opposite Elk Lake on the map, the meadow becomes marsh. A junction with a trail to Winnemucca Creek is at 2.8 miles at the end of the meadow. Beyond it, take the track that winds east through forest and grassy clearings.

At 5 miles, the old road becomes a trail just before a trail branches southeast to Valley Creek and Hindman Lake. From 5.6 to 6.3 miles, the trail is on the south side of the

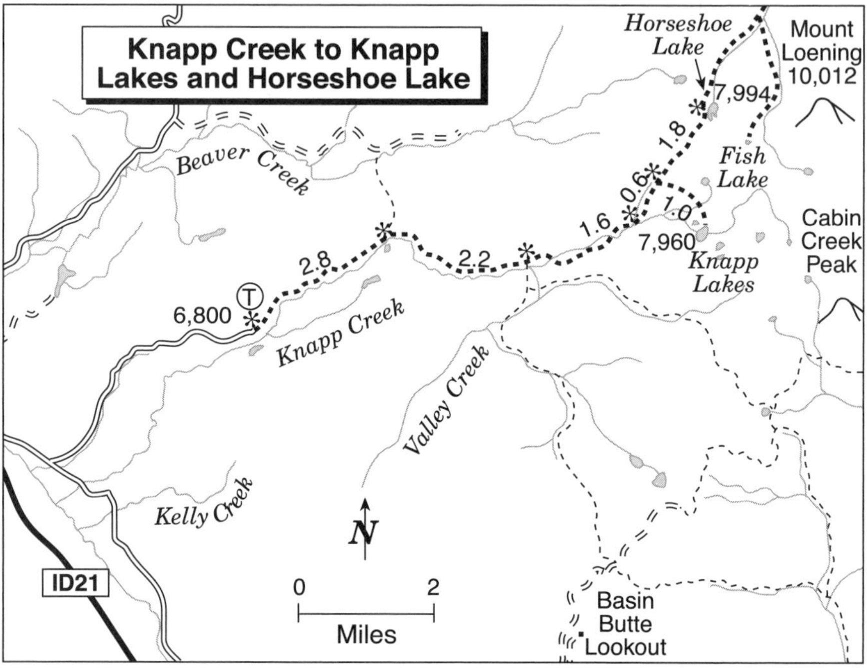

creek. At 6.6 miles on the north side of the creek, the trail crosses a side stream and enters the Frank Church Wilderness.

Beyond the stream, the trail climbs a wooded hillside to a burned-over ridge, with a view of the striped cliffs of Cabin Creek Peak. On this hillside, the side trail to Knapp Lakes turns off. Keep straight ahead on the main trail, which continues through trees to a divide at 8.2 miles. Beyond it and 640 feet below, Horseshoe Lake nestles in trees at 9 miles. Campsites are along the trail side of the lake at the lower end. This trail is listed as a National Recreation Trail, but because of wilderness policy is not signed that way.

4.

Knapp Lakes

Round trip: 16.4 miles
Elevation gain: 1,280 feet; elevation loss (return climb): 120 feet
Highest point: 8,080 feet
Topographic maps: Langer Peak, Knapp Lakes
Trailhead GPS: N 44 24” 38.5” W 115 11’ 5.8”
Time: 2 days: difficulty: strenuous

Access: See Horseshoe Lake from Knapp Creek to go by trail to the intersection of the Horseshoe Lake Trail with the side trail to Knapp Lakes where this description begins.

What you will see: An "X" created by cracks in the rock of the face of an unnamed peak marks the location of Knapp Lakes. East of the lakes, the crags of Cabin Creek Peak and the colorful ridge leading north to the Tango Peaks barricade the end of the canyon.

Directions: To reach Knapp Lakes, turn right (east) off the Horseshoe Lake Trail at 7.2 miles in an old burn. The turnoff is .6 mile beyond the crossing of a side creek in a gully. From the turnoff, follow cairns for 200 yards downhill through sagebrush. The trail may disappear, but go northeast along the edge of the burn for 150 yards and it will reappear. It drops downhill .7 mile from the sign and turns southeast across a creek. The trail continues along the base of a ridge, turns south below knolls, passing northeast of a pond. The first lake is one mile from the main trail and 8.2 miles from the trailhead. It has few campsites because of steep shores. To reach the upper lakes, use the topographic map to follow the streams between them.

SEAFOAM AREA

5.

Mable Lakes

Round trip: 10 miles to first lake
Elevation gain: 2,120 feet; elevation loss (return climb): 580 feet
Highest point: 8,480 feet
Topographic map: Cape Horn Lakes
Trailhead GPS: N 44 24" 44.3" W 115 8' 53.7"
Time: 8.5 hours for round trip; difficulty: strenuous
Access: From Stanley, drive 18 miles northwest on Highway 21. Turn north onto the improved dirt Seafoam Road. Drive 2.3 miles to the Halstead - South Fork Fall Creek trailhead at Beaver Creek.

What you will see: Broken cliffs bulge on the south side of the only one of the Mable Lakes on a trail. Above both ends of the blue-green lake, pale orange talus rises to short cliffs. The trail has a magnificent view of the jagged Sawtooth Range, the pale summits of the White Clouds and the striped, serrated top of Cabin Creek Peak. Six other small lakes within a mile of the first can be reached by cross-country travel. The area around the lakes burned in the 1998 Fall Creek Fire.

Directions: On the Seafoam Road, just beyond a bridge over Beaver Creek at 2.3

miles, take the Halstead - South Fork Fall Creek Trail. It begins as an old road that turns right (north) at a sign for the Bulldog Trail near the west end of the meadow. At .4 mile, it passes an old route coming from the east. The trail climbs the side of the canyon through sagebrush, grass and woods, and at 1.7 miles curves west along the side of a ridge. In the canyon of Halstead Creek at 2.5 miles, the trail crosses the creek near a camp, switchbacks northwest up a ridge, and at 3.5 miles turns north to a saddle on the ridge at 3.7 miles (8,480 feet) with a view of the Sawtooths.

Below to the right (northeast) is a basin with four of the seven Mable Lakes partly hidden in trees and snags. To reach them, follow the trail down to a meadow, then take a side trip cross-country. Beyond the meadow, the trail circles the head of the canyon of Shake Creek, heads up along a ridge and drops to another saddle at 4.5 miles. At this saddle a trail turns right (northeast) to go 2 miles to the Langer Lake-Ruffneck Peak Trail.

Keep straight ahead on the South Fork Fall Creek Trail (signed "Bulldog Trail"), which turns west across talus above the lake. Beyond the talus, a side path winds down to the shore at 5 miles (8,040 feet). The trail continues 3 miles down the South Fork of Fall Creek to the Fall Creek Trail.

The shores of this lake are steep, so camping is poor. A sixth lake is .5 mile to the west and over a 200-foot ridge. A seventh lake can be reached most easily from the trail to Ruffneck Peak from Langer Lakes.

6.

Pinyon Lake and the Beaver Creek - Loon Creek Road

Round trip: 2 miles
Elevation gain: none; elevation loss (return climb) 800 feet
Highest point: 9,240 feet
Topographic map: Pinyon Peak
Trailhead GPS: N 44 34' 46.7", W 114 54' 27.9"
Time: 3 hours; difficulty: easy but road has rocks and is very exposed
Access: A vehicle with four-wheel drive and a high wheelbase is required. From Stanley drive 18 miles northwest on Highway 21. Turn right (north) onto the improved dirt Seafoam Road and drive 5.5 miles to the Beaver Creek - Loon Creek Road. Turn right (east) on the narrow, primitive, very rocky road, driving past Feltham Creek Point and a spur road to Pinyon Peak Lookout. Park at the first sharp corner beyond the lookout road at 23 miles.

What you will see: The Beaver Creek - Loon Creek Road gives access to a trail to tiny, green Pinyon Lake, which nestles among western Labrador tea and red mountain heath below the talus cone of Pinyon Peak. The access road winds above deep canyons with splendid views of the Bighorn Crags, the Sawtooths and colorful mountains near

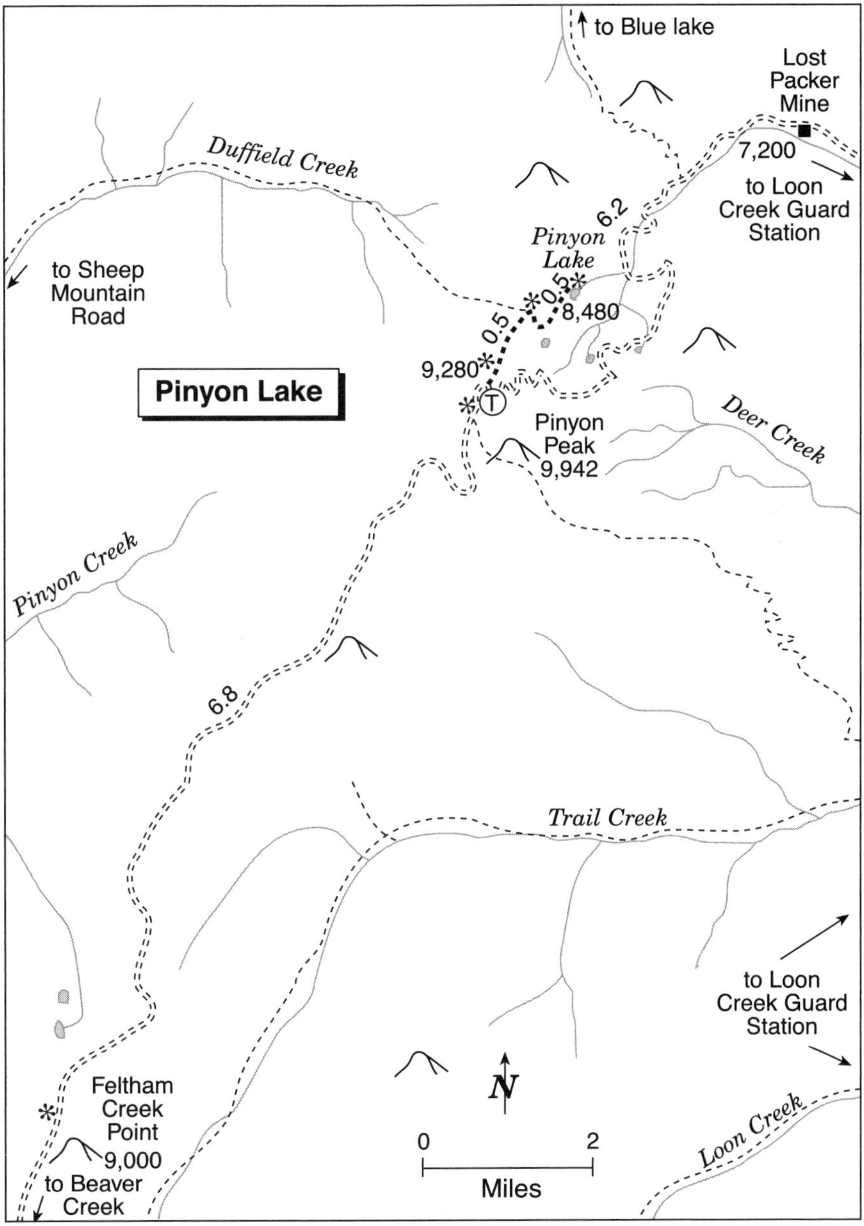

Loon Creek. This road is an adventure with sharp bends, knife edges, mud holes, drop-offs, and football- and softball-size rocks sticking up from its surface. Although the road is steep and narrow with blind corners, it is maintained. From Pinyon Peak Lookout, pink, tan, and blue-green ridges parade to the horizon in every direction. Toward Loon Creek from Pinyon Peak, the road passes tiny ponds, miniature subalpine firs and meadows of wildflowers.

Where the Knapp Creek Cutoff Trail turns right, 8.5 miles from Highway 21, the road fords a stream. Beyond a bridge over Beaver Creek at 11.9 miles, the road switchbacks 800 feet up to an open ridge at 9,000 feet. Beyond the turnoff for Feltham Creek Point at 16 miles, the road has been blasted out of rock and passes above Kidney Lakes and 2,000-foot drop-offs. At 20.5 miles the road traverses a knife edge, then passes a jeep trail to Deadfall Creek that is closed to motor vehicles. At 22.8 miles the side road to Pinyon Peak Lookout (9,942 feet) climbs 500 feet in a mile.

Directions: At the first sharp bend beyond the lookout at 23 miles, park and look for the Pinyon Lake Trail 50 feet beyond the bend. The trail, possibly signed Duffield Creek, turns north (left) down a bank, zigzags and then runs north along the side of a ridge. At a saddle at .5 mile a trail leads 9 miles down Duffield Creek to the Sheep Mountain Road.

From this saddle, the Pinyon Lake Trail hairpins south, then at .7 mile curves north around a pond through red mountain heath and talus. At 1 mile the path goes around the left (northwest) side of the small green lake (8,480 feet). The topographic map shows the trail continuing down the outlet of the lake to the road at Canyon Creek, but this is not evident on the ground. If you want to make your drive more interesting, continue east to Loon Creek.

A little history: That section of the road passes the site of the Lost Packer Mine, important in the history of the Loon Creek area.

The lode of the Lost Packer Mine was discovered in 1902 by Clarence Eddy. The summer after he developed the mine in 1904, he shipped out five railroad carloads of gold ore by mule train. With his earnings from the mine, he started newspapers in Custer and at Thunder Mountain, and published a book of his poems, Pinnacle of Parnassus. He was known for wearing a canvas suit instead of taking a tent and sleeping bag when prospecting, and carrying only a pick, and in his pockets a notebook, raisins and grapenuts.

A settlement named Ivers grew up around the Lost Packer. It was named for James Ivers, president of a Salt Lake mining company that bought the mine in 1904. After the company put in a wagon road over Loon Creek Summit that year. A 100-ton smelter, processed copper, silver and gold. By the time the mine closed in 1914, it had produced $700,000 worth of various metals.

7.

Langer, Island and Ruffneck Lakes

Round trip: 6 miles
Elevation gain: 1,280 feet; elevation loss (return climb): 120 feet
Topographic maps: Langer Peak, Cape Horn Lakes
Trailhead GPS: N 44 22" 50.4" W 115 3" 57.7"

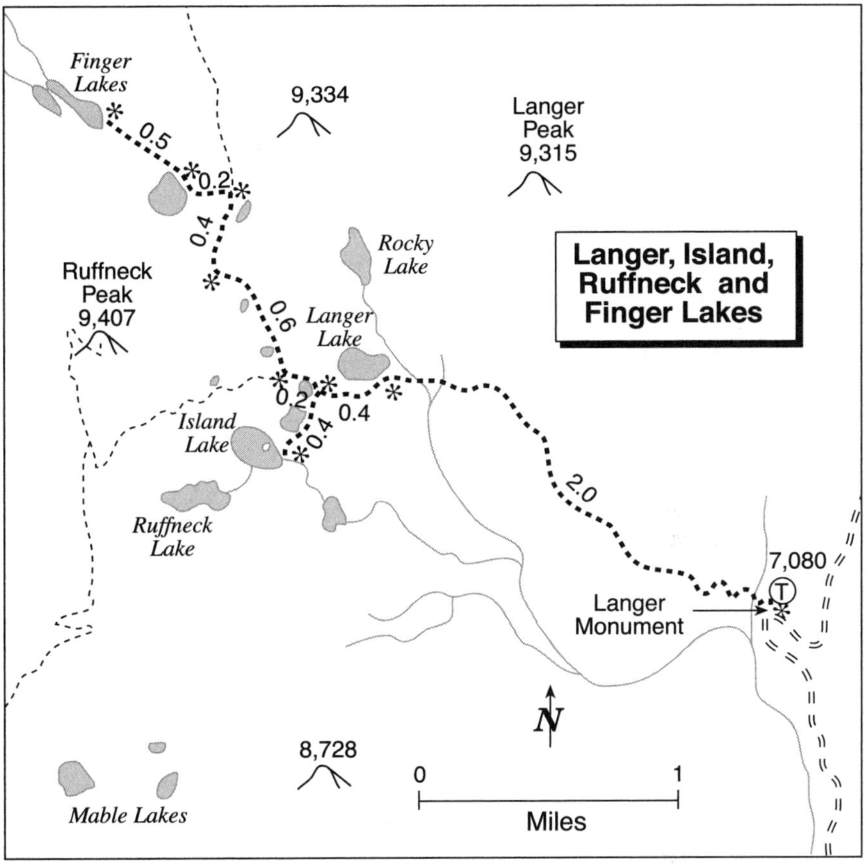

Time: 5 hours; difficulty: moderate; cross-country to Ruffneck Lake

Access: From Stanley drive 18 miles northwest on Idaho 21. Turn right (north) onto the improved dirt Seafoam Road and drive 7 miles to the Langer Monument trailhead.

What you will see: Like a white sugar cube, a lookout on the talus top of Ruffneck Peak overlooks blue-green Langer, Rocky, Island, Ruffneck and Finger lakes. At Island Lake, gray striped cliffs 200 feet high zigzag across from a mushroom-cap island. Talus surrounds the milky-turquoise water of Ruffneck Lake, which partly dries up by August.

The trail begins at the Langer Monument, which commemorates the death of a district ranger and two others in a World War II air search for a downed pilot.

A little history: About a mile before the trailhead was Wagontown. It was established in 1895 on the route to the Seafoam mines by Mose Stohrer as a lodging and store for miners. After constructing a smelter in 1904, Snowstorm Mining and Milling and the Greyhound Mining Company built a toll road over Vanity Summit to the mines in 1905. (Vanity Summit is the pass two miles north of the Langer Monument.) In 1926,

Fishing at Langer Lake

a Coeur d'Alene mining company, Hecla, invested in mines at Seafoam and nearby Sheep Mountain, and installed a 50-ton mill. By 1927, the Seafoam mines had 17 claims, with 40 people spending the winter.

Directions: From the Langer Monument, take the blazed trail that leads northwest up a hillside burned in the 1998 Fall Creek Fire and across the wilderness boundary. It climbs 500 feet in the first .7 mile before the grade lessens. At 1.7 miles, the trail crosses a stream coming from a marsh, and the outlet of Rocky Lake, then arrives at Langer Lake at 2 miles.

Note that the topographic map reverses the names of Island and Ruffneck lakes. To reach Island Lake, go .4 mile around Langer Lake on the main trail towards Ruffneck Lookout to a small pond and sign saying "lake area." From here, the trail climbs 3 more miles in 1,260 feet to the top of Ruffneck Peak. To reach Island Lake, turn left (southwest) at the pond on a path, follow it around a second pond, and descend to the lake, .4 mile from the main trail. The cross-country route to Ruffneck Lake, 3.3 miles from the trailhead, climbs 200 feet in .2 mile along the left (east) side of Island Lake's usually dry inlet.

8.

Finger Lakes

Round trip: 8.6 miles
Elevation gain: 1,520 feet; elevation loss (return climb): 800 feet
Highest point: 8,800 feet
Topographic maps: Langer Peak, Capehorn Lakes, Soldier Creek
Trailhead GPS: N 44 22" 50.4" W 115 3" 57.7"
Time: 8 1/2 hours; difficulty: strenuous
Access: From Stanley drive 18 miles northwest on Highway 21. Turn right (north) on the improved dirt Vanity Summit Road and drive 7 miles to the Langer Monument trailhead.

What you will see: Finger Lakes provide a great view of Ruffneck Peak's north face, the upper half of which is crumbled cliffs, divided into three lobes by avalanche chutes. Below the peak, the scalloped circle of the upper lake is set in a bowl of gravel, and the blue-green fingers of the lower lakes nestle in grooves above the canyon of Fall Creek. From grassy slopes on the trail you can look south to the jagged Sawtooths and southeast to the creamy White Clouds.

Directions: From the trailhead, the trail switchbacks up through forest burned in the 1998 Fall Creek Fire. At 1.7 miles, where the trail crosses a little saddle, the burn was so intense it carved the trees into charcoal sculptures. At 1.8 and 1.9 miles the trail crosses two branches of a creek, and at 2 miles reaches the side path to Langer Lake.

High above Finger Lakes

Continue on the trail, which curves through unburned forest above the lake, then climbs over a little knoll, and passes a pond with a sign saying "lake area" on the left, indicating a turnoff for Island and Ruffneck Lakes. Continue straight ahead on the main trail, which goes around the right-hand side of this pond at 2.3 miles. At 2.8 miles turn right on a trail to the north toward Fall Creek. From here on, the trail is not on the topographic or forest maps, so the mileage given here may not be as great as what is on the ground. The trail is on the wilderness map but is shown incorrectly.

To reach Finger Lakes turn right (north) on this trail through forest, which gives you glimpses of two tiny ponds off to the left. (The trail straight ahead here goes 2.5 miles west and north to the top of Ruffneck Peak in a 1,200-foot climb.) This lookout is one of the few in this wilderness still operated during the fire season. At 2.7 miles the trail climbs a rocky, grass-covered slope with a view of the Sawtooths and White Clouds. After climbing among granite boulders, the trail reaches an 8,600-foot divide at 3.2 miles. On the other side, the trail turns right (east) and goes across talus below cliffs. Here you can look down on the scalloped-edged highest of the Finger Lakes, although it is unnamed on the topographic map. A few yards along the talus section of the trail, a steep rocky path turns off to the north and drops 500 feet to the lake. This is not the trail. The wilderness map shows the main trail descending to the lake here and circling its west side, but instead it stays high above the east side of the lake all the way to its junction with the Fall Creek Trail at 4.5 miles. Reaching the lake is safer if you continue along the trail for another .4 miles to an avalanche area opposite the middle of the lake's east shore, then turn off the trail and descend to the lake cross-country. Before the avalanche area, paths lead to the right to a tiny narrow pond, which has excellent views of Ruffneck Peak's face, and in early summer makes a fine destination in itself.

At the avalanche area at 3.6 miles, the trail crosses a semi-open area of little trees. This is your turnoff for the lakes. From here pick your way cross-country down to the scalloped, highest lake at 3.8 miles. To reach the lower lakes, go around this highest lake and from its lower end cut cross-country to the open area shown on the map. This will enable you to see the other lakes below. Then descend through the forest to the head of the larger one at 4.3 miles. Note that the whole area is heavily forested, so it is easy to get confused.

While looking for the place to descend to the highest lake, be careful not to go too far along the trail, which connects in 1.5 more miles with the Fall Creek Trail, which runs between Seafoam Lakes and the Middle Fork. If you plan a through trip, you need to know that on the Seafoam side, it is safe to drive only as far as the ford of Seafoam Creek, even with four-wheel drive.

9.

Vanity Lakes

Round trip: 5.4 miles for five lakes
Elevation gain: 1,280 feet; elevation loss: 200 feet
Highest point: 8,240 feet
Topographic map: Langer Peak
Trailhead GPS: N 44 22": 43.9" W 115 3" 57.7"
Time: 4 to 5 hours; difficulty: moderate, non-system trail, no signs

Access: From Stanley drive 18 miles northwest on Highway 21, turn right (north) onto the improved dirt Seafoam Road. Drive 9 miles to Vanity Summit and 1 mile beyond the summit to a side road on the right (east).

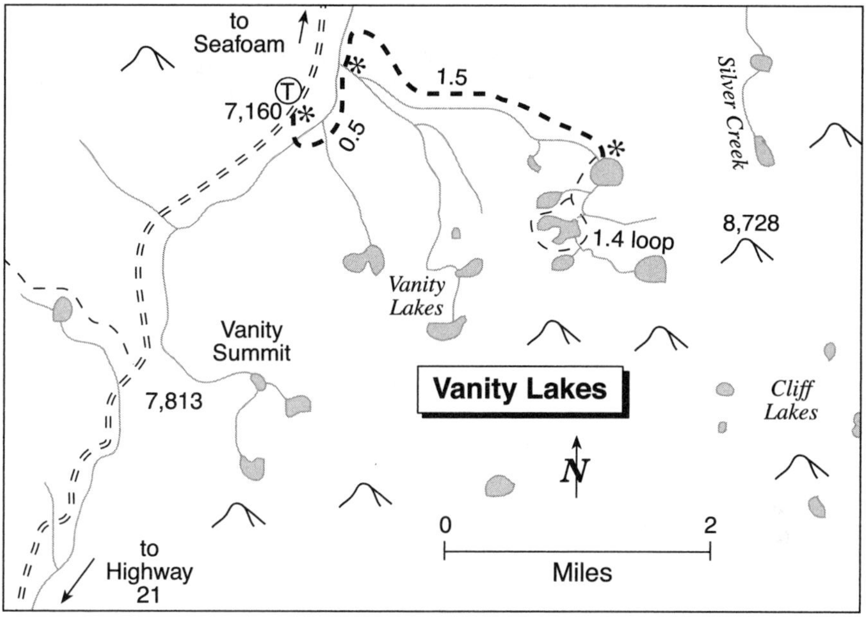

What you will see: An unofficial trail to Vanity Lakes leads to an olive green lake labeled "7872" on the topographic map. South of this lake, the 400-foot face of a peak resembling an upended plowed field turned to stone has snow-filled furrows in early season. Cliffs plunge from the furrowed peak into the pale aqua water of the fourth lake. Four other lakes can he reached by easy cross-country travel.

One car can park at the edge of the main road at 7,160 feet, but the side road (not open to motor vehicles) is too steep for parking. Turnouts farther down the main road have more parking.

Begin the hike by walking down the old road, carefully skirting a six-foot deep pit if it is still there. At 200 yards, the road crosses Vanity Creek, then goes downstream, fording a rushing side creek at .7 mile. Forty yards from this creek, the road disappears in alders, but continues. Beyond these alders at 250 yards, a line of rocks across the road marks a well-worn uphill path turning right (southeast). It has a few overgrown blazes. This trail is not a Forest Service system trail so is not maintained, patrolled, or on any map.

The trail climbs the center of a little ridge on the side of the canyon. When the grade lessens at 1.5 miles at an open area, the trail is at the edge of the outlet's ravine. At 1.7 miles, in another open area, a rock nubbin on a ridge appears ahead, and at 2 miles, the trail ends at the first lake (7,872 feet).

To reach the other lakes, climb cross-country up the streams that connect them, using the topographic map. The fourth lake is 2.5 miles from the Seafoam Road, and the fifth 2.7 miles (8,240 feet). Three smaller lakes can be reached by rough cross-country travel from Lake No. 3, or by going up the right side of Lake 7905's outlet from the trail at the .4-mile point. An additional three (smaller) lakes, separated from the others, are within a mile of Vanity Summit. Although the area nearest Vanity Summit burned in the 1998 Fall Creek Fire, these lakes can easily be reached by cross-country hiking from it.

10.

Rapid River

Round trip: 25.8 miles to the Middle Fork of the Salmon
Elevation gain: 160 feet; elevation loss (return climb): 1,200 feet
Highest point: 5,920 feet at trailhead
Topographic maps: Greyhound Mountain, Little Soldier Mountain, Artillery Dome
Trailhead GPS: N 44 34' 12.9", W115 4' 15.3"
Time: 3 days for round trip to Middle Fork; difficulty: moderate to strenuous
Access: From Stanley, drive 18 miles northwest on Highway 21. Turn right (north) onto the improved dirt Seafoam Road and drive 14 miles to the Seafoam Guard Station, then 2 miles farther on a primitive road. Turn right (northeast) on the primitive Rapid River Road and go .3 mile to a gate.

This tributary of the Middle Fork winds diamond clear and apple green over pale stones. Where the channel narrows, rapids roar into sea-green pools. Along the upper 2.5 miles of the trail, cliffs and knobs constrict the river into a narrow gorge. Below this, the canyon widens, but silvered snags burned in the 1979 Mortar Creek Fire line the four miles below Pearl Creek. (Another, better-known Rapid River is near Riggins.)

From the gate, walk down the old road around a hairpin and then ford the river. This ford will be a problem for hikers until late summer. Just beyond this, where Float Creek joins the river from the west, the trail emerges from a lodgepole-fir forest onto talus. It ascends to cross Lime Creek at .7 mile on a culvert, then the path climbs below a rock tooth covered with green lichen. In the canyon of Lunch Creek at 1.5 miles, 250 feet above the river, it goes along the base of rock ledges.

Below Pearl Creek at 2.3 miles, the track descends to the river as the canyon widens. At 3.2 miles is a ford of Bruin Creek and a campsite. Here, the trail leaves the old road and turns right (southeast) for 200 yards up Bruin Creek, then returns to the canyon of the Rapid River, but stays high above it.

At Lucinda Creek at 4.5 miles, the trail crosses the boundary into the Frank Church - River of No Return Wilderness. It returns to the river near Sheep Creek at 6.8 miles where a trail leads up Sheep Creek 3.5 miles to the Sheep Mountain Ridge Trail. At Cabin Creek at 9.1 miles is a campsite. From here, the Lake Creek Trail ascends Cabin Creek to Little Soldier Mountain and then descends Lake Creek 9 miles to the Middle Fork. The Rapid River Canyon below this has 800-foot walls of cliffs and talus. There is no bridge over the Middle Fork at 12.9 miles, and there is no trail up the Middle Fork to Dagger Falls on this side. Instead, the trail continues 6 miles down the Middle Fork on the east side to a bridge at Indian Creek.

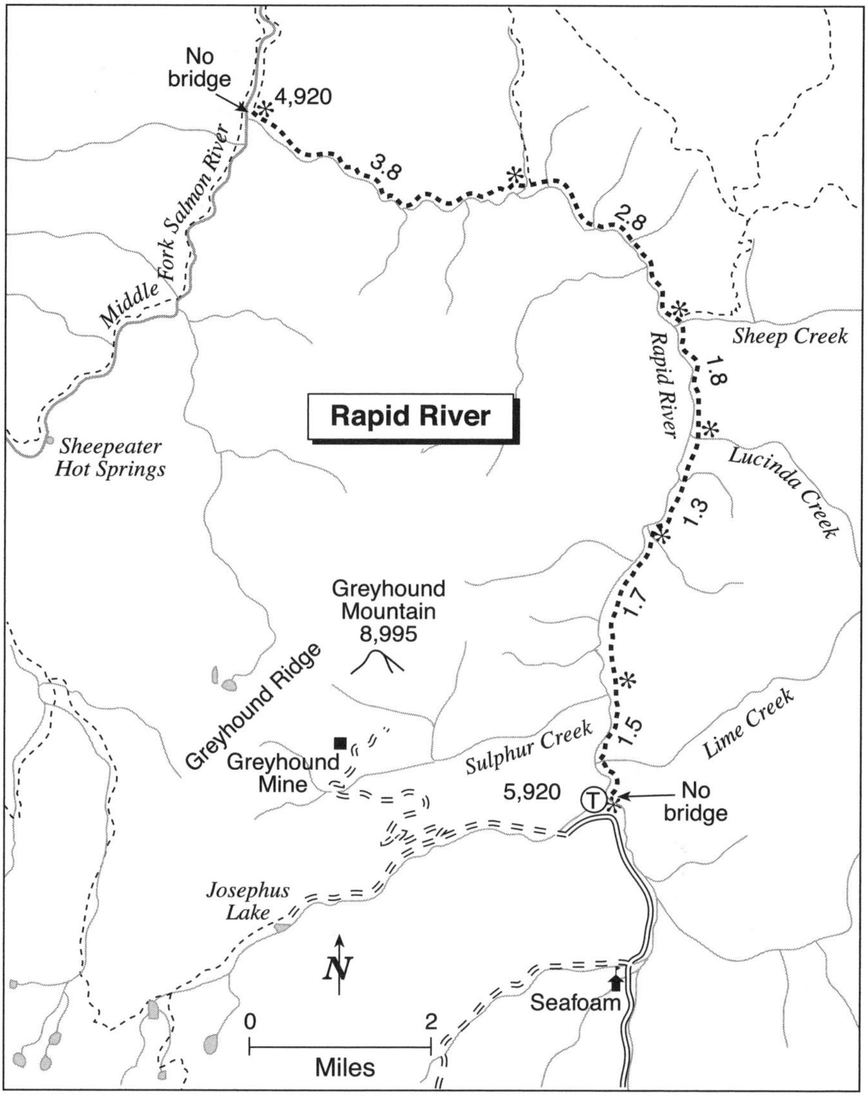

11.

Lost Lake

Round trip: 4 miles
Elevation gain: 520 feet

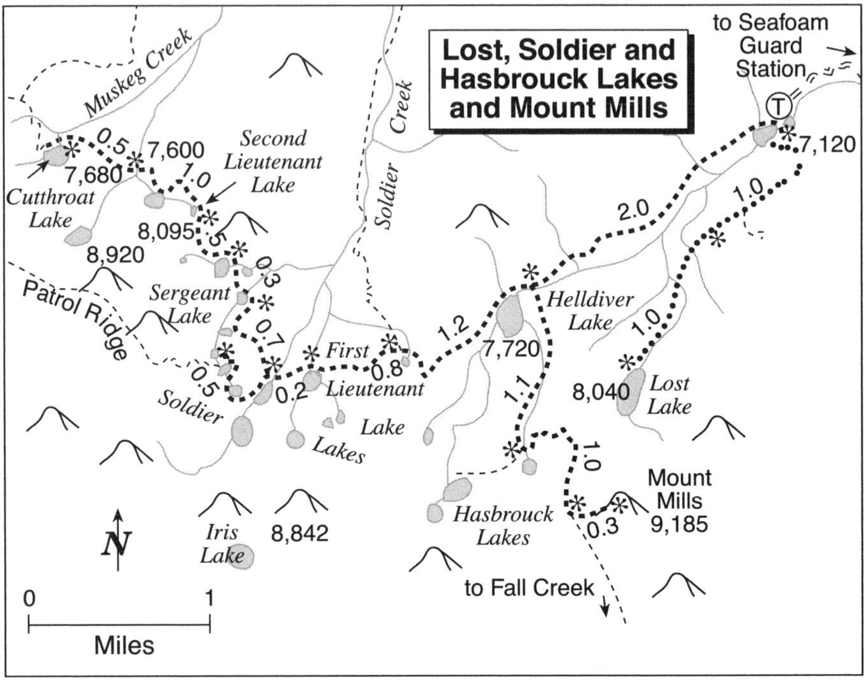

Highest point: 8,040 feet
Topographic map: Soldier Creek
Trailhead GPS: N 44 32" 55.7" W 115 8" 32.8"
Time: 4 hours; difficulty: trail is non-system and may be hard to find
Access: From Stanley drive 18 miles northwest on Highway 21. Turn right (north) onto the improved dirt Seafoam Road. Drive 19.6 miles to Josephus Lake; for the last 4 miles, the road is primitive.

As you drive past the Seafoam Guard Station and several mines on the way to the trailhead, it is interesting to know a little about the area. Seafoam's minerals were first noticed in 1879 when Capt. Bernard's packers and scouts found lead and silver while pursuing the Sheepeater Indians. The next year, Manual Fontez, one of Bernard's packers, and others staked claims on Greyhound Ridge, and in 1882, Fontez found ore on Sheep Mountain. In 1866, the Summit and Josephus mines at Seafoam were discovered. Seafoam was the name of the settlement on Float Creek near the Seafoam Mine.

On the top third of Mount Mills, gray cliffs send rocks down the avalanche chutes between them, plowing furrows in the talus below. This talus drops into blue-green Lost Lake across from wooded shores. Part of the trail is an old mining road and the rest is an informal trail not shown on maps.

Unless your car has four-wheel drive, park at Josephus Lake and ford the outlet. Then walk up the rocky, steep road through woods, past log cabin ruins and a prospect. At .2 mile, the road begins to switchback up the side of the canyon, and at .5 mile, it turns southwest along the side of the ridge. Park four-wheel-drive cars here. Keep right (straight ahead) where a side road turns left uphill. Where a second road curves left uphill at 1 mile, look straight ahead for two paths that join in 25 yards at a wilderness boundary sign.

From the sign, the trail drops to a rocky area below a mountain wall, then enters woods, crosses a creek in moss, and turns left (uphill). Where the path turns right at 1.6 miles it is difficult to find. At the end of a boulder slope below the face of a shoulder of Mount Mills, keep just below the boulders for 200 yards, then move to the right (north) onto a wooded ridge, passing willows and a creek on the left at 1.8 miles. At 1.9 miles, a branch of the trail crosses the creek to a campsite, but continue along the north side of the creek to the lower end of the 8,060-foot lake at 2 miles. Camping at the lake is limited by steep banks.

A loop trip with .3 mile cross-country travel can be made by climbing southwest up grass and scree from the southwest corner of the lake, over the ridge on the north side of Mount Mills and down to the Fall Creek Trail. To complete the six-mile loop, take the Fall Creek Trail past Helldiver Lake back to Josephus Lake. Mount Mills can be climbed from this ridge, but it is easier to climb the peak from the west through a saddle on the Fall Creek Trail. (See Mount Mills and Hasbrouck Lakes.)

12.

Helldiver, Soldier and Cutthroat Lakes

Round trip: 14.4 miles
Elevation gain: 1,340 feet; elevation loss (return climb): 775 feet
Highest point: 8,080 feet
Topographic map: Soldier Creek
Trailhead GPS: N 44 32" 55.7" W 115 8" 32.8"
Time: 2 days; difficulty: strenuous
Access: From Stanley, drive 18 miles northwest on Highway 21. Turn right (north) onto the improved dirt Seafoam Road. Drive 19.6 miles to Josephus Lake; for the last 4 miles the road is primitive.

This hike tours a string of similar small lakes, clustered close together, all wearing the same uniform of emerald water; dark green woods, and a short, gray cliff. Most of the lakes have army names related to their uniformity, from General down to PFC (private first class), which is little more than a mud puddle.

There is a small campground at Josephus Lake, but the road is too steep for trailers. From the trailhead just before the campground, the trail circles the northwest side of the lake to the upper end, where it enters the Frank Church Wilderness. In 2 easy miles, the route climbs 560 feet up the wooded canyon past the oasis of Mushroom Spring to Helldiver Lake, where cliffs of Mount Mills loom beyond a wooded ridge. Just below the lake, a trail leads south to Fall Creek and Ruffneck Lookout.

From Helldiver Lake, the trail to Soldier Lakes climbs 400 feet in a lodgepole-fir forest to a saddle at 2.7 miles. It then zigzags down to a pond and junction with the Soldier Creek Trail at 3.2 miles. Next it circles the head of a canyon, crosses a boulder field, and at 4 miles, arrives at First Lieutenant Lake. The best of three campsites is off the trail beyond the inlet of this lake.

The trail continues over a 100-foot ridge to Colonel Lake at 4.2 miles. Here the Soldier Ridge Trail turns off, providing a one-mile side trip to three more lakes. The first, General, at 200 yards, shines emerald under a rocky, tree-topped peak. After circling General Lake, the trail reaches Major Lake at .5 mile. Back at General Lake a path to the left leads 200 yards to the largest lake, unnamed, which glows green below a long, high ridge of cliffs. A huge boulder masks a campsite.

Back at Colonel Lake, the main trail winds over a ridge to Sergeant Lake at 4.9 miles, and Staff Sergeant at 5.2 miles. Then the trail climbs 200 feet to a saddle (8,095 feet) and zigzags down to tiny Second Lieutenant Lake at 5.7 miles, an unnamed lake at 6 miles, and the puddle of PFC Lake at 6.7 miles 490 feet below the saddle. From here, the main trail wanders over a ridge to Cutthroat Lake (7,640 feet) at 7.2 miles, where 300-foot gabled cliffs hang from a rounded peak.

13.

Mount Mills and Hasbrouck Lakes

Round trip: 8.8 miles
Elevation gain: 2,065 feet
Highest point: 9,185 feet
Topographic map: Soldier Creek
Trailhead GPS: N 44 32" 55.7" W 115 8" 32.8"
Time: 8 to 9 hours; difficulty: cross-country to summit of Mount Mills and to 3 of the 4 lakes
Access: From Stanley drive 18 miles northwest on Highway 21. Turn right (north) onto the improved dirt Seafoam Road. Drive 19.6 miles to Josephus Lake; the last 4 miles of which are on a primitive road.

Along the trail from Helldiver Lake to the Fall Creek Trail is a small, round, green lake under fractured cliffs divided by diagonal ledges. Behind two nearby off-trail lakes stands a large peak. The Forest Service calls these three lakes Hasbrouck Lakes after the former owner of the nearby Silverbell Mine, but they are not labeled on the maps.

Mount Mills is a moderate climb from a saddle on a trail that connects the Soldier Basin Trail with the Fall Creek and Langer Lakes trails. From the summit you see colorful mountains at the head of Loon Creek, the summits of the peaks above Seafoam Lakes, and the vertical wrinkles of Ruffneck Peak.

From the Josephus Lake Campground at 7,120 feet, follow the sign for Soldier Lakes straight ahead to the west. Above the side of shallow green Josephus Lake, the trail crosses talus to the wilderness boundary at the far end. Then the route winds up through forest and over side streams to a campsite and meadow at Mushroom Springs at 1.5 miles. At 2 miles, where a trail leads south to Fall Creek, Helldiver Lake (7,680 feet) is straight ahead (west). The Soldier Basin Trail continues 10 miles from here past the Soldier Lakes to the Middle Fork. To reach Hasbrouck Lakes and Mount Mills, turn left (south) at this junction and cross Helldiver Creek.

The trail follows an inlet of Helldiver Lake, then crosses it at 2.5 miles. At 3 miles, it returns to the east side of this creek just below the first of the Hasbrouck Lakes at 8,320 feet.

To reach the largest of the Hasbrouck Lakes at 8,400 feet, hike west cross-country .6 mile along the edge of the forest beside an open, rocky area. A second lake is only 200 yards above (southwest) this largest lake, and a third lake is in woods 100 feet down and .3 mile north. (Seeing these three lakes adds 2 miles to the hike.)

To climb Mount Mills from the lake that is on the trail, continue east on the trail through firs and boulders, then south in sandy soil. Four miles from the trailhead is a divide, from which the trail descends 800 feet in 1.3 miles to Fall Creek, then climbs above Finger Lakes to the Langer Lake - Ruffneck Peak Trail.

To reach Mount Mills from the divide, turn east off the trail and hike cross-country to the summit ridge, then walk south along it to the top at 4.4 miles (9,185 feet).

BEAR VALLEY AREA

14.

Bear Valley Creek

Round trip: 9 miles
Elevation gain: 320 feet; elevation loss (return climb): 440 feet
Highest point: 6,400 feet
Topographic maps: Blue Bunch Mountain, Cape Horn Lakes
Trailhead GPS: N 44 25' 38" W 115 17' 37.8"
Time: 6 hours; difficulty: moderate, except for four fords
Access: From Stanley drive 21.5 miles northwest on Highway 21. Turn right (north) onto the improved dirt Warm Lake-Stanley Road and go 7.9 miles to a sign for the Fir Creek Campground. Here turn right (north) and, avoiding the road into the campground, go .4 mile to the trailhead next to Bear Valley Creek.

A little history: As you drive through Bruce and Ayers meadows on the way to the trailhead, it is fun to imagine Alexander Ross in 1824 and John Work in 1832 visiting Bear Valley with their fur trappers or John Stanley and his prospectors on their way to Stanley in 1862. Stanley's party named the valley for the great number of bears they saw feeding on spawning salmon. Around 1900, so many cattlemen had arrived that the Forest Service closed most of the land in Bear Valley to homesteading because it was prime land for summer range and the squatters trying to live there were creating problems. The Forest Service actually began razing cabins, which led to a man named Alonzo Cooley being jailed for several months for burning a Forest Service building in retaliation for the Forest Service burning his cabin. A ranger station was built in 1909. A road to Bear Valley, the Warm Lake - Stanley Road, was completed in 1922 with a Holt tractor and six-horse teams.

In the 1950s the valley was dredged for uranium and for the steel alloys, tantalum and niobium (columbium). The author remembers driving up the Clear Creek grade from Lowman to Bear Valley at that time and meeting mining trucks that were dripping onto the roadbed. The mining operation employed 90 men to operate two Yuba dredges there and a concentration plant in Lowman. Before it shut down, $12.5 million worth of minerals had been processed.

That grade was the main road to Stanley from Boise until Highway 21 from Lowman to Stanley was constructed in 1965, and that road wasn't all paved until 1975.

What you will see: Except for three fords of 60-foot-wide Bear Valley Creek and one of Marsh Creek, this hike is a pleasant walk in green forest along a meandering creek. Small cliffs and low bluffs provide accents, and so does an undeveloped hot spring with two or three small pools set in river stones and sand. A one-mile fisherman's trail avoids the first ford, but crosses dangerously steep slopes above cliffs for .2 mile, so wait and hike the trail in late summer when the fords are only knee-deep.

Directions: From the trailhead, cross the footbridge over Bear Valley Creek and turn right (east) on the trail signed Marsh Creek, which at first runs along below a steep hillside. Beyond a flat at 1.5 miles it fords the creek to the south over rounded river stones that can be very slippery. A walking stick, either your own or a dead branch from the forest floor, will be helpful. Just before 2 miles, the trail climbs above the creek 50 feet and crosses a side stream. At 2.5 and 3 miles are other side streams, and at 3.5 miles the hot springs. Then at 3.8 miles the trail fords the creek to the north to avoid cliffs and returns to the south bank just before the confluence of Bear Valley and Marsh Creek. The trail goes up the south side of Marsh Creek for .1 mile, then fords it, and descends Marsh Creek, continuing past Big Hole to meet the Middle Fork Trail at 4.5 miles. It is 10 miles along the river from here to Dagger Falls.

15.

Blue Bunch Mountain

Round trip: 8 miles
Elevation gain: 2,343 feet
Highest point: 8,743 feet
Topographic map: Blue Bunch Mountain

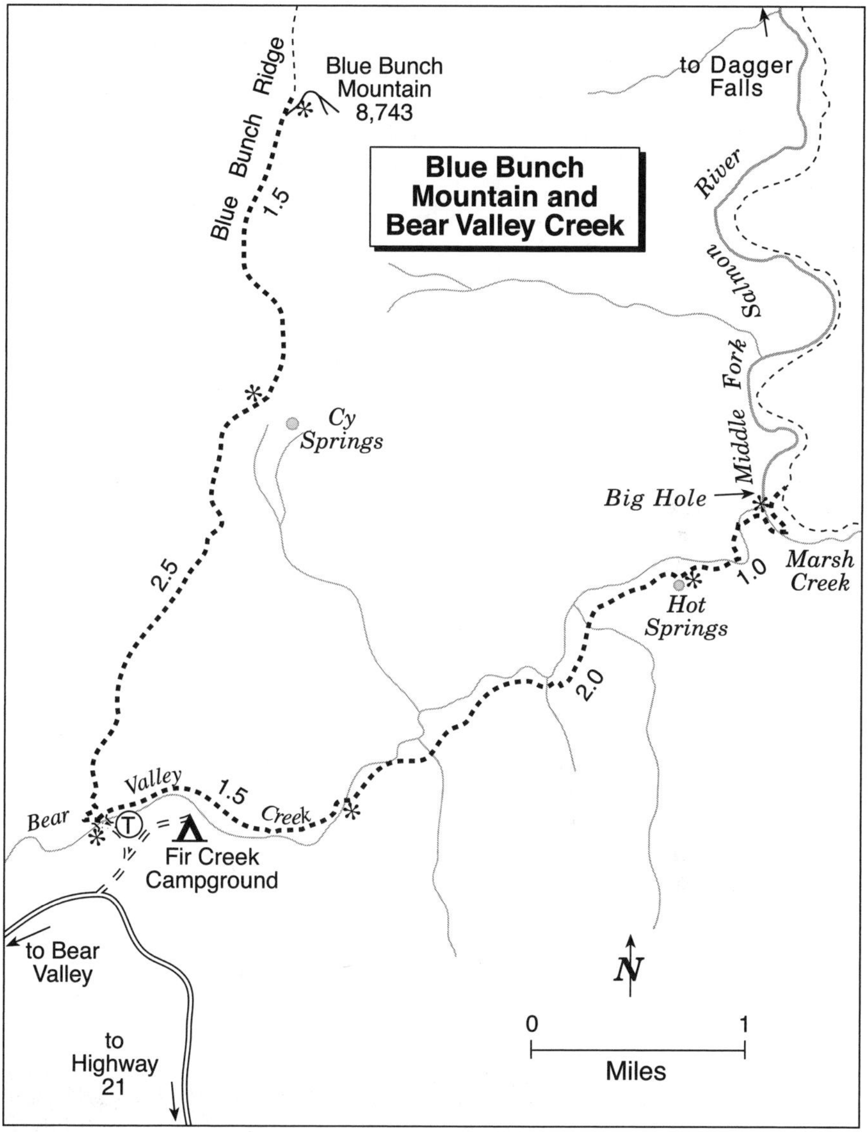

Trailhead GPS: N 44 25' 38" W 115 17' 37.8"

Time: 7 1/2 hours; difficulty: strenuous with route-finding problems

Access: From Stanley drive 21.5 miles northwest on Highway 21. Turn north onto the improved dirt Warm Lake-Stanley Road and go 7.9 miles to a sign for the Fir Creek Campground. Here turn right (north) and, avoiding the road to the campground, go .4 mile to the trailhead next to Bear Valley Creek.

What you will see: Blue Bunch Mountain is a long, grassy ridge with a view of Bear

Valley Creek meandering in great blue curves through the meadows of Bear Valley. From the mountain, you also see the faint blue silhouettes of the White Clouds, the talus top of Capehorn Mountain and the rock-lined canyon of the Middle Fork. The 1987 Deadwood Fire left several nearby ridges and mountains patched with gray lace and silver snags parading up the west side of Blue Bunch Mountain. In midsummer, the grassy summit ridge is brilliant with blue lupine and yellow sulphur plant.

Directions: From the trailhead the trail first crosses a footbridge to a junction with the trail up Bear Valley Creek, Big Hole and Dagger Falls. Turn left (west) here and take the trail toward Blue Bunch Ridge. After 200 yards it turns to the right away from the creek and climbs through alternate woods and sagebrush. After 1 mile you come out on an open grass and sagebrush ridge with a view of Bear Valley Creek twisting through the meadows. Here the trail begins to deteriorate, and you can't tell how much progress you have made because the ridge hides what is ahead. The ridge remains mostly open with snags and downed timber.

At 2 miles, the trail goes to the left of the little summit marked 8,006 feet on the topographic map. Next you must pick your way through and around .5 mile of downed timber. Soon a spring is off to the right in a gully between Cy Springs, which is shown on the map, and the trail. Between the spring and the top of the ridge at 2.7 miles (8,425 feet), the trail tread exists only in patches. When you reach the top, it is a good idea to notice distinctive trees and other markers for where to turn off the ridge on the way back. The trail soon reappears in the center of the open, grassy ridge top.

At the 8,608-foot hilltop at 3.5 miles, trails go on both sides of the ridge, rejoining in a little saddle. From this saddle the trail goes along the left (west) side of the ridge, climbing 200 feet to the summit (8,743 feet) at 4 miles. The similarity of the hilltops on the ridge can be confusing, but the summit is the bare rocky one with grass and a few little trees. Confusingly, a trail of sorts continues north beyond the summit to a last high point (8,640 feet), then descends 300 feet to another saddle and climbs to a wooded hilltop at 8,400 feet, about 5 miles from the trailhead.

16.

Mountain Meadow and the Camptender Trail

Round trip: 23.8 miles

Elevation gain: 1,420 feet; elevation loss (return climb): 480 feet

Highest point: 7,820 feet

Topographic maps: Blue Bunch Mountain, Bear Valley Mountain, Honeymoon Lake, Big Soldier Mountain

Trailhead GPS: N 44 27' 59.3" W 115 19' 31.8"

Time: 9.5 hours; difficulty: strenuous

Access: From Stanley, drive 21.5 miles northwest on Highway 21. Turn right (north)

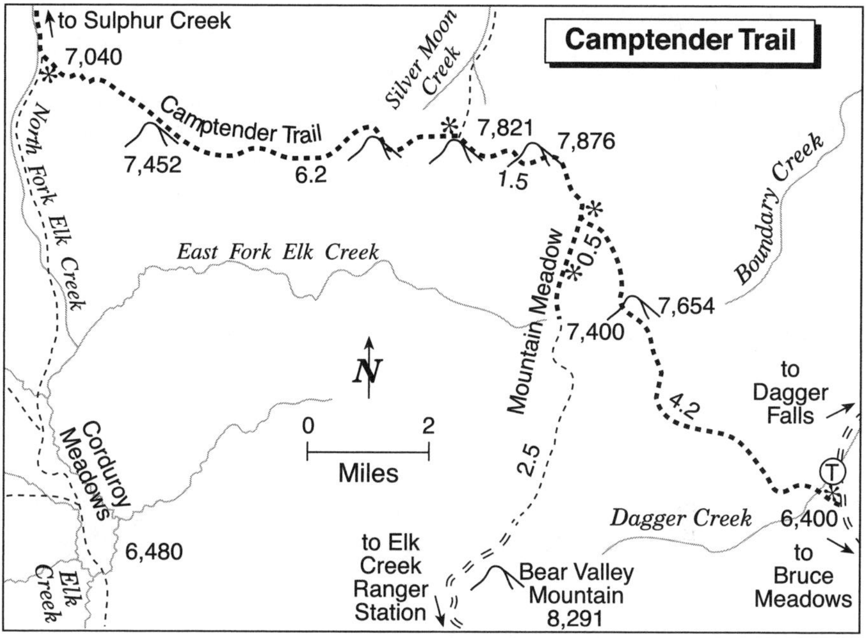

onto the improved dirt Warm Lake - Stanley Road. Drive 9.2 miles to Bruce Meadows, turn north on the Dagger Falls - Boundary Creek Road and drive 3.7 miles to the Camptender trailhead.

What you will see: Below this trail, the green arms of Poker and Ayers meadows sprawl toward furrowed peaks. In the fall, aspens, willows and grasses make these meadows glow with gold and amber. Along the trail in summer, sego lilies, lupines and asters brighten the hillside under burned Douglas firs and lodgepoles. From the high point of the trail is a vista south to the thumb-shape of Mount Regan in the Sawtooths, west to peaks around Bernard Lake and north across Sulphur Creek to the terraced sides of Morehead Mountain. Below, Sulphur Creek curves through meadows and bars of white sand. One-half mile off the main trail, below wooded hills, Mountain Meadow displays brilliant wildflowers in summer. Much of the area around the Camptender Trail burned in the 1987 Deadwood Fire. Because most of the trees burned were lodgepoles and they keep falling over like jackstraws, it is impossible for the Forest Service to keep up with them, so expect some fallen logs across the trail.

From the Frank Church Wilderness boundary sign, the trail goes northwest across the meadow 200 yards to a blaze at the edge of the trees. After fording Dagger Creek at .2 mile, it winds onto a ridge. At 2 miles is a grassy area with a view of Poker and Ayers meadows. After following the east side of the ridge, the route drops to circle the west side of a hill at 3 miles. Mountain Meadow and the peaks near Bernard Lake are in the distance as the trail meanders through woods to a junction at 4.2 miles (9,752 feet).

To reach Mountain Meadow (7,400 feet), take the Mountain Meadow Trail to the left (south) .5 mile through woods. This trail continues through the meadow another

.5 mile and then goes 2 miles through much downed timber up to the Bear Valley Mountain Road near the summit of the mountain. Although Bear Valley Mountain has a fine view, the road to it is in poor shape and not maintained for public use.

From the junction with the Mountain Meadow Trail, the Camptender Trail crosses a stream at 4.5 miles, then turns west around a grassy hilltop, where there is a view southwest. After turning right (north) downhill, the trail bends left (west) again at 5.2 miles on a narrow ridge, where an unsigned path leads right. For a view of Sulphur Creek, go north off the trail 30 yards. The view shows the contour trenching and planting on Morehead Mountain that was done to repair erosion damage from a cloudburst in 1956.

Beyond here, the trail runs west along the grassy ridge to a junction at 7,821 feet and 5.5 miles. Here, a little-used trail leads 3.1 miles down Silver Moon Creek to Sulphur Creek. The Camptender Trail continues along the ridge, then turns north along the North Fork of Elk Creek and descends to the North Fork of Sulphur Creek Trail at 11.9 miles.

17.

Middle Fork Salmon River: Dagger Falls to Marsh Creek

Round trip: 20 miles
Elevation gain: 760 feet; elevation loss (return climb): 640 feet
Highest point: 6,200 feet
Topographic maps: Big Soldier Mountain, Soldier Creek, Cape Horn Lakes
Trailhead GPS: N 44 31' 42.5" W 115 17' 6.6"
Time: 2 to 3 days: difficulty: strenuous
Access: From Stanley drive 21.5 miles northwest on Highway 21. Turn right (north) on the improved dirt Warm Lake - Stanley Road and drive 9.2 miles to a junction in Bruce Meadows. Here, turn right (north) and go 19.2 miles to a junction for Dagger Falls. Turn right and go 1 mile to the trailhead.

What you will see: From Dagger Falls, any length of this trail makes a pleasant hike with plenty of shade. It is prettiest in late June or early July when the grasses are green, wildflowers are out, and flowering shrubs are blooming, although in a high-water year the trail is underwater in some places in mid-June, mostly about 8 miles from Dagger Falls. Much of the canyon is heavily wooded with occasional ledges and big dark cliffs. Dagger Falls is pure white because the water rushes so fast. An old snag lying in it at an angle makes you wonder if it has been there long enough to give the falls its name.

This trail section is not included in the Big Creek-Middle Fork through trip because there is a gap of .8 mile between it and the Middle Fork Trail at Boundary Creek. However, you can walk 1.5 miles on roads between the two trailheads, carefully watching for traffic, if you wish to combine this section with the others. To do this, you would need to start or end your trip on the Marsh Creek Trail.

Directions: The trail first goes down to the river and crosses it to the north bank on a footbridge. On the other side of the bridge, a trail takes off up the canyon wall to Big Soldier Mountain. Most of the way along the river trail there are campsites on flats every mile or so. The trail goes over an intermittent stream, and above and below blocks and cliffs of lichen-patched rock. As it continues, flat forest alternates with steep open hillsides. At 1.7 miles the trail crosses Patrol Creek on a bridge. At 2.5 miles where the river bends to the right (east), the trail is on a steep hillside with ledges and cliffs. A spring flowing over the trail here makes the surface slippery. Beginning at 2.8 miles the trail goes over talus for 200 yards. At 3 miles it crosses Chicken Creek, then Kotch Creek. At 5 miles is a junction with a trail up Fall Creek that goes 3 miles to the trail between Langer and Seafoam Lakes (see Finger Lakes.) From here to Marsh Creek, the Middle Fork Trail crosses only one all-year stream (at 7.5 miles), Jose Creek. From 6 to 7 miles the path climbs 400 feet above the river, then down again before 8 miles is reached. At 10 miles at a pool called Big Hole, the trail joins the Marsh Creek and Bear Valley Creek trails

Dagger Falls on the Middle Fork of the Salmon River

18.

Middle Fork of Salmon River: Boundary Creek to Artillery Creek

(Section 8 of Big Creek-Middle Fork through trip)

This section, one way: 17.4 miles
Elevation gain: 720 feet; elevation loss (return climb): 1,360 feet
Highest point: 5,800 feet
Topographic maps: Artillery Dome, Soldier Creek, Big Soldier Mountain
Trailhead GPS: N 44 31' 41" W 115 17' 59.7"
Time: 4 days round trip from Boundary Creek; difficulty: strenuous
Access: From Stanley drive 21.5 miles northwest on Highway 21. Turn right (north)

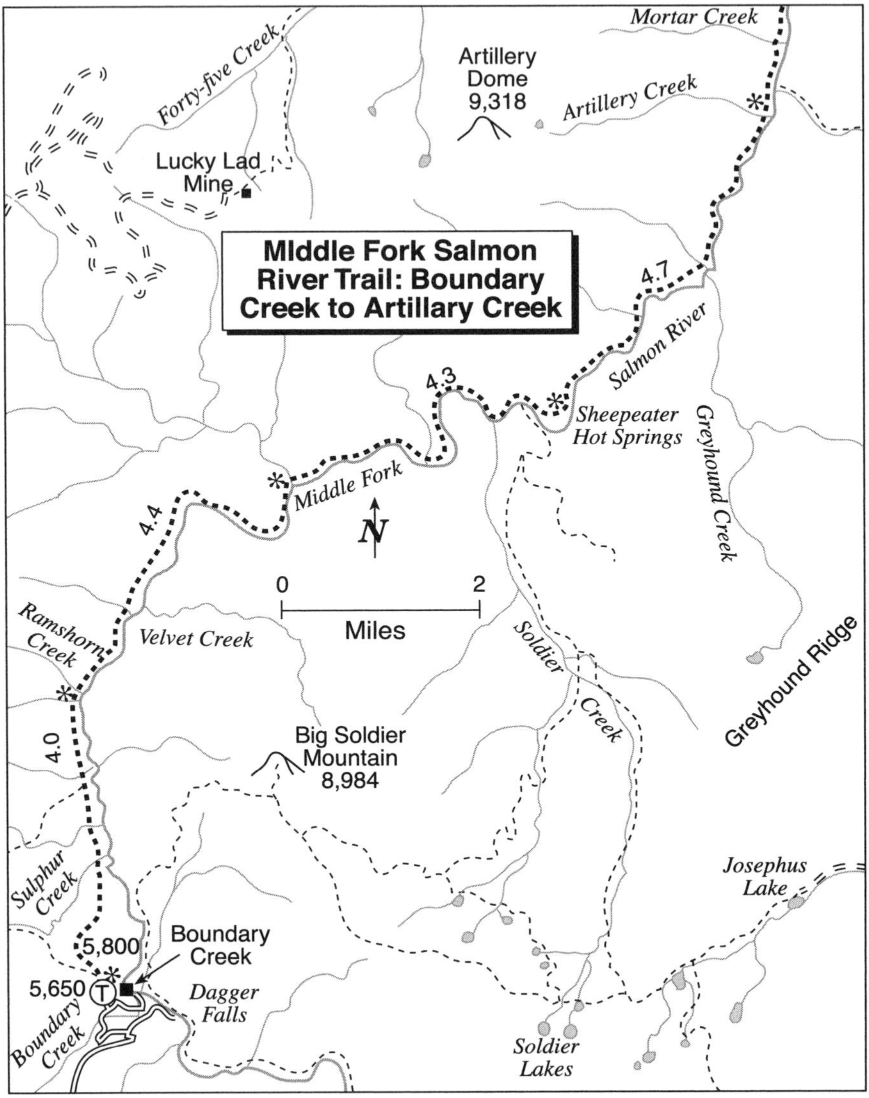

onto the improved dirt Warm Lake - Stanley Road. Drive 9.2 miles to Bruce Meadows. Turn right (north) and drive 13 miles to the Boundary Creek trailhead.

What you will see: In this part of the Middle Fork, dark animal-shaped outcrops alternate with lichen-patched cliffs. Side creeks plunge in cascades and waterfalls, and rapids rushing through rock chutes turn the river white. This section is as rugged as that from Big Creek Bridge to the Flying B, but it is heavily forested and thick willows edge the river. Sheepeater Hot Springs spreads hot rivulets over a rocky flat. At high water (8.2 feet deep on the gauge at the Middle Fork Lodge, or 12,400 cubic feet per second), the trail is knee- to thigh-deep in several places. At this water level, some side creeks are dangerous, but the most dangerous are bridged.

Directions: This hike description begins at Boundary Creek, even though it is the final section of the Big Creek - Middle Fork through trip. It will be useful to people taking day and overnight hikes from Boundary Creek, as well as those making the through trip. At a large parking area before the campground, the official trail begins, going north. The road continues to the launching ramp at the edge of the river, where another trail leads along the river and through the woods to the official trail at .5 mile.

From the horse transfer camp, the Middle Fork Trail starts downhill as an old road in an area burned in the 1987 Deadwood Fire. The first 3 miles also burned in 2019. From here, it is 79 miles to the end of the trail at the Big Creek Bridge on the Middle Fork, where it meets the Big Creek and Waterfall trails.

At .5 mile, the trail joins the path from the raft launch, then climbs a hill for 200 yards to a junction with a trail to the private Sulphur Creek Ranch. It then descends the east side of the fence of the private Morgan Creek Ranch, and at 2 miles, jogs 200 yards up the canyon to bridge Sulphur Creek, which really does smell like sulphur here.

After going along a high bank above the river, the trail turns away from it and at 2.3 miles, fords Prospect Creek. At 2.5 miles it passes another side trail to the Sulphur Creek Ranch, and at 2.8 miles passes the Prospect Creek Trail.

The Middle Fork Trail continues level well above the river, fording tiny Morehead Creek at 3.8 miles and bridging Ramshorn Creek at 4 miles. At 5.3 miles is a ford of Spike Creek in a ravine, then a climb of 250 feet in woods to avoid cliffs. It then returns to the river and at high water is in it. At Trail Flat at 7.5 miles, hot springs bubble at the edge of the river. After climbing 200 feet to avoid cliffs, the path switchbacks down to a bridge over Elkhorn Creek at 8.4 miles.

After climbing above the river, the route descends to cross Deer Horn Creek at 9.8 miles. Next, it goes over talus and through raspberries. Here the trail may be flooded at high water. At a bend at 12 miles, there used to be a wheel attached to an old log building (known as the Powerhouse) across the river. It was used to run a one-stamp mill with water power.

The trail passes the dilapidated Joe Bump Cabin, across the river from Soldier Creek. The cabin was built in the 1930s by Joe Fox and Roscoe Dodge. It was named for the next owner, a prospector and packer, who left the canyon when he got blood poisoning from frostbite in a Bear Valley snowstorm. Next the trail ascends ledges overlooking a rock island. Across from the Soldier Ridge Trail at 12.3 miles, the trail returns to the river. After climbing away from the river, the route drops to Sheepeater Hot Springs at 12.7 miles. (Paths from the river's edge joining the trail may confuse those going south.) Because the hot springs pool is only a foot deep or less, it is not a good place to soak, but there are several campsites.

Beyond the hot springs, wet meadows below rock ledges are flooded at high water. The path crosses Lake Creek at 14.8 miles, climbs grass and scree to avoid cliffs, and returns to the river. After Dome Creek at 15.4 miles, it circles a headland, where metal supports keep tread from sliding away. Beyond this corner at 16.1 miles is an avalanche area and then the trail goes along a hillside to Artillery Creek at 17.4 miles (4,960 feet).

19.

Bernard Lake

Round trip: 14.4 miles
Elevation gain: 1,040 feet; elevation loss (return climb): 280 feet
Highest point: 7,200 feet
Topographic maps: Bear Valley Mountain, Bernard Mountain
Trailhead GPS at N. Fork Elk Cr sign: n 44 25' 26.7" W 115 25' 26.1"
Time: 2 days; ability: expert because part is a non-system trail
Access: From Stanley drive 21.5 miles northwest on Highway 21. Turn right (north) onto the improved dirt Warm Lake - Stanley Road and drive 14.2 miles to the Elk Creek trailhead. Turn right (north) and drive 0.3 mile on a primitive road to the beginning of the trail.

The route to Bernard Lake wanders through immense green meadows embroidered with wildflowers. When awash with blue camas in early June, the meadows resemble lakes. Later in the summer, a mixture of flowers such as shooting star and littleflower penstemon replace the camas. There may be glimpses of three-foot-tall sandhill cranes. Two tiers of 400-foot cliffs, striped with gray and pale orange, tower over the south side of the blue-green lake, with the rocky hump of Bernard Peak adjoining the cliffs. On the west, rock scallops lead north to a pointed peak with a 500-foot face.

The hike begins at the end of the primitive road at the boundary of the Frank Church Wilderness. If you decide to leave your car at the main road, you will need to add 1 mile to the distances given here. Part of the area near Corduroy Meadows and Bernard Lake burned in the 1987 Deadwood Fire.

From the wilderness boundary, the trail tops a 6,720-foot wooded ridge at .7 mile, then descends to Corduroy Meadows (6,480 feet) at 1 mile. Here, a plank bridge crosses a marshy arm of the meadow. Under the planks are the logs of the old "corduroy" road.

The trail skirts the east edge of Corduroy Meadows with a view of Bernard Peak to the west. In early July, the water in a ford of Elk Creek at 2.3 miles can be knee-deep.

After climbing 40 feet up a wooded hill, at 2.5 miles the trail reaches Porter Creek Meadows, and at 2.8 miles is a junction with the Porter Creek Trail. From here the North Fork of Elk Creek Trail continues north 4.5 miles to the Camptender Trail through burned areas. Turn left (west) on the Porter Creek Trail, which may have no path; using the topographic map, cross an unnamed branch of Elk Creek at 3 miles. To help find the route, look for posts.

The trail rounds the south end of a 20-foot hill and becomes plainer west of the hill. It continues west to a blazed trail in forest at 3.5 miles. After following the willows of a creek, the trail at 4 miles enters a narrow meadow. From 5.2 to 6 miles, it outlines the north edge of Crane Meadows (6,600 feet), then turns northwest where a cow path intersects it from the east.

At 6.5 miles (6,720 feet), look for an initialed tree, if it still stands, which is the turnoff for a cross-country route to the lake. Turn west and cross Porter Creek. After two or three paths join, the unofficial trail passes a granite outcrop, then winds steeply. Use

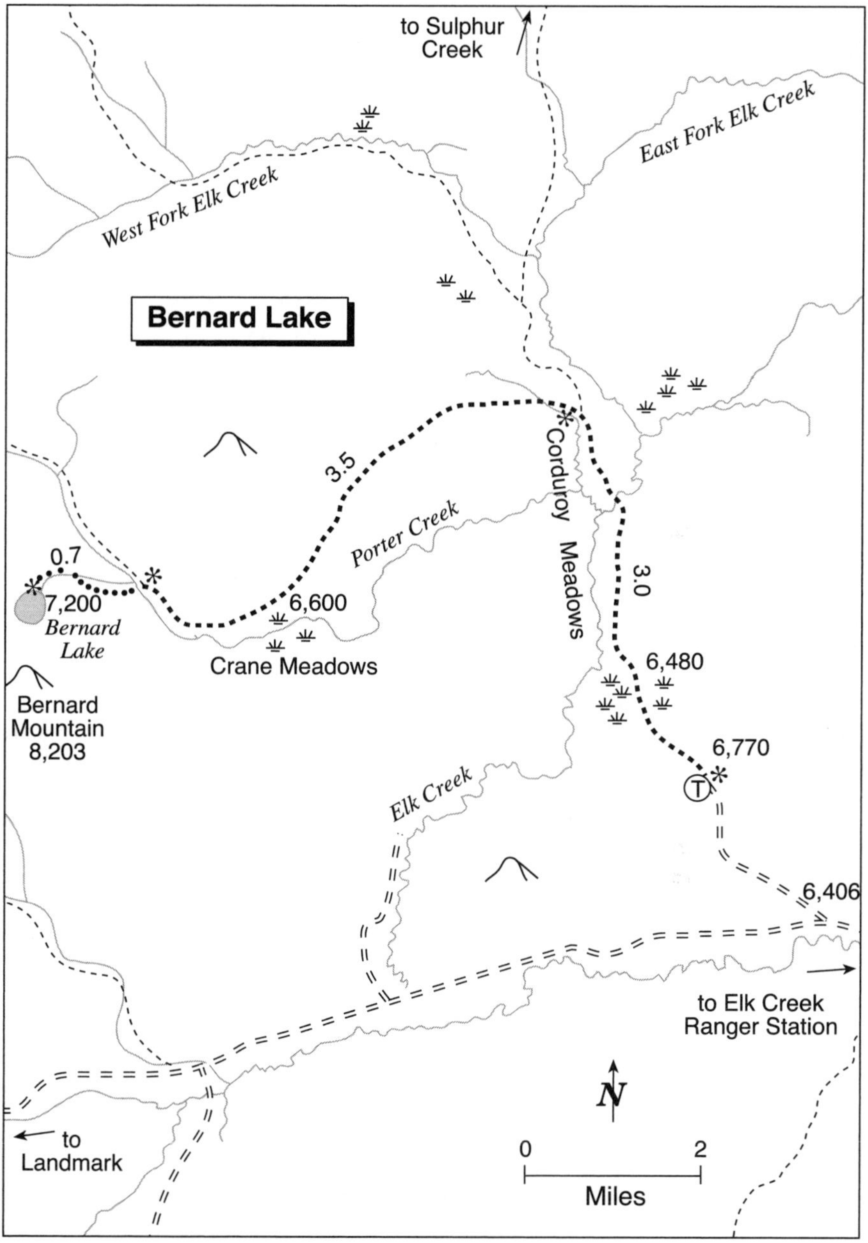

the topographic map to follow a route below cliffs of the pointed peak to the 7,200-foot lake at 7.2 miles. Because no water runs down the outlet, hikers will be unable to find the correct route by looking for the spot where the outlet joins Porter Creek. The Porter Creek Trail continues 7 miles to the historic Deadwood Mine just above the

Warm Lake - Stanley Road, but according to rangers has downed timber from the 1987 Deadwood Fire. The creeks mentioned here are closed to fishing from July 1 to September 1 to protect spawning salmon.

LANDMARK AREA

20.

Sulphur Creek

Round trip: 28 miles
Elevation gain: 80 feet; elevation loss (return climb): 1,360 feet
Highest point: 6,880 feet
Topographic maps: Tyndall Meadows, Honeymoon Lake, Big Soldier Mountain
Trailhead GPS: N 44 33' 42.6" W 115 36' 42.8'
Time: 4 days; difficulty: strenuous
Access: Drive the Warm Lake-Stanley Road from either end to reach the dirt Sulphur Creek Road, which is on the south side of Whiskey Creek 4.5 miles south of the road junction and guard station of Landmark. Landmark was named for a pile of rocks on a ridge that riders could see as they came out of the mountains in the early days; they knew the rocks marked the way to Cascade. (The Warm Lake-Stanley Road runs from Warm Lake to the junction on Highway 21 leading to Bear Valley.) It is paved from Warm Lake to the Landmark junction. The rest is improved dirt. Once on the Sulphur Creek Road, drive 3.3 miles to a faint onsigned trail leading left (east) across a meadow.

A little history: If you drive to this point from Stanley, you will pass the site of the old Deadwood Mine. Mining began here in 1863 with placers. After Nathan Smith (the man who had discovered gold at Loon Creek and Yellowjacket) found better placer gold in 1867, 100 prospectors arrived. That summer, three quartz lodes were discovered and by 1907, these lodes had operating mines that sent ore out by pack trail to be smelted.

After a road was completed from Bear Valley to the mines in 1922, the Bunker Hill Company ran two of the mines as the Deadwood Mine from 1924-32. They constructed a 150-ton flotation mill there, but abandoned it. The mine reopened in 1944, and by 1947, $1 million in lead and zinc had been taken out, but it hasn't operated for many years.

What you will see: The Sulphur Creek Trail descends a forested canyon, broken by open rocky slopes of grass and patches of false hellebore. The creek runs clear as mountain air over orange sand and where it joins the Middle Fork gives off a faint smell of sulphur. Whiskey Creek was named for a freight stop and saloon that once

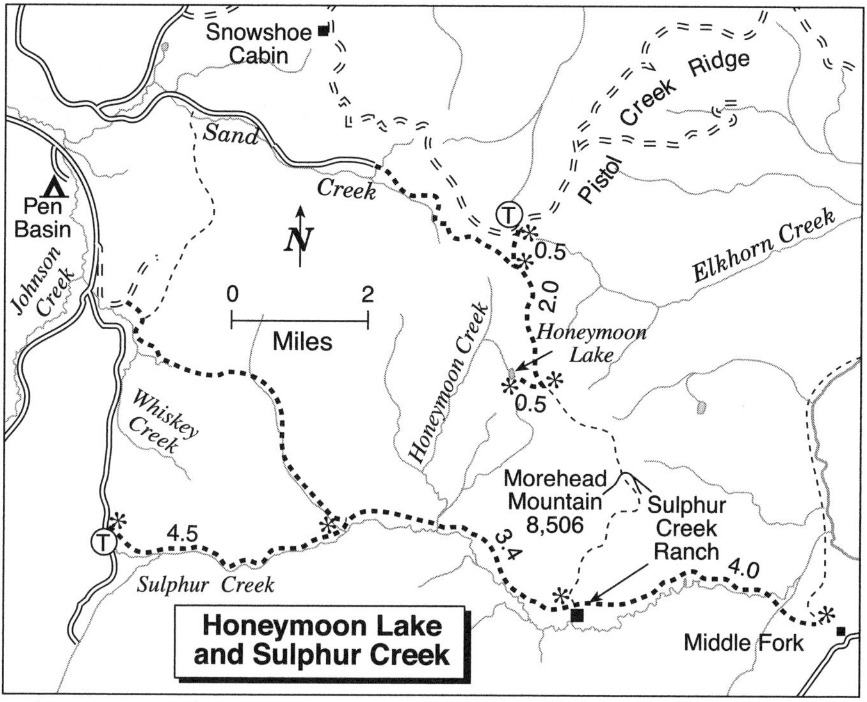

stood here, where freight for Thunder Mountain was loaded from wagons onto mules.

Directions: From the Sulphur Creek trailhead at 6,880 feet, walk east across the meadow on an indistinct path and ford the creek into the trees. The last time I was there (in 2018) the trailhead signs had vanished due to vandalism. From the ford, the trail runs south along the left (east) side of the meadow and creek. At .5 mile, it heads uphill away from the creek across from clear-cuts, then at 1 mile drops into the canyon at the Frank Church Wilderness boundary. After the trail descends to a grassy flat and campsite beside the creek at 1.8 miles, it may be unclear but continues. Some of the Sulphur Creek drainage burned in 1987.

At 1.8 miles, the creek joins the South Fork of Sulphur Creek. The trail continues down Sulphur Creek, passing at 3.7 miles a junction with the North Fork of Elk Creek Trail, which leads south 6 miles to Elk Meadows. At 4.5 miles, the Sulphur Creek Trail joins the North Fork of Sulphur Creek Trail, which is maintained as one of the main trails in this wilderness, but it is .7 mile longer to this junction on it than on the Sulphur Creek Trail. From here the trail on down Sulphur Creek is confusingly called by the Forest Service the North Fork of Sulphur Creek Trail. It continues in an 880-foot drop to the privately owned Sulphur Creek Ranch and airstrip at 8.9 miles. There is access for the trail through the ranch with a gate at each end. From the ranch, trails run north to Morehead Mountain and south up Silver Moon Creek to the Camptender Trail. The main trail continues 4 miles to meet the Middle Fork Trail .5 mile below the Boundary Creek trailhead.

21.

Honeymoon Lake

Round trip: 6 miles (1 mile cross-country)
Elevation gain: 680 feet; elevation loss (return climb): 920 feet
Highest point: 8,638 feet
Topographic map: Honeymoon Lake, Pistol Lake
Trailhead GPS: N 44 37' 29.9" W 115 25' 439.3"
Time: 7.5 hours; ability: expert

Access: From the road junction near the Landmark guard station, 12 miles east of Warm Lake on a paved road, drive east on the improved dirt Burntlog Road. (From this junction, roads also go north to Yellow Pine and south to Highway 21 west of Stanley.) Do NOT turn left on the road signed Burntlog Trail a half mile from Landmark) Instead at 2 miles take the left (north) fork. Take the 8-mile-long Sand Creek Road to the Honeymoon trailhead at the end of that road.

What you will see: A forest of fernlike algae grows in the shallow, green water of Honeymoon Lake, which is surrounded by dead trees, killed by a beaver dam. The lake is .5 mile from the Honeymoon Trail, which has a view east of wooded canyons turning blue with distance toward the chasm of the Middle Fork of the Salmon River. The hike is prettiest in midsummer when wildflowers like yellow sulphur plant and blue littleflower penstemon cover the ridges. Directions: From the Artillery Dome Road, take a trail that descends .5 mile to meet the Honeymoon Trail, which has come 2 miles from the old Sand Creek Road trailhead. (Note that the access road and beginning of the hike to Honeymoon Lake has changed since the first edition of this book because of the washout of the Sand Creek Road.) From this junction, the trail climbs south along a partly open ridge. After dropping into a gap at 1.3 miles, it follows the narrow second section of the ridge to a crest at 8,638 feet. Here at 2.3 miles, the trail overlooks Honeymoon Lake, but do not turn off yet because the hillside is too steep.

At 2.5 miles, where the trail begins to descend (southeast) off the ridge, turn southwest off-trail, keeping to the ridge crest. There is no marker or path at the turnoff , but in 300 yards a path appears and drops to a saddle northeast of an unnamed 8,300-foot peak. It is a non-system trail so is not maintained. From the saddle, follow the path north down to the lake (7,840 feet) at 3 miles. Back on the ridge, the Honeymoon Trail continues 2.8 miles with a 400-foot gain and a 560-foot loss to Morehead Mountain Lookout.

22.

Pistol Lakes

Round trip: 12.2 miles
Elevation gain: 1,220 feet; elevation loss (return climb):1,480 feet
Highest point: 8,733 feet
Topographic map: Pistol Lake
Time: 10 hours; difficulty: strenuous

Access: From the road junction near the Landmark Guard Station, drive east on the improved dirt Burntlog Road. At 2 miles take the left (north) fork. At 4 miles turn right (east), and avoiding a logging road to the right, drive straight ahead up the primitive Artillery Dome Road, which climbs 1,300 feet on its way to the beginning of the Summit Trail to Pistol Lakes at 6.7 miles. This trailhead is before the Snowshoe Cabin trailhead. The road is not suitable for passenger cars, and early in the season and in wet weather requires four-wheel drive. From here on the road is four-wheel-drive only with car-eating holes.

A little history: Snowshoe Cabin was the second cabin that stood at this trailhead. The original cabin stood on the other side of the spring. It was built by Jim Voller and Michael McNerney and a man named Crothers as a stopover place for people riding horseback to Cascade from the Middle Fork of the Salmon as early as the 1890s. (Voller lived at the site of the Middle Fork Lodge beginning in 1889.) In 1925 Cy Johnson replaced this cabin with a new one, and several tent frame cabins as a base for his outfitting business. At that time the road ended here. The business was later carried on by his son, Lafe Johnson of Emmett. Past Snowshoe Cabin the road continues out along Pistol Creek Ridge to the Lucky Lad and other mines, which together have produced $465,000 in gold and tungsten.

What you will see: Between two 200-foot gray cliffs a strip of willows reaches the blue-green water of Pistol Lake. At the upper and lower ends are wildflower meadows. Northeast of the lake, the talus dome of Big Baldy Ridge peers from behind the granite point of Chinook Mountain.

Directions: From the Pistol Lakes sign take the trail that leads north, the Summit Trail. It descends through a Douglas fir forest and climbs over a hill. At .7 mile, where the trees thin, it descends the north end of a hill to a grassy saddle at 1.2 miles. In its zigzags up the side of the next ridge, the trail passes an early-season spring. It continues north along the ridge through wildflower meadows with a view of mountains northwest of Landmark.

At 3.1 miles, the path drops to another saddle, then climbs, crossing streams on the left side of another ridge. At 4.5 miles, the Forty-Four Creek Trail turns northeast to descend in 8 rough miles to Pistol Creek.

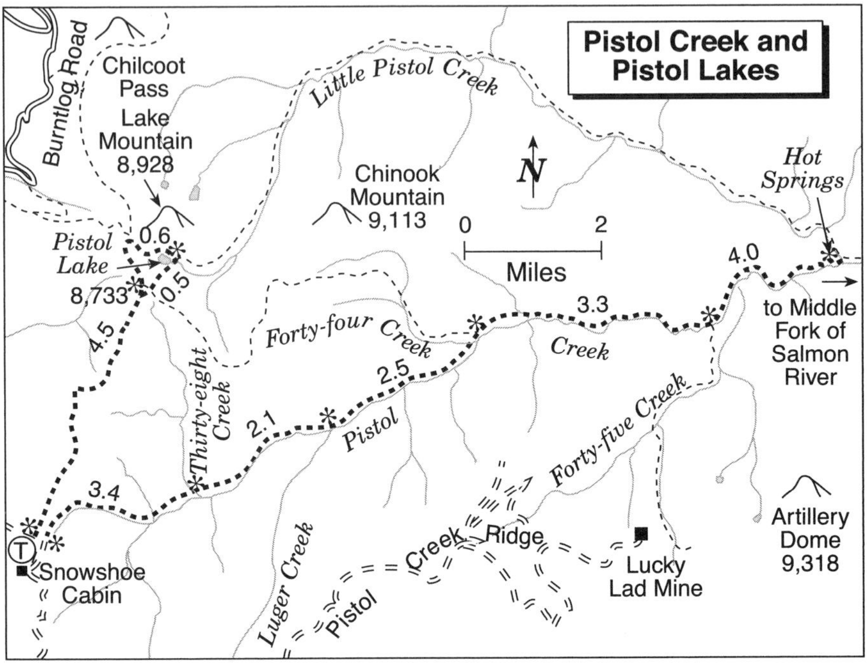

Take the main signed trail north to a narrow saddle at 5 miles. Go up a hill and down to a junction at 5.5 miles (8,480 feet) with the Little Pistol Creek Trail. Here, leave the Summit Trail, which continues along the ridge for 12.2 miles past Chilcoot Pass to the Old Thunder Mountain Road near Meadow Creek Lookout (see Chilcoot Pass and Pistol Rock map.) From the Summit Trail closer to the Little Pistol Lake Junction, a trail goes .6 mile west out of the wilderness to a jeep trail, the East Fork of Burntlog Creek Road, a branch of the Burntlog Road. This jeep trail is closed to motor vehicles due to a washed-out bridge; it provides shorter (4 miles), but not as scenic, access to Pistol Lake.

To reach the lakes from the junction with the Little Pistol Creek Trail, turn east and climb a few feet over a narrow ridge, then down in switchbacks over scree and across the inlet into a meadow. The trail curves around the north shore of the lake, then drops to the lower end at 6.1 miles (7,812 feet). This trail continues down Little Pistol Creek below the lake for 15.2 miles to the Pistol Creek Trail at Pistol Creek Hot Springs. Much of this drainage burned in the Snowshoe Fire of 2001.

Experts can save distance on the return by taking an alternate trail, which is not on the topographic map and may be hard to find. To do this, follow a path west around the lower end of the lake and climb a wooded gully to a marsh and stream where a 200-yard cross-country walk reaches the upper lake. Beyond the marsh, the path turns southwest to an unsigned junction with the Forty-Four Creek Trail, .5 mile from the lower lake. Turn right and take it up a wooded ridge back to the Summit Trail, .7 mile from the lake.

23.

Pistol Creek Trail

Round trip: 41 miles to Middle Fork of Salmon
Elevation gain: 160 feet; elevation loss (return climb): 3,195 feet
Highest point: 8,000 feet;
Topographic maps: Pistol Lake, Chinook Mountain, Artillery Dome
Trailhead GPS: N 44 39' 42,2" W 115 26' 51.4"
Time: 5 days for round trip to Middle Fork: difficulty: strenuous
Access: From the road junction near the Landmark Guard Station, drive east on the dirt Burntlog Road. At 2 miles take the left (north) fork. At 4 miles turn right (east) onto the primitive Artillery Dome Road and drive to Snowshoe Cabin at 7.1 miles, a climb of 1,300 feet in 2.7 miles. Four-wheel drive may be needed, and passenger cars shouldn't attempt it.

In July, the canyon of Pistol Creek is a medley of flowers: wild geranium, paintbrush, pearly everlasting, lupine, aster, Queen Anne's lace and sego lily, which glow in the late afternoon sun like stained glass. In the lower meadows, the creek flows transparent over pebbles and golden sand. From the head of Pistol Creek, a procession of hills cloaked with forest slides away into the blue haze of the Middle Fork Canyon. In an ironic contrast with the peaceful mountains, the side creeks draining into Pistol Creek are all named after guns, such as Thirty-Eight, Luger, Twenty-two, Winchester, Remington and even Popgun Creeks. Note that the forest along the trail from Luger Creek to Popgun Creek burned in the 2001 Snowshoe Fire.

Park at or near the four-way road junction at the Snowshoe Cabin trailhead. From here the Artillery Dome Road, a rough four-wheel-drive road, goes straight ahead along Pistol Creek Ridge to mines. The road to the right leads 100 yards to the site of Snowshoe Cabin.

From a spur road to the left of the trailhead notice board, take a trail to the left (north-northeast) across the meadow and into the trees. It descends the right side of a ridge for .2 mile, where a path joins it from the right. After several springs and open grassy areas, the trail at 1.3 miles goes over a stream in a gully.

At 2.5 miles, it heads back into a ravine to cross a side creek, then descends the steep canyon, crossing three sections of Thirty-Eight Creek at 3.4 miles near a campsite. The trail continues through meadows and past two waterfalls on the canyon wall at 4.7 miles. At 5.5 miles, near a sign for Luger Creek, is another campsite.

The trail descends through the burned area for 6 miles to Popgun Creek. From there it is 9 more miles down to the Middle Fork of the Salmon River at 4,800 feet. A 64-mile loop trip can be taken down Pistol Creek to the Middle Fork, down the Middle Fork to Indian Creek, up Indian Creek to the Summit Trail and along the Summit Trail back to Snowshoe Cabin.

At 8 miles is a junction with a primitive trail that goes 8 miles up Forty-Four Creek to the Summit Trail. At 13 miles is a junction with a six-mile trail up Forty-Five Creek to the Artillery Dome Road. Just past Pistol Creek Hot Springs at 15.5 miles a trail

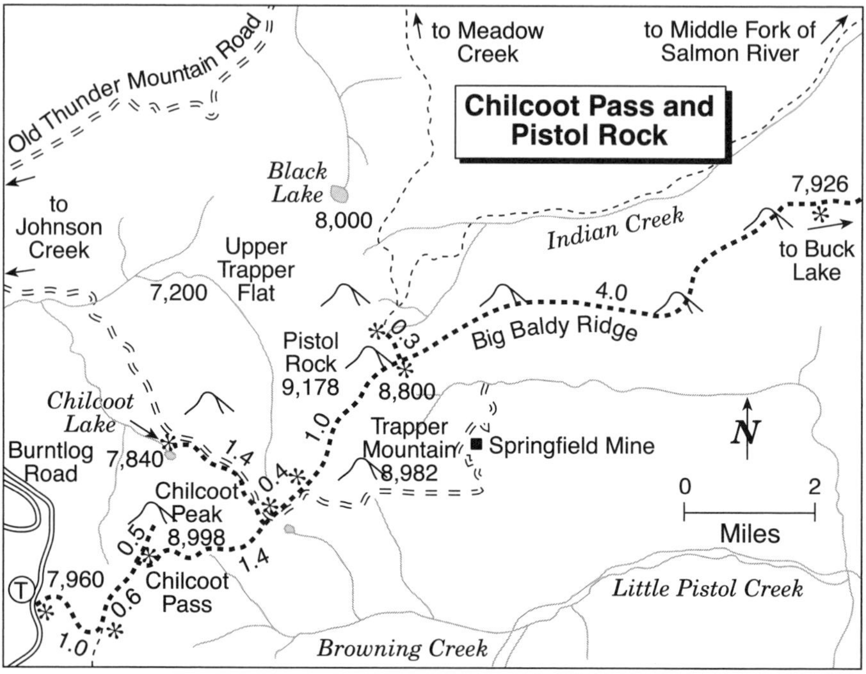

turns up Little Pistol Creek to go 16 miles to the Summit Trail. The crossing of Little Pistol Creek here is bridged. At 15.7 miles, the Big Baldy Ridge Trail takes off to join the Summit Trail at Pistol Rock in 19 miles. At 20.5 miles, the trail reaches the Middle Fork.

24.

Chilcoot Pass and Pistol Rock

Round trip: 9.4 miles
Elevation gain: 1,480 feet: elevation loss (return climb): 1,120 feet
Highest point: 8,800 feet
Topographic maps: Chilcoot Peak
Trailhead GPS: N 44 45' 343.3" W 115 26' 32.8"
Time: 2 days; difficulty: strenuous

Access: From the road junction near the Landmark Guard Station, drive east on the dirt Burntlog Road. At 2 miles turn left (north) where Sand Creek Road turns right. At 4 miles, where Artillery Dome Road turns right (east), keep straight ahead on the improved dirt Burntlog Road. Drive north to a trailhead about 150 yards before the Burntlog Creek - Trapper Creek Divide (8,000 feet) at 18 miles.

What you will see: From Chilcoot Pass a .5 mile trail leads to Chilcoot Peak, which has an excellent view north to red peaks near Monumental Summit and the dark helmet of Pistol Rock. Between Chilcoot Pass and Pistol Rock, a short side trip reaches tiny, dark green Chilcoot Lake where white talus contrasts with an 800-foot gray wall. Below the granite hat of Pistol Rock, a spring bubbling out of green turf and wildflowers begins Indian Creek.

Directions: The trail begins by angling up the side of a ridge, then turns northeast at .8 mile in a sandy area. At 1 mile, it joins the Summit Trail at 8,400 feet. From here, the Summit Trail runs north 9.4 miles to the Old Thunder Mountain Road, and 9 miles south to the Artillery Dome Road near the site of Snowshoe Cabin.

From the junction, take the Summit Trail north along the ridge and over a boulder slope to Chilcoot Pass (8,560 feet) at 1.6 miles. Here, you can take a one-mile side trip that climbs 440 feet above the pass to the top of Chilcoot Peak, site of a former lookout.

From the pass, the Summit Trail zigzags east into a cirque, edges a meadow and follows a stream down the canyon. This stream is one of two water sources between the trailhead and the spring below Pistol Rock. After dipping past a round meadow at 2.9 miles, the trail meets a jeep trail at 3 miles (8,800 feet).

To take a 2.8-mile side trip to Chilcoot Lake from here, follow the jeep trail left (northwest) across the head of a canyon and over a low saddle (8,080 feet) at .7 mile. This jeep road, the Trapper Creek Road, is a private mining road, with a locked gate on the west side of the saddle. Below the gate, turn southwest off the road where it curves back to the right, and walk .2 mile cross-country to the lake (7,840 feet), 1.4 miles from the Summit Trail. Campsites are limited. The Trapper Creek Road is a spur of the Old Thunder Mountain Road, which is not recommended for travel from Johnson Creek at the west end to the trailheads near Thunder Mountain due to its extreme steepness.

Back at the junction of the Summit Trail and the jeep road, the trail on to Pistol Rock first follows the jeep road northeast uphill. After .4 mile (at 3.4 miles), where the road hairpins to the right (south), leave the road, which used to go off to the right (east) around the south side of Trapper Mountain to the Springfield Mine.

A little history: The tungsten of the Springfield Mine was discovered in 1945 by H.D. Bailey and Lafe Cox and mined by the Bradley Mines. One of the miners once told camp manager Clark Cox to throw used carbide from the miners' lamps down the privy to keep it from smelling. Another gave him a can of new carbide instead and said it would work better than the used, and even better if he dumped a pail of water on it and then threw in a lighted match. When he did this, the outhouse blew up in his face, singeing his eyebrows and hair.

From the road hairpin, climb northeast up the road cut to rejoin the trail, which goes north. At 3.7 miles, a branch of Trapper Creek 100 feet below the trail (not shown on the map) has water. The trail angles up along the west side of Trapper Mountain to a saddle at 8,800 feet. Beyond the saddle, the path climbs around the southeast side of Pistol Rock, and at 4.4 miles drops to a narrow shelf east of Pistol Rock. From the shelf, the Big Baldy Ridge Trail 227 leads along a ridge to Buck Lake.

To find a campsite with water at Pistol Rock, descend the Summit Trail north .3 mile to the Pistol Rock Spring at 8,440 feet. (Note: There is no water along the eight-mile

Big Baldy Ridge Trail to Buck Lake.) This spring is the headwaters of Indian Creek. The Indian Creek Trail 225 turns off the Summit Trail .3 mile below the spring and descends 24 miles to the Middle Fork. From this junction, the Summit Trail continues 5 miles to the Old Thunder Mountain Road near Meadow Creek Lookout.

25.

Big Baldy Ridge Trail to Buck Lake

Round trip: 24.8 miles
Elevation gain: 2,790 feet; elevation loss (return climb): 3,125 feet
Highest point: 9,080 feet
This section, one-way: 8 miles; 1,310 feet gain; elevation loss (return climb): 2,005 feet
Topographic maps: Chilcoot Peak and Big Chief Creek
Trailhead GPS: N 44 45' 343.3" W 115 26' 32.8" at the Burntlog Road
Time: 4 days; difficulty: strenuous
Access: See Chilcoot Pass and Pistol Rock to go by trail to the junction of the Summit Trail with the Big Baldy Ridge Trail

What you'll see: On Big Baldy Ridge, gaunt whitebark pines stand sentinel on volcanic outcrops and on hillsides of aster, yarrow and sulphur flower. The ridge has a wonderful view of the dark knoll of Pistol Rock, red-orange peaks near Monumental Summit and green Papoose Lake in a black basin. Buck Lake resembles clear turquoise glass set in a pewter brooch, below two tiers of charcoal-gray cliffs and the talus summit of Big Baldy.

This description begins at the junction of the Summit Trail with the Big Baldy Ridge Trail at Pistol Rock at 8,740 feet. If you didn't camp at the spring, you'll want to detour to fill your water bottles .3 mile north of this junction because there is no water between it and Buck Lake.

Directions: From the junction, take the Big Baldy Ridge Trail east down a sandy, wooded ridge, from which you will soon see buildings and orange diggings of the Springfield Mine below. Beyond a flat at .5 mile, the trail climbs, then drops to a saddle at 1.5 miles. (The trail shown on the map leading down to the Springfield Mine from the saddle no longer exists.)

After ascending a grassy hill, the trail continues along a ridge in the trees, then drops off the end of the ridge to another saddle at 3 miles. It next switchbacks up 910 feet onto a ridge at 5 miles and climbs 300 feet along the ridge to the high point of the trail (9,040 feet) at 6.5 miles, where it overlooks Papoose Lake. Then the route zigzags east down to a gap at 6.7 miles, curves into a saddle above cliffs and winds to a drop-off at 7.3 miles, where a great cliff falls toward meadows.

Beside this cliff, the trail hairpins down treacherous scree for 450 feet. At 7.7 miles

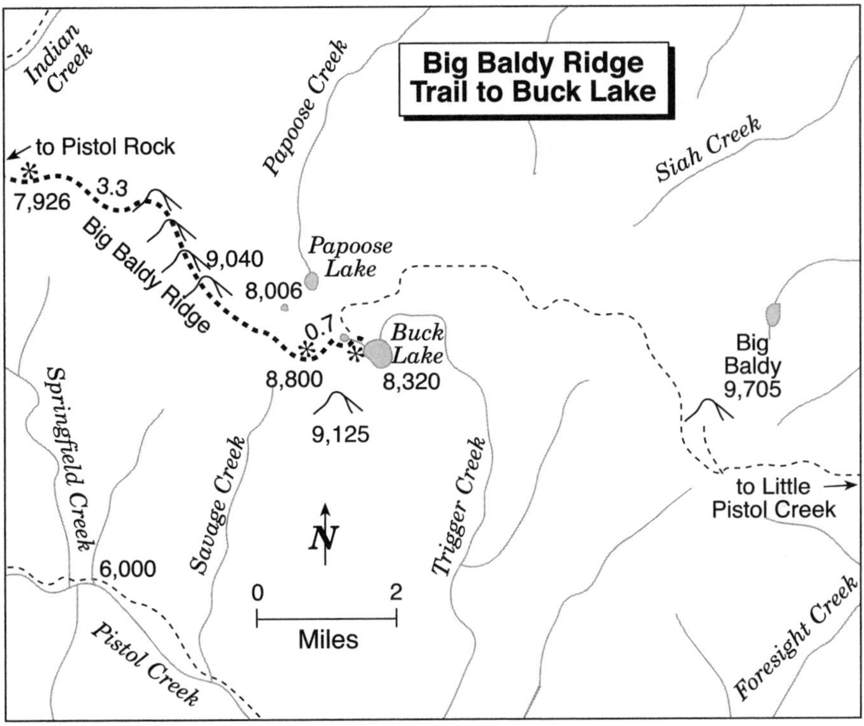

at a pond, the tread may disappear, but the trail circles the south (right) side of the pond, crosses its outlet, and continues to Buck Lake (8,320 feet) at 8 miles.

There are two or three campsites on the trail side of Buck Lake. Avoid camping on the grass by the pond to prevent damaging the meadow around it. To reach Papoose Lake, begin at the pond, and take a path northwest up to an 8,760-foot saddle. Here turn north and descend cross-country to the lake (8,000 feet) at .5 mile. From the saddle, the trail climbs 11.2 miles over Big Baldy and down to Pistol Creek near the hot spring

26.

Middle Fork of Salmon River: Loon Creek To the Middle Fork Lodge

(Section 6 of Big Creek-Middle Fork through trip)

This section one-way: 15.2 miles

Backpacking along the Middle Fork of the Salmon River

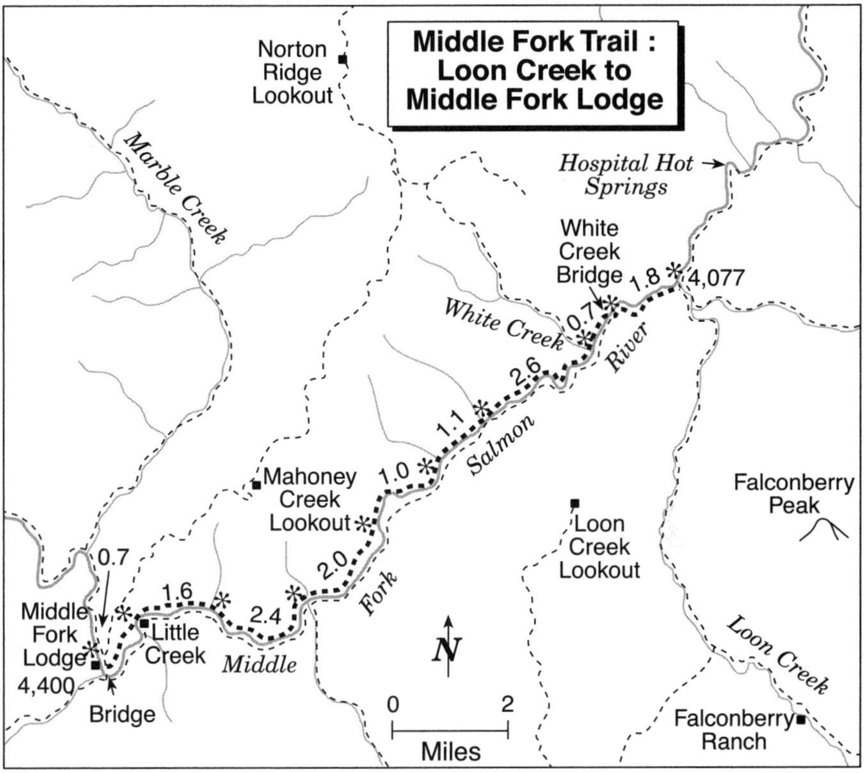

Elevation gain: 1,360 feet; elevation loss (return climb): 980 feet

Highest point: 4,640 feet

Topographic maps: Ramey Hill, Norton Ridge, Sliderock Ridge, Little Soldier Mountain

Trailhead GPS at Big Creek: N 44 45' 343.3" W 115 26' 32.8"

Trailhead GPS at Boundary Creek: N 44 31' 41" W 115 17' 59."

Time: 2 weeks for entire through trip from Big Creek to Boundary Creek; difficulty: very strenuous

Access: See other sections of Big Creek - Middle Fork through trip to go by trail to Loon Creek on the Middle Fork where this description begins.

What you will see: In this gentle section of the Middle Fork, the canyon walls are grassy hills, dotted with trees and outcrops. The west side of the canyon is dry and bare, and the east side has some forest, but sagebrush grays wide bars on both sides. Near White Creek, two rock towers resemble multipoint jester hats. At Mahoney Creek, another outcrop looks like a boat with a stone captain at the prow. The buildings, pastures and lawns of the Middle Fork Lodge are so elegant they appear to be pictures from a magazine. In this section, old snags from the Mortar Creek Fire of 1979 begin to appear.

From the White Creek Bridge, 1.8 miles above Loon Creek, to the Middle Fork Lodge, there are trails on both sides of the river. The trail on the east side has more shade and a bridge over Little Loon Creek, but it climbs more: a 2,000-foot gain and 1,000-foot loss in 12 miles. Therefore, above the White Creek Bridge this hike description is of the west side. For directions to Loon Creek on the Middle Fork Trail, see the first five sections of the Big Creek - Middle Fork through trip. This hike description begins at Loon Creek and is written for those traveling south.

Beyond the bridge over Loon Creek, the Middle Fork trail crosses a sagebrush flat then goes into woods. It hugs the bank as the river spreads around an island at 1.4 miles near Shelf Creek. At high water (8.8 feet or 14,800 cubic feet per second at the Middle Fork Lodge), this section may be knee-deep for 40 yards, but hikers can detour through the brush.

At 1.8 miles, cross the White Creek Bridge to the west side of the river. At 2.5 miles, the trail runs into a shrubby canyon to ford White Creek. Here, a side trail climbs 5.3 miles to the trail to Norton Lake. On the main trail at 3.2 miles is a pine flat with campsites, and at 3.4 miles, at a big rock in the river, is the Rock Island rafting campsite. At 3.5 miles, the trail is across from the white-streaked slope of Cox Hot Springs. At the hot springs is the grave of Whitey Cox, a packer and placer miner who was killed in 1954 when the creek bank caved in on him.

Next the path climbs 150 feet above cliffs. The trail crosses Foundation Creek in shrubs at 4.5 miles, drops to the river and treads the marshy bar of Bacon Creek at 5.1 miles. At 5.5 miles, Red Bluff Creek comes in on the opposite side beside orange cliffs. Grassy slopes and a sagebrush bar bring you to Pine Creek at 6.2 miles.

A grassy area with an old orchard at the back is at 7.5 miles. Near tiny campsites in high grass at 8.1 miles, Mahoney Creek flows down a steep hillside. From here, the trail climbs around a corner to the Mahoney Creek Landing Strip at 8.5 miles, 360 feet above the river. Across the river here are the log cabins of the Cougar Creek Ranch,

A little history: It is owned by the Idaho Department of Fish and Game. After the death of Dutch John Helmke, who started Cougar Creek Ranch, Charley Warnock packed and raised stock there. He helped pack in Zane Grey from Meyers Cove when Grey was working on his novel, Thunder Mountain, a fictionalized account of the drowning of the town of Roosevelt.

More directions: The trail winds in and out of ravines on the side of grassy hills and across sagebrush bars to a ford of Cameron Creek at 10.1 miles. On a sagebrush bar at 12.4 miles, it goes over Range Creek. At 13.5 miles, the trail reaches an immense bar at Sunflower Creek from which Sunflower Hot Springs bubbles at 13.6 miles. Beyond the spring, the Hood Ranch Cabin, owned by the Idaho Department of Fish and Game, stands on a grassy flat. The cabin is open for public use but is primarily for river-rafting emergencies. At the Hood Ranch, John Chestnut grew peaches to sell to Thunder Mountain miners. After leaving Thomas Creek, Milt and Mary Hood came here to continue their outfitting business.

Watch for rattlesnakes from here to the Middle Fork Lodge, although many of the snakes are gopher snakes (also called bull snakes.) They resemble rattlesnakes except for narrower heads and smaller spots. They may even coil, hiss and lunge at those who get close but are non-poisonous.

At 14 miles, the trail reaches the huge sagebrush bar of the Thomas Creek Landing Field, a public air strip, where a side trail leads over a bridge to the Little Creek Guard Station. The main trail follows the landing strip to a bridge at 15.2 miles for the Middle

Fork Lodge. Although this is a private lodge with no trespassing allowed, an outfitter for hunting, trail rides and backpacking is based here. Beyond the bridge, the Norton Lake Trail turns north to go 21 miles over the summits of Mahoney and Norton Ridge Lookouts to Norton Lake. The trail along the opposite (east) side of the river stops at the Middle Fork Lodge, and there is no trail on that side from there to Indian Creek.

27.

Middle Fork of Salmon River: Middle Fork Lodge to Artillery Creek

(Section 7 of Big Creek-Middle Fork through trip)

This section one way: 17.3 miles
Elevation gain: 720 feet; elevation loss (return climb): 160 feet
Highest point: 4,960 feet
Topographic maps: Artillery Dome, Little Soldier Mountain, Pungo Mountain
Trailhead GPS at Boundary Creek: N 44 31' 41" W 115 17' 59.7"
Time: 2 weeks for entire through trip; difficulty: strenuous
Access: See other sections of the Big Creek-Middle Fork through trip to go by trail to the Middle Fork Lodge on the Middle Fork where this description begins.

What you'll see: At the Middle Fork Lodge, dark gray cliffs and thick woods force the river into a gorge where charcoal-gray lichens turn pale granite cliffs black. Above the green river, the trail passes a huge landing field at Indian Creek Guard Station and a smaller one at the private Pistol Creek Ranch. Near Artillery Creek are old snags from the Mortar Creek Fire of 1979. This hike description begins at the Middle Fork Lodge and is written for hikers traveling south.

A little history: Thomas Creek, site of the Middle Fork Lodge, was named for miners living there in the 1880s. Around 1900, Jim Bollard and Mac MacNerney mined and built a cabin here. In 1913, Freeman Nethkin, Edward Osborne and Henry Clay bought the property for a cattle ranch. When they sold it in 1919, a severe winter killed all the stock, so the bank foreclosed. Nethkin's group took it back and tried again, but by 1928 the group had gone broke and Nethkin bought out his partners. In the early 1930s, Milt and Mary Hood leased the property and ran the first commercial dude ranch on the Middle Fork here. Tom and Nell McCall bought the ranch in 1938 for a fly-in ranch that they ran until 1955. After a number of owners, including Harrah's Club, the property was purchased by the Nature Conservancy.

Directions: Beyond the Middle Fork Lodge (4,400 feet), the trail travels a wooded hillside across the river from a rock face. At a bend in the river at 1 mile is a pine-covered bar called Sunflower Flat. At 2.2 miles, the trail spans Marble Creek, where a

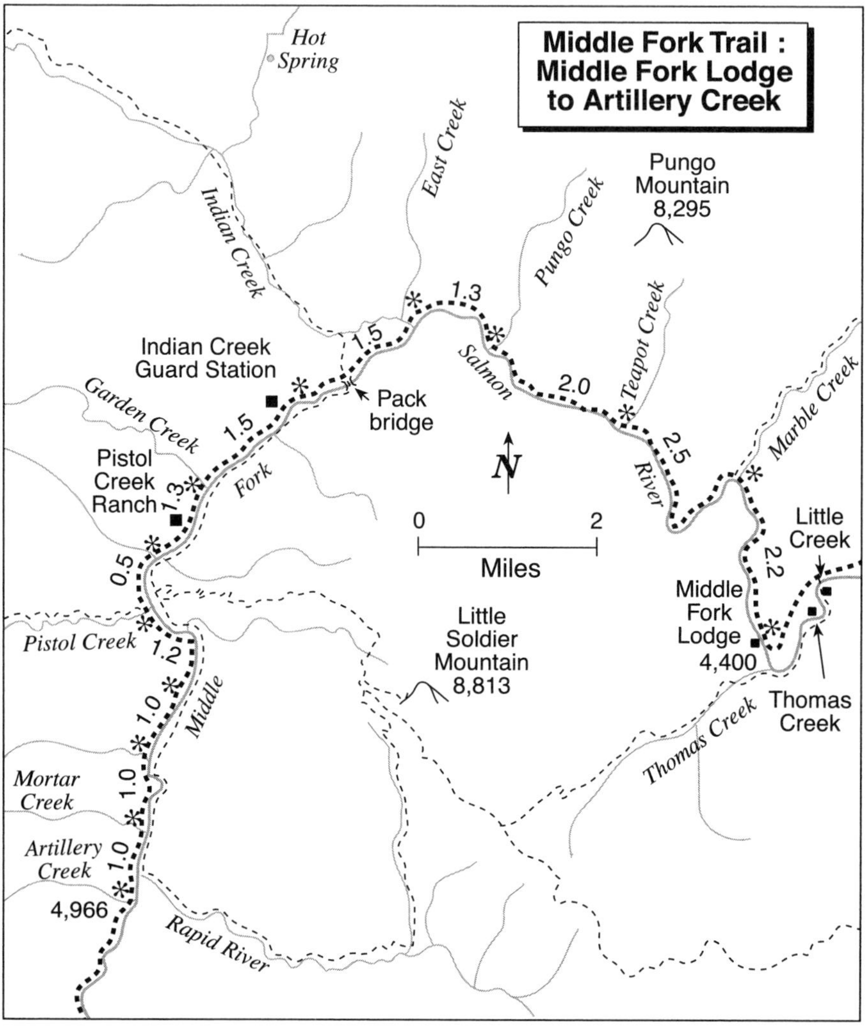

side trail ascends Marble Creek 25 miles with about 40 fords of that creek to the site of the Sunnyside Mine and new trailhead that is reached by the road that also goes to the Lookout Mountain Ridge trailhead. The Marble Creek Trail is a section of the Idaho Centennial Trail, but is not signed as such.

On the Middle Fork Trail at 2.5 miles is a large campsite in a pine flat. At 3.3 miles, the trail makes a hairpin turn. Near Teapot Creek at 5 miles, it travels ledges close to the river, passing a campsite at 6.2 miles. At 7 miles, just beyond Pungo Creek, is a campsite below the trail, and still another is at 7.5 miles.

Where the canyon widens at 8.3 miles, a trail up Indian Creek goes 24 miles to the Summit Trail at Pistol Rock. The Middle Fork Trail bridges Indian Creek, and in .5

mile comes to another junction (at 8.8 miles) Here a trail leads across a bridge over the Middle Fork and up the other side of the river 8 miles to the Rapid River Trail. The main trail skirts the north side of the fenced Indian Creek Landing Field to the Indian Creek Guard Station at 9.8 miles. From near here to beyond Pistol Creek, the hillsides burned in 2000.

At Garden Creek at 11.3 miles, a side trail climbs 6 miles to the Big Baldy Ridge Trail. Beyond Garden Creek, the Middle Fork Trail meets and follows a road from the Pistol Creek Airstrip past some private cabins, several of which burned in the 2000 fires and have been rebuilt.

More history: A packer named Sam Hopkins was the first settler here at the Pistol Creek Ranch in 1892. It was patented by a later owner, George Risley, in 1924. After several different owners, the property was subdivided into summer home lots.

At a junction, take the right (west) road through a gate that must be opened and closed. After following the west (right) edge of the landing strip, the track disappears. A road angles left (south) from the end of the landing strip and crosses Ranch Creek at 12.6 miles where a gate provides access to continue south on the trail.

In the canyon of Pistol Creek, the river trail bridges the creek near a campsite at 13.1 miles. Here a trail turns up the creek to go 21.5 miles to the Snowshoe Cabin trailhead. The river trail reaches a flat at 13.6 miles near the site of a log cabin. Beyond tiny Cap Creek at 14.3 miles, black outcrops are above and willows and a gravel island below. Then the route scrambles up talus above the river to get around a high point that is above the Big Snag campsite and the backwater eddy known as Dolly Lake, where trapped logs go round and round. At 15.7 miles, a treacherous footpath leads from the trail down to a campsite. After crossing Mortar Creek at 16.3 miles, the trail passes four campsites in succession. At 17.3 miles is Artillery Creek (4,960 feet), which is split into two parts.

LOON CREEK AREA

28.

Crimson Lake

Round trip: 21 miles
Elevation gain: 2,040 feet; elevation loss (return climb): 260 feet
Highest point: 8,330 feet
Topographic maps: East Basin Creek, Mount Jordan, Knapp Lakes
Trailhead GPS: N 44 22' 14.1" W 114 44' 40.6"
Time: 2 to 3 days; difficulty: strenuous

Dragline along Loon Creek Road

Access: From Stanley, drive 12 miles east on Idaho 75 to Sunbeam. Turn left (north) on the paved, then improved dirt road and drive 7.4 miles to Bonanza. Turn left (west) and at the guard station keep left. At a split in the road at 7.8 miles where a road goes off to a group campground keep right, and 0.5 mile beyond it avoid a road that goes off to the left to a private campground. Go straight ahead. In another 0 6 mile at another junction, take the road to the left. Drive to the trailhead, at which is at a junction at 10.8 miles with a half mile side road to the Boot Hill cemetery.

A little history: It is worth driving or walking the extra half mile to Boot Hill to see the graves of Lizzie King and her two husbands. She operated a saloon in Bonanza while her husband, Richard, speculated in real estate. When Richard was killed over a real estate deal, Lizzie left for Butte, Montana, where she met Bob Hawthorne, who told her he was rich from mining in England. After returning to Bonanza and opening the Yankee Fork Dance Hall and Saloon, she married Hawthorne in 1880. When people in Bonanza discovered that Hawthorne wasn't rich after all, he killed Lizzie and then himself.

The cemetery was one of two for the town of Bonanza. Because miners had success at nearby Loon Creek in 1869, in 1870 D.B. Varney and Sylvester Jordan tried placer mining for gold on the Yankee Fork of the Salmon River. Their mining drew others to the area; in 1875 William Norton discovered the Charles Dickens lode and in 1876, James Baxter, E.K. Dodge and Morgan McKeim discovered the General Custer lode. In 1879 a pack train brought in the 10-foot flywheel for the mill for the General Custer. It required six mules to carry each half of the wheel. During the trip, lightning struck one wheel half and killed all the mules carrying it.

The towns of Bonanza and Custer grew up around the mines. There are still a few weathered log and board cabins and the towns are now an Idaho state park with a museum and interpretive trails.

What you will see: On a calm day, blue-green Crimson Lake reflects the 400-foot cliffs of two red-orange peaks. South of them, two 600-foot gray prongs of a spur of Cabin Creek Peak lean toward each other.

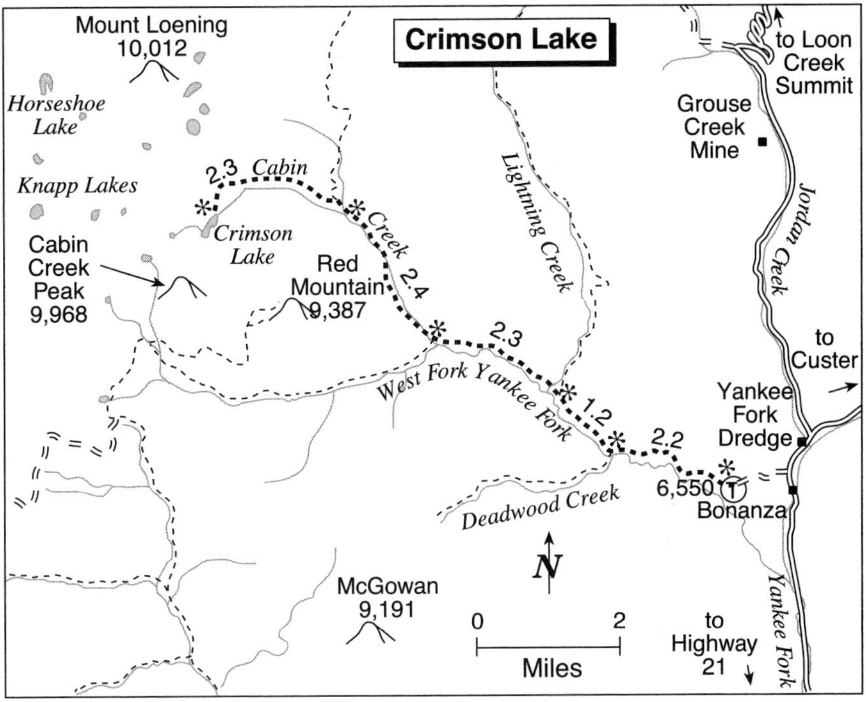

Directions: From the point where the road to Boot Hill turns right at the trailhead, the trail begins as a road going straight ahead. It is gated and signed as the West Fork Yankee Fork Trail in 50 yards. The trail, at first still an old road, climbs along the side of the canyon in sagebrush and firs. In an open area at 1.2 miles, the salmon-pink summit of Red Mountain appears ahead. The way passes behind a wooded knoll, then switchbacks 1down an open slope at 1.7 miles and edges the river at 2.1 miles. At 2.3 miles a side trail turns off to the south along Deadwood Creek. Continue on the main trail through willow flats. At 3.3 miles, the path circles a 500-foot gray lava bluff. In a sagebrush flat at 3.5 miles is a junction with a trail north up Lightning Creek.

At 3.7 miles, the West Fork Trail fords Lightning Creek, below a burnt orange tooth. The trail crosses a dry flat, then returns to the creek in grass and willows at 4.3 miles. Beyond a lodgepole forest, it edges the canyon wall at 5 miles, and crosses a mossy side creek at 5.5 miles. At 5.8 miles, the Cabin Creek Trail, which has come up Pioneer Creek from Loon Creek and down Cabin Creek to this point, joins the West Fork Trail in a grassy flat.

Turn northwest onto the Cabin Creek Trail, which crosses to the west bank of the West Fork at 6.3 miles. Here the tread may disappear, so look for blazes. At a side stream at 6.8 miles, is a close view of Red Mountain to the west. At 7.3 miles, among avalanche-strewn trees, the trail returns to the east bank of the creek.

The trail crosses to the west bank of the North Fork of Cabin Creek at 8.2 miles. Beyond the crossing 100 yards, a blazed spur trail goes 200 yards left (west) into the trees to a campsite. Stay on the main trail to a junction at 8.5 miles at the end of the first big switchback beyond the creek crossing. The Crimson Lake Trail goes straight ahead here, while the Cabin Creek Trail turns right (north.)

From the junction, the trail to Crimson Lake goes west-northwest up the canyon wall in forest. At 9 miles, it climbs the edge of a talus slope, crosses it, and then heads up a gully in woods beside a tiny ridge. The path jogs sharply left for 50 yards, and then continues up the left side of the gully going west.

After crossing more talus, it comes to the boundary of the Frank Church Wilderness at 9.5 miles. After three more narrow talus slopes, and a wooded ravine, the trail goes north of a tiny wooded hill. At the end of a flat, it turns left downhill, crosses a creek and follows its bank southwest. Next, it switchbacks south up one side of the gorge of the outlet of Crimson Lake to a ridge above this gorge and follows the ridge to the lake at 10.5 miles.

29.

Mystery Lake

Round trip: 5 miles
Elevation gain: 2,230 feet
Highest point: 9,070 feet
Topographic maps: Casto, Mount Jordan
Trailhead GPS: 44 31' 7.96" W 114 46' 33.56"
Time: 8 hours; ability: expert; 2 miles cross-country

Access: From Stanley, drive 12 miles east on Highway 75 to Sunbeam. Turn right (north) onto the paved, then improved dirt, Yankee Fork Road. Drive 8.8 miles to Jordan Creek. Turn left (north) on this dirt road and drive over Loon Creek Summit at 17.7 miles to Mystery Creek, 23.5 miles from Highway 75.

What you will see: Above the turquoise water of Mystery Lake, buff and bright orange stripes scribble the cliffs of The General and its neighbors. Below the cliffs, avalanche chutes claw the scree. A peninsula of bare rock accents the scene, and opposite it, whitebark pines sprinkle green on rock benches. A half-mile below the lake, a granite peninsula, a miniature bay and disappearing waterfall distinguish a smaller aqua-green lake.

This is one of the shortest but most difficult hikes in the Frank Church Wilderness. The traces that exist of a trail were probably built by the Civilian Conservation Corps in the 1930s because there was a CCC camp where Mystery Creek crosses the Loon Creek Road at the beginning of the hike. The route climbs beside two waterfalls, gaining 2,230 feet in only 2.5 miles. It is not recommended for children or for those bothered by steep trails or by drop-offs. Sturdy boots are essential, and a walking stick or trekking poles are strongly recommended.

Directions: Park above the road just before Mystery Creek, beside the site of the CCC camp. Cross the road bridge over Mystery Creek and turn left up an open area

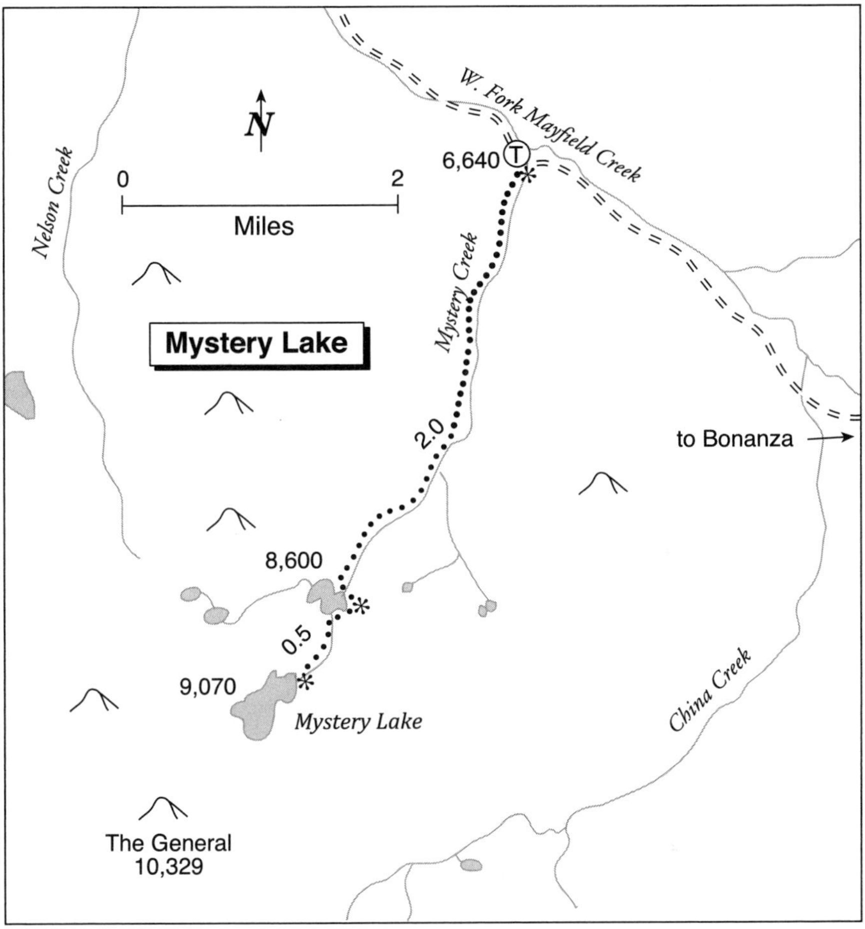

of grass and river stones. The non-system trail begins in 100 yards behind a wilderness boundary sign at the edge of the trees.

The trail first skirts the base of a steep slope in firs and aspens, amid downed timber. The steepness lessens in a few yards. The route continues along the bases of talus slopes. At .8 mile, where the path goes along the creek, talus extends to the creek on both sides. Here, it turns up away from the creek to cross the talus. Ahead on the left is a flat knoll resembling frowning eyebrows and on the right a rock face. Just below the face, the trail disappears in talus for 150 yards, then reappears in the forest 25 yards from the creek. At the base of a second rock face, the route again turns up, away from the creek, first in talus, then in forest. At 1.2 miles, the canyon and creek split, but the east branch of the creek, which descends in two branches from three little ponds, is shown only on the Mount Jordan quadrangle, not on the Casto quadrangle. Beyond the split, the route climbs the right (west) side of the west branch.

Where the talus descends to the creek, keep 100 feet above the creek, which enters a gorge. At 1.5 miles, the trail is even with the rock eyebrows and ascends the grass and rock ledges of a wrinkle above the gorge. Take a cautious glimpse of a 50-foot waterfall and cascades below.

The path creeps up steep rock and dirt close to the creek just above ledges that line the gorge. As the ground begins to level out at 1.7 miles, the trail disappears in an old burn. Stay 100 yards from the ledges along the creek, and cross lodgepole benches to the first lake, which is unnamed, at 2 miles. An inlet on the west side of this small lake descends from two tiny lakes at 8,900 and 9,200 feet.

To go on up to Mystery Lake, you follow a different inlet, this one at the south end of the first lake. To reach it circle the left (east) shore on a fisherman's path. It crosses a talus slope below the inlet, which much of the summer flows underneath the talus. Halfway between the talus and the large peninsula on the west side of the lake, turn left off the path and walk cross-country southeast up a sloping grassy shelf between ledges to a wooded ravine. (Be sure to find the shelf, because climbing directly from the lakeshore into the ravine requires scrambling.) Go south up the ravine 150 yards from the waterfall and parallel to it on the west. When the ground flattens, walk over rock benches to Mystery Lake at 2.5 miles. There are possible campsites along the northwest shore near the outlet.

30.

East Fork of Mayfield Creek to Ibex Creek

Round trip: 10.6 miles
Elevation gain: 860 feet; elevation loss (return climb): 240 feet
Highest point: 6,240 feet
Topographic maps: Casto, Sherman Peak
Trailhead GPS: N 44 30' 15.9" W 114 45' 0.7"
Time: 7.5 hours for round trip: difficulty: expert, due to 8 fords of creek

Access: From Stanley, drive 12 miles east on Highway 75 to Sunbeam. Turn left (north) onto the paved, then improved dirt, Yankee Fork Road. Drive 8.8 miles to Jordan Creek. Turn left (north) on the dirt Loon Creek Road and drive over Loon Creek Summit at 17.7 miles to the East Fork of Mayfield Creek, 25.4 miles from Highway 75.

What you will see: Above the East Fork of Mayfield Creek, pinnacles top 400-foot beige cliffs, and charcoal-gray towers resemble giant firs. Colorful talus dapples the upper canyon walls with yellow, cream, gray, pink, brown and purple. Alders, willows and thimbleberries have overgrown the trail, which fords Mayfield Creek once and the East Fork seven times between the trailhead and Ibex Creek. Most years, the first two crossings will be dangerous for foot travelers until mid-August.

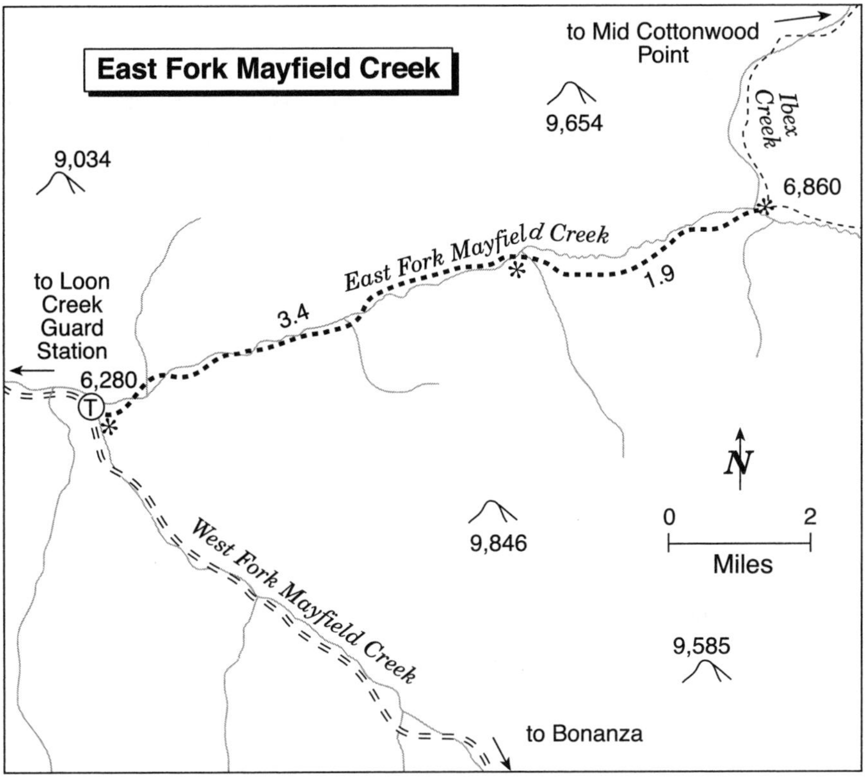

Directions: From the Loon Creek Road, the trail first fords Mayfield Creek at 6,280 feet, then wanders through a Douglas fir flat on the south side of the East Fork. At .3 mile, the trail fords to the north side of the East Fork, which is wider and deeper than Mayfield Creek, and may be knee-deep even in September.

Once across, the route roams through forest, crossing a side creek at .5 mile and wading back over the East Fork in willows at .7 mile. The overgrown trail goes back to the north side of the creek at 1.2 miles, and at 1.3 miles is another ford to the south. At 1.8 miles the route is along a grassy flat with a campsite below a cliff. Then there is steep forest, a side stream at 2 miles, a ford to the north side at 2.1 miles, and another to the south at 3.4 miles.

The trail fords a side stream, climbs around the south side of a wooded knoll, and at 5.2 miles returns to the north side of the creek. In a sagebrush flat at 5.3 miles is a junction (6,860 feet) with the Ibex Creek - Cold Creek Trail, which climbs 12 miles over Mid-Cottonwood Point and down Cold Creek to the Warm Springs Creek Trail. On the main trail, just beyond a sagebrush flat is an algae-filled pond, with a view of colorful canyon walls. The trail continues up the canyon, then climbs the side of it to a junction at 12 miles (8,200 feet) with the eight-mile Trapper Fork Trail to Warm Spring Creek.

31.

Loon Creek Trail to Horseshoe Lake

Round trip: 18 miles
Elevation gain: 2,190 feet
Highest point: 7,994 feet
Topographic maps: Casto, Pinyon Peak, Knapp Lakes
Trailhead GPS: N 44 32' 57" W 114 51' 0.1"
Time: 2-3 days; ability: expert
Access: From Stanley drive 12 miles east on Highway 75 to Sunbeam. Turn left (north) onto the paved, then improved dirt, Yankee Fork Road. Drive 8.8 miles to Jordan Creek. Turn left (north) on the dirt Loon Creek Road and drive over Loon Creek Summit at 17.7 miles to the Loon Creek Guard Station at 29 miles.

What you will see: Below Horseshoe Lake, gray needles, corrugated walls and charcoal inverted cones overlook the upper end of Loon Creek Canyon. At the lake, a pale orange ridge crumbles into the blue-green water, which is split at the upper end by a long wooded peninsula. For an alternate route to Horseshoe Lake, see Horseshoe Lake from Knapp Creek.

Directions: From the Loon Creek Guard Station at 5,800 feet, walk northwest from the corral through a gate and along an old road toward Loon Creek. In 100 yards, is a path from the Diamond D Ranch next door. Turn left (southwest) on the path, which within a few yards crosses the Frank Church Wilderness boundary through a gate where there is a register box.

From here follow the trail across grassy flats dotted with Douglas firs. Where the trail to Pinyon Peak turns off at .4 mile, keep straight ahead. Soon the trail goes down through shrubs along the creek before returning to the flat. After angling uphill to a grassy shelf, the trail descends to a side stream, No Name Creek, at 1.5 miles. Avoid a path up to a campsite just before it. There are some burned areas along here. At 2.2 miles is a junction with a trail that goes 8 miles up Pioneer Creek and down Cabin Creek to the West Fork of Yankee Fork trail.

Beyond the Pioneer Creek junction, the Loon Creek Trail fords Pioneer Creek, which is a problem in early season. At 2.5 miles, it crosses Loon Creek to the north bank in a ford that could be dangerous in early season. This ford is not shown on the topographic map.

Once across, the trail continues through a Douglas fir forest below gabled towers, passing a hot spring on the opposite bank at 3 miles. Between 4 and 5 miles, the creek curves to the south. The trail goes over a side creek at 5 miles, then crosses back to the left (now east) side of Loon Creek, where it spreads into shallow streams.

Next the trail climbs away from the creek into lodgepoles and goes through the first

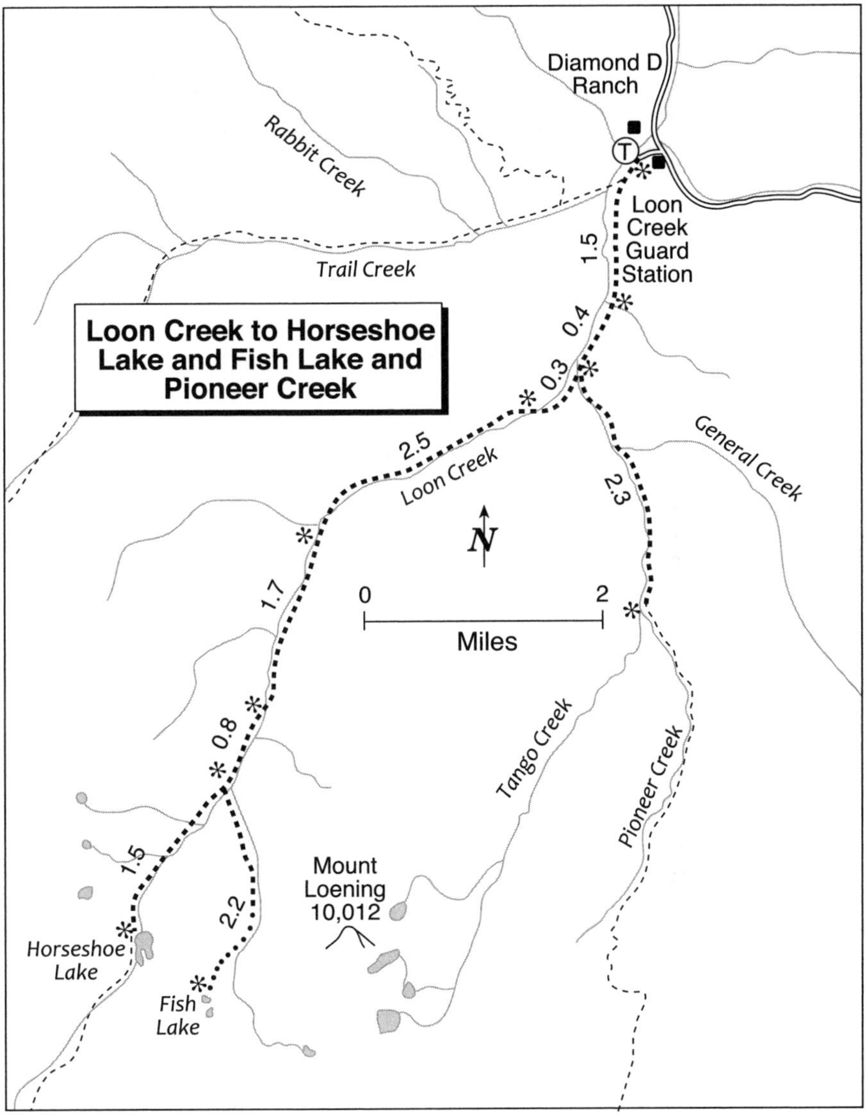

of four strips of aspens at 5.5 miles. At 6.7 miles it returns to the right (west) side of Loon Creek. In the remaining 2.3 miles the trail climbs 1,100 feet. At 7.5 miles the trail passes an old junction with a former primitive trail to Fish Lake (There is another Fish Lake near the Chamberlain Ranger Station.)

Beyond this former junction, the Loon Creek Trail ascends through brush, forest and mud, to the lake at 9 miles (7,994 feet.) Campsites are at the lower end and on the peninsula, but bears frequent them. The trail continues for 7.5 miles over a divide and down to the Asher/Knapp Creek trailhead.

32.

Pioneer Creek to Tango Creek

Round trip: 9 miles
Elevation gain: 840 feet
Highest point: 6,840 feet
Topographic maps: Casto, Mount Jordan
Trailhead GPS: N 44 32' 57" W 114 51' 0.1"
Time: 7 hours; difficulty: moderate
Access: From Stanley, drive 12 miles east on Highway 75 to Sunbeam. Turn left (north) on the paved, then improved dirt Yankee Fork Road, and drive 8.8 miles to a junction with the Jordan Creek Road. Turn left (north) on this dirt road and drive over Loon Creek Summit at 17.7 miles and down to the Loon Creek Guard Station at 29 miles.

What you will see: Pioneer Creek splashes down a rugged canyon topped with high crumbled cliffs and little pointed towers. The view of the canyon walls is excellent because you can see through the trees, most of which have burned. The trail up the creek gives access to Tango Creek, whose headwaters contain some of the most spectacular lakes and peaks in the Frank Church Wilderness.

Directions: To reach the trail, park by the main road and walk to the guard station's corral Go through a gate to the right (north). Cross a grassy area to a path coming from the Diamond D Ranch next door and join it as it goes west through a gate at a register box. at the end of the fenced pasture, Hike up Loon Creek for 2.2 miles (see Loon Creek Trail to Horseshoe Lake for details) to a junction with the trail up Pioneer Creek, just before the Loon Creek Trail fords Pioneer Creek. The Pioneer Creek Trail first climbs a steep, grassy, brushy hillside with a view across the canyon of a mountain dotted with outcrops. Much of the way from Loon Creek to Tango Creek the trail is in burned forest. As it contours along the steep hillside, it has slid away in places, so watch your footing. At 3 miles the trail fords General Creek. In early season, you will want to look for logs to cross on. At 3.5 miles, a complex of teeth and towers is on the right (west) canyon wall, with a big talus slope below the last of these towers. The trail continues in burned forest, and at 4.5 miles begins to curve southeast, continuing up the canyon of Pioneer Creek.

Here Tango Creek splits off from Pioneer Creek. If you want to try to go on up Tango Creek to Tango Lakes, this is the place to turn off. However, the route is mostly rough cross-country travel and there is a lot of downed timber along it. It is recommended only for the rugged and patient. You may find bits of the ancient trail by looking for cut logs, horse manure and faint trail tread above the confluence of the two creeks. These bits are first found by fording to the right (west) side of Tango Creek and looking in the forest slightly above the bank. Early in the summer, high water will make fording the creek difficult. It is also possible and probably much easier to reach these lakes by cross-country hiking from the cirque above Crimson Lake.

The trail up Pioneer Creek is formally considered a part of the Cabin Creek Trail. From Tango Creek it continues up Pioneer Creek over an 8,600-foot saddle 5.5 more miles to meet the trail that goes down Cabin Creek to the West Fork of the Yankee Fork, and a spur trail that goes up Cabin Creek to Crimson Lake.

33.

Fish Lake

Round trip: 19.4 miles
Elevation gain: 2,440 feet
This section (one way): 2.2 miles; 1,080 feet gain
Highest point: 8,280 feet
Topographic map: Knapp Lakes
Trailhead GPS: N 44 32' 57" W 114 51' 0.1" at Loon Creek Guard Station
Time: 2-3 days; ability: expert; rangers say former trail is mostly gone.
Access: See Loon Creek to Horseshoe Lake to go by trail to the obscure junction of the Loon Creek Trail with the trail to Fish Lake where this description begins.

What you will see: The topographic map shows an open area south of Fish Lake, but in wet years it is really another lake, so there can be two small lakes of glowing green. They nestle in ovals of pale green sphagnum moss that bounces when you walk on it. Across the canyon a row of rock needles towers 400 feet, next to a splintered peak with tiny leaning spires. The side trail to Fish Lake is an old Forest Service trail but is not on any map.

Directions: The hike begins on the Loon Creek Trail at the Fish Lake junction (7,200 feet) at 7.5 miles. The indistinct, 2.2-mile trail from the junction to Fish Lake climbs 1,080 feet. It first heads up the canyon of Loon Creek, fording it at 200 yards. At .5 mile, the trail crosses below talus of the west canyon wall, then climbs through woods and fords Fish Creek to the east at 1 mile. At 1.2 miles, it returns to the west side and climbs through forest to the top of creekside cliffs.

The path edges talus at 1.7 miles, then crosses a grassy ravine and a stream to the left and goes up onto a granite bench at 2 miles. From here, it follows a ridge on the left (east) side of the ravine below orange and gray towers to the first lake at 2.2 miles (8,240 feet). The second lake is a few yards south of the first.

Fish Lake may also be reached by cross-country hiking from Horseshoe Lake. To do this, go .5 mile up the trail above the lake toward the Knapp Creek Divide, then cut over to the three small ponds shown on the map. From the highest pond, climb to a saddle (8,680 feet) and then down a scree-filled gully to the first lake.

34.

Loon Creek Hot Springs

Round trip: 12 miles to the junction with the Warm Spring Trail
Elevation gain: 280 feet; elevation loss (return climb): 680 feet
Highest point: 5,411 feet
Topographic maps: Casto, Falconberry Peak, Rock Creek
Trailhead GPS: N 44 36' 8" W 114 48' 25,9"
Time: 7.5 hours; difficulty: strenuous
Access: From Stanley, drive 12 miles east on Highway 75 to Sunbeam. Turn left (north) 75 onto the paved, then improved dirt, Yankee Fork Road. Drive 8.8 miles to Jordan Creek. Turn left (north) and drive over Loon Creek Summit at 17.7 miles past the Loon Creek Guard Station and turnoffs for the roads to Pinyon Peak and Indian Springs to the end of the road at 33.7 miles.

What you will see: Along the Lower Loon Creek Trail lichens paint a row of cliffs and an 800-foot face dark gray and lime green. At one of five springs, hot waterfalls spray over moss into Loon Creek and into a rock-lined pool. None of the hot pools is large enough for more than one person. Because of the low elevation, this hike is best for fall or early summer.

The Loon Creak Road to the trailhead is a spectacular drive, with views of pink, rust-brown and cream-colored mountains. Seven switchbacks, each .2 mile long, climb 2,000 feet to the 8,700-foot summit. Below the Loon Creek Guard Station at 29 miles, the road passes sites of the gold mining camps of Casto and Orogrande.

A little history: In 1869, Nathan Smith found placer gold at Loon Creek. When he reported his discovery to the people at the mining camp of Leesburg near Salmon, miners came to Loon Creek with him and by that fall there were 1,000, some of whom stayed all winter. Spring supplies were packed into camp at night to avoid soft snow. By the fall of 1870, two sawmills were producing 11,000 board feet of lumber a day at Orogrande.

When the boom ended in 1871, the Chinese bought most of the claims and the town. On February 12, 1879, the remaining five (or so) Chinese were murdered in the episode that started the Sheepeater War.

The site of Orogrande is now known as Casto because the next settler was miner Billy Casto, who also ran a hotel there in 1903. When the Lost Packer Mine was developed in 1904, after Clarence Eddy discovered gold there, Casto became its supply center and post office.

Directions: The trail descends only 400 feet in 6 miles, but climbs up and down as it does so. It begins at a parking area at the base of orange and gray outcrops. At .5 mile it is across the canyon from the 800-foot face. In grassy flats at 1.2 miles, the trail crosses four branches of Shell Creek. Talus follows, and at 2 miles there is a wall of lichen-covered cliffs. At 3 miles, it bridges Loon Creek to the east side, then passes a

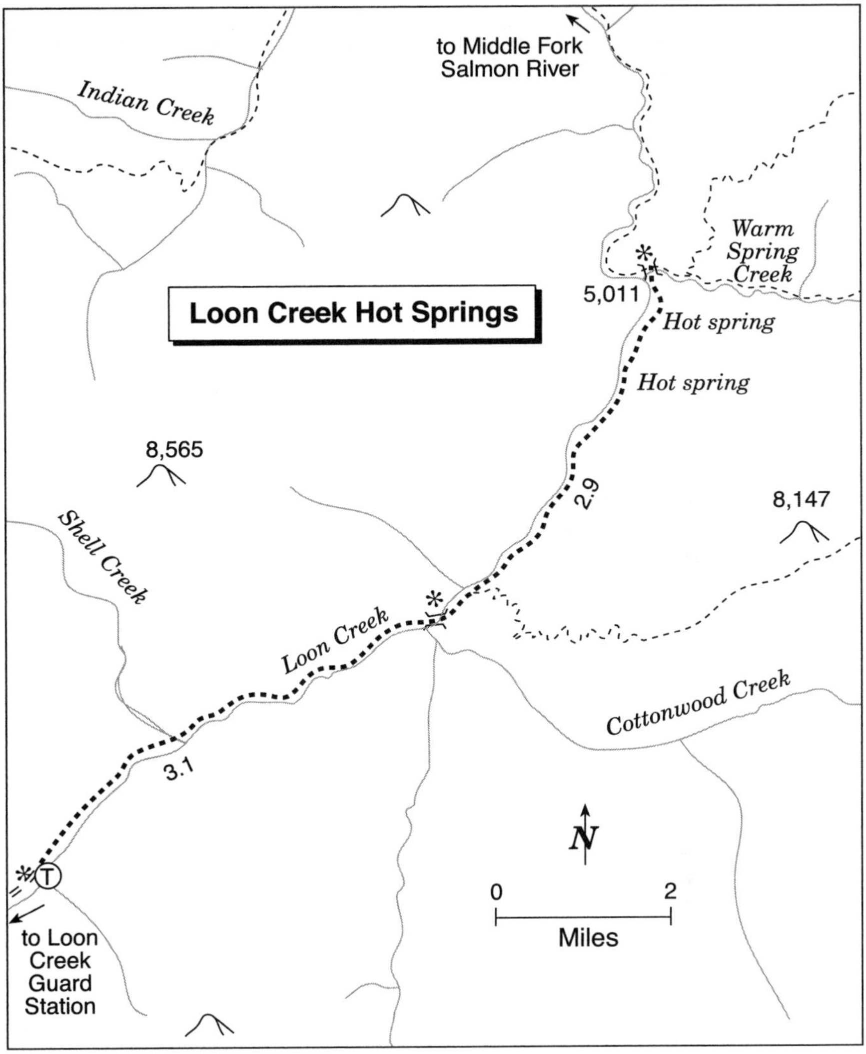

turnoff for a little-used trail up Cottonwood Creek at 3.3 miles. (This trail climbs 6.8 miles to the Ibex-Cold Creek Trail at Mid-Cottonwood Point.)

From 4 to 4.5 miles, the Loon Creek Trail goes over three side streams that dry up by summer's end, and at 4.5 miles curves left across a bare hillside. Below a historic cabin at 5.2 miles, the first spring trickles down into lukewarm pools beside the creek. Around the next bend, the two largest hot springs tumble over cliffs to the creek. At 5.7 miles are two more algae-filled pools and an old cabin called the Owen cabin. Beyond a crumbled black monolith at 6 miles, the trail bridges Warm Spring Creek to meet the trail that has come down that creek. From here, the Loon Creek Trail descends 16 miles to the Middle Fork with all crossings bridged. A 4- by 10-foot cement-sided hot pool is .4 mile above the Middle Fork.

35.

Cougar Point

Round trip: 6 miles
Elevation gain: 980 feet; elevation loss (return climb): 480 feet
Highest point: 8,099 feet
Topographic map: Falconberry
Trailhead GPS: N 44 40'16.3" W 114 50' 22.4"
Time: 5 hours; difficulty: moderate

Access: From Stanley drive 12 miles east on Highway 75 to Sunbeam. Turn left (north) on the paved, then improved dirt, Yankee Fork Road, and drive 8.8 miles to Jordan Creek. Here turn left (west) on the Loon Creek Road and drive over Loon Creek Summit at 17.7 miles. Continue past the Loon Creek Guard Station at 29 miles to a junction with the Indian Springs Road at 32 miles. Here turn left (west) on that road and drive over Grouse Creek Summit to a switchback just before a spur road to the Indian Springs Guard Station turns off at 41.7 miles. The trail begins at the switchback, but parking is better at the little campground beside the guard station at 42.2 miles.

What you'll see: The views from Cougar Point demonstrate the main characteristic of the Frank Church Wilderness: a sea of mountains and ridges rolling in every direction. Also it is a good place to see one of the stages in the fire regeneration cycle: bare grass and brush-covered hillsides. This drainage burned in the 1979 Mortar Creek Fire. To the northeast is Falconberry Peak's heap of orange talus and Sleeping Deer Mountain's white curved top and dark nubbins. In the distance to the south is the cone of Pinyon Peak, flanked by saw-toothed gray peaks at the head of Tango Creek. On the grassy hilltop of Cougar Point the cement foundation of the former lookout draws a white square in paintbrush and lupine.

Directions: Two trails begin at the switchback in the road where the guard station road turns off. One leads 9 miles down Jack Creek to Falconberry Ranch on Loon Creek. In the 1880s Jack Ferguson started this ranch. He was the first long-term rancher on Loon Creek. About 1900, he sold his place to Len Falconberry and the site of the ranch became known as Falconberry. The other trail leads to Cougar and Loon Creek points and was built by the CCC; Take this trail, which angles up a grassy hillside and contours along in the woods to a junction at .8 mile with the Cold Springs trail, which descends 7.5 miles to the site of the Biggs Ranch on Loon Creek. From here the main trail switchbacks down 400 feet through a Douglas fir forest to a saddle at 1.2 miles, from which a primitive trail leads west into the canyon of Little Loon Creek.

From the saddle the main trail climbs along the side of a ridge, partly on sagebrush hillsides and partly through Douglas fir forest, passing the cliffs of a 30-foot outcrop at about 1.5 miles. From here you can look out across the Middle Fork to the rounded top of Big Baldy, patched with snow until late summer. At 2.5 miles, the trail to the former Loon Creek Lookout turns off to the right (north), passing a spring at .5 mile. This trail

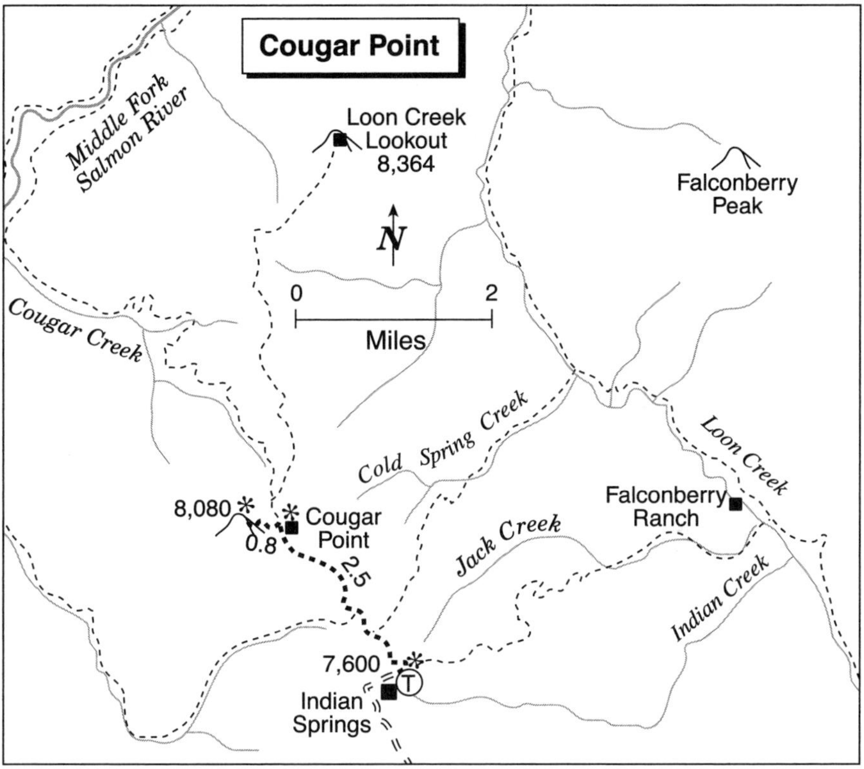

goes 5 miles to the lookout site, which has an excellent view of the Middle Fork canyon.

To reach Cougar Point from the saddle, keep straight ahead at the junction on an overgrown path instead of turning north. This little-used trail winds back and forth across the face of the hill, then climbs past rock outcrops to the summit at 3 miles.

SLEEPING DEER AREA

36.

Sleeping Deer Lookout

Round trip: 4 miles
Elevation gain: 760 feet; elevation loss (return climb): 120 feet
Highest point: 9,881 feet

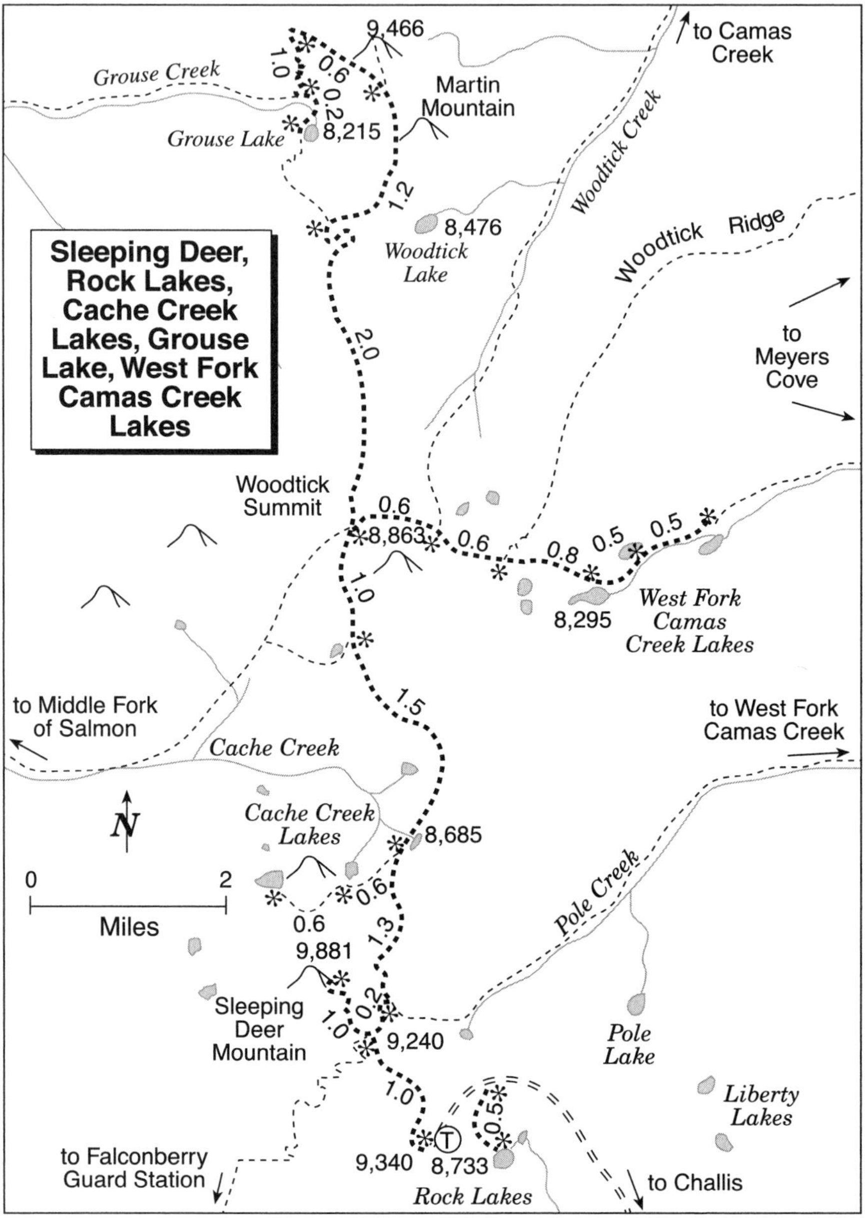

Topographic map: Sleeping Deer

Trailhead GPS: N 44 45' 13.2" W 114 40' 47.2"

Time: 4 hours; difficulty: easy but rocky and the access road is trying

Access: In Challis, turn left (west) off Highway 93 onto Main Street. At .5 mile, turn right (north) off Main Street onto the paved Challis Creek Road. The pavement ends at 9.3 miles and the road intersects with one to Mosquito Flat Reservoir at 10.4 miles. Passenger cars and trailers are not recommended beyond this point. Four-wheel drive is a good idea. Keep straight ahead. Open and shut two ranch gates if they are closed. Continue on the primitive and rocky Sleeping Deer Road over Twin Peaks Saddle at 19 miles and on out to the end of the road at 42.9 miles. Most of the trees along the road from the Mosquito Flat turnoff on have burned in the last 20 years. Snow and/or landslides often block the last 4 miles before August 1, so call ahead.

What you will see: The view from Sleeping Deer Lookout (9,881 feet) resembles a gigantic relief map stretching in every direction for more than 50 miles. To the north, below 800-foot cliffs, Cache Creek Lakes decorate this map with blue-green ovals and triangles. Views to the south are of orange-pink sandy peaks near Crimson Lake, dark green canyons of Warm Spring and Loon Creeks and blue silhouettes of the White Clouds. Southeast stand the double points of Twin Peaks. To the east, a buffalo-shaped outcrop obscures the golden valley of Meyers Cove. To the northwest, the deep chasm of the Middle Fork divides the peach-colored needles of the Bighorn Crags from the wooded ridges of Chamberlain Basin. West of the lookout, the ground drops thousands of feet to the Middle Fork.

The Sleeping Deer Road is one of the most scenic and challenging in Idaho, hairpinning up and down along ridges above 2,000-foot-deep canyons for more than 30 miles. It ends abruptly 400 feet above Rock Lakes, 2 miles from Sleeping Deer Lookout. At 18.6 miles the road passes a junction with the two-mile road up to the Twin Peaks Lookout, which sits on a triangular peak of chocolate-colored talus. From Challis, it is only 45 minutes (19 miles) to Twin Peaks Saddle (9,190 feet) at the Frank Church Wilderness boundary. Snow landslides 4 miles before the end often block the road, so be sure to call ahead.

Directions: From the end of the road, the Sleeping Deer Lookout trail circles west around the south end of a sandy ridge, studded with whitebark pines, then turns north and west again. At 1 mile, the trail to the lookout splits off from the trail to Cache Creek Lakes. From this junction, the Cabin Creek Trail descends to the south 9 miles to the site of Falconberry Ranch on Loon Creek. Take the lookout trail, which heads northwest along the side of Sleeping Deer Mountain, switchbacking up in scree. It passes a small shoulder of the peak at 1.3 miles;. After two more big switchbacks across talus, it reaches the 9,881-foot summit at 2 miles.

37.

Cache Creek Lakes and Woodtick Summit

Round trip: 10 miles
Elevation gain: 380 feet; elevation loss (return climb): 860 feet
This section: 4 miles one way; 340 feet gain; elevation loss (return climb): 860 feet
Highest point: 9,280 feet

Third Cache Creek Lake

Topographic map: Sleeping Deer Mountain
Trailhead GPS: N 44 45' 13..2" W 114 40' 47.2" at road's end
Time: 8 hours; difficulty: moderate, cross-country to upper lakes
Access: In Challis turn left (west) off Highway 93 onto Main Street. At .5 mile, turn right (north) off Main Street onto the paved Challis Creek Road. The pavement ends at 9.3 miles and the road intersects with one to Mosquito Flat Reservoir at 10.4 miles. Passenger cars and trailers are not recommended beyond this point. Four-wheel drive is a good idea. Keep straight ahead. Open and shut two ranch gates if they are closed. Continue on the primitive and rocky Sleeping Deer Road over Twin Peaks Saddle at 19 miles and on out to the end of the road at 42.9 miles. From the end of the road hike 1 mile to a junction with the Sleeping Deer Lookout Trail where this description begins.

What you will see: Lime-green marsh grass echoes the emerald water of the first Cache Creek Lake. Above it to the southwest, crumbled cliffs sweep in a wide triangle to the top of Sleeping Deer Mountain. On the opposite shore, talus spills into the water from a ridge of needles. Down the trail, the second lake creates concentric green ovals, with blue-green in the center, yellow-green water ringing the edge of the lake, lime-green grass around it and then a larger oval of meadow punches a hole in the forest. To the southwest of this lake rises a black 1,000-foot wall of vertical rock cylinders.

The off-trail lakes are overlooked by a dark volcanic neck decorated with snow slivers on the ridge of Sleeping Deer. Each summer an island of boulders in the highest lake becomes a peninsula. Above the lower of these off-trail lakes, a small stream tumbling down Sleeping Deer Mountain nourishes an alpine meadow.

From the junction (9,240 feet) with the trail to Sleeping Deer Lookout, 1 mile northwest of the trailhead, the trail to the Cache Creek Lakes drops to a junction with a trail down Pole Creek at .2 mile. (The Pole Creek Trail descends 6.2 miles to the West

Fork of Camas Creek Trail, giving rough, cross-country access to Pole Lakes.)

From this junction, continue down the Cache Creek Trail across talus to a saddle at .5 mile, then down between granite slabs and young trees to a meadow at the upper end of the first lake (8,685 feet) at 1.5 miles (2.5 miles from the trailhead.) Below this lake the trail descends a grass-covered ridge to a mossy stream at 2 miles with a view of the green-ringed second lake (8,525 feet) well below the trail. At 2.7 miles, the third small lake sits in a muddy basin. At 3 miles is a junction with a trail that goes west down Cache Creek 7.5 miles, passing a fourth lake, to the Loon Creek Trail, just above the Middle Fork.

Keep straight ahead toward Woodtick Summit. The area between here and Grouse Lake burned in 1988. Near the summit there used to be log tripods that once held a telephone line to the former Martin Mountain Lookout. At 4 miles, Woodtick Summit is an 8,863-foot saddle between two ridge spurs sprinkled with silver logs.

To reach the two off-trail upper lakes, start at the meadow at the upper end of the first Cache Creek Lake on the trail and follow a white rounded ridge southwest. Descend to the lower lake (8,558 feet) by climbing down gullies or the inlet stream. This lake is .6 mile from the trail.

To reach the upper off-trail lake (8,691 feet) from the lower, follow the inlet up and cross the 9,040-foot saddle between Peak 9340 and Peak 9753. Then scramble down the rocky benches to the shore, 1.2 miles from the trail. If you walk quietly, you may see wildlife.

38.

West Fork of Camas Creek Lakes

Round trip: 16 miles
Elevation gain: 540 feet; elevation loss (return climb): 2,030 feet
This section: 3 miles; 160 feet gain; elevation loss (return climb): 1,170 feet
Highest point: 8,863 feet
Topographic map: Sleeping Deer
Time: 2-3 days; difficulty: strenuous
Access: Follow the directions for the Sleeping Deer Road and the directions in the preceding hike, Cache Creek Lakes and Woodtick Summit, to go by trail to Woodtick Summit where this description begins.

What you will see: At the head of the canyon of the West Fork of Camas Creek, two little ponds perch below stair steps of a dark gray peak. Below them in the woods the green water of the largest lake is shaped like a bottle. Farther down the canyon under gray rock benches, a wooded point divides the tea-colored middle lake into two bays. Well below it hides the sliver-shaped lowest lake.

From 8,863-foot Woodtick Summit, take the trail to West Fork Lakes, which zigzags east down the ridge and then cuts under cliffs across the head of the canyon of

Woodtick Creek, where there is a view into the canyon of Camas Creek. At .6 mile near a spring, a trail turns down Woodtick Creek to descend 12 miles to Camas Creek. Stay on the West Fork Lakes Trail, which crosses a stream and climbs to a grassy flat with two marshy ponds.

Beyond the ponds and a grassy saddle at 1.2 miles, the Woodtick Ridge Trail branches northeast 10.9 miles to the West Fork of Camas Creek Trail 2.7 miles above Meyers Cove, offering cross-country access to Martindale Lakes.

The main trail descends a talus slope, from which you can see the miniature and largest lakes below. It then drops through woods to the lower end of the large lake (8,295 feet) at 2 miles across from a campsite. Below this lake, the trail to the middle lake (8,128 feet) descends 160 feet in .5 mile through a lodgepole forest to a meadow, which is a few steps southeast of the lake. The trail drops another 180 feet to the narrow lower lake (7,852 feet), which is 200 yards off the trail at 3 miles. By midsummer, there is no water between the stream above the second Cache Creek Lake and West Fork Lakes. Below the West Fork Lakes, the trail continues down the West Fork of Camas Creek 10 miles to Meyers Cove.

39.

Grouse Lake

Round trip: 18.4 miles
Elevation gain: 820 feet; elevation loss (return climb): 1,950 feet.
This section: 5 miles; 440 feet gain; elevation loss (return climb): 1,090 feet
Highest point: 9,300 feet
Topographic map: Sleeping Deer Mountain
Time: 2-3 days; difficulty: strenuous
Access: Follow the directions for the Sleeping Deer Road and the directions in the preceding hike, Cache Creek Lakes and Woodtick Summit, to go by trail to Woodtick Summit.

The trail to Grouse Lake gives you a view of blue-green Woodtick Lake below dark crumbly cliffs and rows of rounded pink mountains across the Middle Fork canyon. Above Grouse Lake a ridge of woods and talus forms the backbone of Martin Mountain. The spongy ground around the shallow, marshy lake is studded with burnt snags, some of them with grotesque burls.

This hike description begins at Woodtick Summit (8,863 feet) 5 miles from the trailhead. To reach Grouse Lake from there, take the Martin Mountain Trail north. The trail follows the top of a narrow ridge through sparse whitebark pines. At 1 mile, it angles left onto the west side of the ridge, and at 1.5 miles, returns to the ridge top that overlooks Woodtick Lake.

Next, the path hairpins down to a junction (9,000 feet) at 2 miles with an old foot trail to Grouse Lake, which is impassable because of burnt, fallen logs from a 1988 fire. To take a side trip to Woodtick Lake (8,476 feet) from this junction continue straight ahead .2 mile to a saddle, then leave the trail and descend cross-country over talus for .2 mile, dropping 500 feet. To reach Grouse Lake, continue straight ahead on the Martin Mountain Trail. This trail is an old CCC trail with beautifully crafted retaining walls. It first climbs 400 feet onto Martin Mountain. At 3.2 miles an old trail turns off to the former lookout. Continue on the main trail, which descends 600 feet to a saddle at 3.8 miles. From here take the Grouse Creek Trail, which drops 450 feet south to Grouse Creek at 4.8 miles and descends west to the Middle Fork. From the point where the trail reaches the creek, take a side trail .2 mile south to Grouse Lake at 5 miles (8,215 feet). Back at the saddle, the Martin Mountain Trail continues along Macarte Ridge, descending 9 miles to the Middle Fork near Tappan Falls. Note that there is no water between the creek just above the second Cache Creek Lake and Grouse Lake.

40.

Rock Lakes

Round trip: 1 mile
Elevation gain: none; elevation loss (return climb): 425 feet
Highest point: 9,160 feet
Topographic map: Sleeping Deer Mountain
Time: 2 hours
Difficulty: easy, but difficult road
Access: Turn left (west) off U.S. 93 onto Main Street in Challis. At .5 mile, turn right (north) off Main Street onto the paved Challis Creek Road. The pavement ends at 9.3 miles, and the road intersects with one to Mosquito Flat Reservoir at 10.4 miles. Passenger cars and trailers are not recommended beyond this point and four-wheel drive is a good idea. Keep straight ahead toward Twin Peaks. Open and shut two ranch gates if they are closed. Continue on the primitive and rocky Sleeping Deer Road over Twin Peaks Saddle at 19 miles to the Rock Creek - Pole Creek sign at 41.9 miles, .5 mile before the end of the road.

Rock Lakes wink among lodgepole pines below Sleeping Deer Mountain's cap of crumbled cliffs. In August, wildflowers create little gardens below the lakes' terraced meadows. The outlet runs into Loon Creek, a tributary of the Middle Fork of the Salmon.

Begin hiking at the Rock Creek - Pole Creek sign at 9,200 feet, about .5 mile before the end of the road. Parking is limited, but there is a small campsite with no water. From the road the trail descends west but parallel to it for 200 yards, then turns south and plunges down terraces to the lakes. To reach the larger lake at 8,735 feet, stay on a path to the left that crosses a meadow to the rounded slabs of the lakeshore. The lower lake, one-fourth the size of the upper one, is 150 yards down the connecting stream.

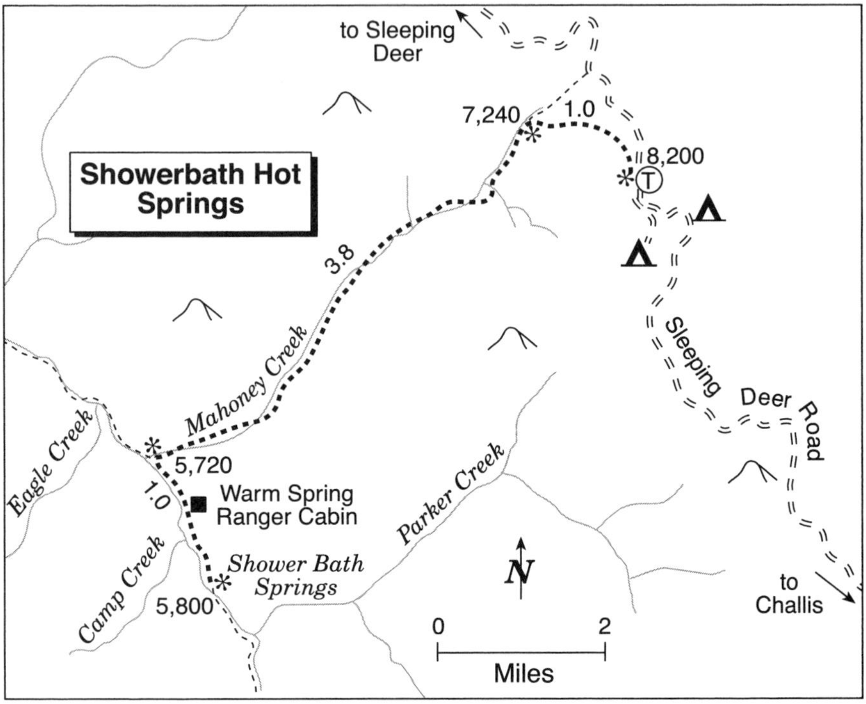

41.

Showerbath Hot Springs

Round trip: 11.6 miles
Elevation gain: 100 feet; elevation loss (return climb): 2,360 feet
Highest point: 8,160 feet
Topographic map: Sheldon Peak
Trailhead GPS: N 44 45' 33.18" W 114 40' 25.82"
Time: 9 hours; difficulty: expert; must walk in the deep creek to reach springs.

Access: In Challis turn left (west) off U.S. 93 onto Main Street. At .5 mile turn right (north) off Main Street onto the paved Challis Creek Road. The pavement ends at 9.3 miles, and the road intersects with one to Mosquito Flat Reservoir at 10.4 miles. Passenger cars and trailers are not recommended beyond this point, and four-wheel drive is a good idea. Keep straight ahead. Open and shut two ranch gates if they are closed. Continue on the primitive and rocky Sleeping Deer Road over Twin Peaks Saddle at 19 miles and on out to the first sign for the Mahoney Creek Trail at 28.4 miles.

What you will see: At Showerbath Hot Springs, hot water cascades over bright green

Old Warm Spring Creek ranger cabin

moss from the wall of a 200-foot-deep gorge. Alders and other shrubs make the canyon seem as green as those along the Columbia River in Oregon. Above the springs, gray-green mountain mahogany juts from walls that are coated with black, orange and lime-green lichens. Other walls are decorated with towers resembling feather headdresses. Because Warm Spring Creek completely fills the narrow gorge, the trail is underwater for 400 yards much of the summer. Not until late August can hikers walk safely through the gorge to the hot pools. On Warm Spring Creek near the gorge stands the historic log cabin of the Warm Spring Ranger Station, constructed in 1910, one of the first Forest Service buildings in the area. The Forest Service has stabilized and repaired it.

Directions: On the Sleeping Deer Road, start hiking at the first Mahoney Creek trail sign at 28.4 miles, which is .3 mile beyond the turnoff for the Mahoney Springs Campground below the road. An additional small campground is off to the right .5 mile before Mahoney Springs. (There is a second branch of the trail at 29.1 miles.)

The first Mahoney Creek Trail descends through lodgepoles, crosses a stream and meets the other trail at 1 mile beside a spring. (The other trail descends 800 feet in only .5 mile so is not recommended.) The main trail continues down the creek, passing a meadow and two ponds. After passing orange-colored outcrops at 1.5 miles, it switchbacks down to cross a side creek at 1.7 miles. At 1.9 miles, the trail fords the main creek to the north then crosses a side stream in aspens at 2.2 miles.

The route returns to the south side of the creek at 2.5 miles, and at 3.2 miles, is along a steep hillside with aspens. At 4 miles, it crosses to the right (north) side of the creek, and returns to the south side at 4.7 miles. It joins the Warm Spring Creek Trail at 4.8

miles on a sagebrush flat. The Warm Spring Trail descends 8 miles to Loon Creek with six fords and also goes upstream to the Sleeping Deer Road.

Turn left on the trail up Warm Spring Creek, passing the Warm Spring Ranger Cabin on a sagebrush flat at 5.2 miles. The Warm Spring Trail enters a gorge at 5.7 miles, passes two springs, dips into the creek for 25 yards, and then crosses it in water still knee-deep in late July. After 25 yards on the bank, the trail plunges into swift water that is often waist-deep.

In late summer, hikers can continue 300 yards in the water to dry land on the west side of the creek where tiny hot springs come out of the cliffs. Past these at 6 miles, the trail turns a corner into a little alcove 100 yards long, where larger hot springs spray off the canyon wall into three rock tubs. Beyond the pools, the trail continues 12.3 miles up the creek to the Sleeping Deer Road with 15 fords. Because of toxic metals from mining at Kerr Creek upstream, it is safest to obtain water for your filter from side streams, not from Warm Spring Creek.

MORGAN CREEK AREA

42.

White Goat and West Fork Lakes

Round trip: White Goat Lake, 14 miles
Elevation gain: 2,980 feet; elevation loss (return climb): 620 feet.
Highest point: 9,421 feet
Topographic maps: Blowfly Creek, White Goat Mountain
Time: 2-3 days ; difficulty: strenuous
Access: From Challis drive 8 miles north on Highway 93 to a sign for Cobalt. Turn left (northwest) onto the paved then improved dirt, Morgan Creek Road. Drive 6.3 miles to the West Fork of Morgan Creek Road. Turn left (west) on that dirt road and drive to Blowfly Creek at 11.5 miles.

What you will see: The trail to White Goat Lake passes the site of a former lookout on White Goat Peak that when in operation was only a log platform. From the peak, the view includes the blue crags of the Sawtooths, the cliffs of Sleeping Deer Mountain and the peach-colored towers of the Bighorn Crags. Farther along the trail, rock benches dotted with trees and wildflower meadows flank the light green water of White Goat Lake. A spur trail reaches West Fork Lakes, but they are not within the Frank Church Wilderness. On the south side of the marshy lower West Fork Lake, logs have avalanched into amber-colored water, opposite grassy cliffs. Above the pale green upper lake bulges a rounded black crag, cracked at a 45-degree angle.

Directions: On the West Fork of Morgan Creek Road at 11.5 miles, the road turns up Blowfly Creek to a picnic area. The trail begins at the turn (6,600 feet). It crosses Blowfly Creek and goes up the right (northeast) side of the West Fork of Morgan

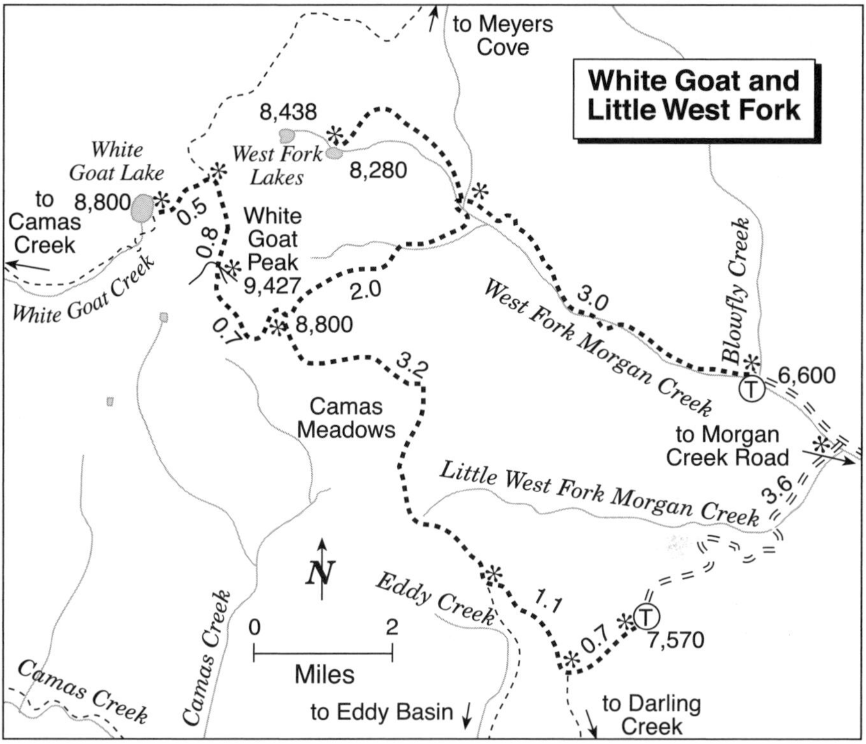

Creek over rocks and through willow and Douglas fir. At 1.5 miles, the trail crosses to the west side of the creek for 100 yards, then returns. At 2.8 miles is a side creek in a ravine and at 3 miles a junction with a trail north to West Fork Lakes.

Here, take the left trail west toward Castle Creek. It crosses two branches of the West Fork, then climbs a third stream on its north bank, crossing this stream at 3.8 miles, near a large outcrop. At 4.2 miles, the trail goes over a marsh then ascends to a junction with the Darling-Castle Creek Trail at 5 miles. From here, turn southwest on the trail to White Goat Peak. It scrambles up the summit ridge among whitebark pines, with a view south of the White Clouds, then at 5.3 miles turns northwest.

At 5.7 miles (9,421 feet) is the summit of White Goat Peak. (From here, a stock driveway runs west down a ridge 6.2 miles to the Camas-Eddy Creek Trail.) Continue on the White Goat Trail, which descends the ridge north to a saddle at 6.5 miles where the trail splits. The Darling-Castle Creek Trail straight ahead leaves the wilderness within .3 mile and goes north 16 miles to the head of Castle Creek.

From the saddle, turn left (southwest) on the trail to White Goat Lake, which plunges past outcrops to the lake (8,800 feet) at 7 miles. There are campsites at both ends. Below the lake, the trail continues down White Goat Creek 4 miles to Camas Creek. A route to White Goat Lake with 1,000 feet less elevation gain is by the Little West Fork Trail (see that hike.) Back at the junction with the Darling - Castle Creek Trail expert hikers can leave the Frank Church Wilderness and follow a cut-off trail to the upper one of the West Fork Lakes to make a loop trip of about the same length as a round trip to White Goat Lake. This cutoff trail is not described here because there is a gap in it (see below.)

To reach West Fork Lakes by the regular trail turn right (north) off the trail to White Goat Lake onto a spur trail 3 miles above the trailhead. This trail runs through parklike forest along a branch of the creek and across it at 3.5 miles, climbs above the creek, crosses a side stream and reaches the first lake (8,280 feet) at 4.5 miles. Reaching the upper lake (8,438 feet) is difficult because it requires cross-country travel through downed timber. The upper lake lacks campsites, but there are a few at the lower.

43.

Little West Fork Trail

Round trip: 10 miles to a junction with the Darling-Castle Creek Trail
Elevation gain: 1,460 feet; elevation loss (return climb): 460 feet
Highest point: 8,720 feet
Topographic map: Blowfly Creek, White Goat Mountain
Trailhead GPS: N 44 41' 0.3" W 114 20' 36.2"
Time: 7 hours for round trip to the West Fork Trail junction; Difficulty: strenuous
Access: At a sign for Cobalt 8 miles north of Challis, turn left (northwest) off Highway 93 onto the paved, then improved dirt, Morgan Creek Road. Drive 6.3 miles to the West Fork of Morgan Creek Road. Turn left (west) on that road and at 10.8 miles turn left (southwest) on the Little West Fork Road and drive to the trailhead at 14.4 miles (7,570 feet)

What you will see: Along these trails, lodgepole forests alternate with grass and sagebrush hillsides scattered with pink bitterroot and purple lupine in season. There is a panoramic view that includes the cone of Van Horn Peak and ridges along the Sleeping Deer Road. This route to White Goat Lake is the same length as the trail up the West Fork of Morgan Creek, but the elevation gain is about 1,000 feet less.

Directions: The trail follows an old road for a few hundred yards, climbing through Douglas fir, over a stream, and across a sagebrush hillside. Then it drops to a junction at .7 mile where it joins the Darling-Castle Creek Trail. From the junction, this trail goes south 7 miles to the Darling Creek Road. Take the right (north) branch up a sagebrush hill and along the left side of it to a notch. Then traverse to a wooded gap at 1.8 miles, just before a junction.

A trail from this junction to Eddy Basin and Pats Creek turns left (south) here. Keep right (northwest) on the Darling - Castle Creek Trail, which runs down the side of a fir-covered ridge. At 2.5 miles is a spring at the head of the Little West Fork of Morgan Creek. The Frank Church Wilderness boundary is at 3.3 miles in lodgepoles where a side trail to Camas Meadows turns off. The main trail goes along the side of a ridge, following the wilderness boundary north and then west, to a notch at 4 miles. Then it crosses an old burn and circles a lodgepole ridge to meet the West Fork of Morgan Creek Trail at 5 miles, 1,180 feet above the Little West Fork trailhead. This junction is 5 miles and a 2,280-foot climb up that trail from the West Fork trailhead. From here it is .7 mile to White Goat Peak and 2 miles to White Goat Lake. For a description of these 2 miles see the White Goat and West Fork Lakes hike.

44.

Camas Creek Trail

Round trip: 29.2 miles to the Middle Fork of the Salmon
Elevation gain: 400 feet; elevation loss (return climb): 1,800 feet
Highest point: 5,200 feet
Topographic maps: Meyers Cove, Yellowjacket, Aparejo Point
Trailhead GPS: N 44 49' 45.01" W 114 29' 21.37"
Time: 6 days; difficulty: strenuous
Access: From Challis, drive 8 miles north on Highway 93 to a sign for Cobalt. Turn left (northwest) onto the paved, then improved dirt, Morgan Creek Road. Drive 19.5 miles to Morgan Creek Summit. Continue to a junction at 27.5 miles, turn left (west) on the Meyers Cove Road and drive over Rabbitsfoot Summit and down past an old campground at 38 miles to a trailhead at 41.6 miles. You can drive to 42 miles, but the only parking is at the trailhead. . The trailhead is called the Everett Decora trailhead, after an early rancher and packer in the Salmon area.

A little history: Near Meyers Cove placers were found in 1869 on Silver Creek, 15 miles west of the road down Panther Creek from Morgan Creek Summit. The cove, rolling meadows surrounded by forested hills and lava towers, was named for B.F. Meyer, a former Pennsylvania congressman who owned mines on nearby Arrastra Creek. From 1906 to 1940, Meyers Cove had its own post office. L.L. (Andy) Anderson began an outfitting business from Meyers Cove in 1939 and pioneered Middle Fork float trips starting in 1945.

Here in 1941, Reese Miles and Roy Johnson of Salmon discovered fluorspar, which is the non-metallic raw material in fluorine chemicals such as the refrigerant Freon and in fluorocarbon plastics like Teflon. In 1949, J.R. Simplot acquired the 75 unpatented claims and two mill sites, and from 1951-53 the Simplot Corporation produced 11,000 tons of fluorspar. In 1970 another company, the Seaforth, planned to mine and reduce the ore, but the venture failed and the mine closed.

What you will see: In the 3,000-foot-deep canyon of Camas Creek, fins of jointed

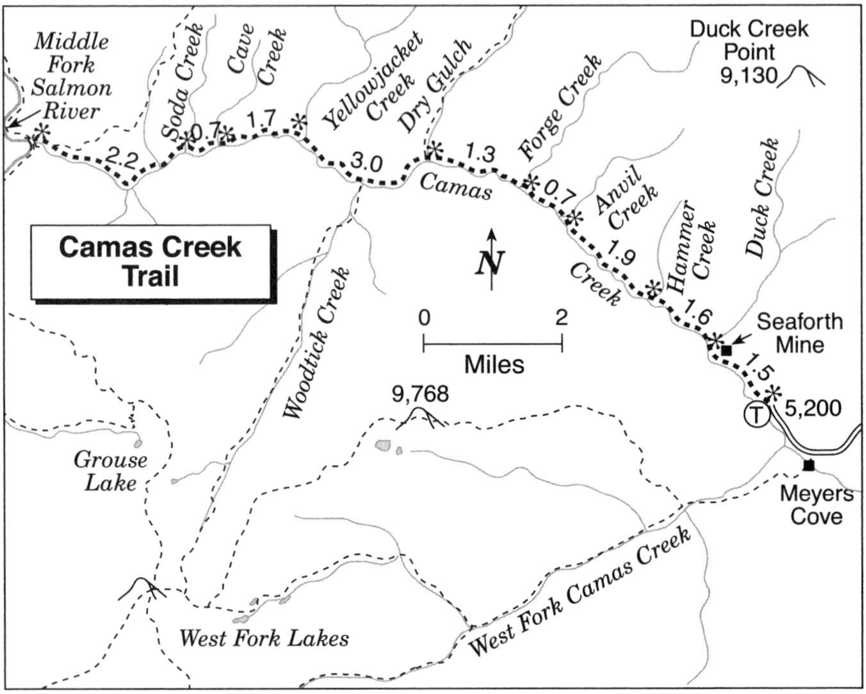

rock top 600-foot walls. Below them, buff-colored precipices pinch the thundering creek between immense boulders. Charcoal-gray lichen coats the tops of outcrops and dribbles down the cliffs, with lime-green and orange accents. Above Little Dry Gulch, 6.2 miles from the trailhead, trees shade the trail, but below that trees are few and in summer it can be 110 degrees. In June, until the trail is rerouted, it may be underwater just beyond Forge Creek

Directions: From the gate, the trail begins by following an old mining road below an open hillside beside aspens and willows. At 1.5 miles are the silver tarpaper buildings of the Seaforth Mine. The Forest Service has a right-of-way for the trail through this private land.

At 2.6 miles, the track becomes a trail. It plunges through shrubs past the trickle of Hammer Creek at 3.1 miles, then at 3.7 miles goes through an old burn. At 4.2 miles, the trail climbs a bluff that looks down on Camas Creek as it stairsteps down through 10-foot boulders.

Around a bend at 4.7 miles, the canyon becomes spectacular with lichen-splashed rock walls and towers. At 5 miles, it fords Anvil Creek. Near Forge Creek, where walls squeeze Camas Creek into a slot at 5.5 miles, the trail creeps under the prow of a cliff and passes an old blacksmith forge made of rock and dirt, used to sharpen the tools of the CCC crew building the trail.

At 5.7 miles, the trail crosses Forge Creek beside a small campsite, then skirts a cliff. It rounds a corner above another cliff, then goes through sloping woods to Little Dry

Gulch at 6.2 miles. From Meyers Cove, the eastern boundary of the Frank Church Wilderness runs along the opposite side of Camas Creek from the trail, On this trail you enter the wilderness between Little Dry Gulch and Dry Gulch where the boundary turns north. At Dry Gulch at 7 miles, a trail climbs north 7 miles to meet the trail along Little Jacket Creek, a tributary of Yellowjacket Creek. At 10 miles at Yellowjacket Creek a trail climbs north 5.4 miles up that creek to the Middle Fork Peak Road. Right before this junction is a cave just north of the trail with Sheepeater pictographs and excellent shade. The main trail descends 4.6 more miles to the Middle Fork of the Salmon.

NORTH FORK DISTRICT: YELLOWJACKET - BIGHORN CRAGS AREA

45.

Lake Creek Lakes from Middle Fork Peak

Round trip: 5 miles (2 miles cross-country)

Elevation gain: 240 feet; elevation loss (return climb): 1,090 feet

Highest point: 8,840 feet

Topographic map: Aparejo Point

Trailhead GPS: N 44 58' 5.9" W 114 39' 18.6"

Time: 5 hours; difficulty: partly cross-country

Old store at Forney

Access: From Challis, drive north 8 miles on Highway 93 to a sign for Cobalt. Turn left (northwest) on the paved, then improved, dirt Morgan Creek Road and drive over Morgan Creek Summit at 19.5 miles. Continue down to Porphyry Creek at 32.9 miles. Turn left (northwest) on a dirt road for the Bighorn Crags. At 40.2 miles at a four-way junction for the Crags, turn left (west) on the road to the ghost town of Yellowjacket. At Yellowjacket at 48.5 miles, the road becomes primitive but has bridges and culverts. Four-wheel drive is

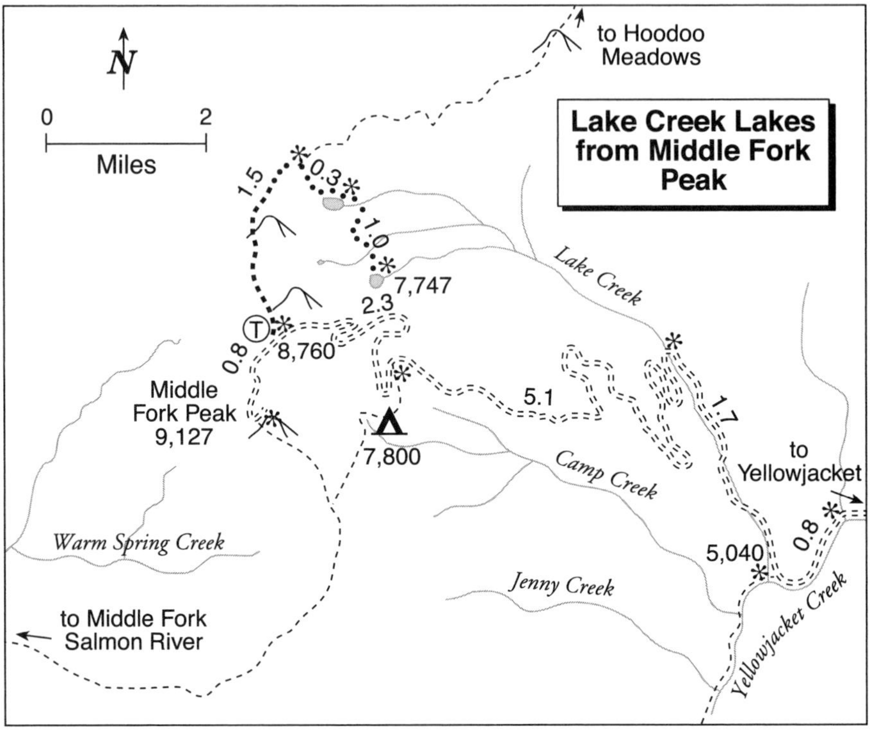

recommended. Drive to a saddle at 62.4 miles, .6 mile below Middle Fork Peak.

A little history: By 1895, a wagon road had been completed from Salmon to Panther Creek by way of Leesburg and on up to the village of Forney, which once stood at the intersection of the road to the Bighorn Crags with the Panther Creek Road. Stages ran from there to Yellowjacket, the starting point for pack trains going to the Middle Fork and Thunder Mountain. The post office and stage station at Forney were named after Henry Forney, an early settler. There was a ranger station at Cabin Creek near Forney. It was moved in 1920 to the present site of the Cobalt Ranger Station on Panther Creek. In 1925, the Morgan Creek Summit Road was constructed as far as Napias Creek, but below that there was only a trail down Panther Creek to the Salmon River.

What you will see: Middle Fork Peak, a grassy hill topped by rock outcrops and a lookout, overlooks a half-moon of grass and a blue curve of the Middle Fork of the Salmon River. To the south, snow-filled furrows slash the dark wall of Sleeping Deer Mountain. The trail to these lakes follows a grassy ridge through lupine, paintbrush and dead whitebark pines. The trail overlooks two small blue-green lakes set below crumbling 800-foot cliffs.

Directions: About 4 miles beyond Yellowjacket is a new trailhead for the Yellowjacket Creek Trail, which descends to Camas Creek. A mile beyond this, the road to Middle

Snags above Lake Creek Lakes

Fork Peak turns right (northwest) up Lake Creek. At this point, the road has sloughed away as a result of the Clear Creek Fire of 2000. This short section may be difficult to travel even with four-wheel drive. Inquire first. The campground still shown on some maps up on Middle Fork Peak is not maintained.

A little history: Near Yellowjacket the road passes several old mines. The first was started by Nathan Smith, the man who discovered gold at Leesburg and Loon Creek, and three friends in 1869. They found placer and lode gold and named the place Yellowjacket after a nest of yellowjackets stirred up by their pack horses. In 1876, a three-stamp mill was installed.

By the end of 1894 the mill had 60 stamps. After a wagon road was built in 1895, two cyanide mills were brought in, but high-grade ore ran out and they shut down in 1897.

The Yellowjacket Mine reopened in 1910, closed during World War I and then was bought by Charles Peters of Salt Lake City. In 1923, Peters constructed a hotel, which was five stories in front and three stories in the rear. His money ran out before it was finished, but there are still remnants of the old hotel.

Directions: After driving to the saddle at 62.4 miles, .8 mile below the Middle Fork Peak lookout, look for a Frank Church Wilderness boundary sign and from it take a trail north, which leads 9.5 miles along the crest of the Yellowjacket Mountains to Hoodoo Meadows. It is primitive and in poor condition but fairly plain as far as the turnoff for the lakes. Note that the whole area burned in the 2000 Clear Creek Fire. The trail contours the hillside to a notch at .7 mile, and circles a hill to another notch at 1.2 miles, which has a view of the northernmost of the two lakes. Then it skirts a hill to a saddle at 1.5 miles.

Here, turn right (southeast) off the trail, and drop cross-country through grass and talus to the 7,966-foot upper lake at 1.5 miles. To reach the lower, smaller lake at 2.5 miles (7,747 feet), circle the first lake on the north. Then from its outlet, climb southeast over the ridge separating the two cirques.

46.

Middle Fork of Salmon River Trail: Big Creek Bridge to the Flying B

(Section 4 of Big Creek-Middle Fork through trip)

This section one-way: 11.9 miles
Elevation gain: 1,220 feet; elevation loss: 940 feet
Highest point: 3,680 feet
Topographic maps: Puddin Mountain, Aparejo Point
Reached from Big Creek
Time: 2 weeks for entire through trip from Big Creek to Boundary Creek; difficulty: strenuous
Access: See the three sections of the Big Creek Trail or Heart, Terrace and Barking Fox Lakes in the Bighorn Crags to go by trail to the Big Creek Bridge over the Middle Fork where this description begins.

What you will see: Downriver from this part of the Middle Fork, the only trail along

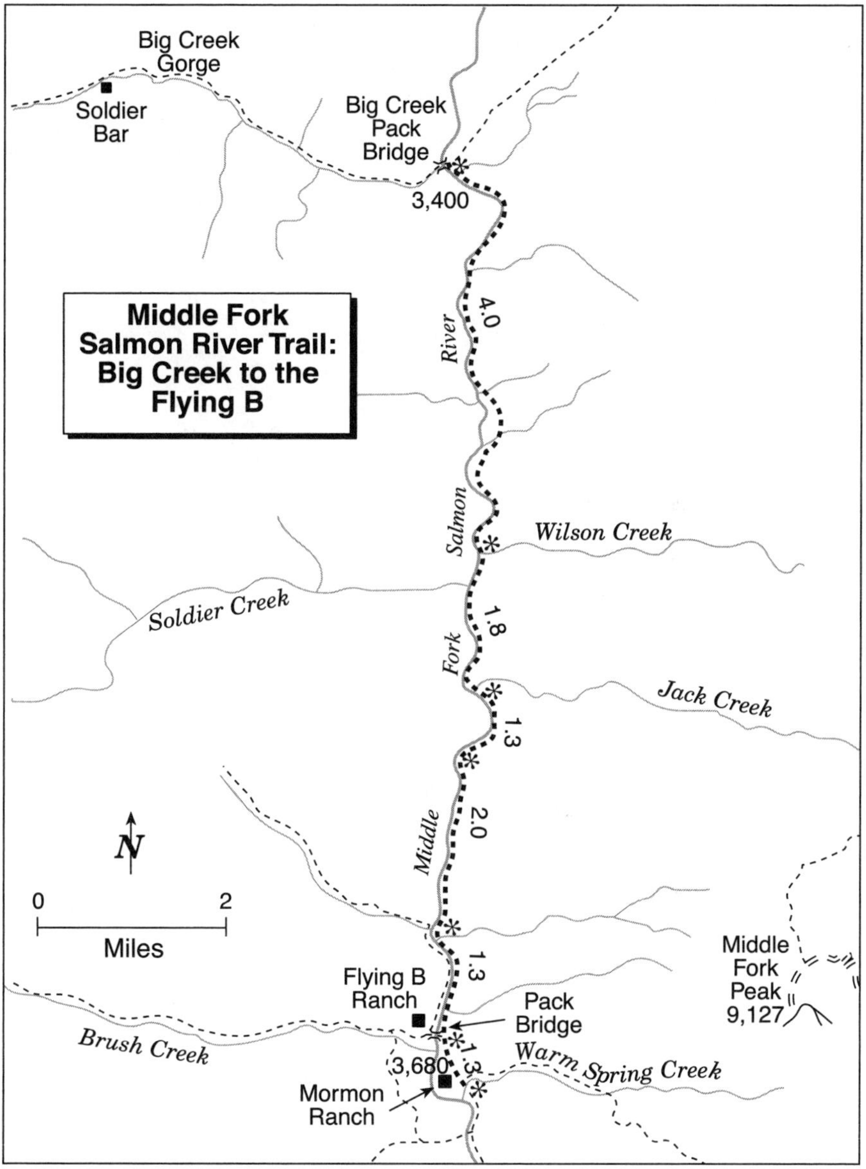

the river is thousands of feet above it. The canyon walls in this trail less 18-mile section, nicknamed the "Impassable Canyon" by Bernard's troops in the Sheepeater War, rise 2,000 feet straight up, with a total depth of 6,700 feet. The most rugged section of the river-level trail is this one, the one just above the Impassable Canyon. Here, great peaks of crinkled cliffs and soft grass cascade to pines at the edge of the twisting silver river. Grassy slopes soften the precipices, but the small river terraces are so rare that

Middle Fork from near Rattlesnake Creek

in spring they appear to be bits of paradise dropped along the river. In June, sediment colors the river chocolate brown, but later in the summer it changes to turquoise. From Rattlesnake Creek to above the Flying B, both sides of the canyon burned in the 2000 Shellrock Fire.

See the first three sections of the Big Creek Trail for directions for hiking to the Big Creek Bridge (3,400 feet) where this description starts, which is written for travelers going south. From the bridge, the Waterfall Trail climbs east 5,000 feet in 11 miles to Terrace Lakes in the Bighorn Crags, and the Middle Fork Trail goes 79 miles south to its other end at the Boundary Creek trailhead and then after a short gap continues 10 miles more to the beginning of the Middle Fork at the confluence of Marsh and Bear Valley creeks.

Directions: From the bridge, the Middle Fork Trail first climbs along the talus past mountain mahogany and cliffs, bridging Waterfall Creek at .2 mile, Fox Creek at .8 mile and Bobtail Creek at 1.7 miles. At bubbling Woolard Creek at 3.2 miles, a side path drops to a 150-yard long grassy bar with poison ivy and several campsites.

Beyond Woolard Creek, the trail corkscrews up a 500-foot grassy hill with an excellent view. In summer it is best to hike this in the evening or early morning. From the top, the trail zigzags down rocks and sagebrush to cross Rattlesnake Creek in a tangle of shrubs at 4 miles. Here, two paths go to the right to the pictographs and poison ivy of Rattlesnake Cave. Camping is prohibited at or near the cave.

The trail next traverses a sloping bar, ledges and talus, and the canyon becomes rockier and narrower. At 5.5 miles is the Wilson Creek Bridge. A trail formerly went up Wilson Creek to Hoodoo Meadows, but all but the upper 3 miles was obliterated by dead trees and slides after a 1929 fire. Driftwood Camp at 6.4 miles is on a long sandbar, but the only drinking water is the river. After climbing 120 feet up a grassy hillside, the trail drops to the bank below cliffs, where rocks and cribbing hold the trail above high water. Before this construction was done, the trail in June often led through waist- or chest-deep rapids. It crosses a bridge over Jack Creek at 7.3 miles to a small campsite.

Above Jack Creek, talus flanks the river and the trail wanders above and below cliffs with a magnificent view of the walls ahead. At 8.6 miles, it fords Cold Spring Creek at a campsite, and at 10 miles threads a narrow gorge opposite Short Creek. When the canyon opens out, the trail wanders in and out of gullies in sagebrush. On the other side of the river is the Bernard Creek Guard Station and its airstrip, constructed in 1932 with a horse-drawn plow and Fresno scraper, brought in by pack string. Crews stay in the guard station in summer, but they don't keep office hours. There is a trail from the guard station to the Flying B ranch, but it goes through private land.

A little history: A homestead was established on the Bernard Creek property by Sam Laing and family in 1900; after Sam and his wife left, their son David stayed on until 1905 when he was appointed the first ranger for Chamberlain Basin. About 1916, Asa Clark came here; the Forest Service later built the guard station on the foundation of his cabin.

More directions: At 10.6 miles above Haystack Rapids, the Middle Fork Trail crosses Pole Creek, then goes out on a sagebrush flat across from the Flying B airstrip. At 11.9 miles a suspension bridge gives access to this ranch and the Brush Creek Trail, which climbs 7.1 miles to the Bear Creek Point Trail.

More history: At the time of the Sheepeater War, a village of Sheepeater Indians lived at the site of the Flying B, the last ranch on the Middle Fork before the Impassable Canyon. After buying the property from two squatters in 1912, Albert Kurry ran cattle there with his brother, Henry. He lost 270 of his 300 cattle in the severe winter of 1919 and that June his wife died. But he stayed on and patented the land in 1920. (A patent for land is a grant made by the government to an individual, giving him or her title to an area of public land.) After George Crandall and his wife bought the ranch in the late 1920s, Mrs. Crandall didn't leave the place for 16 years. Crandall sold to A.A. Bennett, who was an early director of the Idaho Department of Aeronautics. The Flying B Ranch is named for him. It is now a fly-in hunting lodge.

47.

Middle Fork of the Salmon River Trail: Flying B to Loon Creek

(Section 5 of Big Creek-Middle Fork through trip)

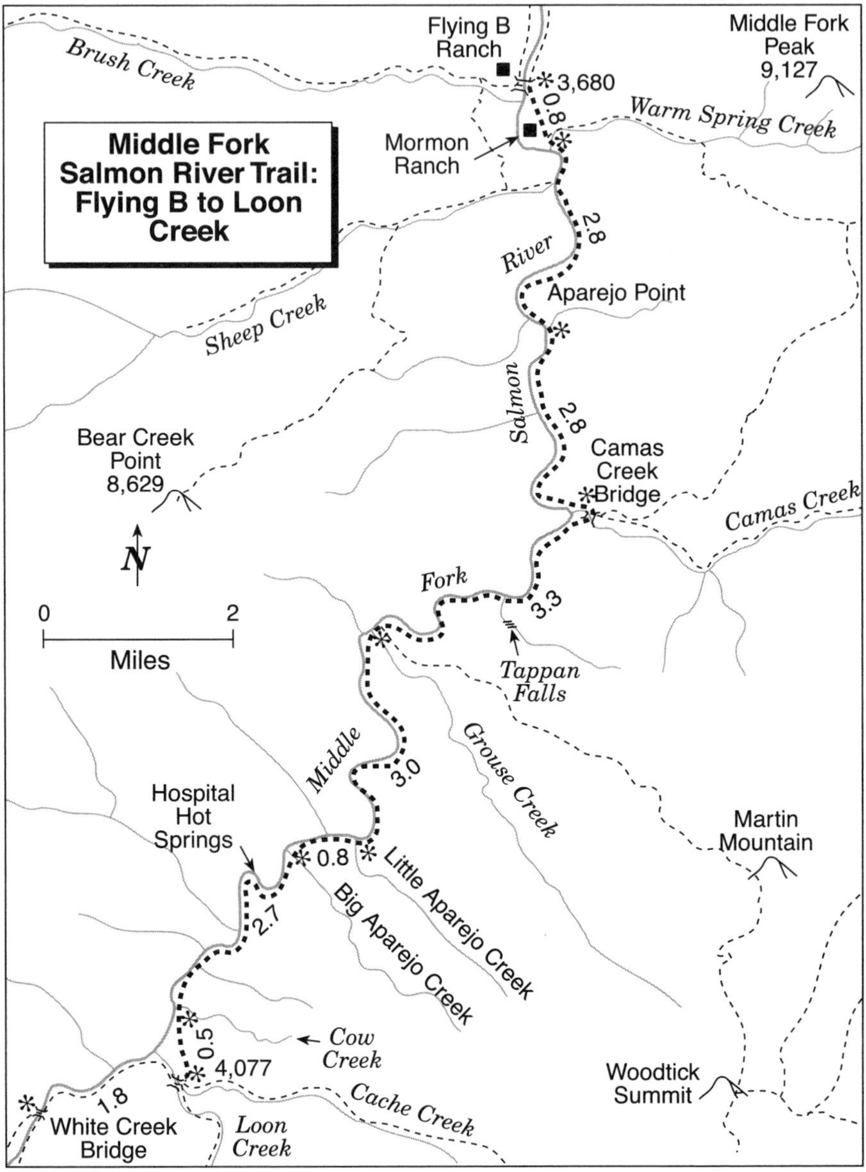

This section one-way: 17.2 miles
Elevation gain: 1,090 feet; elevation loss (return climb): 610 feet
Highest point: 4,160 feet
Topographic maps: Aparejo Point, Bear Creek Point, Ramey Hill
Reached by trail from Big Creek
Time: 2 weeks for entire through trip; difficulty: strenuous

Access: See the three sections of the Big Creek Trail and Big Creek Bridge to the Flying B to go by trail to the Flying B Ranch where this description begins.

What you will see: High, grassy hills and 1,200-foot cliffs border this part of the canyon, with water-loving shrubs at side streams and springs. Across the river from a tower on the canyon wall at Aparejo Point, the trail creeps along under overhanging cliffs. There are several towers and outcrops such as the one near Cow Creek resembling a stone rhinoceros. At Loon Creek a half-mile off the trail is a hot spring with a 4- by 10-foot cement-sided pool. From the Flying B to Camas Creek and Sheep Creek the canyon burned in 2000.This description, written for hikers traveling south, begins at the Flying B Bridge over the Middle Fork. About .3 mile below the Flying B, Sheep Creek flows in across the river.

A little history: Charlie Ernst and his wife, Frankie, came to the Middle Fork to prospect in 1915. When they tried to take the ranch on Sheep Creek owned by Jake Reberk, Reberk was shot. Frankie and Charlie accused each other of killing him. Charlie Ernst was convicted of second-degree murder and Frankie of manslaughter. While in prison, Frankie confessed and Charlie was pardoned in 1921, although he went to prison again for shooting a man in 1942.

Directions: From the Flying B, an old road runs upstream .8 mile to the Mormon Ranch, but the trail stays above this road on a bench. About 1900 the Beagle brothers – Bill, Ben and Perry – lived and constructed stone cellars on the land that became known as the Mormon Ranch at the mouth of Warm Spring Creek. The Beagles were Mormons so that was how the place got its name. In 1919, Bill Wilson bought the ranch to raise cattle. Today it belongs to the Fish and Game Department. From here a side trail goes up another Warm Spring Creek to the Middle Fork Peak road.

At 2.3 miles, the main trail passes a pine bar with a campsite (marked "Trail" on the river maps.) The way begins to round the cliffs of Aparejo Point at 3 miles, where the water can be thigh-deep in June. Before 1923, the trail climbed over the top of the point. Horses and mules often fell off there, leaving their aparejos (Spanish-style pack saddles padded with moss or hay) lying in a heap among the remains of the animals. There is a tiny campsite just beyond Aparejo Creek at 3.6 miles.

In June at Camas Creek at 6.4 miles, there may be water over the trail, because it climbs along the creek for .3 mile to reach a bridge over the creek near campsites. Once across the creek, it goes along a high sagebrush bench then returns to the river. At 7.5 miles, the canyon narrows with cliffs on both sides and Tappan Falls Rapids on the river. Across the river here is the tombstone of Eldon Handy, an outfitter who drowned in these rapids about 1980. At Grouse Creek at 9.7 miles, below the trail is the site of a log cabin at what is called the Tappan Ranch. It flanks a grassy bar and campsite, but the trail remains on the hillside above. The cabin was built by Willis Jones, who came to the Middle Fork in 1927 hoping to cure his tuberculosis. Fred and Daisy Tappan purchased the ranch from him, and it became the Tappan Ranch. They constructed more buildings, ran cattle and grew a large garden. Bob Simplot later bought this ranch and sold all but the cabin to the Fish and Game Department.

Beyond Grouse Creek, the trail winds along open slopes and through shrub jungles. At 12.7 miles, it fords Little Aparejo Creek and at 13.5 miles Big Aparejo Creek, near a campsite on a pine flat. At 14.2 miles, the trail is across from Hospital Hot Springs,

Cabin on Panther Creek near Porphyry Creek

where rafters often stop. Beyond here, the river changes directions from northwest to south. At 14.7 miles Norton Creek runs down a V-shaped canyon across the river. The stone rhinoceros at Cow Creek is at 16.2 miles.

At Loon Creek at 16.7 miles is the .2-mile-long Simplot Landing Field belonging to the Idaho Department of Fish and Game. Originally Bob Ramey had a farm and cattle ranch at this spot before Sam and Amie Lovell raised horses here. Bob Simplot bought the ranch, then traded it to J.R. Simplot, who kept the cabins and sold the rest of the land to the Idaho Fish and Game Department.

The trail skirts the edge of the landing field, then passes through a gate to a bridge over Loon Creek at 17.2 miles. On the other side of the bridge, a trail up Loon Creek goes 22 miles to the Loon Creek Road, passing at .5 mile the hot spring mentioned earlier.

48.

Wilson Creek from Hoodoo Meadows

Round trip: 2.6 miles to viewpoint; 6 miles to bottom of canyon
Elevation gain: 140 feet; elevation loss (return climb): 2,540 feet
Highest point: 8,300 feet
Topographic map: Hoodoo Meadows

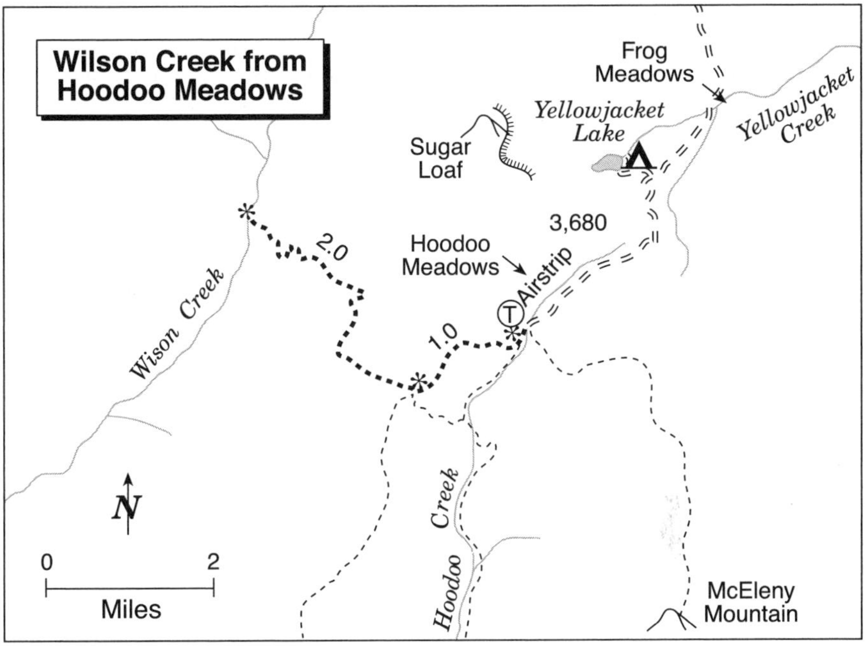

Trailhead GPS: N 44 58' 5.9" W 114 39' 18.5"

Time: 2 hours to viewpoint; difficulty: easy to viewpoint, strenuous to expert to bottom of canyon, but access road is in bad shape

Access: From Challis drive 8 miles north on Highway 93 to a sign for Cobalt. Turn left (northwest) onto the paved, then improved dirt, Morgan Creek Road and drive over Morgan Creek Summit at 19.4 miles. At 32.9 miles at Porphyry Creek, turn left (northwest) on the rocky, dirt road and drive to a four-way intersection at 39.9 miles. Here, keep straight ahead (north) on a primitive road over Quartzite Mountain to a junction with the road to Yellowjacket Lake at 48.4 miles. Take the left fork toward the lake, but be aware that the road in 2018 had deep ruts and washes that are impassable for some 4-wheel drive vehicles. Go past the lake turnoff at 5 miles and then 2 miles farther to the end of the road at the far (south) end of Hoodoo Meadows at 55.4 miles.

What you will see: This trail is a short walk to a spectacular canyon view, even if you descend into the canyon only as far as the first open area. Cream-colored rock lines the canyon walls, except for one dark mountain. The head of the canyon is ringed with the peach, beige and gray teeth and fins of Fishfin Ridge.

Yellowjacket Lake has a developed campground, but Hoodoo Meadows does not. The trail begins by fording Hoodoo Creek to the west side. Climbing gently, it then wanders along through a lodgepole forest underlain by grouse whortleberry. At 1 mile is an intersection. A trail to the left (south) leads 8.5 miles to the Middle Fork Peak Road along the crest of the Yellowjacket Mountains, passing above the Lake Creek Lakes on the way. A primitive trail down Hoodoo Creek also is supposed to go east from this junction, but it is not readily apparent. Continue straight ahead over a little saddle into the canyon of Wilson Creek.

Granite slabs at 1.3 miles make a fine viewpoint. If you choose to continue farther to see more of the canyon, the trail deteriorates, and the steep part at 2.5 miles has treacherous footing. It used to continue along the bottom of the canyon 2 more miles, but that section has mostly disappeared. Originally the trail descended to the Middle Fork, but a fire in 1929 caused landslides that obliterated it.

49.

Golden Trout Lake

Round trip: 1 mile
Elevation gain: none; elevation loss (return climb): 310 feet
Highest point: 8,460 feet
Time: 2 hours for round trip; difficulty: easy, but steep and slippery
Topographic map: Hoodoo Meadows
Trailhead GPS: N 45 6' 22.4" W 114 31' 17.1"
Access: From Challis drive north 8 miles on U.S. 93 to a sign for Cobalt. Turn left (northwest) onto the paved, then improved dirt, Morgan Creek Road. Drive over Morgan Creek Summit at 19.4 miles to Porphyry Creek at 32.9 miles. Here, turn left on a rocky dirt road and go to a four-way intersection at 39.9 miles. Keep straight ahead (north) on a primitive road over Quartzite Mountain, which passes through a little of the 2000 Clear Creek Fire and drive to a junction with a road to Yellowjacket Lake at 48.4 miles. Take the right (northwest) fork and go 2.2 miles to Crags Campground at 50.2 miles.

What you will see: Above the green water of Golden Trout Lake, outposts of the Bighorn Crags perch on a wooded ridge. The middle tower, larger than the others, seems to rule the row of granite gnomes.

Directions: To reach the lake, park at the main trailhead and walk back on the road to the beginning of the campground. Here a spur road goes north a few yards to the beginning of the trail to Golden Trout Lake, which is 300 feet below. This trail goes through a gap in the granite benches, then descends a gully in forest to the lake (8,149 feet) at .5 mile. The path often disappears where it runs over sloping granite outcrops.

50.

Welcome Lake

Round trip: 14 miles

Elevation gain: 1,400 feet; elevation loss (return climb): 1,520 feet

Highest point: 9,000 feet

Topographic maps: Hoodoo Meadows, Mount McGuire

Trailhead GPS: N 45 6' 15.2" W 114 31' 27.9"

Time: 2 - 3 days; difficulty: strenuous

Access: From Challis drive north 8 miles on U.S. 93 to a sign for Cobalt. Turn left (northwest) onto the paved, then improved dirt, Morgan Creek Road. Drive over Morgan Creek Summit at 19.4 miles to Porphyry Creek at 32.9 miles. Here, turn left (northwest) on a rocky, dirt road and continue to a four-way intersection at 39.9 miles. Keep straight ahead (north) on a primitive road over Quartzite Mountain, which passes through a little of the 2000 Clear Creek Fire, and drive to a junction at 48.4 miles with the road to Yellowjacket Lake. Take the right (northwest) fork and go 2.2 miles to Crags Campground at 50.2 miles.

Rock tower on main trail into the Bighorn Crags from Crags Campground.

What you will see: From Welcome Lake, the orange and gray triangular towers of Fishfin Ridge resemble the fins of a 400-foot prehistoric fish, with a square tower forming the head. Northwest of the lake stands a blunt peak split by a great chimney. Meadows of buttercups, cinquefoil, and red and white mountain heath surround the water. Along the trail, jointed granite towers resemble grotesque toes, ski hats and the worm-eaten prow of a ship.

Directions: The foot trail, which begins at a wooden map and register box at the north end of the campground (8,450 feet) is not on the topographic map until it meets the horse trail, which is on the map. The horse trail begins a few yards to the south of the trailhead and switchbacks up the hillside. From the trailhead, the foot trail zigzags up a ridge of lodgepoles, contours above Golden Trout Lake to an 8,720-foot summit at 1 mile and descends to a saddle at 1.4 miles (8,687 feet) where it meets the horse trail and a trail from Frog Meadows near Yellowjacket Lake.

The main trail climbs west onto another ridge and follows it north to the first of the towers at 2 miles. There are nine or ten towers in the next .7 mile. The way descends to a saddle at 3.4 miles where the Gant Ridge Trail branches northeast below Cathedral Rock. This trail, which gives access to Cathedral and Deer lakes, goes 21.3 miles to the Panther Creek Road through a forest that mostly burned in the Clear Creek Fire of 2000.

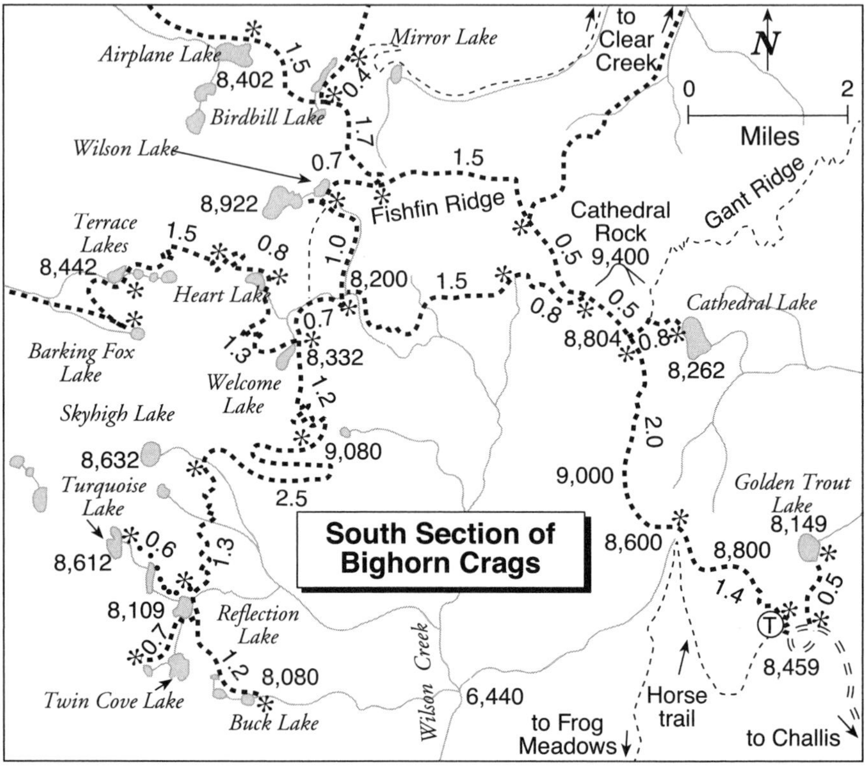

The main trail descends under the west side of Cathedral Rock to a muddy spring at 3.7 miles, 100 feet below the trail. It is the only water source between Crags Campground and Wilson Creek. Beyond here, the trail turns northwest to a junction at 3.9 miles with the trail to Wilson Creek and Welcome Lake.

Take the trail toward Welcome Lake, which is not shown on the topographic map. It hairpins down into Wilson Creek Canyon through trees to cross a branch of Wilson Creek at 4.7 miles. (Here an old trail, not maintained but on the topographic map, leads northeast to the Clear Creek Trail junction.) Beyond the crossing, the Welcome Lake Trail is on the map. It goes across the canyon to a second branch of the creek at 5.5 miles, climbs 100 feet, turns west, then north. At 6.2 miles is a junction with a one-mile trail to Wilson Lake. Continue on the Welcome Lake Trail, which immediately fords the creek (8,120 feet.)

The trail zigzags west into the canyon of Welcome Lake's outlet and climbs along the south side of it to a junction at 6.9 miles. Here, a trail goes west to Heart and Terrace Lakes. Take the trail that goes south toward Buck Lake. Fifty yards beyond the junction, a side trail goes .1 mile to Welcome Lake (8,332 feet) at 7 miles.

51.

Cathedral Lake

Round trip: 8.4 miles
Elevation gain: 640 feet; elevation loss (return climb): 1,280 feet
Highest point: 9,090 feet
Topographic maps: Hoodoo Meadows, Mount McGuire
Trailhead GPS: Trailhead GPS: N 45 6' 15.2" W 114 31' 27.9"
Time: 7 hours; difficulty: strenuous; slippery footing for last .5 mile on non-system path

Access: From Challis drive 8 miles north on U.S. 93 to a sign for Cobalt. Turn northwest onto the paved then improved dirt Morgan Creek Road. Drive over Morgan Creek Summit at 19.4 miles to Porphyry Creek at 32.9 miles. Here, turn left (northwest) on the rocky, dirt road and go to a four-way intersection at 39.9 miles. Keep straight ahead (north) on a primitive road over Quartzite Mountain, which passes through a little of the 2000 Clear Creek Fire and drive to a junction at 48.4 miles with a road to Yellowjacket Lake. Take the right (northwest) fork and drive 2.2 miles to Crags Campground at 50.2 miles.

What you will see: From the lower end of Cathedral Lake, Cathedral Rock resembles an immense gray molar. On two sides of the lake, granite knolls drop into the water, and on the other two sides the hoof prints of elk and moose indent muddy spots in the meadows. The trail passes several orange and gray granite teeth, from 100 to more than 200 feet high.

Hiking in the Bighorn Crags

Directions: For the first 1.5 miles there are two trails from this trailhead, one for horses and one for people on foot. (The horse trail begins at the corral just south of the trailhead.) Take the foot trail up a steep sandy and rocky hillside and past an overlook of Golden Trout Lake. The trail crosses over a wrinkle at the north end of the ridge at .8 mile, turns southwest and descends to a saddle at 1.4

miles, where the horse trail joins the foot trail and a less distinct trail comes in from Frog Meadows near Yellowjacket Lake. On the way down to the saddle are glimpses of Cathedral Rock and Fishfin Ridge ahead.

From the junction, the trail switchbacks up the end of a ridge, passing a little rock tower full of holes at 1.7 miles. The way is now mostly level through stands of whitebark pines to a 120-foot tower resembling a morel mushroom at 2 miles. You can now see the head and fins of Fishfin Ridge in the distance. From here the trail continues to a little saddle, climbs along the right side of a tower complex, and drops to another saddle at 3.4 miles. The trail straight ahead from it continues 9.8 more miles to Ship Island Lake.

To reach Cathedral Lake, turn right (east) at this junction onto the Gant Ridge Trail, which leads 21 miles to Panther Creek, passing near Cathedral and Deer Lakes. (Beyond Deer Lake the trail is within the perimeter of the 2000 Clear Creek Fire.) From the junction, the trail plunges down along a usually dry stream to a meadow 250 feet below at 3.7 miles. Here at the near side of the meadow, which is shown as marsh on the topographic map, turn off the trail to the right (east). Follow a path around the meadow to its east corner, from which the path drops down a steep slippery hillside. The path makes a few curves and switchbacks on its way to a campsite at the northwest corner of the lake at 4.2 miles. For the best view, circle the lake through the meadows on the north and east sides to the outlet at 4.7 miles. On the west side of the lake is a granite peninsula with a view of the lower end of the lake and the nubbin-topped hills surrounding it.

52.

Heart, Terrace and Barking Fox Lakes

Round trip: 22.4 miles
Elevation gain: 2,070 feet; elevation loss (return climb): 2,200 feet
This section: 3.7 miles; 670 feet gain; elevation loss (return climb): 680 feet
Highest point: 9,000 feet
Time: 3-4 days
Topographic map: Mount McGuire; difficulty: strenuous
Reached from Crags Campground
Trailhead GPS: N 45 6' 15.2" W 114 31' 27.9"
Access: From Crags Campground; see Welcome Lake to go by trail to that lake where this description begins.

What you will see: A bend in the shore pushes the blue-green water of Heart Lake into two lobes of a very wide heart. At one side of the heart, an alpine meadow stands below a pointed peak and switchbacks of the trail leading over a divide to Terrace Lakes. There an 800-foot black cliff with rock needles leads a line of dark scallops above the four small green lakes. Below these lakes, the Waterfall Trail plunges 5,000 feet in 11 miles to the Middle Fork of the Salmon River at the Big Creek Bridge, with a view of the purple depths of the canyon on the way.

Reflection Lake

Directions: Heart, Terrace and Barking Fox lakes can be reached from Welcome Lake, where this hike description begins. The trail to Heart Lake fords the outlet and skirts the north end of Welcome Lake (8,332 feet), then turns west across the head of the canyon and back to the northeast. The path climbs the canyon wall to the outlet of Heart Lake and then along it to the lake (8,623 feet) at 1.3 miles.

Above Heart Lake, the trail makes two long switchbacks just below the 9,000-foot divide at 2.1 miles. As the trail descends the other side, it turns southeast at 2.5 miles and hairpins down to the upper Terrace Lake (8,458 feet) at 3 miles. From here, the trail edges the north shore of the two smaller middle Terrace Lakes, then crosses a natural dam to the south shore of the lowest Terrace Lake (8,442 feet) at 3.6 miles.

To reach Barking Fox Lake from here, descend the Waterfall Trail .2 mile across rocks to the lake's outlet. Just before a ford of the outlet, an unsigned path turns left (east) up the north side of the creek to the lake (8,335 feet) at 4.3 miles. The Waterfall Trail continues 11 miles with 5,000 feet elevation loss to the Middle Fork Trail at the Big Creek Bridge.

53.

Reflection Lake

Round trip: 23.8 miles

Elevation gain: 2,260 feet; elevation loss (return climb): 2,600 feet

This section: 5 miles (one way); 850 feet gain; elevation loss (return climb): 1,080 feet

Backpacker on Fishfin Ridge in the Bighorn Crags

Highest point: 9,080 feet
Topographic maps: Mount McGuire, Hoodoo Meadows
Trailhead GPS: N 45 6' 15.2" W 114 31' 27.9"
Time: 3 - 4 days; difficulty: strenuous
Access: From Crags Campground, see Welcome Lake to go by trail to that lake where this hike description begins.

What you will see: Over a granite hill above the south end of oval, green Reflection Lake is a 1,000-foot black wall. The lake water reflects its irregular curves. Drifted logs have raised the water level, which exits the lake through a garden of bluebells and pink mimulus. Reflection Lake is one of the Puddin Mountain Lakes, called that for a high peak to the west. From a divide above Welcome Lake, Reflection Lake is in the shadows below the black cliff ahead with Skyhigh Lake just to the west below a pointed tower. The trail for this section is not on the topographic map, but it is an official trail.

From the lower end of Welcome Lake, take the trail south toward Reflection Lake and the other Puddin Mountain Lakes. It climbs in 200-yard switchbacks to the 9,080-foot divide at 1.2 miles. Then it descends into a wooded canyon, turning west, making two .2-mile-long switchbacks and a .7-mile-long one to a boulder-strewn meadow. Here, the trail turns southeast into trees and across Skyhigh Creek at 3.7 miles.

After descending the end of a ridge, the route overlooks a pond in marsh grass at 4 miles. Beyond a ford of the pond's inlet, the trail contours along a ridge and zigzags downhill, reaching an 8,000-foot low point at 4.7 miles. From here, it zigzags up rocks to the lake (8,109 feet) at 5 miles. A few small campsites are above the trail.

54.

Buck, Doe, Fawn, Echo, Twin Cove and Turquoise Lakes

Round trip: 28.8 miles
Elevation gain: 3,170 feet; elevation loss (return climb): 2,720 feet
Highest point: 9,080 feet
This section: 2.5 miles ones way; 930 feet gain; elevation loss (return climb): 120 feet
Topographic map: Hoodoo Meadows
Trailhead GPS: N 45 6' 15.2" W 114 31' 27.9"
Time: 5 days; difficulty: partly cross-country
Access: From Crags Campground: see Welcome and Reflection lakes to go by trail to Reflection Lake, where this description begins.

What you will see: Above Buck Lake, a crumbled rock ridge leads to the notched top of a 1,000-foot black cliff, from which a low ridge runs north to granite hills above Doe Lake. This marshy lake stretches out toward round, green Buck Lake, which is surrounded by woods, beargrass and grouse-whortleberry. South of Reflection Lake gray rock towers descend a ridge from the immense cliff into deep, green Twin Cove Lake. Here, two peninsulas of gray-green striped rock at either end of the lake form twin coves. Two unnamed tarns are west up an inlet, below the furrows, caves and chimneys of the black cliff. Northwest of Reflection Lake are Echo and Turquoise Lakes. At narrow Echo Lake, ledges drop into the water from rock knolls, and to the north, a rock tower resembles a sombrero. On the west side of Turquoise Lake, a peninsula of talus and little trees marks the shoreline below colorfully striped cliffs.

Directions: At Reflection Lake, take the trail south along its east shore, which leaves the lake at .2 mile and descends to two ponds at .4 mile. It switchbacks down past Fawn Lake at .7 mile to Doe Lake, then down to Buck Lake (8,080 feet) at 1 mile, where it circles the north shore of the lake to a dead end at 1.2. miles. Campsites are on the west side.

Twin Cove Lake can be reached from Reflection Lake by a path along the shore to its south inlet. Cross the inlet to the west side and climb a faint path along it to the lake at .5 mile. To reach the two small unnamed lakes under the black cliff, climb .2 mile along the north side of Twin Cove Lake's inlet.

To reach Echo Lake, take a fisherman's path west along the north shore of Reflection Lake. Climb 200 yards up the north side of the west inlet, then go up onto a ridge to the right and follow it west to the lake (8,320 feet) at .3 mile.

For Turquoise Lake (8,612 feet), go north along the east shore of Echo Lake to a campsite at the end of the lake. Continue north through a beargrass-covered valley that turns northwest. Climb between granite benches to the lake, .6 mile from Reflection Lake.

55.

Wilson and Harbor Lakes

Round trip: 13.4 miles
Elevation gain: 1,900 feet; elevation loss (return climb): 1,320 feet
This section: 3 miles one way; 820 feet gain; elevation loss (return climb): 360 feet
Highest point: 9,200 feet
Topographic map: Mount McGuire. Hoodoo Meadows
Trailhead GPS: N 45 6' 15.2" W 114 31' 27.9"
Time: 2 to 3 days; difficulty: strenuous
Access: From Crags Campground; see Welcome Lake to go by trail to the junction of the Waterfall and Ship Island trails, where this description begins.

What you will see: Above small, blue Wilson Lake rises the head of Fishfin Ridge. Next to the square-topped head, an orange spire resembling a carved African mask guards the neck of the fish, followed by two large triangular fins and three smaller ones. Only .1 mile from Wilson Lake is Harbor Lake. Two granite peninsulas on the north side of Harbor Lake and one on the south side enclose a harbor at its lower end. On the peninsulas, small subalpine firs, tiny whitebark pines, and red and white mountain heath resemble Japanese gardens. Above the harbor stands the charcoal-gray helmet of a peak that is cracked down the middle.

Directions: The shortest way to Wilson and Harbor lakes from Crags Campground is by way of the Ship Island Lake Trail. For a description of the Ship Island Trail from Crags Campground to the junction with the Waterfall Trail under Cathedral Rock where this hike description begins, see Welcome Lake. From this junction, 3.9 miles from Crags Campground, take the Ship Island Trail north through woods on a ridge to an 8,880-foot saddle at .5 mile. From here, the Clear Creek Trail goes 18.3 miles down Clear Creek to the Panther Creek Road, except that now it is in bad shape with downed trees and landslides.

Continue on the Ship Island Trail up a sandy slope to the east end of Fishfin Ridge (9,200 feet) at 1 mile. The trail climbs along the side of Fishfin Ridge, then changes to the north side of the ridge at 1.7 miles. Here three 250-foot triangular towers are just ahead. At 2 miles is a junction at 9,000 feet with a side trail to Wilson and Harbor Lakes. From here, the Ship Island Trail descends across cliffs into a usually snowy cirque and on to Birdbill Lake. To go to Wilson Lake, take the left (west) trail from this junction. It has been rerouted from its location on the topographic map, so it goes directly to Wilson Lake (8,880 feet) at 2.6 miles. The trail skirts the west shore to join the trail down Wilson Creek at 2.7 miles, 6.6 miles from Crags Campground. A trail continues around the south side of the lake to Harbor Lake (8,922 feet) at 2.8 miles.

Another way to Wilson Lake is to take the Waterfall Trail into Wilson Canyon from the junction near Cathedral Rock. At the crossing of Wilson Creek 6.2 miles from Crags Campground, go up the creek instead of down. This trail goes over granite benches to Wilson Lake, 7.2 miles from Crags Campground.

56.

Birdbill Lake

Round trip: 15.2 miles
Elevation gain: 1,280 feet; elevation loss (return climb): 1,480 feet
This section: 1.7 miles one way; 200 feet gain, 520 feet loss
Topographic map: Mt. McGuire
Trailhead GPS: N 45 6' 15.2" W 114 31' 27.9"
Highest point: 9,000 feet
Time: 2 to 3 days; difficulty: strenuous
Access: From Crags Campground; see Welcome Lake and Wilson and Harbor lakes, to go by trail to the junction on Fishfin Ridge with the trail to Wilson and Harbor Lakes where this description begins.

What you will see: On the way to Birdbill Lake, you pass the 200-foot orange and gray triangles of Fishfin Ridge. The tiny blue-green lake is amid white granite benches below the square gray head of the fish.

Directions: From the junction on Fishfin Ridge with the trail to Wilson Lake 5.9 miles from Crags Campground, the trail to Birdbill Lake descends a vertical wall into a cirque in two breathtaking switchbacks, then cuts northwest along the side of Fishfin Ridge. Snow covers the trail in the cirque until mid-August most years. After rounding

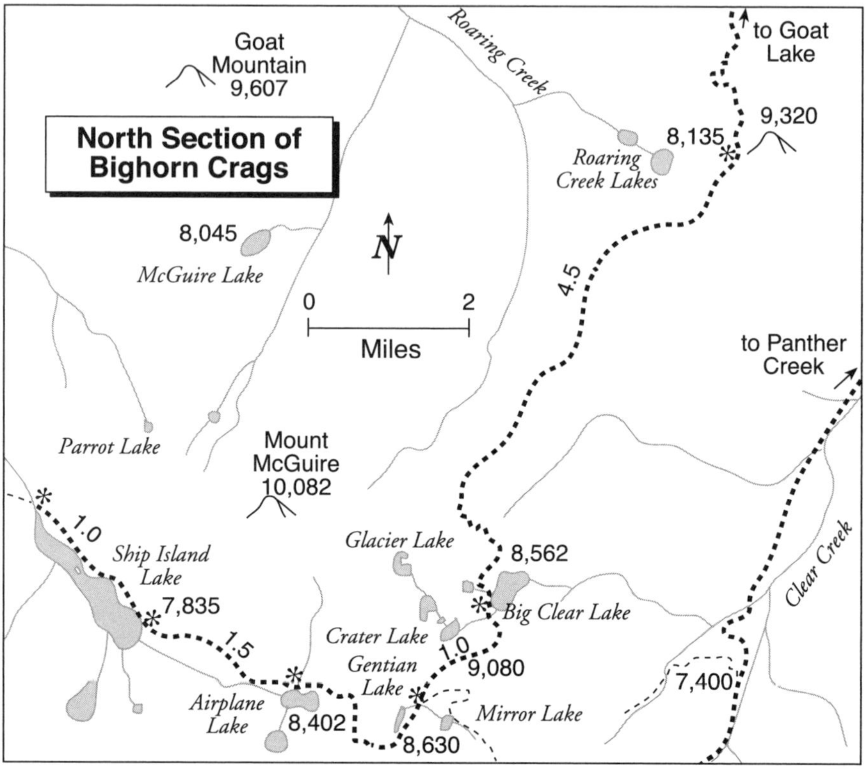

the end of the ridge, the trail descends to the lake (8,670 feet) at 1.7 miles, 7.6 miles from Crags Campground. To avoid the snow in summer you will need to take the Clear Creek trail downhill and then go up a side trail to Mirror Lake and from it to Birdbill.

57.

Gentian and Big Clear Lakes

Round trip: 18 miles
Elevation gain: 1,730 feet; elevation loss (return climb): 2,000 feet
This section: 1.4 miles one way; 450 feet gain; elevation loss (return climb): 520 feet
Highest point: 9,080 feet
Time: 3 days; difficulty: strenuous
Topographic map: Mount McGuire

Trailhead GPS: N 45 6' 15.2" W 114 31' 27.9"

Access: from Crags Campground: see Welcome Lake, Wilson and Harbor lakes and Birdbill Lake to go by trail to Birdbill Lake, where this description begins.

What you will see: A shoulder of Mount McGuire crouches behind a rocky ridge above the cobalt blue water of Gentian Lake. In late summer, equally blue gentians cover the grassy shores. Beyond the lake is a tiny pond where the trail to Big Clear Lake passes 500 feet above silvery Mirror Lake in the forest below. From a saddle between Gentian and Big Clear Lakes, you can see seven lakes. Three of them are blue-green Crater Lake, which shades to dark turquoise in the center, Gooseneck Lake with its elongated neck under the dark cliffs of Mount McGuire and Big Clear Lake with crystal water and white sand below outcrops resembling pink erasers. The other four are Glacier and Pothole under Mount McGuire ahead and Gentian and Birdbill back to the south.

Directions: To reach Big Clear Lake from Birdbill Lake, take the trail north from the junction with the Ship Island Trail at the lower end. (For directions for reaching this junction, see Birdbill, Wilson and Harbor and Welcome lakes.) The trail first descends 200 yards to narrow Gentian Lake (8,630 feet), then winds .2 mile along its east shore and past a pond to a junction at .4 mile with a trail that drops 1 mile to Mirror Lake and another 2.9 miles to the Clear Creek Trail.

Here, stay on the main trail, which zigzags north up a sandy ridge to a 9,080-foot saddle at .8 mile. Beyond this it angles northeast across talus, descends through trees, and crosses an inlet in a cleft to Big Clear Lake (8,562 feet) at 1.4 miles, 9 miles from Crags Campground. Campsites are at the south end near the inlet. The trail continues 6.5 miles north to Goat Lake, passing trees burned in the Clear Creek Fire of 2000 on the way.

To reach Crater Lake (8,707 feet) from Big Clear Lake, climb to Pothole Lake (8,640 feet) by taking the trail north .2 mile and a path that goes west 100 yards. Then go south and west around the end of a ridge to the lake. Or you can descend to the lake cross-country from the saddle between Gentian and Big Clear Lake, but don't try to hike down the gorge between Crater Lake and Big Clear Lake. To reach Gooseneck and Glacier Lakes (8,760 feet and 8,945 feet), hike up the stream from Crater Lake.

58.

Airplane and Ship Island Lakes

Round trip: 21.6 miles
Elevation gain: 1,480 feet; elevation loss (return climb): 2,600 feet
This section: 3 miles, 200 feet gain; elevation loss (return climb): 1,120 feet
Highest point: 8,960 feet
Time: 3 days; difficulty: strenuous

View above Airplane and Ship Island Lakes

Topographic map: Mount McGuire
Trailhead GPS: N 45 6' 15.2" W 114 31' 27.9" at Crags Campground
Access: from Crags Campground; see Wilson and Harbor lakes, and Birdbill Lake to go by trail to Birdbill Lake, where this description begins.

What you will see: West of a saddle above Birdbill Lake, waterfalls cascade into the brilliant blue of Airplane Lake from the hanging valley containing Shoban and Sheepeater lakes. (A hanging valley is one with a drop-off at the lower end, caused by a glacier in the main canyon below down cutting faster than the one in the valley.) Farther down the canyon the sapphire platter of Ship Island Lake is inlaid in dark green woods below orange towers and charcoal peaks. At 1.3 miles long, it is the largest lake in the Frank Church Wilderness. Above the white granite of its island-ship, a peak resembles a huge bird with outstretched wings. Along the lakeshore in midsummer bloom three-foot-tall white plumes of beargrass. From the lower end of the lake, orange and gray gargoyles march down into the Impassable Canyon of the Middle Fork.

Directions: From the junction with the Ship Island Trail at the lower end of Birdbill Lake, where this description begins, take the Ship Island Trail, which switchbacks west .5 mile and 180 feet up to the saddle with the view of Airplane and Ship Island lakes. On the other side, the trail descends talus and slabs into forest. At 1.5 miles a side trail leads .2 mile to Airplane Lake (8,402 feet). Below this turnoff, the main trail descends through forest and between rock shelves. At 1.7 miles, an orange granite buttress 800 feet high looms across the canyon. The upper end of Ship Island Lake (7,835 feet) is at 3 miles.

To look down into the Middle Fork Canyon, take a path along the north shore of the lake, passing the island at 3.5 miles, to the lower end of the lake at 4 miles. Here, cross the outlet and climb 100 vertical feet to the top of a granite ridge. It is easy to trip and fall on the smooth granite, so be very careful. Back at the upper end of the lake, if you can ford Ship Island Creek to the south side, you can hike south cross-country for .5 mile to an unnamed, half-mile-long lake under the cliffs of Aggipah Mountain.

Panther Creek Area

59.

Clear Creek Trail

Round trip: 36 miles
Elevation gain: 5,390 feet; elevation loss: (return climb): 120 feet
Highest point: 8,680 feet
Topographic maps: Pine Creek Rapids, Bighorn Crags, Gant Ridge, Mount McGuire
Trailhead GPS: N 45 17' 23.1" W 114 20' 57.6"
Time: 4 days; difficulty: expert, center section of trail is in poor condition, maybe impassable
Access: At a sign for Cobalt 8 miles north of Challis, turn left (northwest) off Highway 93 onto the paved, then improved dirt, Morgan Creek Road. Drive over Morgan Creek Summit at 19.4 miles and down Panther Creek past Cobalt to the Clear Creek Trailhead, 62 miles from Highway 93. Or on U.S. 93 at North Fork 21 miles north of Salmon, turn left (west) onto the Salmon River Road, and go 26.6 miles to Panther Creek, 4.3 miles up it and .2 mile on a side road to the trailhead.

A little history: If you take the route to the trailhead over Morgan Creek Summit and down Panther Creek, you will pass the settlement of Cobalt; three miles below it a road comes in from the east from the old town of Leesburg, which is on the National Register of Historic Places.

At the height of mining at Cobalt in the 1950s, 2,000 people lived there. Located in a grassy flat along Panther Creek, Cobalt is a modern ghost town of white buildings behind a chain-link fence. If the price of cobalt climbs enough, the town may live once more.

Gold was discovered near Cobalt in 1893, copper in 1896 and cobalt itself, which is used as a steel alloy, in 1901. From 1913 to 1921, silver, nickel and copper were mined and beginning in 1917, cobalt as well at the Blackbird Mine. After acquiring the Blackbird and building a mill in 1949, the Calera Mining Company took out $47.5 million in ten years. At its height the mine fulfilled one-quarter of U.S. cobalt needs, but it closed in 1959 when the government stopped cobalt price supports. Because the cobalt deposits extend into the Frank Church Wilderness, the Central Idaho Wilderness Act of 1980, which designated that wilderness, set up a special mining

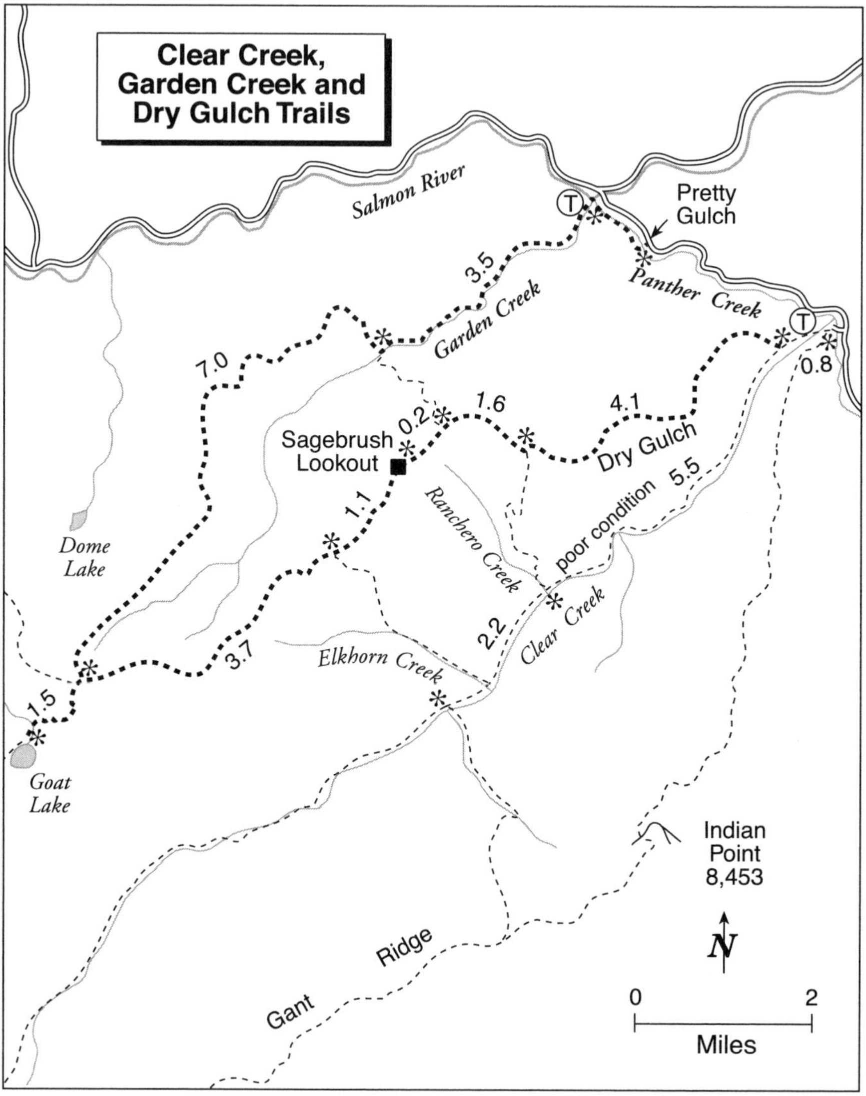

management zone for the cobalt.

Leesburg started In July 1866, when five Montana miners – Frank "Barney" Sharkey, Elijah Mulkey, Joseph Rapp, William Smith and Ward Girton – discovered gold on Napias Creek in the Leesburg Basin, about 20 miles west of Salmon. "Napias" means gold in Shoshoni. Within a few months there were 3,000 people, served by the supply center of nearby Salmon. Col. George Shoup, who later became the first governor of Idaho, opened a store here and sent in supplies with freighter William J. Bryan. This gold rush led to many other mining discoveries in the area. By 1946, when all the residents had finally left, 600,000 ounces of gold had been taken from Leesburg.

Ford of Panther Creek at Clear Creek

What you will see: This trail climbs the beautiful canyon of Clear Creek. From a height such as Dome Mountain, the canyon seems gentle and wooded, but from the trail you see the dramatic rock faces and towers that hide within it, patched with dark gray and lime-green lichen. The trail begins in sagebrush, grass and mountain mahogany, then climbs through a burned forest of ponderosa pine and Douglas fir. Rock nubbins on Gant Ridge near Cathedral Rock decorate the head of the canyon. In early or late season, when the road to Crags Campground is closed by snow, the Clear Creek Trail used to be traveled to reach the Bighorn Crags. The lower two-thirds of the trail is within the perimeter of the 2000 Clear Creek Fire. Because of this fire the Forest Service has not been able to do all the maintenance needed, -cutting downed trees and repairing landslides- so trying to travel the whole trail up into the Bighorn Crags now is not advised and probably impossible.

Directions: The trail begins by fording Panther Creek at 3,400 feet. The ford can be knee-deep even in mid-August. It is best to start up the trail in early morning because it can be 110 degrees in summer. Before July 1 each year this ford is impassable. To avoid it, drive 2 more miles up Panther Creek to Beaver Creek, walk across a bridge over Panther Creek, and then hike back down Panther Creek along a dirt road to the trail.

From the ford of Panther Creek at the Clear Creek trailhead, the trail begins as a primitive road across a pasture to Clear Creek. Just before it reaches the creek at .5 mile, the unsigned Gant Ridge Trail turns off to the left to go 21.3 miles through burned forest to the Bighorn Crags Trail above Cathedral Lake. The main trail crosses Clear Creek to the north side, then angles up a grassy hill and turns west up the creek. At .8 mile is a junction with the Dry Gulch Trail to Sagebrush Lookout and Dome Mountain. The old road turns into a trail soon after this. Grassy hillsides alternating with creek-bottom shrubs give way to cliffs at 2 miles. At 4 miles, the trail crosses the creek to the south side.

Beyond a ford of tiny Cougar Creek at 4.1 miles, the route climbs onto a grassy knoll across from a big cliff, then descends to Clear Creek and wades back to the north side at 4.4 miles. In early season, try to find a foot log. The trail now winds through snags to a meadow at Rancherio Creek at 5.5 miles, where a Spaniard once homesteaded. In the woods near the creek is a campsite. From here a trail up Rancherio Creek used to go 2 miles to the Sagebrush Lookout Trail. If you have gotten this far it is probably time to turn around.

The Clear Creek Trail continues through woods along the base of cliffs, then edges the creek. Here in June it would be underwater. At 6.1 miles, at two huge boulders, the trail goes into the creek for 20 yards. Those on foot will want to take a path above the creek.

At 7.1 miles is a junction with a trail up Elkhorn Creek that connects with the Sagebrush Lookout Trail over Dome Mountain. Beyond a ford of Elkhorn Creek, the main trail skirts cliffs to reach another junction at 7.7 miles. From here, a trail goes south 3.4 miles up Deadhorse Creek to the Gant Ridge Trail about 2 miles west of Indian Point.

The Clear Creek Trail formerly continued up the creek 11 miles more to the Ship Island Trail. On the way, it fords the creek three more times at 9, 10 and 15 miles. The fords are no problem, but there are boggy places and much downed timber.

60.

Dry Gulch Trail to Sagebrush Lookout and Dome Mountain

Round trip: 23.8 miles
Elevation gain: 5,990 feet; elevation loss (return climb): 440 feet
Highest point: 8,960 feet
Topographic maps: Pine Creek Rapids, Bighorn Crags, Mount McGuire
Trailhead GPS: N 45 17' 23.1" W 114 20' 57.6"
Time: 4-5 days; ability: expert; water scarce
Access: From Challis drive 8 miles north on U.S. 93 to a sign for Cobalt. Turn left (northwest) onto the paved, then improved dirt, Morgan Creek Road and drive over Morgan Creek Summit at 19.4 miles, then down Panther Creek to the Clear Creek Trailhead, 62 miles from Highway 93. Or from North Fork, 21 miles north of Salmon on U.S. 93, turn left (west) on the paved, then improved dirt, Salmon River Road and go 26.6 miles to Panther Creek. Turn left (south) and drive 4.3 miles up Panther Creek and .2 mile on a side road to the trailhead. On foot, ford Panther Creek, and hike .8 mile to a junction with the Clear Creek Trail, where this description begins.

What you will see: The Dry Gulch Trail to Sagebrush Lookout climbs through meadows, forest, brush and burned snags. The trail gives a great view of the deep chasm of Panther Creek and the rugged canyon of Clear Creek. Far to the south of Dome Mountain rise the spires and turrets of the Big Horn Crags.

It is best to take this hike as soon as the snow on Dome Mountain has melted because the meadows will be green and full of flowers and the five springs, the only water sources, will have plenty of water. It can be 110 degrees at the trailhead and the trail climbs nearly 6,000 feet so it's a good idea to start hiking at dawn and stop by early afternoon.

Sagebrush Lookout

Directions: After fording Panther Creek at the Clear Creek trailhead where the water is knee-deep even in late summer, hike .8 mile to a junction. In early summer, park at Beaver Creek 2 miles upstream so you can cross Panther Creek on a bridge. Then hike down the creek to the junction of the Clear Creek and Dry Gulch trails. The Clear Creek Trail goes 16 miles up that creek to meet the Ship Island Trail in the Bighorn Crags.

Take the Dry Gulch Trail northwest over a bare ridge to the canyon of Dry Gulch at 1 mile. A spring runs cold and clear to the left at 1.8 miles, just before the trail turns south. Trees and snags begin at 2.3 miles, where the path curves west. A smaller, closer spring is at 2.5 miles. At 3 miles, the canyon levels in grass, but at 3.3 miles narrows and steepens, then circles a miniature hill. The next spring at 4.2 miles is 100 yards south of the trail near a grassy campsite that has several rattlesnakes. At 4.5 miles, the trail climbs south out of Dry Gulch to a saddle at 4.9 miles. From here, the Rancherio Creek Trail descends 2 miles to Clear Creek.

The Dry Gulch Trail now traverses a ridge northwest through snags and grass to a saddle at 6 miles and along a little ridge to another saddle at 6.5 miles. Here a little-used trail turns off to drop 1.8 miles to Corral Flat on Garden Creek. Also, a path goes left around the summit of Sagebrush Lookout. Keep straight ahead up another 200 feet to the white-painted log lookout (7,147 feet) at 6.7 miles, which was constructed in 1925. Be sure to watch for rattlesnakes.

To find the only campsite near the lookout, take the trail southwest down the ridge. In 200 yards a side trail turns left (southeast) .5 mile to a spring and campsite, 400 feet below the lookout.

Beyond the campsite junction, the main trail follows the top of an open ridge and descends to a saddle at 7.8 miles where the trail is indistinct. Here the Elkhorn Trail, which is in poor condition, drops 3.2 miles to Clear Creek. Beyond it, the main trail follows the ridges southwest, mostly in woods and burned trees.

Two campsites northeast of a saddle are at 9 miles. To find water, go left (south) from the second campsite, which is closest to the trail. This spring is the only water between the lookout spring and a spring on Dome Mountain at 12 miles.

Beyond here, the trail zigzags 900 feet up the center of a wide ridge in 1 mile to the 8,697-foot ridge top. At 10 miles, it turns right (west) along a ridge towards Dome Mountain. Beyond a saddle, the path climbs to a junction with the Garden Creek Trail at 11.5 miles.

61.

Garden Creek Trail to Dome Mountain

Round trip: 23 miles
Elevation gain: 5,720 feet; elevation loss (return climb): 160 feet
Highest point: 8,960 feet
Topographic maps: Mount McGuire, Long Tom Mountain, Bighorn Crags
Trailhead GPS: N 45 19' 25.9" W 114 23' 38.7"
Time: 3 days; ability: expert, water scarce
Access: From Challis drive north 8 miles on U.S. 93 to a sign for Cobalt. Turn left (northwest) onto the paved, then improved dirt, Morgan Creek Road. Drive over Morgan Creek Summit and down Panther Creek to the new trailhead at Pretty Gulch at 65.3 miles. Or from North Fork 21 miles north of Salmon on U.S. 93, turn left (west) on the paved then improved dirt Salmon River Road and drive 26.6 miles to Panther Creek and up it one mile to a ford that begins the trail..

What you will see: For the first 4.5 miles to Corral Flat, the trail up Garden Creek plunges through shrubs with cliffs hanging close above. Farther up, the cliffs give way to grass. Soon, dark green moss softens the cliffs closest to the stream. Between the Salmon River and Corral Flat, the trail fords the small creek 16 times. Remember it can be 110 degrees here in summer, so plan accordingly. The lower two-thirds of the trail is within the perimeter of the 2000 Clear Creek Fire, and that burn follows the east side of the trail clear to Dome Mountain.

Above Corral Flat, the trail follows grassy ridges dotted with snags. From here you can look down on dark blue curves of the Salmon River, which runs in a chasm. Two springs 200 feet below the trail are the only water between Corral Flat and a stream above Goat Lake. The Garden Creek Trail is one way to reach Goat Lake, but the Dry Gulch Trail is less difficult and has more reliable springs.

Directions: At the confluence of Panther Creek with the Salmon River where the topographic map shows the Garden Creek Trail beginning, it is blocked by fenced and posted private land. A new trailhead has been constructed one mile up the Panther Creek Road at Pretty Gulch. The trail begins by fording Panther Creek, which is passable each season beginning in mid-July. From the ford the trail goes away from Panther Creek to the head of a meadow and then leads over rugged terrain parallel to Panther Creek to Garden Creek and northwest across it to the trail found on the topographic map.

That trail goes along the creek and at the first creek crossing at 1.5 miles drops into the creek bed and stays next to the creek, crossing back and forth a few more times than shown on the topographic map. Although the creek is small, be cautious when crossing it early in the season because the footing is treacherous.

At 4.5 miles at Corral Flat (4,956 feet), the trail disappears in tall grass on the north side of the creek before an outfitter's camp. Here, a side trail goes south 1.8 miles to Sagebrush Lookout. From Corral Flat, the Garden Creek Trail turns right (northwest) up a side canyon.

At the top of a gully, the main trail turns left (southwest) up the end of a ridge to a summit at 5.8 miles. For the next 3 miles, the route follows grassy ridges. At 7 miles, a side path leads left (south) 200 feet below the trail to a spring that is stagnant in late summer. At 7.5 miles, the trail turns south again across a hillside with a view of the Salmon River below. At 8 miles is a turnoff for a reliable spring 400 feet west.

At 8.5 miles, ignore a path downhill to the right. The correct route climbs the end of a ridge and turns southeast, crossing two grassy hills at 9 miles. You'll view Sagebrush Lookout across Garden Creek at 10 miles, and at 10.7 miles the trail passes above outcrops splintered into page like pieces.

At 8,800 feet is a junction with a side trail to the top of Dome Mountain. The main trail curves southeast here across the head of Garden Creek through scree with difficult footing until it joins the trail from Sagebrush Lookout at 11.5 miles.

62.

Dome Mountain to Goat Lake

Round trip: 25 miles
Elevation gain: 5,760 feet; elevation loss (return climb): 1,170 feet
This section: 1.5 miles; 40 feet gain; elevation loss (return climb): 1,010 feet
Highest point: 9,000 feet
Topographic map: Mount McGuire
Trailhead GPS: N 45 17' 23.1" W 114 20' 57.6" at beginning of Dry Gulch trail
Time: 4 days; ability: expert
Access: See Dry Gulch Trail to Sagebrush Lookout or Garden Creek Trail to go by trail to the junction of these trails on Dome Mountain, where the description begins.

What you will see: Over the west side of sapphire Goat Lake looms an 800-foot cylinder of dark rock. Gray and pale orange crags enclose the cylinder and lake on three sides, with the wooded summit of Dome Mountain on the fourth. As the trail descends to the lake, you can look down Goat Creek into both the Middle Fork and Main Salmon River canyons. While the Clear Creek, Garden Creek and Dry Gulch

Goat Lake in the Bighorn Crags

trails are within the perimeter of the 2000 Clear Creek fire, the fire spared Goat Lake.

Directions: Where the Garden Creek and Sagebrush Lookout trails join on Dome Mountain (8,960 feet,) the trail to Goat Lake climbs southwest around the side of Dome Mountain. At .5 mile on a saddle it joins three other trails and a path. The path goes south to a spring. One of the trails goes north to the summit of Dome Mountain. Another, a continuation of the Garden Creek Trail, goes northwest from this junction to Horse Heaven Mountain and then dwindles as it descends Shell Creek to a ford of the main Salmon River in 8.5 miles.

The third trail descends southwest to Goat Lake, first in seven long switchbacks and then in smaller zigzags across talus to the outlet at 1.2 miles. On the other side of the outlet, it climbs over rock benches to the lake (7,988 feet) at 1.5 miles, 13 miles from the Sagebrush Lookout trailhead and 13.5 miles from the Garden Creek trailhead. Campsites are near the outlet and at the upper end.

63.

Goat Lake to Big Clear Lake

Round trip: 37.4 miles from Panther Creek to Big Clear Lake, or 30.4 miles from Crags Campground to Goat Lake.

Elevation gain: 7,550 feet; elevation loss (return climb): 2,450 feet from Panther Creek

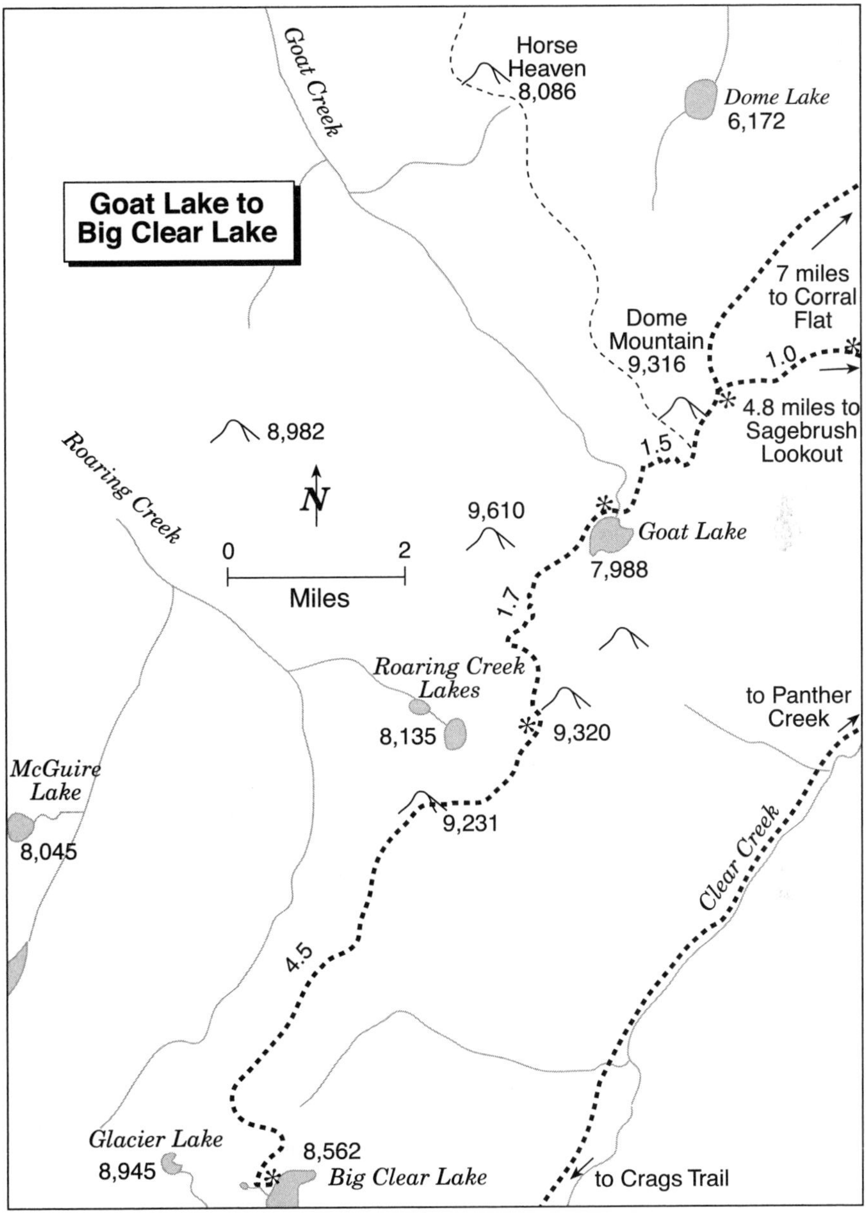

This section: 6.2 miles; 1,790 feet gain; elevation loss (return climb): 1,280 feet

Highest point: 9,340 feet

Topographic map: Mount McGuire

Reached from the Dry Gulch or Crags Campground

Trailhead GPS: Trailhead GPS: N 45 17' 23.1" W 114 20' 57.6" at Dry Gulch trailhead

Time: 5 - 6 days; difficulty: strenuous

Access: See Dry Gulch Trail to Sagebrush Lookout and Dome Mountain to Goat Lake to go by trail to Goat Lake, where this description begins.

What you will see: On the other side of a saddle, above the west side of Goat Lake, an old burn stretches down to Roaring Creek Lakes, silver gems inlaid in a forest recovering from the 1979 Ship Island Fire. Across the canyon, spires flank the dark triangle of Mount McGuire, and the cream-colored dome of Goat Mountain. From a rocky knoll .7 mile beyond the saddle you can see the fangs of Fishfin Ridge to the south.

Directions: From the lower end of Goat Lake (7,988 feet), the trail to Big Clear Lake circles the lake and climbs southwest along a stream, crosses it and a talus slope, and traverses an avalanche area to a cirque. After zigzagging 400 feet up, the trail reaches an 8,960-foot saddle at 1.2 miles. From the saddle, expert hikers can descend through the dead snags and fallen trees to Roaring Creek Lakes. Most will want to stay on the trail to Big Clear Lake, which climbs south along the side of a ridge. At 1.7 miles is a 9,340-foot knoll of sharp rocks, then a ridge. At 3.7 miles, the trail drops 400 feet, climbs 240 feet and rounds the end of a spur. It drops another 400 feet, passing Pothole Lake, to the shore of Big Clear Lake (8,562 feet) 6.2 miles from Goat Lake (18.7 miles from Panther Creek.) Big Clear Lake can also be reached by 9 miles of trail from Crags Campground. For directions for this route, see Welcome, Wilson and Harbor, Birdbill and Gentian and Big Clear lakes.

NORTH FORK AREA

64.

Salmon River Trail; Corn Creek to Lantz Bar

Round trip: 24 miles
Elevation gain: 350 feet; elevation loss (return climb): 220 feet
Highest point: 2,960 feet
Topographic maps: Butts Creek Point, Square Top, Waugh Mountain
Trailhead GPS: N 45 22' 13.5" W 114 45' 16.2"
Time: 3 days; difficulty: strenuous

Access: At North Fork 21 miles north of Salmon on Highway 93, turn left (west) onto the paved, then improved dirt, Salmon River Road. Drive to the end of the road at Corn Creek Campground at 46 miles.

A little history: Along the road to the trailhead, you pass the village of Shoup. Placer gold was discovered there in the 1860s, but mining didn't start in earnest until

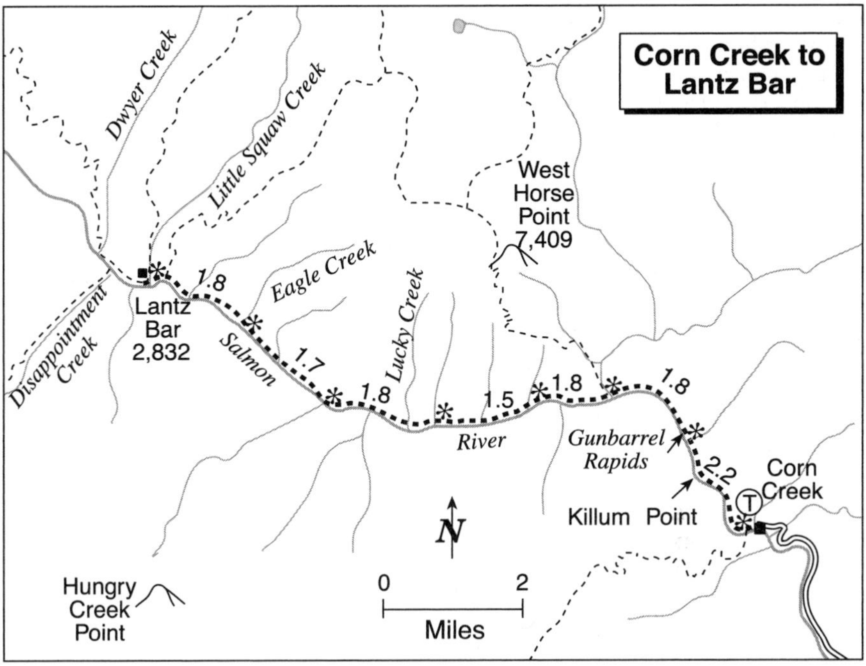

two prospectors from Leesburg, Sam James and Pat O'Hara, discovered the Grunter and Kentuck lodes in 1881 and 1882. By 1886, five water-powered stamp mills churned at the village, first called Boulder City, and then Shoup, after Idaho's first governor. By the 1890s, Shoup had 300 claims and 1,500 residents. In the early 1900s the closest road was still six miles away and supplies were carried in by barge or pack trail. The barges were taken apart and used for buildings, since they couldn't go back up the river.

The trailhead at Corn Creek is also the launch site for raft trips on the Salmon River. The first regular trips down the river were made by a prospector, John McKay, a Scotsman who first came to the canyon about 1872. Each spring he would build a wooden scow, load it with supplies and set off from Salmon down the river to prospect, spending the winter in the canyon and returning to Salmon each spring.

Beginning in 1896 Harry Guleke began to make regular trips down the river in wooden boats. He was perhaps the first outfitter for trips on the Salmon. One of the parties he guided was organized by the editor of the New York Times, Cissy Patterson, in 1921; the trip was written up in Field and Stream. Guleke's boats, called scows, were flat-bottomed with high sides and sweeps (long oars) at each end. He made the boats of green lumber for flexibility and tarred them inside and out for water resistance. Each time Guleke reached Riggins, he sold his boats and returned by land. Perhaps that was what the National Geographic party who went down the river in 1935 was referring to when they gave it the nickname "River of No Return."

What you will see: Along the trail to Lantz Bar on the Salmon River, western tanagers often dart through the shrubs and ponderosa pines with flashes of red, black and yellow. Near Corn Creek, gray granite towers, coated with black lichen, hang above the grassy bars, sandy beaches and lime-green water of the river. Side creeks tumble down shrub-filled gulches from 5,000-foot canyon walls. The hike can be a challenge in July and August, because the temperature in the canyon can reach 110 degrees. In addition, poison ivy lines the trail and rattlesnakes often sun themselves here. Much of the canyon wall across the river from the trail burned in 2000.

Directions: The trailhead at Corn Creek Campground is .5 mile farther west than shown on the topographic map. It begins above the boat ramp by traversing a steep rocky slope, then drops to the river to bridge Wheat Creek at 200 yards. At 1.5 miles, it is 150 feet above the river, when it rounds the cliffs of Killum Point above Gunbarrel Rapids. Jack Killum, who lived at Gunbarrel Creek, built his cabin right on the river trail. Anyone on the trail from 1935 to 1941 had to walk through his house, where he lived with his wife and five children.

At 2.2 miles, the trail spans Gunbarrel Creek, and at 4 miles crosses sandy bars and then Horse Creek. On the west side of the bridge over Horse Creek, the Horse Creek Trail turns off to the north. This trail is difficult several miles up due to landslides. The Horse Creek Trail gives access by a six-mile side trail to the site of West Horse Lookout.

Just beyond Horse Creek are supports for a former bridge over the river. The trail runs under cliffs above rapids and at 5.2 miles, crosses dry Legend Creek at a campsite. At Bow Creek at 6 miles, black towers jut from the woods on the canyon walls. Spindle Creek fountains down a steep, brush-filled canyon at 6.7 miles. Here a rock tower resembles a spindle, and there is a campsite on a grassy bench. The trail winds back into shrubs to span Lucky Creek on a log at 7.2 miles.

Across from a pine bar with campsites, Cottonwood Creek rushes white down a deep canyon. After threading cliffs above rapids, the trail descends to a beach across from Phantom Creek at 8.5 miles. At 9 miles, just above Rainier Rapids, is tiny Rainier Creek on another pine bar with campsites. At 10.2 miles, the trail goes across Eagle Creek.

At Fawn Creek at 11.2 miles, the trail fords the creek to a small campsite. At Lantz Rapids at 11.7 miles is a dry wash, then at 12 miles are the meadows, orchards, tree-dotted hills and guard station of Lantz Bar. Beyond a campsite, the path bridges Little Squaw Creek. From Lantz Bar the Fawn Ridge Trail climbs 5.5 miles to the Waugh Mountain-West Horse Trail, and the Eakin Ridge Trail climbs a vertical mile in 8 miles to Eakin Point.

A little history: Oscar Eakin, a trapper, had a cabin at Lantz Bar about 1916, followed by Milt Haynie and then John McCoy and his brother Walter, who were wanted in Owyhee County for stealing 100 horses. The bar is named for Frank Lantz, who moved there in 1925. While Lantz was bringing his belongings to the site that year his boat turned over in Gunbarrel Rapids, but he succeeded in his second try. After that, he built a new boat each year at Shoup to float his supplies down the river. In 1935, he married a Montana cook and brought her to the river. In 1964, a Forest Service summer guard accidentally set fire to Lantz's house. That fall, without government authorization, rangers built a new house, where Lantz lived until he died in 1971.

More directions: Beyond Lantz Bar, the river trail becomes the primitive Dwyer-Smith Gulch Trail, which continues along the river for a short distance, then climbs partway up the canyon wall and back down. From the beginning of that climb a primitive spur trail continues along the river for 1.8 miles to a dead end at Corey Bar. The Dwyer-Smith Trail ascends more than 7,000 feet in 16 miles to the Mount Harrington Trail at Black Creek Saddle.

The trail from Lantz Bar to Corn Creek has no problems at normal high water of 30,000 cubic feet per second, but higher flows may put sections underwater, so it's a good idea to check with the North Fork Ranger District before hiking this trail in May or June.

65.

Stoddard Trail: Salmon River to Reese Creek

Round trip: 16 miles
Elevation gain: 4,100 feet; elevation loss (return climb): 1,130 feet
Highest point: 6,680 feet
Topographic map: Long Tom, Butts Creek Point
Trailhead GPS at site of former Stoddard Bridge: N 45 17' 57.5" W 114 35' 45.4"
Time: 2 days; difficulty: strenuous, water scarce
Access: From North Fork 21 miles north of Salmon on U.S. 93, turn left (west) onto the paved, then improved dirt, Salmon River Road. Drive .6 mile past the Middle Fork confluence to the Stoddard Pack bridge site at 38.6 miles. The bridge was destroyed by a landslide in 2017 and is scheduled to be rebuilt in 2021.

What you will see: From the dark, rock-lined canyon of the Salmon River, the Stoddard Trail hairpins up a brushy slope to run along cliffs 3,500 feet above the Impassable Canyon of the Middle Fork. From the trail, you look down on the white curlicues of rapids embroidering the blue-green river. Across the river, canyons plunge down between cliffs from the delicate towers of the Bighorn Crags. Along the trail, tilting slabs decorate rock knolls where mountain goats and bighorn sheep live. On the canyon walls, the ravines of Color, Nolan and Reese creeks resemble giant claw marks. Although the trail runs above precipices in many places, it is well-maintained. The whole area along it burned in 1988.

Directions: Because temperatures in the canyon can reach 110 degrees in summer and there is little shade, it is best to hike the 4.8 miles to the first water, Color Creek, before 9 a.m., or plan the hike for spring or fall. Be sure to watch for rattlesnakes and poison ivy.

To begin the hike, walk 200 yards down a jeep trail (not open to motor vehicles) from the Salmon River Road to the pack bridge (3,000 feet.) The trail starts in grass, rocks and chaparral with burned snags and mountain mahogany higher up. At the top of the switchbacks at 2 miles is a view up the Middle Fork and a campsite with no water.

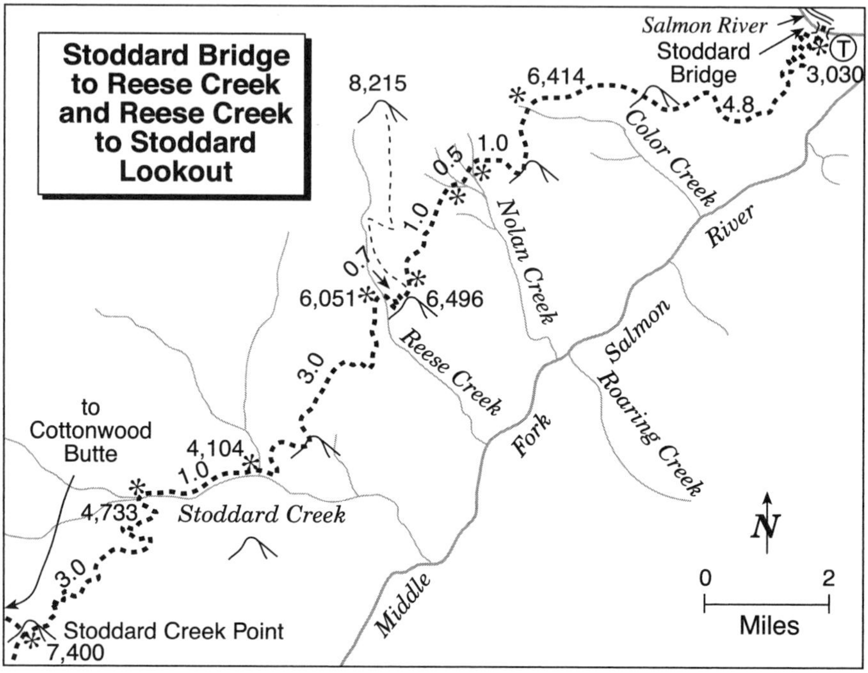

Sections of the Middle Fork can be seen below at 2.4 and 2.8 miles. The trail edges a drop-off at 3.5 miles and passes above a grassy saddle with another waterless campsite at 3.8 miles. Color Creek (6,414 feet) at 4.8 miles is lined with alder and water birch. Here two tiny tent sites are carved into the slope. The site does have water.

Beyond Color Creek, the trail climbs through alders and willows. At 5.5 miles is a flat, grassy point and a path to a waterless campsite. The main trail descends through burned forest to four branches of Nolan Creek at 5.8, 6, 6.2 and 6.3 miles. All lack campsites because of the steep hillside. Next, the route traverses a precipice, then at 7 miles, passes under a rock tower. Across the river from where Roaring Creek descends from the Bighorn Crags at 7.2 miles, the trail looks down on another bit of the Middle Fork. At 7.3 miles, at 6,520 feet is a flat saddle from which the main trail hairpins down to the shrubs of Reese Creek at 8 miles. Here tent sites are cut into the pine-needled hillside.

66.

Stoddard Trail: Reese Creek to Stoddard Lookout

Round trip: 31.2 miles

Stoddard Lookout

Elevation gain: 7,560 feet; elevation loss (return climb): 3,090 feet
This section one way: 7 miles; 3,460 feet gain; elevation loss (return climb): 1,950 feet
Highest point: 7,536 feet
Topographic maps: Aggipah Mountain, Butts Creek Point
Trailhead GPS at river: N 45 17' 57.5" W 114 35' 45.4"
Time: 4 days; difficulty: strenuous, water scarce
Access: See Stoddard Trail - Salmon River to Reese Creek to go by trail to Reese Creek, where this description begins. To reach Reese Creek the hike requires crossing a foot bridge that is scheduled to be rebuilt in 2021.

What you will see: Below the old eight-foot-square Stoddard Lookout, furrowed cliffs drop into the abyss of the Middle Fork of the Salmon River, with side canyons forming a row of dark notches. The historic lookout is still standing although the area around it and all along the trail burned in 1988. Across the Middle Fork, organ-pipe towers descend from the Bighorn Crags.

Directions: From a saddle south of Reese Creek, the trail descends 2,000 feet on a bare, grassy hillside with a view of the Stoddard Creek Canyon below. The main obstacle on this trail is that 2,000-foot descent from Reese to Stoddard creeks, because it leaves a 3,300-foot climb from there to the lookout.

Beyond Reese Creek (6,051 feet), the trail climbs south along the gorge of the creek to a saddle at .5 mile that has a nearby campsite with a spring. From the end of a switchback at .7 mile on the other side of the saddle, a blue curve of the Middle Fork appears below.

The main trail circles west across talus past wild raspberries and at 2 miles curves

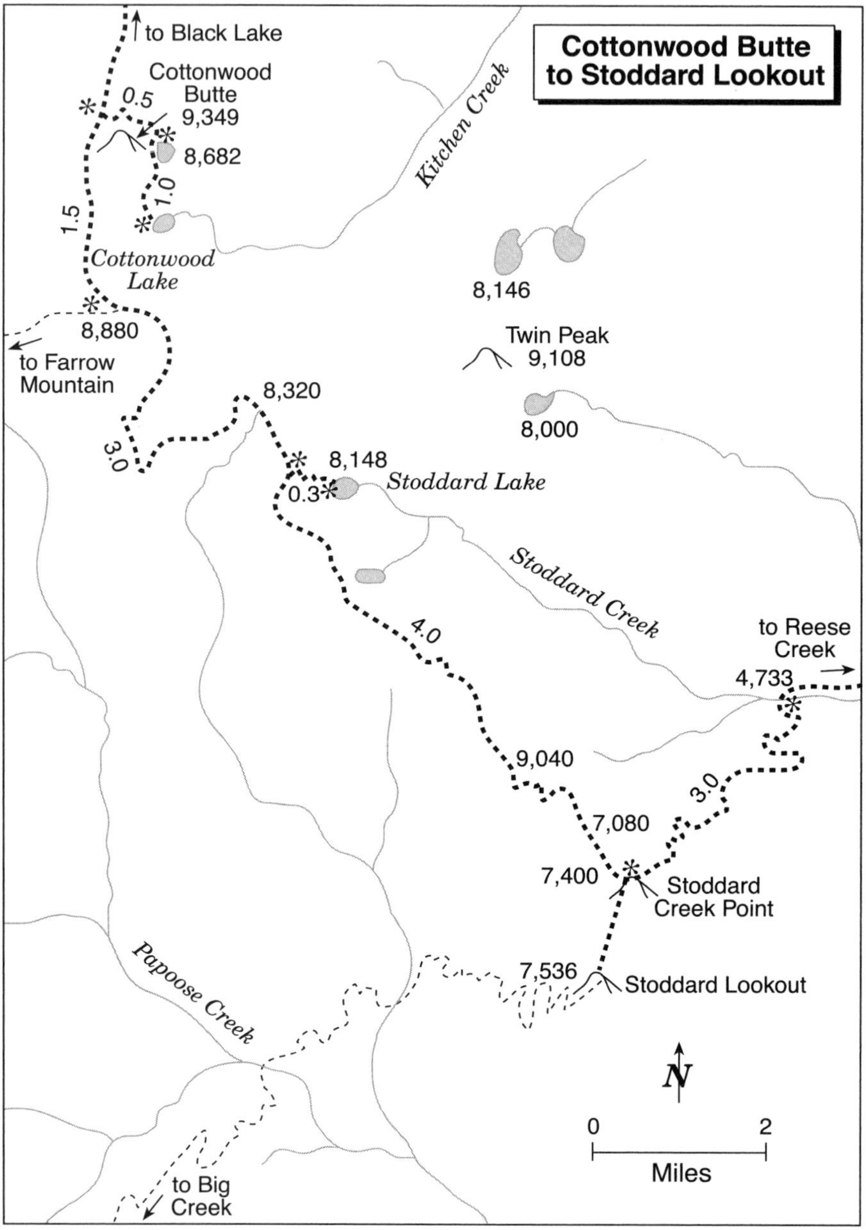

into the canyon of the North Fork of Stoddard Creek. At 2.3 miles, it turns south down a bare ridge. Just above Stoddard Creek at 2.8 miles, a path leads east to a grassy campsite. The main trail climbs west up Stoddard Creek to cross its north fork at 3 miles (4,104 feet) near a campsite.

Trout fishing at Cottonwood Butte Lake

The route then ascends Stoddard Creek to a crossing of it at 4 miles and switchbacks through huckleberry and snags to a narrow saddle at 5 miles, From the saddle a path leads south towards Cradle Creek. After ascending it is much easier to be flown in to Cold Meadows and reach the lookout rom there,. a ridge spur, the main trail climbs the end of Stoddard Creek Point to a junction with the Cottonwood Butte Trail at 7 miles, which is 15 miles from the Stoddard Pack bridge.

The eight-foot-square lookout is .6 mile to the south on a bare, grassy hill (7,536 feet). Beyond the lookout, the Stoddard Trail descends to Papoose Creek 4 miles below, then Goat Creek, a tributary of Big Creek.

The only water near the lookout is a spring at the head of Nugget Creek .4 mile northeast and 250 feet below. You can reach it by heading east down a ridge below the lookout on a path towards pointed granite knolls for .2 mile, then turning north and descending .2 mile farther.

67.

Cottonwood Lakes to Stoddard Lake and Stoddard Creek Point

Round trip: 42.5 miles from Chamberlain airstrip
Elevation gain: 5,720 feet; elevation loss (return climb): 5,580 feet
This section: 8.5 miles; 1,680 feet gain, elevation loss (return climb): 3,300 feet
Highest point: 9,120 feet
Topographic maps: Cottonwood Butte, Aggipah Mountain, Papoose Peak

Trailhead GPS at Cold Meadows: (The lakes are most easily reached from Cold Meadows.)

Time: 6 days from Chamberlain; difficulty: strenuous; water scarce

Access: See Chamberlain to Cold Meadows, Cold Meadows to Black Lake, Black Lake to Cottonwood Lakes (or both sections of the Stoddard Trail) to go by trail to the 8,920-foot notch above the highest of the two Cottonwood Lakes, where this description begins.

What you will see: Rows of black outcrops north of dark green Stoddard Lake resemble vertebrae. Beyond the lake, the trail from Cottonwood Butte to Stoddard Creek Point plunges 2,000 feet, giving magnificent views of the Middle Fork of the Salmon River Canyon, the Bighorn Crags and the gorge of Papoose Creek.

Directions: From the notch above Cottonwood Lakes, the main trail continues south along Cottonwood Butte. At .9 mile is a saddle with a view of the lower Cottonwood Lake, but there is no good way to descend to it. Next, the route overlooks Black Lake on the west and Kitchen Creek on the east. At 1.5 miles is a junction with a 2-mile trail that connects with the Farrow Mountain Trail 2 miles from Coyote Springs.

From the junction, take the left (east) trail toward Stoddard Creek Point, which goes through areas burned in 1988. The trail drops off the end of a ridge at 2.5 miles. At 3.6 miles are a meadow and campsites with a spring. The path follows a stream down to a notch at 3.8 miles. This stream is the only water from Black Lake to Stoddard Creek. From the notch, the trail climbs to a junction with the Stoddard Lake Trail at 4.5 miles. That side trail drops 400 feet in .3 mile to the lake.

Beyond the junction, the main trail tops a summit at 4.8 miles, then descends to a saddle at 5 miles. Below cliffs south of this saddle is a small yellow-green lake. The trail ascends the ridge to its highest point, 9,040 feet, then plunges over dangerous scree towards the Middle Fork, switchbacking down. At 7.2 miles, on a grassy tongue, is a view of the canyon. The trail zigzags down the tongue and on a notch at 8.2 miles are grass, flowers, and scattered trees and snags. This parklike slope continues up to Stoddard Creek Point, (7,400 feet) where the trail joins the Stoddard Trail at 8.5 miles.

HORSE CREEK PASS AREA

68.

Horse Creek from Gattin Ranch to Cayuse Creek

Round trip: 6 miles
Elevation gain: 120 feet; elevation loss (return climb): 240 feet
Highest point: 5,600 feet
Topographic map: Horse Creek Butte
Trailhead GPS at Gattin Ranch: N 45 29’ 15.3” W 114 32’ 11.1”
Time: 5 hours; difficulty: moderate
Access: At North Fork, 21 miles north of Salmon on U.S. 93, turn left (west) on the

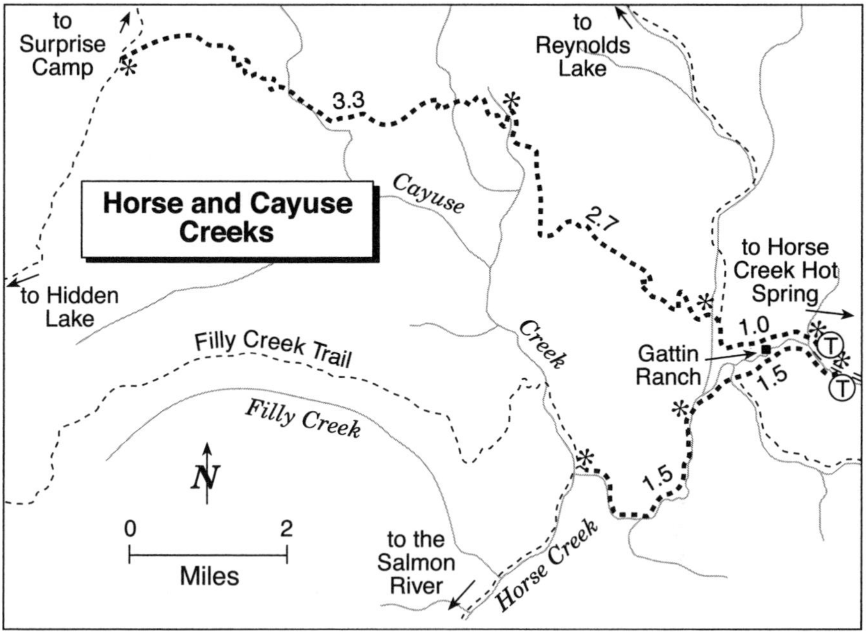

paved Salmon River Road. At 16.7 miles turn right (north) on the rocky, dirt Spring Creek Road and drive over Horse Creek Pass to 50 yards before Woods Creek Pass, at 35.8 miles. Turn left (south) on the road to Horse Creek Hot Springs. It descends Horse Creek, passing the hot springs at 46.3 miles, to a sign for the Horse Creek Trail at 50.3 miles, about .2 mile before the road is closed and gated for private property. There is no trespassing: The cabins are occupied and the owners are serious about it. The main trailhead is at the hot springs, but you can drive 4.2 miles beyond it to the gate.

It is also possible to reach the hot springs from U.S. 93 from Darby, Montana, but it is 50 miles north of North Fork on the highway. To do this, turn left (west) off U.S. 93 onto the paved Connor Cutoff 7.5 miles south of Darby or onto the West Fork Road 4 miles south of Darby. The 1-mile-long Connor Cutoff meets the West Fork Road 3 miles from Highway 93. Continue 11.4 miles on the West Fork Road to a junction. Here turn left (south) towards Painted Rocks Lake. At 22 miles is the reservoir, where the pavement stops. At 26 miles the road is paved again until a junction at 34.1 miles. Here keep right on an improved but rocky dirt road that switchbacks up to Woods Creek Pass at 42.8 miles.

A little history: If you drove through Montana to reach the trailhead, you passed through part of the Bitterroot Valley. In 1805 Lewis and Clark traveled north through it with their Indian guide, Toby, on their way to Lolo Pass. In 1824, Alexander Ross and his fur-trapping party of 55 men, 25 women, 64 children and 392 horses got snowed in here for a month. Finally, when the snow froze hard enough to support their weight, they were able to get over the mountains to the south by walking 18 miles in one day.

The upper end of the valley, where they camped for so long, is known as Ross's Hole. While in the area Ross found a ram's skull embedded in a pine tree. Today you can't see the skull – if it is still there – but this tree, known as the Medicine Tree, stands unmarked beside the highway, decorated with ribbons for good luck.

What you will see: The trail down Horse Creek from the Gattin Ranch descends a rugged canyon, where talus and jumbled towers punctuate the wooded walls. Beside granite boulders the creek flows crystal-clear over white sand. In its setting the creek is so pretty it seems out of a fishing dream, and indeed, there are plenty of catch-and-release trout. Except for two fords of the creek, the trail is pleasant exercise for those who come here to enjoy the undeveloped sand- and rock-bottomed hot springs, which consist of a hot-tub-size really hot pool and two much larger but cooler pools.

Directions: Because the place where the trail begins has little or no parking, you may wish to look for a pullout before the sign or continue to the gate across the road, where there is more parking, and walk back to the trail. The first thing the trail does is ford the 20-foot creek to the left (east) side. This crossing and new trail section are not shown on the topographic map. The ford was shin-deep on July 7 in a dry year, so could be difficult or impassable that early in wet years for hikers, although it may be possible to cross on logs. Once across, the trail goes along a pole fence on a lodgepole hillside 50 feet above the creek. At .7 mile there are cabins across the creek-bottom meadows. At 1 mile the trail crosses Stud Creek, where a side trail goes off up that creek. After willows and more woods, the trail at 1.5 miles turns down to Horse Creek, fords it to the right (west) side, and enters the Frank Church Wilderness. Now the route is right along the creek beside boulders and sand. At 1.8 miles, the trail goes under a big cliff, then climbs 100 feet in forest. It descends to a gravel beach at 2 miles, where a side stream not shown on the map enters the creek. At 2.3 miles, the trail goes under another set of cliffs and talus, where the creek bends 90 degrees to the west.

Now the trail becomes rockier and is overgrown in places. At 2.6 miles, the creek, canyon and trail curve sharply 90 degrees to the north. At 3 miles, you can look up the side canyon of Cayuse Creek and across at the rugged canyon of Horse Creek on its way to the main Salmon River. Within 200 yards the trail fords Cayuse Creek and continues down Horse Creek. Between here and Filly Creek the trail suffers from landslides that make it difficult but the trail continues 6.5 miles down to the Salmon River.

69.

Cayuse Creek

Round trip: 14 miles
Elevation gain: 2,340 feet; elevation loss (return climb): 300 feet
Highest point: 7,640 feet
Topographic maps: Horse Creek Butte, Blue Joint, Wood Hump

Trailhead GPS at Gattin Ranch: N 45 28' 15.3" W 114 32' 11.1"

Time: 10 hours; difficulty: strenuous

Access: At North Fork, 21 miles north of Salmon on U.S. 93, turn left (west) on the paved Salmon River Road. At 16.7 miles turn right (north) on the rocky, dirt Spring Creek Road and drive over Horse Creek Pass to 50 yards before Woods Creek Pass, at 35.8 miles. Turn left (south) on the road to Horse Creek Hot Springs. It descends Horse Creek, passing the hot springs at 46.3 miles, to a sign for the Horse Creek Trail at 50.3 miles about .2 mile before the road is closed and gated for private property. There is no trespassing: The cabins are occupied and the owners are serious about it. The main trailhead is at the hot springs, but you can drive 4.2 miles beyond it to the gate.

It is also possible to reach the hot springs from U.S. 93 from Darby, Montana, but it is 50 miles north of North Fork on the highway. To do this turn left (west) off U.S. 93 onto the paved Connor Cutoff 7.5 miles south of Darby or onto the West Fork Road 4 miles south of Darby. The 1-mile-long Connor Cutoff meets the West Fork Road 3 miles from Highway 93. Continue 11.4 miles on the West Fork Road to a junction. Here turn left (south) towards Painted Rocks Lake. At 22 miles is the reservoir, where the pavement stops. At 26 miles the road is paved again until a junction at 34.1 miles. Here keep right on an improved but rocky dirt road that switchbacks up to Woods Creek Pass at 42.8 miles.

The Cayuse Creek Trail gives shorter access to Hidden Lake and Stripe and Waugh lakes west of it than the trail past Reynolds Lake. It also has a much better access road, is 4.5 miles shorter and has 700 feet less elevation gain.

What you will see: From the trail you see meadows and wooded hills reminiscent of Vermont, and higher up, there are views of the chasms of Horse Creek and the Salmon River.

Directions: Due to development of the Gattin Ranch as a cabin area, the trails take different routes than the ones shown on the topographic map. From the trailhead at the Gattin Ranch gate, the trail leads off to the right (north) of the gate through willows and then makes a couple of switchbacks up a sandy, ponderosa-pine hillside. Then it goes along above the fence around the cabin property, detouring back into the canyon of a stream to cross it at .5 mile. Please be as silent as possible along here to avoid disturbing the cabin residents. At .8 mile the trail turns uphill to the right (north) to a junction with the Reynolds Creek Trail at .9 mile. That trail climbs 2,360 feet in 6.5 miles to the trail between Reynolds Lake and Surprise Creek Camp. Continue on the main trail, which drops to Reynolds Creek and fords it at 1 mile. From here on up the side of the canyon a contractor created new switchbacks on the trail in 1997, making it 1 mile longer than shown on the topographic map.

From the ford, the trail climbs up into a side canyon crossing an open area at 1.5 miles with a view of surrounding wooded ridges. Then it climbs the side of a ridge and rounds the end of a ridge at 6,600 feet at 2.8 miles. The trail drops 300 feet into the head of the canyon of Cayuse Creek, crossing three branches of the creek, at 3.7, 4.2 and 6 miles. Above the third crossing, it switchbacks up to join the Reynolds Lake-Surprise Camp Trail on a flat 7,640-foot saddle at 7 miles, which has no nearby water.

70.

Reynolds Lakes and Surprise Creek Camp

Round trip: 18 miles
Elevation gain: 1,980 feet; elevation loss (return climb): 1,840 feet
Highest point: 8,640 feet
Topographic map: Blue Joint
Trailhead GPS: N 45 34' 3.4" W 114 31' 30.8"
Time: 2 days; difficulty: strenuous

Access: At North Fork, 21 miles north of Salmon on U.S. 93, turn left (west) on the paved Salmon River Road. At 16.7 miles turn right (north) on the rocky, dirt Spring Creek Road and drive over Horse Creek Pass to 50 yards before Woods Creek Pass, at 35.8 miles. Continue straight ahead on a four-wheel-drive road to the trailhead at 48.7 miles. It is also possible to reach the Reynolds Lake trailhead from U.S. 93 near Darby, Montana, but it is 50 miles north of North Fork on the highway. To do this turn left (west) off U.S. 93 onto the paved Connor Cutoff 7.5 miles south of Darby or onto the West Fork Road 4 miles south of Darby. The 1-mile-long Connor Cutoff meets the West Fork Road 3 miles from Highway 93. Continue 11.4 miles on the West Fork Road to a junction. At 14.4 miles turn left (south) towards Painted Rocks Lake. At 22 miles is the reservoir, where the pavement stops. At 26 miles the road is paved again until a junction at 34.1 miles. Here keep right on an improved but rocky dirt road that switchbacks up to Woods Creek Pass at 42.8 miles.

What you will see: Above the emerald water of the largest Reynolds Lake, beargrass, talus and granite outcrops form repeating layers. Beyond the marshy lake, the trail wanders along wooded ridges past dark granite spindles, caps of pink or white talus, and views of the Bitterroots and Bighorn Crags. The spring at Surprise Creek Camp is the only water between Reynolds Lake and Hidden Lake.

Directions: At the trailhead (7,280 feet) park before a mud hole near undeveloped waterless campsites. Beyond this, the trail starts off to the left, signed Reynolds Creek and Divide Trails. It skirts a meadow, crosses a stream at .7 mile, and climbs over a ridge at 1.2 miles. At 1.5 miles, across a bridge over the outlet of a pond, a path leads 100 yards northwest to Reynolds Lake (7,523 feet). To reach the other two off-trail lakes, turn left (southeast) and descend a faint path .4 mile down the creek to the first lake (7,400 feet). The second lake is .4 mile farther up a ravine south (left) of the large talus slope.

From Reynolds Lake, the main trail climbs the inlet to a grassy 8,000-foot saddle at 2.5 miles. After turning north, the way drops to a junction with the Reynolds Creek Trail at 3.2 miles. This trail descends 2,360 feet in 6.3 miles to the Cayuse Creek Trail, 1 mile west of the Gattin Ranch trailhead, giving cross-country access to the Reynolds Creek Lakes, west of the trail. The main trail climbs to a notch, then turns west to a grassy flat with a campsite, spring and junction at 3.4 miles.

The trail to the right, the Divide Trail, follows the Idaho-Montana line 14 miles

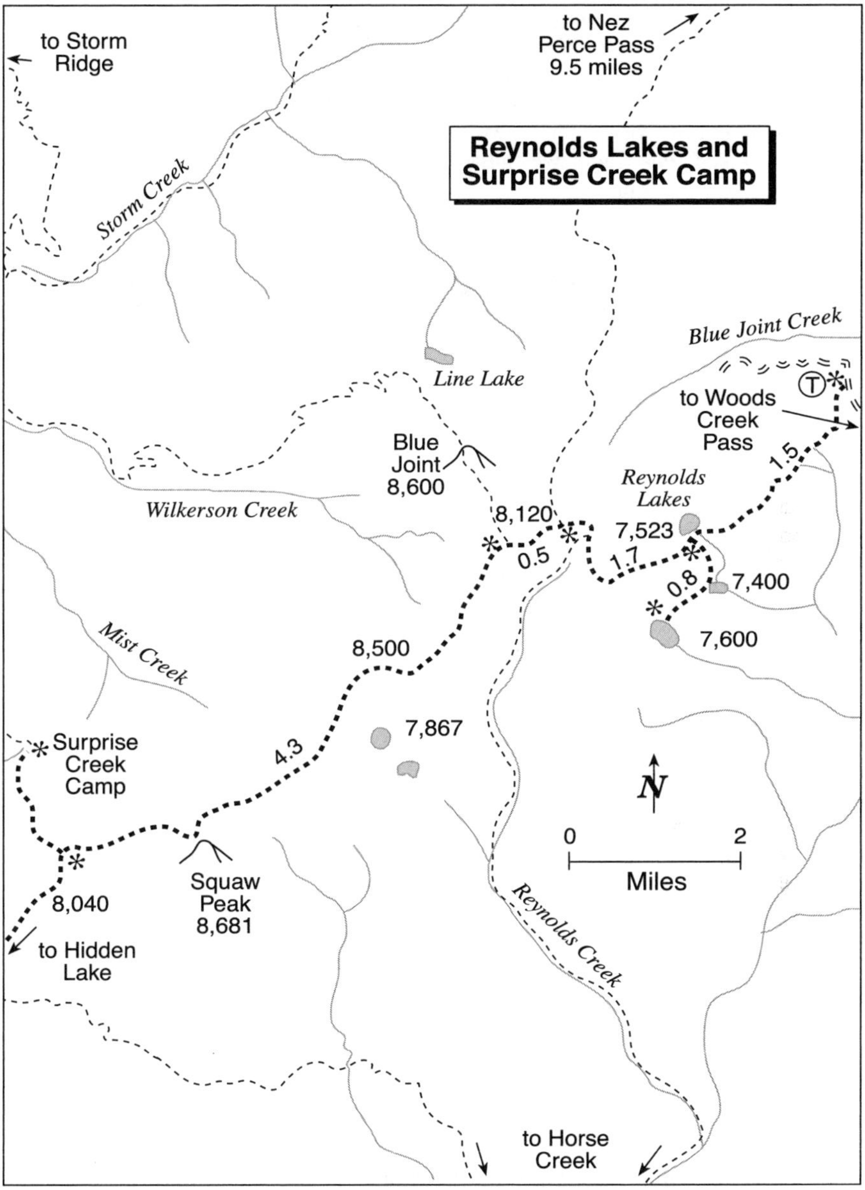

north to the Nez Perce Trail Road at Nez Perce Pass. Go left (southwest) on the trail towards Parker Mountain and Hidden Lake. In about .5 mile is a second junction labeled the Blue Joint Trail. This trail climbs 5 miles over Blue Joint, above Line Lake and down to the Storm Creek Trail .5 mile from Storm Creek Flat on the Selway River. Continue on the main trail up a sandy slope to a flat of dead whitebark pines along a ridge and up a hill of pink talus at 4.8 miles, which gives a glimpse of Reynolds Creek

Lakes below. The talus mound of Squaw Peak (8,681 feet) soon appears ahead, and the trail switchbacks up to its high point (8,640 feet) at 6.7 miles on the side of this peak. After more ridges, it reaches, at 8 miles, a junction with the Wood Hump Trail, which descends 11 miles to Thompson Flat on the Selway River.

To find a campsite with water, take the Wood Hump Trail north 1 mile and down 640 feet to Surprise Creek Camp, which has two large campsites and a spring underneath a boulder below the trail.

71.

Surprise Camp Junction to Hidden Lake and Parker Mountain

Round trip: 28 miles
Elevation gain: 3,000 feet; elevation loss (return climb): 3,180 feet
This section, one way: 6 miles, 1,020 feet gain
Highest point: 8,503 feet
Topographic maps: Blue Joint, Wood Hump, Square Top
Reached from Reynolds Lake or the Gattin Ranch
Time: 3-4 days; difficulty: strenuous
Access: See Reynolds Lake and Surprise Creek Camp to go by trail to the junction with the Wood Hump Trail above Surprise Creek Camp, where this description begins.

What you will see: The rock tabletop of Square Top Mountain perches above Hidden Lake. Below it, gullies divide the sloping wall into three sections overhanging the green water. The other three sides of the lake are rimmed with marsh grass and yellow pond lilies. From the grassy summit of Parker Mountain southeast of the lake, you can see the towers of the Bighorn Crags, the great dark chasm of the Salmon River Canyon and the pale scallops of the Bitterroots. Much closer, to the northwest, three horizontal white stripes line the face of Stripe Mountain.

The topographic map has Square Top incorrectly located because in 1965, the U.S. Bureau of Geographic Names changed its name to Parker Mountain to honor the 1835 missionary, Samuel Parker, and designated the 8,402-foot peak right above Hidden Lake as Square Top.

Directions: This hike description begins at the 8,040-foot Surprise Camp junction with the Wood Hump Trail. From this junction, take the trail toward Hidden Lake which climbs up and down along wooded ridges. At 1.3 miles is a flat saddle where the Cayuse Creek Trail turns east to descend 7 miles to the Gattin Ranch trailhead.

The main trail continues to another saddle, climbs 400 feet, turns west with the ridges at 3 miles, and on a sandy ridge at 4 miles overlooks a tiny lake near the head of Cayuse Creek. At 5 miles is a junction (8,200 feet) with a .5 mile side trail up Parker Mountain.

Fifty yards beyond the junction a side trail plunges north 5 miles down the South

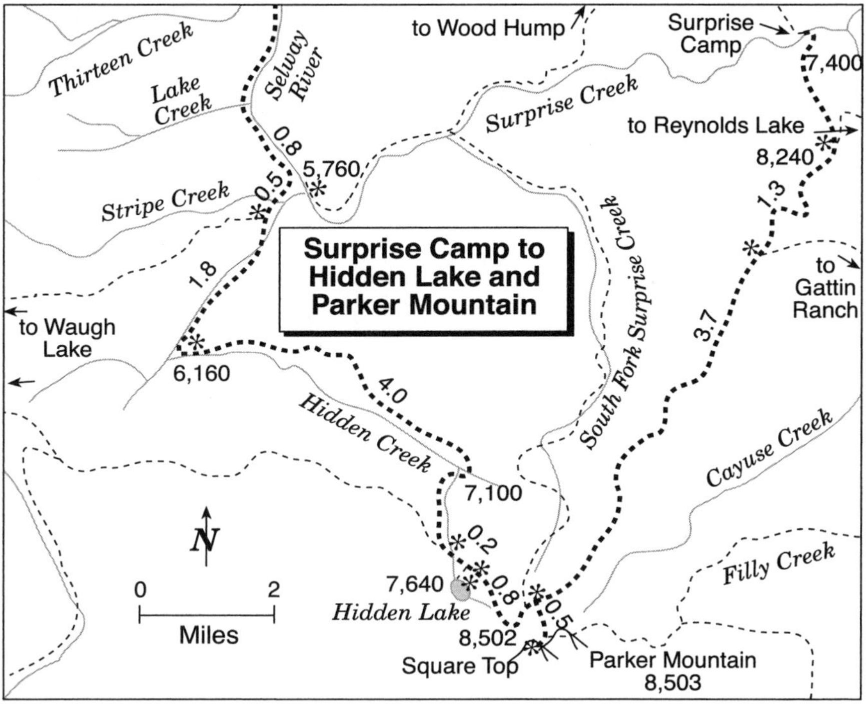

Fork of Surprise Creek to the Wood Hump Trail. The main trail descends to another junction at 5.3 miles, where a path leads west to an outfitter's camp.

Here, turn right (north) on a trail down the inlet of Hidden Lake. At 5.8 miles, a path turns left (southwest) 200 yards to campsites at the lower end of the lake (7,640 feet). At 6 miles the main trail crosses Hidden Creek just before a junction with a trail that goes down the Selway River 24 miles to Magruder Ranger Station and the Shoup-Elk City Trail, which leads to Waugh Lake and eventually to the Base Camp trailhead.

BITTERROOT NATIONAL FOREST
WEST FORK RANGER DISTRICT

72.

Divide Trail

Round trip: 35 miles
Elevation gain: 3,460 feet; elevation loss (return climb): 1,820 feet

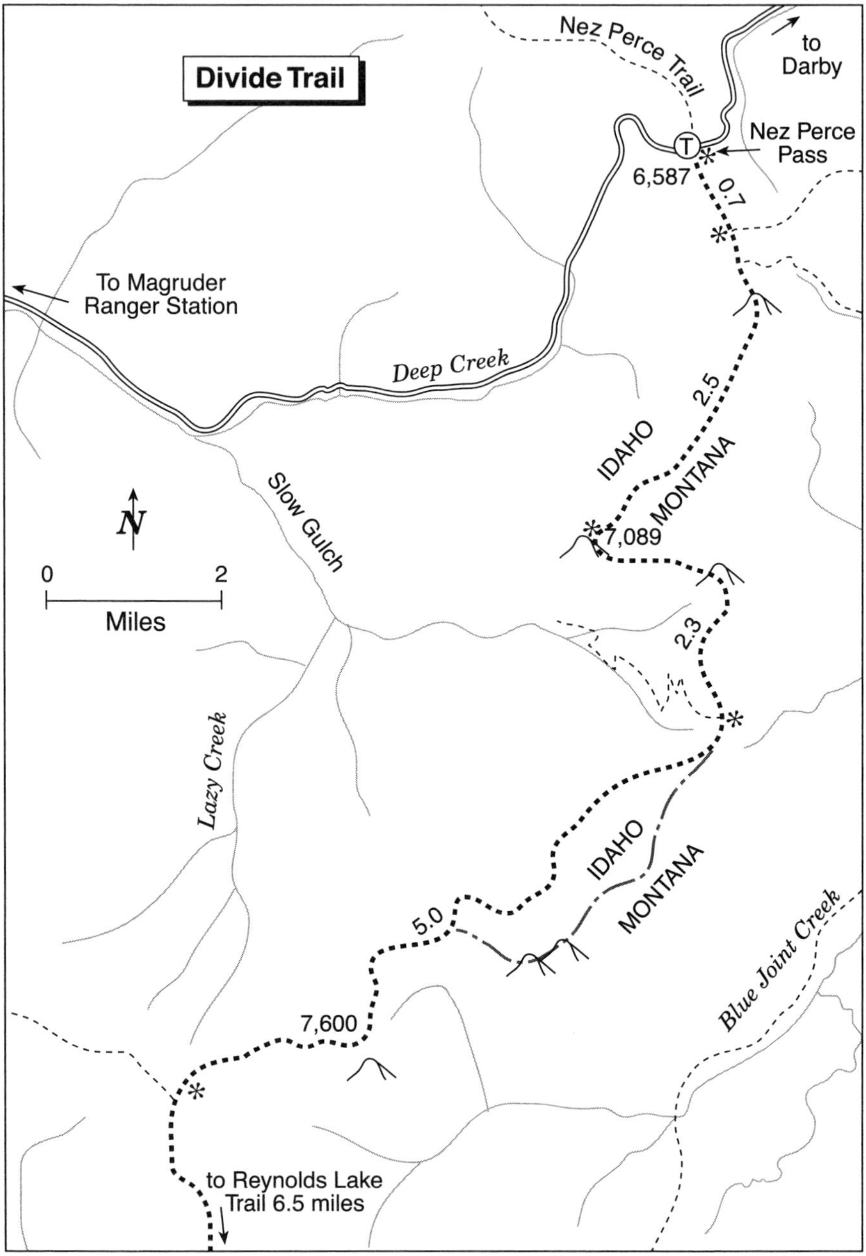

Highest point: 8,460 feet
Topographic maps: Horse Creek Pass, Nez Perce Peak, Blue Joint
Trailhead GPS: N 45 43' 0.14" W 114 30' 11.1"
Time: 4 days; difficulty: strenuous

Access: Turn left (west) off U.S. 93 onto the paved Connor Cutoff 7.5 miles south of Darby, Montana, or onto the West Fork Road 4 miles south of Darby. The 1-mile-long Connor Cutoff meets the West Fork Road 3 miles from Highway 93. Continue 11.4 miles on the West Fork Road to a junction. Turn right (west) onto the paved Nez Perce Trail road and drive to Nez Perce Pass, 28.7 miles from Highway 93 via the Connor Cutoff.

A little history: The route of today's access road was once the Southern Nez Perce Trail. In the 1860s, it was the main route for miners from Elk City, Idaho, to Bannack and Virginia City, Montana, and a branch of this trail, the Shoup-Elk City (Parker) Trail was their main route to Salmon. W.A. Tinkham and his party of the Stevens Railway Survey of 1854 crossed the Southern Nez Perce Trail from east to west. Leaving Fort Owen on November 20, 1853, they went up the West Fork of the Bitterroot River and crossed the mountains on snowshoes, taking almost a month to do so. The Civilian Conservation Corps constructed the present Nez Perce Trail Road beginning in 1934. Two crews worked from opposite ends and met at Observation Point in 1936. The 108-mile road follows the general route of the Southern Nez Perce Trail from Darby, Montana to Elk City, Idaho.

What you will see: On a hilltop 3 miles along the Divide Trail, sapphire larkspur, lavender mariposa lily and yellow sulphur plant embroider the grass. From here, the view is of the brown mushroom stalk of nearby Castle Rock, notched cliffs of the Bitterroots, and pink scree and slabs of Salmon Mountain.

Directions: From Nez Perce Pass, the Divide Trail climbs south through Douglas fir and beargrass, along the right side of a ridge. A side trail, the Castle Rock - South Nez Perce Trail, turns left (east) at .7 mile. The main trail descends the center of the ridge to a junction with the Jack the Ripper Creek Trail at 1 mile. After climbing up and down along three more ridges, you reach a large grassy knoll at 3.2 miles.

Here, the trail turns east along the ridge crest; then at 4.5 miles, curves with the ridge to the top of another hill. After descending, it continues south 12 miles along the divide (with a high point of 8,400 feet) to the Reynolds Lake-Hidden Lake Trail .7 mile west of the largest Reynolds Lake.

73.

Selway River Trail: Magruder Ranger Station to Hidden Lake

Round trip: 45.6 miles
Elevation gain: 3,460 feet; elevation loss (return climb): 140 feet
Highest point: 7,640 feet
Topographic map: Beaver Jack Mountain, Wood Hump, Square Top

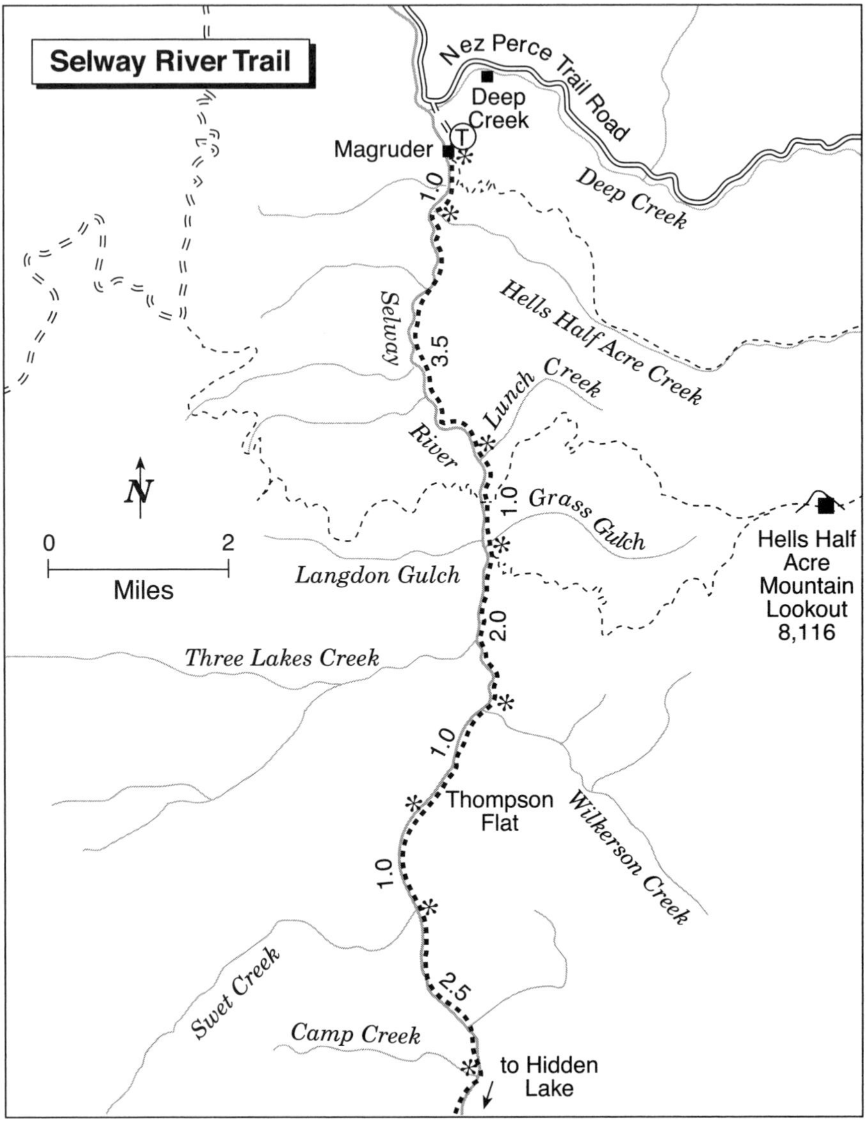

Trailhead GPS: N 45 42' 0.36" W 114 43' 0.6"

Time: 6 days; difficulty: strenuous

Access: Turn left (west) off U.S. 93 onto the paved Connor Cutoff 7.5 miles south of Darby, Montana, or onto the West Fork Road 4 miles south of Darby. The 1-mile-long Connor Cutoff meets the West Fork Road 3 miles from Highway 93. Continue 11.4 miles on the West Fork Road to a junction. Here turn right (west) onto the improved dirt Nez Perce Trail road and drive over Nez Perce Pass, 28.7 miles from Highway 93 via the Connor cutoff. Continue to the junction with the road to Magruder Guard Station at 45 miles. Turn left (south) here and drive .5 mile to the guard station.

What you will see: Along this trail, the upper Selway River eddies in olive-green pools, foams under mossy cliffs and splits to go around gigantic boulders. Below the wooded canyon walls, wild rose, raspberry and alder grow along the river. Opposite Kim Creek 2 miles above the ranger station, dark cliffs with scalloped tops stairstep up Horsejaw Mountain. Similar cliffs and outcrops decorate the canyon much of the way, with perhaps the most spectacular near Wilkerson Creek.

Directions: The trail starts a few yards from the guard station behind a barn (4,120 feet). In thirty yards, the Pasture Ridge Trail turns east to climb 5 miles to the Hells Half Acre-Salmon Mountain Trail. Keep on the Selway River Trail, which plunges into thick undergrowth often dripping with dew. It drops to the river at .2 mile, bends west with it at .7 mile and bridges Hells Half Acre Creek at 1 mile. As the river turns south, the trail traverses a cliff 100 feet above it, then across from Kim Creek at 2 miles, returns to the river. The trail crosses a small, grassy flat and open hillsides across from Gold Pan Creek at 3 miles.

At 3.5 miles, just before Tepee Creek is across the river, is a small campsite. At 4 miles, the river hairpins east below an overhang. The trail goes over Lunch Creek at 4.5 miles across from a 200-foot black tower. Next, it traverses ledges that may be underwater in June. At 5 miles is the sandy meadow called Upper Crossing. From here a trail angles northeast to Hells Half Acre Mountain. On the opposite side of the river, another section of this trail climbs west along the ridge above Langdon Gulch.

The main trail goes along an open slope to ford Grass Gulch Creek in a ravine at 5.5 miles. From here, the Grass Ridge Trail climbs 5 miles to Hells Half Acre Mountain. A campsite is on a grassy flat 50 feet above the river.

The trail continues up the river, crossing it on a bridge to the west bank near Wilkerson Creek at 7.5 miles. At 8.8 miles, the Wood Hump Trail turns off across the river and switchbacks up the river breaks to the top of the hill called Wood Hump. Just beyond Thompson Flat the trail crosses Witter Creek at 9 miles. At 10 miles, a trail turns west up Swet Creek to climb 11 miles to the Shoup - Elk City Trail near Eakin Point. On the main trail there are five fords in the next 2.5 miles between this junction and Camp Creek – one of Swet Creek and four of the Selway.

At 15 miles, the Surprise Creek Trail turns off up Surprise Creek to go 6 miles to a divide near Wood Hump. On the Selway River Trail at 15.7 miles is a junction with the Stripe Creek Trail, which climbs 3.7 miles to the Shoup - Elk City Trail east of Waugh Lake, passing near Stripe Lakes.

At 17.3 miles, the Selway River Trail bends east up Hidden Creek. After fording the river back to the west side at 20 miles, the trail comes to a junction with the Shoup - Elk City trail at 20.7 miles. Take the trail toward Hidden Lake, passing it at 21 miles and reaching a junction with a .5 mile side trail to the top of Parker Mountain at 21.7 miles.

74.

Salmon Mountain Lookout

Round trip: 3 miles
Elevation gain: 800 feet
Highest point: 8,943 feet
Topographic maps: Magruder Mountain, Stripe Mountain
Trailhead GPS: N 45 57' 57.3" W 114 49' 54.3"
Time: 3 1/2 hours; difficulty: easy, but trailhead is hard to find

Access: Turn left (west) off U.S. 93 onto the paved Connor Cutoff 7.5 miles south of Darby, Montana, or onto the West Fork Road 4 miles south of Darby. The 1-mile-long Connor Cutoff meets the West Fork Road 3 miles from Highway 93. Continue 11.4 miles on the West Fork Road to a junction. Here turn right (west) onto the Nez Perce Trail road and drive to Nez Perce Pass, 28.7 miles from Highway 93 via the Connor Cutoff. (The road is paved to the pass.) Drive to the undeveloped trailhead on the side of Salmon Mountain 63.1 miles. It is only 45.4 miles from Grangeville, but the road from that direction is primitive, except for the first 14 miles, so directions are given from the Montana side.

A little history: On the way to the trailhead, as the road climbs above the Selway River, it passes a sign commemorating the Magruder Murder of 1863. That year, freighter Lloyd Magruder was one of the most respected men in the territory and planned to run for Congress. That October, he started with a 60-mule team to go over the Nez Perce Trail from Lewiston, Idaho, to Virginia City, Montana. At Virginia

Salmon Mountain Lookout

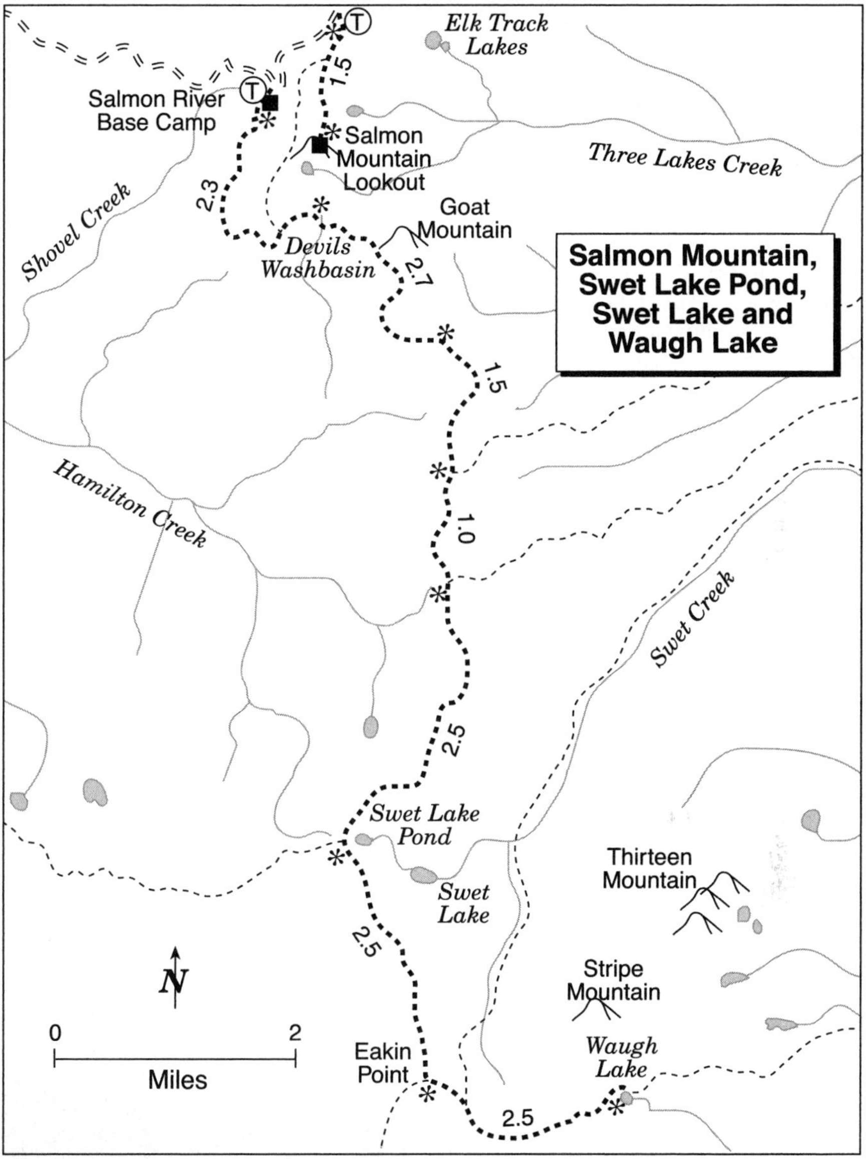

City, Dr. David Howard, William Renton, Chris Lowry, Jim Romaine, Bob Zachary and William Page, who were probably members of the Plummer gang, persuaded Magruder to hire them to help sell his goods.

So it was natural for Magruder to hire Howard, Lowry, Romaine and Page for the return journey to guard the $25,000 he had earned. Four other men joined Magruder on the return also. When the party camped near where the Nez Perce Trail crossed the Selway, Lowry, Romaine and Howard murdered Magruder, and killed his packers and the four men who had recently joined him. They made Page help them throw the bodies over a cliff.

The outlaws continued on the trail to Lewiston, where they left the horses; outside of town they stole a boat intending to float down the Columbia. The water was too dangerous, so they bought stage tickets from hotel owner Hill Beachy instead. When Beachy saw the horses and recognized Magruder's own horse, he and Thomas Pike chased the men to Portland.

By then the outlaws were on a ship to San Francisco, so Beachy and Pike rode to the telegraph office at Yreka, California, and telegraphed ahead. Beachy brought the four men back with him and kept them in his house until the trial. Page turned state's evidence; and Howard, Lowry and Romaine were hanged.

Because Montana residents realized the crooked Virginia City sheriff, Henry Plummer, and his band may have planned Magruder's murder, vigilantes hanged Plummer and two of his aides.

What you will see: Several miles above the murder site, this short climb gives magnificent views of pale blue and cream-colored mountains and ridges undulating off into the distance in every direction. In addition a round, bluish-green lake is set in cliffs just below. The lookout is a standard 14-foot-square building of white-painted boards. A meadow north of it gives a view into a deep cliff-lined cirque holding two tiny ponds and an oval lake of deep turquoise. At the edge of the meadow grow stands of subalpine larch, a tree rare in Idaho. The tiny twigs to which the clumps of needles are attached are so swollen they resemble tiny volcanoes spewing needles.

Directions: From the trailhead, the trail begins climbing through forest as an old road, which is not open to motorized travel because it is within the wilderness. At .5 mile, the track reaches the grassy ridge top. Here two trails turn off, but they are hard to find. Both start near the benchmark marker that is shown on the topographic map. The one to the right (southwest) goes about 2 miles to intersect the trail from Base Camp to Swet Lake Pond in the rolling, rocky area called the Devils Washbasin. The other, turns northeast and skirts the summit of the prominent wooded hill, giving views of and access to Elk Track Lakes at 1 mile and Gold Pan Lake at 2 miles.

Continue along the main trail up the grassy ridge, but be careful. Stop and enjoy the views and continue hiking only when you can watch your steps. It is easy to step off the cliffs that run below the east side of the trail. At 1 mile, the ground steepens and the trail wanders back and forth through rocks and grass to the lookout at 1.5 miles.

75.

Shoup-Elk City (Parker) Trail: Base Camp to Swet Lake Pond

Round trip: 20.4 miles
Elevation gain: 1,200 feet; elevation loss (return climb): 1,000 feet

For side trip to Swet Lake: additional 2 miles round trip; additional elevation loss (return climb): 720 feet

Highest point: 8,280 feet

Topographic map: Stripe Mountain

Trailhead GPS: N 4537' 23.4" W 114 50' 43.8"

Time: 2 to 4 days; difficulty: strenuous; expert ability for 1 mile from pond to lake

Tree possibly peeled by Indians to eat the inner bark

Access: At Grangeville turn right (north) off U.S. 95 onto the main street. At the north end of town near the Nez Perce-Clearwater National Forest office turn right (east) onto the paved Elk City Road and drive 48 miles to the Elk City Junction. Turn right (south) and go 14.7 miles along the Red River. Turn left (east) on the Nez Perce Trail Road. Drive 14 miles on improved dirt, and 30.5 miles on rocky, primitive road to Base Camp on Salmon Mountain.

OR

Turn left (west) off U.S. 93 onto the paved Connor Cutoff 7.5 miles south of Darby, Montana, or onto the West Fork Road 4 miles south of Darby. The 1-mile-long Connor Cutoff meets the West Fork Road 3 miles from Highway 93. Continue 11.4 miles on the West Fork Road to a junction. Here turn right (west) onto the improved dirt Nez Perce Trail road and drive over Nez Perce Pass, 28.7 miles from Highway 93 via the Connor Cutoff. (The road is paved again from 22.2 miles to the pass.) Continue to Base Camp at 63.5 miles. (This end of the road is in better shape than the Idaho end.)

A little history: This hike follows part of the Parker Trail, named for the Rev. Samuel Parker, who in 1835 was the first European to travel this branch of the Southern Nez Perce Trail. He was the earliest Christian missionary to preach in Idaho, Montana or Wyoming. The combined Board of Missions for the Presbyterian and Congregational churches had turned down his request for funds at first because they said he was too old at 56. While raising funds to make the trip anyway, he met Marcus Whitman and recruited him as a companion. They finally obtained funds and permission to go west with an American Fur Company expedition. This group was unfriendly until Whitman removed an arrow from the back of Jim Bridger at the fur trappers' Green River Rendezvous, which was held at a spot near today's Pinedale, Wyoming. One reason they weren't accepted was that Parker kept criticizing the conduct of the fur traders. The Flathead and Nez Perce at the Rendezvous were so enthusiastic about the missionaries that Whitman went back east to recruit more missionaries and funds.

Waugh Lake

That was the official version, but some accounts say that Parker and Whitman didn't get along, partly because Parker insisted Whitman do all the camp chores. Parker went on with the Indians to select a site for the mission, crossing the mountains in only 25 days. He was to meet Whitman at the 1836 Rendezvous with a full report, but after reaching the Columbia and traveling down it went home by sea.

In his diary published in 1837, Parker wrote about the trail: "Parts of the way the ascent and descent was at an angle of 45 degrees, and in some places even more steep and sometimes was down shelves of rocks where my Indian horse would jump from one to another; and in other places would brace himself on all fours and slide down."

Researchers located Parker's route by finding trees which had been partially peeled by the Indians to eat the inner bark when food was scarce. The Forest service has dated some of the peeled trees along the Parker Trail to 1833. Peeled trees are most easily seen today at Fale's Flat Campground on the west side of Nez Perce Pass.

What you will see: Along Parker's Trail, the little white granite cliffs, tiny subalpine firs, and small green pool of Swet Lake Pond create a landscape in miniature. Below the pond at the end of a rough side trail rests the luminous green oblong of Swet Lake, with three crumpled caps of solid rock stair-stepping above it and a chimney splitting the 400-foot wall of the highest cap.

Directions: From Base Camp, the trail drops to a spring at .5 mile and a second spring at 1 mile, then ascends outcrops. It turns east at 1.5 miles around the end of a ridge, then goes north. At 2.3 miles the trail circles the head of the Devils Washbasin, then descends over rocks, goes along the side of a wooded ridge below Goat Mountain and at 3.7 miles drops down the end of a ridge.

At 5 miles, it fords a creek at Arrow Camp (7,600 feet) near campsites. From here, the trail wanders up and down along ridges, leveling at 6.5 miles at a junction with the Goat Creek Trail, which descends 8 miles to Thompson Flat on the Selway River. At Witter Camp at 7.5 miles, a side trail along Witter Ridge also descends 8 miles to the Selway. A spring with a lumpy campsite is off-trail west of the junction.

The trail continues along the side of Witter Point, then drops to a saddle at 8 miles. At 8.5 miles, it climbs onto a narrow ridge and follows it to a grassy notch at 9.3 miles. Here it curves west around a hill with a view of Salmon Mountain and Hamilton Lakes. Much of the area around Hamilton Lakes and Swet Lake was burned in the 2000 fires. The first side trail for Swet Lake Pond (8,014 feet) is at 10 miles and the next at 10.2 miles. It is .2 mile down either path to the pond.

To reach Swet Lake, take a path (a non-system trail) below the pond down the north side of the pond's outlet, traversing two small meadows and crossing a stream .5 mile below the pond. From this point, the route is blazed with non-system blazes that require a sharp eye. Below the stream, it descends a boulder field then curves east through trees to the lake (7,280 feet) near its upper end at 1 mile. Camping is poor because of clumps of beargrass.

76.

Shoup-Elk City (Parker) Trail: Swet Lake Pond to Waugh Lake

Round trip: 30.4 miles

Elevation gain: 2,400 feet; elevation loss (return climb): 2,600 feet

This section, one way: 5 miles, 1,200 feet gain; elevation loss (return climb): 1,600 feet

Highest point: 8,560 feet

Topographic maps: Waugh Mountain, Stripe Mountain

Trailhead GPS: N 4537' 23.4" W 114 50' 43.8" at Base Camp

Time: 4 days; difficulty: strenuous

Access: See Shoup-Elk City (Parker Trail): Base Camp to Swet Lake Pond to go by trail to the junction of the Shoup-Elk City Trail with the Mount Harrington Trail .2 mile beyond the first path to Swet Lake Pond.

What you will see: From the gentle crest of Waugh Mountain, 400 feet of jumbled cliffs, talus and slabs fall into the blue water of Waugh Lake. The lake also features pink outcrops etched with white stripes and a white island pillared with lodgepoles. Just below the lake, a series of waterfalls tumbles 300 feet. From a notch above the lake, it is a 400-foot cross-country hike to the top of Waugh Mountain, which has a splendid view of the Salmon River Canyon and several mountain ranges.

Dry Saddle

Directions: From the junction, the Mt. Harrington Trail runs west 11 miles to the Dennis Creek Trail, giving cross-country access to Dennis Lakes. From here the Shoup-Elk City Trail angles up past a spring at .5 mile, crosses a stream below a marsh and at .8 mile goes over a saddle beside Swet Point. The trail then descends through whitebark pines beside a snow pond at 1.1 miles, then climbs to the top of Eakin Point (8,115 feet) at 2.5 miles. From here, the Eakin Ridge Trail plunges southwest a vertical mile in 8 miles to Lantz Bar on the Salmon River.

Take the left (east) trail at the junction. It goes down a narrow ridge to a notch at 2.8 miles. From here, the Swet Creek Trail leads north 11 miles to the Selway River; a path to a campsite in a meadow leads south.

Turn left (southeast) on the Shoup-Elk City Trail. It climbs along the side of a ridge to a junction with the eight-mile-long Waugh Mountain-West Horse Trail at 3.5 miles. Turn east to continue on the Shoup-Elk City Trail, which scrambles up to an 8,500-foot pass on the side of Waugh Mountain at 3.8 miles.

To climb Waugh Mountain (8,887 feet), just walk south for .3 mile up the center of the ridge from the pass, keeping away from the edge of the cliffs.

Below the pass, the trail switchbacks down through elk thistle and beargrass, then cuts northeast. At 4.5 miles, it goes over a stream, then wanders down rock slabs to the north side of Waugh Lake at 4.9 miles. Just above here, a path runs over to a campsite on the lakeshore. The trail continues along the north shore to two small campsites at 5 miles.

NEZ PERCE-CLEARWATER NATIONAL FOREST
RED RIVER RANGER DISTRICT

77.

Sheep Hill Trail: Dry Saddle to Lake Creek Lakes

Round trip: 13.6 miles
Elevation gain: 840 feet; elevation loss (return climb): 1,480 feet
Highest point: 8,190 feet
Topographic maps: Sabe Mountain, Spread Creek Point, Sheep Hill
Trailhead GPS: N 45 40' 37.6" W 114 54' 38.3"
Time: 2-3 days; difficulty: strenuous
Access: At the east end of Grangeville, turn right (south) off the main street and drive 45 miles to the Elk City - Red River Junction. Turn right (south) and drive 14.2 miles along the Red River, passing the Red River Guard Station just before a junction with the Nez Perce Trail Road. Then turn left (east) on that road and drive 31.5 miles to the Dry Saddle trailhead, or go in from the Montana end of the road for 76.5 miles. The road from Red River is gravel for 14 miles and then primitive, narrow, winding and rocky.

Or turn left (west) off U.S. 93 onto the paved Connor Cutoff 7.5 miles south of Darby, Montana, or onto the West Fork Road 4 miles south of Darby. The 1-mile-long Connor Cutoff meets the West Fork Road 3 miles from Highway 93. Continue 11.4 miles on the West Fork Road to a junction. Turn right (west) onto the Nez Perce Trail road and drive over Nez Perce Pass, 28.7 miles from Highway 93. Continue over Salmon Mountain on a mostly rough road to Dry Saddle at 76.5 miles. The road west of the Selway River is unimproved dirt; west of Salmon Mountain, it is primitive and rocky, some of it with deep ruts that are difficult to travel even with four-wheel drive.

What you will see: This ridge-top trail has sweeping views of cream-colored towers of the Bitterroots, the pink ridge of Salmon Mountain, blue ridges of the Chamberlain country, pinnacles of the Bighorn Crags and a chain of blue-green lakes. It is also an excellent place to observe fire recovery, since the fires of 1988 left a mosaic of burns of different intensities here. The trailhead at Dry Saddle is among burned trees on the Nez Perce Trail Road, which follows the route of the historic Nez Perce Indian Trail across Idaho from Elk City to Darby, Montana. Driving time for the 108-mile dirt road is eight hours, and there are no services between Elk City and Darby. The road is usually open to through traffic about July 15 but may be closed by early snows in September. In rainy weather, it will be very slippery in places. Watch for little markers with two feathers. They show where the original Nez Perce Trail crosses the road. Campgrounds near the trailhead are Poet Creek and Granite Springs. Note that there

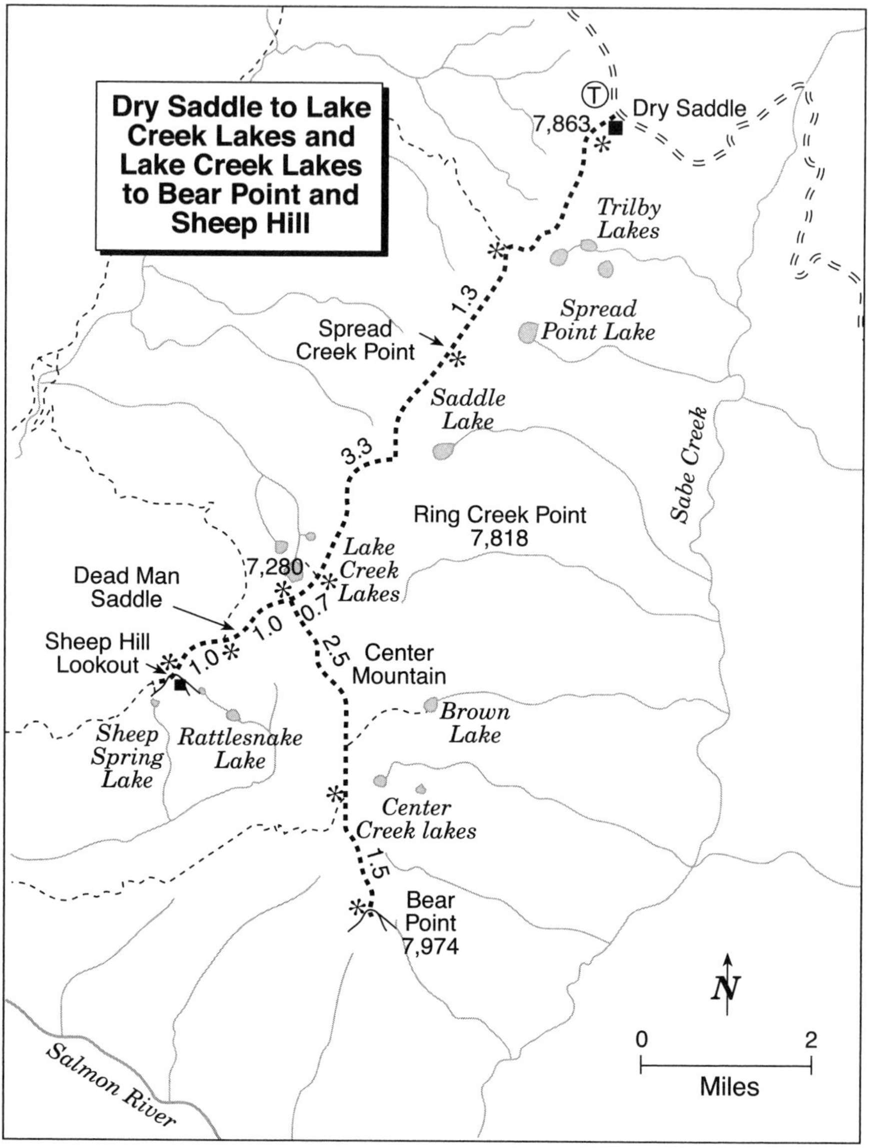

is little water on or near the trail for the first 6.5 miles.

Directions: From Dry Saddle (7,863 feet), the Sheep Hill Trail starts as a primitive road (not open to vehicles) up a ridge to the south. It descends the side of the ridge to a saddle at 1.3 miles, where a path drops 400 feet east in .5 mile to the highest Trilby Lake (7,136 feet). Beyond the saddle, the main trail splits. Take the right branch which avoids a 280-foot climb. (A spring is 200 yards up the left branch.) At 1.8 miles, the

Bleak Creek Trail turns off to go 4 miles to Bargamin Creek. From the main trail at 2.5 miles, tiny Bleak Creek Lake appears in the trees below. At a saddle at 2.6 miles, an unsigned path descends .8 mile east to Spread Point Lake 800 feet below.

The Sheep Hill Trail then climbs to Spread Creek Point at 3 miles, traveling over a rocky slope as it passes above Saddle Lake. At the end of a ridge at 5 miles, a path leads east. To take a side trip to Saddle Lake, turn left (northwest) in 100 yards with the path as it plunges down a grassy slope, then turns east into woods. At .7 mile, leave the path and drop to the lakeshore, 650 feet below the main trail. Campsites are sloping and lumpy.

From the 5-mile point, the Sheep Hill Trail dips, then climbs a ridge and at 5.7 miles begins descending to the Lake Creek Lakes. At a stream crossing at 6.3 miles, a sign points northwest to a path to Lake Creek Lakes. Descend the path to where it meets another at 6.6 miles. Turn left (south) to the largest lake (7,280 feet) at 6.7 miles. (The lowest lake is .4 mile north along the trail to the right here, and the middle lake is northwest .2 mile cross-country from the first lake.)

78.

Bear Point and Sheep Hill

Round trip: 26.4 miles total from Dry Saddle
Elevation gain: 2,200 feet; elevation loss (return climb): 1,800 feet
Highest point: 8,405 feet
Topographic map: Sheep Hill
Trailhead GPS: N 45 40' 37.6" W 114 54' 38.3" at Dry Saddle
Time: 3 - 4 days; difficulty: strenuous
Access: See Sheep Hill Trail: Dry Saddle to Lake Creek Lakes to go by trail to the junction with paths down to the Lake Creek Lakes, where this description begins.

What you will see: From Bear Point, furrowed charcoal-gray walls drop 5,000 feet to blue-green curves of the Salmon River. Northeast of the rocky, barren ridge of Sheep Hill, creamy points of the Bitterroots contrast with the pink talus and dark green woods of the nearby mountains. Below the lookout, the silver ovals of Rattlesnake and Sheep Spring Lakes gleam in the shadows. Most of the trees between Dry Saddle and the Lake Creek Lakes have burned.

Directions: This description begins at the first Lake Creek Lakes junction at 7,480 feet. From here, the trail climbs toward Bear Point and Sheep Hill. At .2 mile is an upper trail for Lake Creek Lakes and a stream and large meadow with campsites. At .7 mile the trail splits into the Bear Point and Sheep Hill trails.

To reach Bear Point, which lacks water, take the left (east) trail, which contours along the right (west) side of a grassy ridge. Avoid two paths to the west. At 1.3 miles from the junction, the trail descends to a saddle where a sign points to Brown Lake

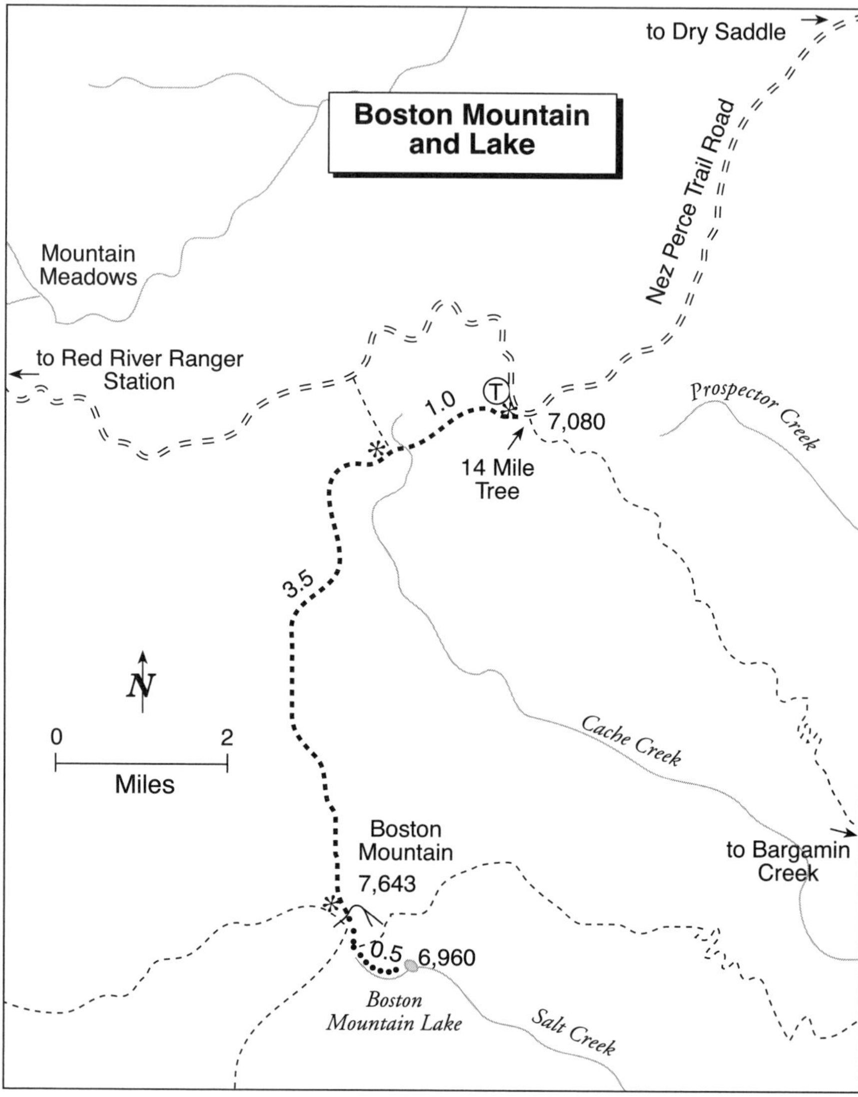

behind Center Mountain. Here the Brown Creek Trail turns off to drop to the lake, but disappears before it gets there.

The main trail circles the west side of Center Mountain to another saddle at 2 miles. From here a side trail descends southeast .7 mile and 600 feet to the highest of the two Center Creek Lakes. From here on, you are within the perimeter of the Flossie/Three Bears Fire of 2000. The trail to Bear Point climbs a grassy hill, then runs along the east side of a ridge above the higher lake. At 2.5 miles, the Rattlesnake Trail turns off to Rattlesnake Spring and the Salmon River in 9 precipitous miles, all of which burned in 2000.

The main trail continues along the center of the ridge to a drop-off at 4 miles. From here a path to the right (west) has the best view. The trail shown on the topographic map descending to the river from Bear Point is no longer maintained.

To reach Sheep Hill from the Sheep Hill - Bear Point Junction, turn right on the trail that leads west uphill. This trail goes along the southeast side of a ridge and past a small spring, then curves right (west) to Dead Man Saddle 1 mile from the junction. There is a junction here with the Cache Creek Trail, which drops 6 miles to Bargamin Creek. From Dead Man Saddle, the trail to Sheep Hill climbs the end of the summit ridge to the lookout (8,405 feet) at 2 miles.

To reach Sheep Spring Lake, take a trail that hairpins west down .7 mile to a notch. From this notch, a side trail drops .2 mile to the lake (7,680 feet), 680 feet below the lookout. A second trail from the notch, the Crofoot Trail, descends 10 miles to the Salmon River; the lowest 3 miles through a burn.

79.

Boston Mountain and Lake

Round trip: 10 miles
Elevation gain: 1,030 feet; elevation loss (return climb): 1,090 feet
Highest point: 7,648 feet
Topographic map: Boston Mountain
Trailhead GPS at 14-mile tree: N 45 41' 20.5": W 115 10' 10.7"
Time: 8 hours; difficulty: strenuous; cross-country from Boston Mountain to lake

Access: At the east end of Grangeville, turn right (south) off the main street onto the paved Elk City Road and drive 48 miles to the Elk City - Red River Junction. Turn right (south) and drive 14.7 miles along the Red River, passing the Red River Guard Station just before a junction with the Nez Perce Trail Road. Turn left (east) on this road, which is gravel as far as the trailhead. In about 1 mile the road forks. Keep to the right on Road 468. Drive 13.7 miles to the improved trailhead at "14-Mile Tree," which parking, a notice board and a toilet.

A little history: On the way to the trailhead from Grangeville, which is the best road for reaching this trailhead, you will pass the turnoff for Elk City. Elk City began when 52 men from Pierce set out in May 1861 to prospect on the South Fork of the Clearwater, although prospecting south of the Clearwater was prohibited by the treaty of 1855 with the Nez Perce Indians. When Chief Looking Glass caught the prospectors, 30 of them turned back, but the rest sneaked in anyway. Four of them – Capt. L.B. Monton, Mose Milner, Charles Hand and Charles Painter – discovered gold at the site that became known as Elk City. By August, 1,000 miners were living there in brush huts.

To mine the Elk City gold, the miners constructed six ditches for hydraulic mining, one of which was more 10 miles long.

By 1872, most of the miners had left except for Chinese ones. Most of them soon went elsewhere when a federal judge ruled that aliens couldn't hold mining claims. In 1884, when S.W. Smith and H.E. McKinney located the Buster Claim, interest in mining revived and in 1889 C.D. Gavin shipped in a dredge by pack mule. Quartz mining began in 1902 and caused a second boom that lasted until 1910.

What you will see: Lupines, beargrass and whitebark pines circle the grassy, open summit of Boston Mountain, which is the site of a former lookout. Above the dark green chasm of the Salmon River to the south, wooded ridges roll toward pale blue mountains, and to the north rise the cream-colored ramparts of the Bitterroots. A half-mile below the summit, the marshy, tea-colored lake hides under granite ledges.

Directions: From the trailhead at 6,840 feet take the Boston Mountain Trail, which leads west and then south along a ridge of lodgepoles, beargrass and huckleberry. Another trail from 14-Mile Tree, the Cache Creek Trail, goes southeast 20 miles to Bear Point, first dropping hundreds of feet into Bargamin Creek to a bridge over it. Below 6,400 feet, the Cache Creek and Bargamin Creek canyons burned in the 2000 fires. The ridges on the way to Boston Mountain show a mosaic of burns of different intensities left by the 1988 fires. Thus the trail gives an excellent opportunity to watch the fire recovery process at work.

Directions: The Boston Mountain Trail drops to a stream in a meadow at .9 mile. Across the stream, at 1 mile, a trail leads northwest to the road, joining it 2 miles west of the Boston Mountain trailhead. After climbing a gentle ridge and dropping to a flat saddle at 2 miles, the main trail goes up a gully at 2.7 miles and ascends a spur ridge to the summit of Boston Mountain (7,648 feet) at 4.5 miles. Southwest of the summit is a junction with the Cook Ranch and Bat Point trails. The Cook Ranch Trail leads out of the Frank Church Wilderness to the Cook Ranch at 8 miles and the Mallard Creek Road at 10.5 miles. The primitive Bat Point Trail descends south toward Yellowpine Bar on the Salmon River, dwindling as it approaches the final steep 3 miles.

Beyond the summit, the Boston Mountain Trail does not go directly east along the ridge as shown on the topographic map. To continue along it to Boston Mountain Lake, take the left (east) trail from the junction and go south with the Cook Ranch and Bat Point trails, downhill, ignoring other paths. The trail descends over a steep headwall in four switchbacks to a spring in a small bowl. From the spring, the Boston Mountain Trail leads north up the side of the bowl to the ridge top, but that is not the way to the lake.

To reach Boston Mountain Lake, descend a path on the left (north) side of the stream a short distance from the bowl. (Paths from campsites in the bowl may cause confusion.) When the path down the stream ends, walk east cross-country and descend outcrops above the stream to the 6,960-foot shore at 5 miles.

Jim Moore Place

80.

Salmon River Trail: Whitewater Ranch to Jim Moore Place

Round trip: 8 miles
Elevation gain: 520 feet; elevation loss (return climb): 560 feet
Highest point: 2,560 feet
Topographic maps: Whitewater Ranch, Sheepeater Mountain
Trailhead GPS: N 45 31' 57.4" W 115 18' 1.1"
Time: 6 hours for round trip; difficulty: moderate

Access: At the east end of Grangeville, turn right (south) off the main street onto the paved Elk City Road and drive 48 miles to the Elk City - Red River junction. Turn right (south) and drive 14.7 miles along the Red River, passing the guard station. Where the Nez Perce Trail Road turns off to the left (east), turn right (south) on the improved dirt Mallard Creek Road and drive up a grade to a junction of the Whitewater and Jack Mountain Roads at 2.6 miles. Take the Whitewater Ranch Road, which goes along Jack Creek, passing the Mallard Creek Ranch at 7 miles, and then descends as a primitive road, making 13 switchbacks down to the Whitewater Ranch at 21.3 miles. Then take a primitive road to a campground at 21.5 miles and continue downriver to a trailhead at 22 miles.

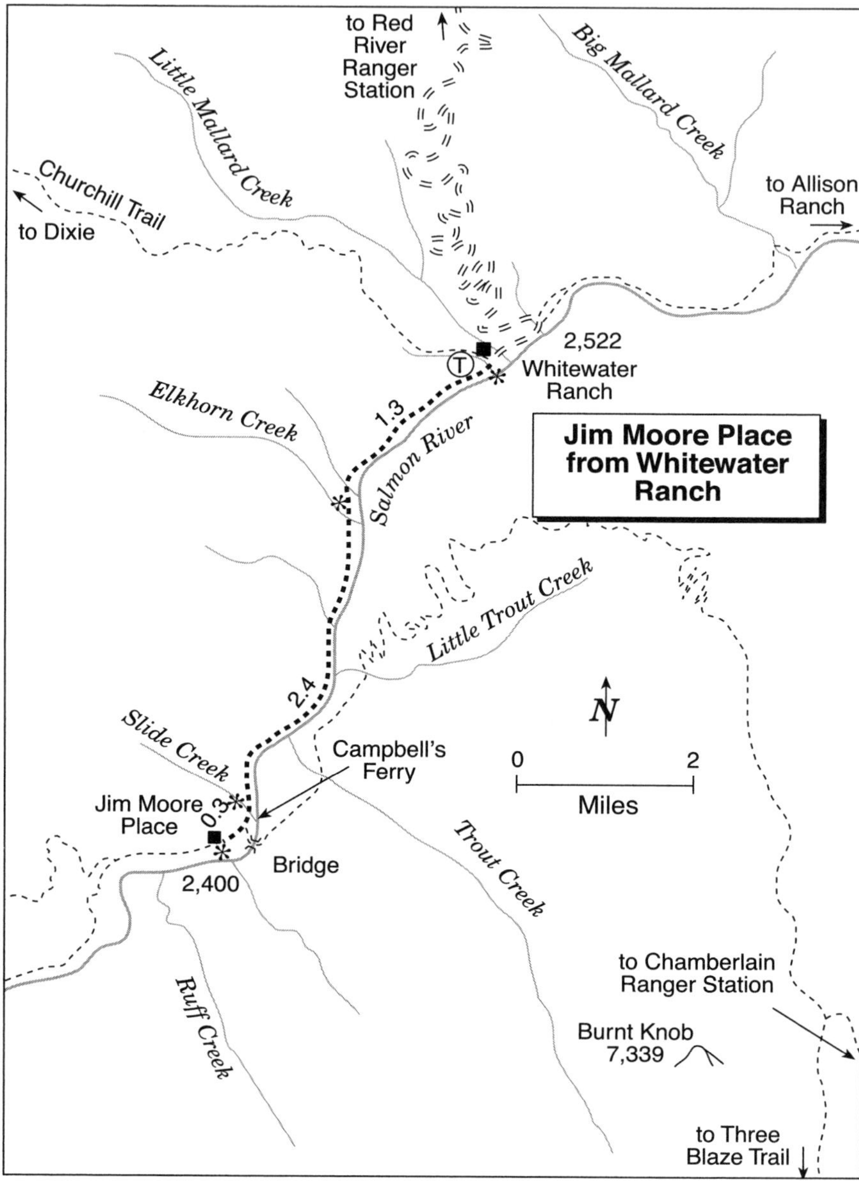

A little history: The Whitewater Ranch, which you drive past near the trailhead, was homesteaded by Eugene Churchill. He had a hook for a hand and supposedly he had amputated the hand himself. He drowned near Richardson Creek trying to bring a boat down to the ranch. When his wife, Ella, heard he had drowned, she is supposed to have said, "Good! There goes the meanest man in Idaho."

Four miles downstream from the Whitewater Ranch, Jim Moore lived on a mining claim, beginning in 1898. As he cleared the land, he constructed 10 buildings of hand-hewn timber, which he used as a walk-in rentals for miners on their way to Thunder Mountain. Moore also sold beef, vegetables, deer meat and hides to the travelers. The hides were used to drag gear and supplies over the snow in winter. When the Thunder Mountain boom faded, he continued to live on the ranch until he died in 1942. The cabins are on the National Register of Historic Places and have been partially restored.

What you will see: Jim Moore's rust-brown cabins of hand-hewn squared logs sit among gnarled fruit trees on a bench above the Salmon River. The cabins include a two-story house, blacksmith shed, chicken house, bunkhouses and storage sheds. In June, the trail is decorated by the white blossoms of syringa and other shrubs below cliffs covered with charcoal-gray lichen. Although most of the trail is shaded, the canyon can be 110 degrees in summer and there are also rattlesnakes and poison ivy. The road usually opens about Memorial Day so cool days in June and in the fall are the best times for this trail.

The road is passable for passenger cars with stick shift in dry weather, providing drivers watch for rocks. (At the other end of the campground from the trailhead, a trail also leads east up the river past Yellow Pine Bar to its end at Deer Park Bar. This trail goes through areas.

Directions: From the end of the spur road, take the trail west down the river, which crosses Churchill Creek at 200 yards. From this creek, a side trail goes 11 miles over Churchill Mountain to Dixie. At .7 mile, the river trail edges a bluff, at 1 mile goes over Dry Can Creek, at 1.3 miles bridges Elkhorn Creek and at 2 miles crosses Little Elkhorn Creek in a shady glen. At 2.4 miles, Little Trout Creek rushes down the opposite canyon wall. After climbing 150 feet across talus, the route drops to the river at Slide Creek at 3.7 miles.

Beyond Slide Creek is a junction with the Three-Blaze Trail that goes 23 miles south to the Chamberlain Guard Station from the Campbell's Ferry Bridge over the Salmon River. Just beyond the junction the main trail reaches the Moore Ranch buildings at 4 miles. This trail continues 15 miles along the river to the Painter Mine trailhead near Mackay Bar.

On the land across this bridge, William Campbell started a ranch in 1896 and built a ferry here in 1900 to serve the Three Blaze Trail to Thunder Mountain. He was lost in a snowstorm on the way home from Thunder Mountain in 1902. After five other owners, Bob Hilands patented the homestead in 1927. In 1935, Joe Zaunmiller acquired the place and ran the ferry until the Forest Service built the bridge in 1956. Frances Zaunmiller Wisner lived here until she died in 1986. In 1983, she received an award from the National Weather Service for her continuous weather reporting and in 1987 the Idaho County Free Press in Grangeville published a book of the columns she had written for them, called My Mountains: Where the River Runs Downhill.

PAYETTE NATIONAL FOREST
KRASSEL RANGER DISTRICT
SOUTH FORK SALMON RIVER AREA:

81.

Buckskin Bill's Museum

Round trip: 6 miles
Elevation gain: 340 feet; elevation loss (return climb): 280 feet
Topographic map: Fivemile Bar
Trailhead GPS at east end Mackay Bar airstrip: N 45 22'56.7" W 115 30' 15,7"
Highest point: 2,400 feet
Time: 6 hours; difficulty: expert (treacherous footing, difficult route finding)

Access: At the east end of Grangeville, turn right (south) off the main street onto the paved Elk City Road and drive 48 miles to the Elk City - Red River junction. Turn right (south) and drive 14.7 miles along the Red River, passing the guard station. Where the Nez Perce Trail Road turns off to the left (east), turn right (south) on the improved dirt Mallard Creek Road and drive up a grade to a junction of the Whitewater and Jack Mountain Roads at 2.6 miles. Turn right (southwest) on the road toward Dixie and Mackay Bar. From the Red River Road it is 16 miles to the village of Dixie and 43 to the Mackay Bar footbridge. The last 5.5 miles of this road descends 3,600 feet.

Buckskin Bill's historic cabins along the Salmon River

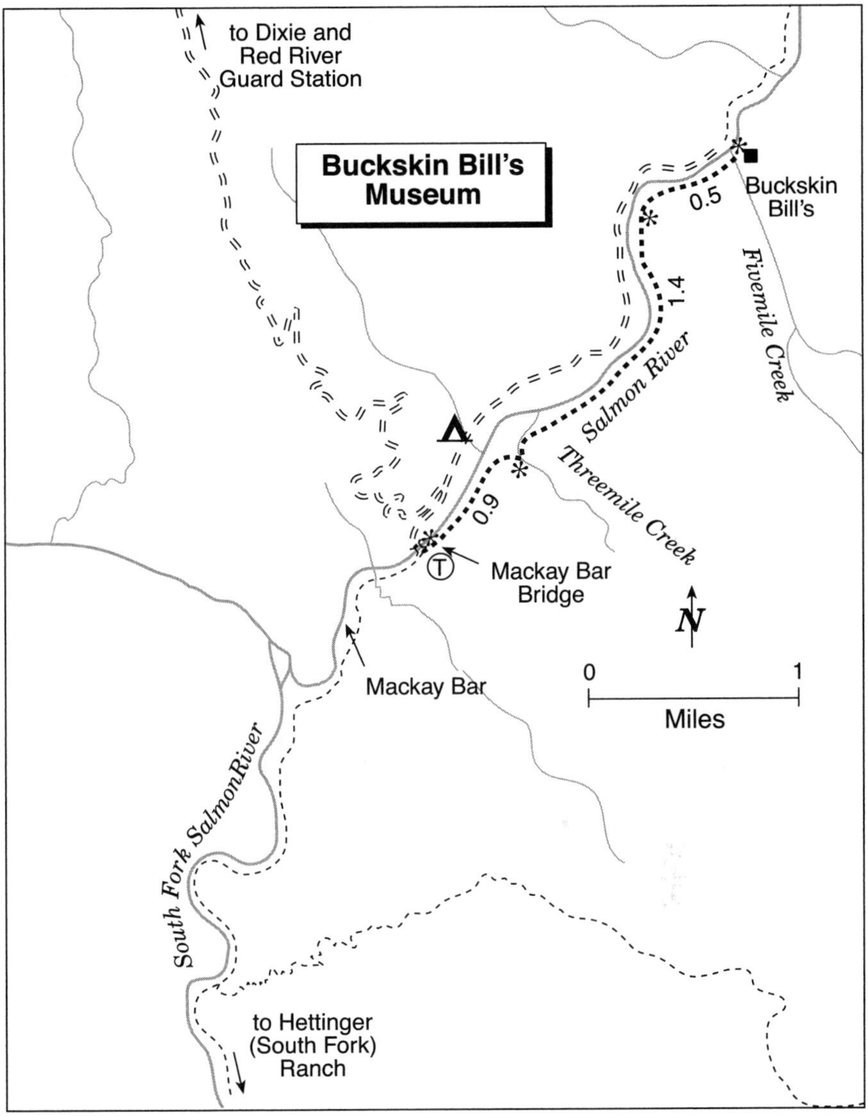

Because it is so steep, rangers recommend using four-wheel-drive low for this section if you have it. If not, stopping often to cool your brakes will help prevent them from burning out.

A little history: The site of the former mining town of Dixie is on the road to Mackay Bar to the trailhead. The town began in 1864 when Sam Killinger and others from Elk City staked claims in Dixie Gulch. Most of the mining at Dixie was placer mining done with sluice boxes in the 1880s. Some lode mining occurred between 1890 and 1910, with a boom beginning in 1893. More mining occurred between 1931 and 1936 when some of the old mines reopened and a drag line did placer mining.

Buckskin Bill's real name was Sylvan Hart. He had graduated from the University of Oklahoma with a degree in English and had done graduate work in petroleum engineering. He first came to live on the Salmon River during the Depression with his brother Tom. Bill stayed there on the Salmon River all the rest of his life, except during World War II when he worked on the Norden bomb site for the air force. He became an expert gunsmith and metalsmith; gathered, grew or caught almost all his food; and made his own buckskin clothes and his own tools, some of them unique inventions. Many of his things are in the State Historical Museum in Boise, including a copper samovar decorated with squirrels with beaded eyes.

Mackay Bar, 3 miles below Buckskin Bill's, was once the site of a Nez Perce village called Wa-toss-pa, "meaning place of fording the river." William Mackay and his wife constructed a log house here to placer mine and ranch about 1900. In 1937, John Oberbillig bought the ranch and built the road to haul supplies to placer mine there. When Oberbillig died, Al and Mary Tice purchased the ranch for a hunting and fishing lodge. In 1969 it was bought by Robert Hansberger for a lodge and dude ranch and run by the Mackay Bar Corp.

What you will see: The road to Mackay Bar and the trail to Buckskin Bill's give you a thorough introduction to the ruggedness of this country, where canyon walls rise 1,000 feet in less than half a mile. Cliffs and outcrops darkened with black lichen alternate with tangles of shrubs like mountain spray. Along the river, flat river bars with orange-trunked ponderosa pines provide pleasant campsites. Buckskin Bill used this trail for access before the road to the Painter Mine was built on the other side of the river. He also used it at high water when he couldn't boat across the river safely, so it is a historic route. Although it can be 110 degrees here, it is best to wear leather boots and long pants because of occasional rattlesnakes and poison ivy.

Directions: Park at the north end of the Mackay Bar bridge, as the bridge is not wide enough for vehicles. The Mackay Bar property is a no-trespassing area unless you have reservations at the ranch. The trail begins at the south end of the bridge as an old road covered with grass and plants. At present, walking it still requires patience and great care because it is so overgrown and in places the tread has slid away, leaving hidden holes.

The old road begins by angling up the canyon wall in brush until it is 100 feet above the river at .2 mile. Then it comes out on a grassy, rocky hillside. At Ludwig Bar at .9 mile, the trail runs above fenced private property that includes a corrugated steel cabin. The track loops back into the canyon of Threemile Creek and fords it in alders. To avoid losing your way, it is best to stay on the track here. Cutting a few branches with a small wood saw will made fording easier. Beyond the ford the track narrows to a trail and climbs up and along a steep grassy hillside, so if you lose it, look for it uphill, not down, as a downhill game trail can be confusing. Across from the upper end of the landing strip across the river, the trail begins to cross talus slopes where the footing is difficult, the tread is indistinct and shrubs block the trail in places. The trail descends to the river and then goes up a few feet onto the pine flat of Haney Bar at 2.5 miles. Once on Haney Bar the trail is much better. Beyond the bar it climbs the side of a bluff of dark rock, then drops to the river at 2.7 miles. Here Buckskin Bill built a catwalk out of poles and wire against the cliff to get by when the water was high (in May and June). From here the trail goes along the sand to Fivemile Creek. Just before the creek a path goes off to the right, allowing people to see Buckskin Bill's historic wire and board bridge. But don't use it; because it is so fragile you might fall through. In addition the private property of a small cabin area begins at the bridge.

Instead, stay close to the river, ford Fivemile Creek near it, and walk along the river 200 yards to the museum at 3 miles. If rafters are here, you may be able to hitch a ride across the river with them and return to the Mackay Bar road on the much easier Painter Bar road. All but the first mile of it is a rough, rocky four-wheel-drive road. Any boating on the river requires a permit arranged the winter before.

82.

South Fork of Salmon River Trail From the South Fork (Hettinger) Ranch

Round trip: 10 miles to junction with Chicken Peak Trail
Elevation gain: 40 feet; elevation loss (return climb): 380 feet
Highest point: 2,975 feet
Topographic maps: Pilot Peak, Chicken Peak, Burgdorf Summit
Trailhead GPS: N 45 22' 56.7" W 115 30' 15.7"
Time: 6 hours; difficulty: strenuous
Access: In McCall, turn north off Highway 55 onto the paved Warren Wagon Road. Drive 23 miles north on a paved road to Burgdorf Junction, then 16 miles east on a dirt road over Steamboat Summit to Warren and 4 miles east to Warren Summit. Then descend 11 miles northwest on a primitive road, partly through a recent burn to the South Fork Ranch (marked on maps as the Hettinger Ranch) on the South Fork of the Salmon River, 58.7 miles from McCall.

A little history: On the way to the South Fork Ranch the road goes through the village of Warren, an old mining town. In 1862, James Warren and others discovered gold at Warrens (now known as Warren.) This settlement was first called Richmond, but miners loyal to the Union moved a mile downstream and named their settlement Washington. Their town became the first county seat of Idaho County. By 1863, 600 people lived there. After Mount Idaho, near Grangeville, got the county seat in 1875, Washington was renamed Warrens.

Warrens is famous in history for the story of Polly Bemis. In China, Lalu Nathoy's father sold her into slavery to get crop seed. A man named Hong King bought her in Portland and took her by pack trail to Warrens in 1872, where she became known as Polly. The story is that Hong King lost her in a poker game to saloon owner Charley Bemis. However, Bemis may just have bought her freedom. In 1892 when Bemis, who had been shot in the face over a card game, had the bullet removed, Polly nursed him back to health.

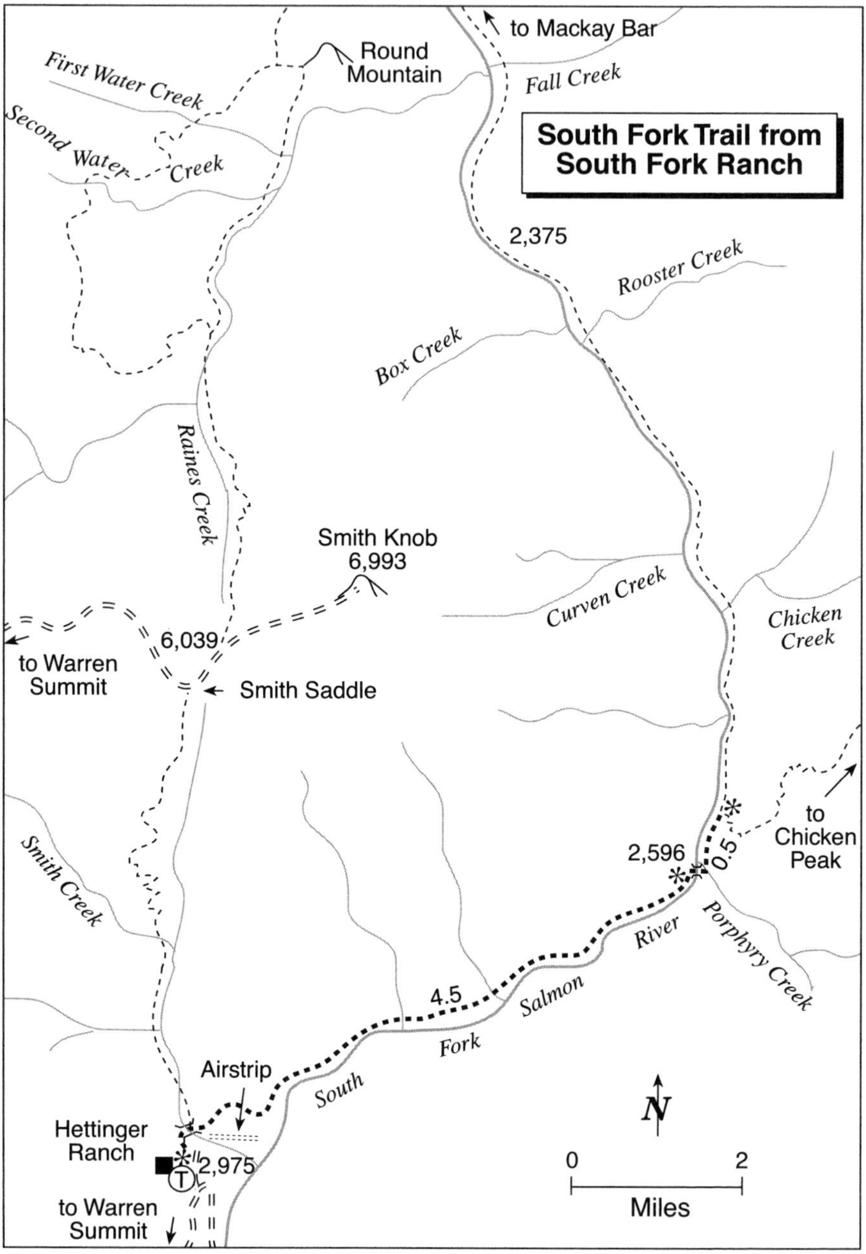

Bemis married Polly in 1894 to keep her from being deported as an alien. After the marriage, they moved down to the Salmon River, where Polly gardened and fished. In 1922, two months after their house burned, Bemis died. Polly left the canyon but returned to live until her final days in a tiny new cabin that neighbors put up for her.

Hay shed at the South Fork (Hettinger) Ranch

Her story is told in the book and movie, Thousand Pieces of Gold, by Ruthanne Lum McCunn.

The South Fork Ranch ten miles down the river was first settled about 1876 by C.F. (Frank) Smith, a cousin of "Three-Finger Smith." He received his homestead patent in 1913. After several other owners, Lawrence Hettinger bought the ranch in 1944. He built a sawmill on the property, but it was never used. Robert Hansberger and the Mackay Bar Corp. purchased the ranch in 1969. It is used for hay and pasture for the Mackay Bar horses.

As the road descends to the ranch from Warren Summit, it passes Hays Station, an old way station on the road. Here Chinese miners once grew vegetables for the Warren miners. The terraces of the Chinese gardens are still visible, and a brochure about them is available from the Payette National Forest

If you go straight ahead from Warren Summit and descend to the river on that road instead of turning left to the South Fork Ranch, you come to the South Fork Guard Station. At this spot Solon Hall established a ranch in 1872. In 1897 Jack and Frankie Shafer (Shiefer) purchased it. Jack drowned when he fell off the bridge in 1905. Later, Carl Brown owned the ranch, followed by Tom McCall, who gave it as a wedding present to his son Cyrus (Ted). After Ted died, his wife, Mamie, gave it to her brother Tom Carrey, who patented it in 1917. His youngest son, John, born here in 1914, is the co-author of three books of history on Idaho rivers. The ranch became the property of the Forest Service through a land exchange in 1925, and the service built the South Fork Guard Station on it.

What you will see: Blackened by charcoal-gray lichen, inner canyon peaks with 3,000-foot cliffs rise from this section of the South Fork of the Salmon River. Rock fins and needles outline their interlocking triangles and grasses, shrubs and trees soften their ledges and cliffs. Along the river banks, ponderosa pines with vanilla-scented bark alternate with poison ivy and open areas of wildflowers. Fall is the best time of year for this hike because in June the trail may be underwater; in summer rattlesnakes are out and temperatures can be 110 degrees.

Directions: Once down at the bottom of the canyon, drive along beside the ranch to a trail sign at a tumbledown cabin. Follow the trail into the canyon of Smith Creek and over the creek on a bridge at .2 mile. Two hundred yards beyond the bridge an old road (the beginning of the trail to Smith Saddle on the road to Smith Knob) turns up to the left. Here, the river trail goes downhill to the right a few yards, then goes over to the left to skirt the fences around the rolling hayfields and airstrip.

The trail stays 150 feet above the river along grassy slopes and under ponderosas, descending gradually to the riverbank by the time Rattlesnake Creek Canyon comes in at 1.5 miles on the opposite side of the river. At 2.2 miles, it crosses the Frank Church Wilderness Boundary on a pine flat above the river. The path returns to the riverbank at 3 miles at a sandy campsite. Beyond here, it climbs across cliffs and beneath rock outcrops where high water blocks the way.

At 4.5 miles, the trail crosses the river to the east side on the Porphyry Creek Bridge. Here the jagged chasm of Porphyry Creek repeats the design of the main canyon. At 5 miles is a junction (3,120 feet) with a maintained foot trail that ascends 5,760 feet in 8.2 miles to the summit of Chicken Peak. The 80 switchbacks have narrow, steep sections, but there is an excellent view of the South Fork Canyon.

The South Fork Trail continues north for 8.5 miles along the river to Mackay Bar on the Salmon River. However, it is not maintained between the Porphyry and Badley bridges, so is dangerous for stock. There is also no trespassing through the Mackay Bar Ranch near the end of the trail. A trail that bypasses most of the Mackay Bar property high above it is hard to find and dangerous for stock. A trail along the South Fork also runs south from the South Fork Ranch up the river to the Elk Creek Road near Pony Creek but the private property of the ranch makes access confusing at this end.

THUNDER MOUNTAIN AREA

83.

Roosevelt Lake

Round trip: 2.8 miles
Elevation gain: 100 feet; elevation loss (return climb): 100 feet
Highest point: 6,160 feet
Topographic map: Rainbow Peak
Trailhead GPS: N 44 57' 09,47" W 115 12' 51.6"
Time: 2.5 hours round trip Difficulty: easy, but partly over loose rocks
Access: From Cascade, drive north 1 mile on Highway 55. Turn right (east) and go

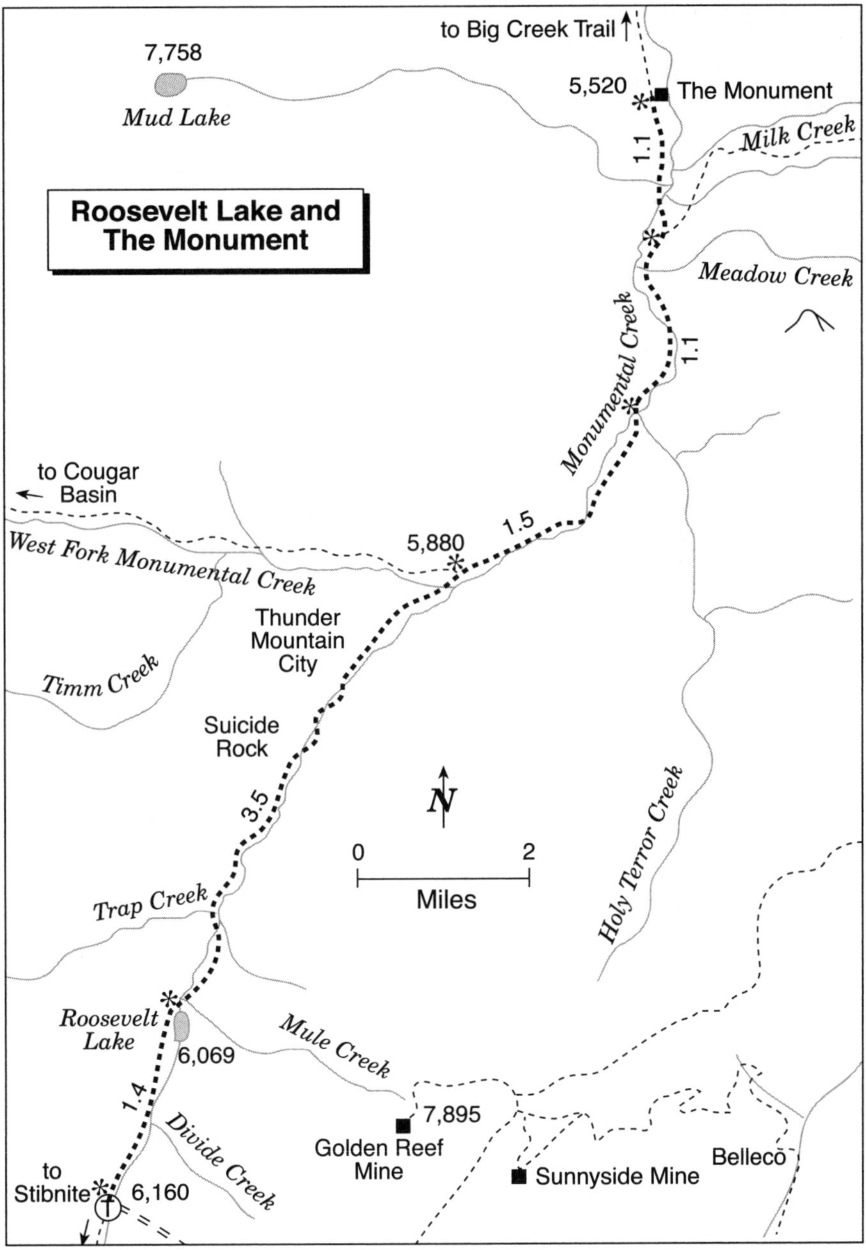

25 miles to a junction with the paved, one-lane South Fork of Salmon River Road. Turn left (north) and go 31 miles. Turn right (east) on the East Fork of South Fork of Salmon River Road and drive 14.7 miles to Yellow Pine. Or take the gravel Johnson Creek Road that leads directly from Landmark to Yellow Pine. From Yellow Pine

Old snow cat at Yellow Pine

continue 8 miles to Stibnite and drive over Monumental Summit and down through burned forest to the Monumental Creek Trailhead 23 miles from Yellow Pine.

A little history: On the way to the Roosevelt Lake trailhead, the road goes through the village of Yellow Pine and the site of the former mining town of Stibnite. The first European to settle at the site of Yellow Pine was a placer miner named Regan who had cabins here at the junction of Johnson Creek with the East Fork of the South Fork of the Salmon River in 1876. One cabin was papered with the Sunday New York Times. Another early settler was Theodore Van Meter in 1902. Albert Behne came to Yellow Pine over the Three Blaze Trail in 1902, pushing a one-wheel cart with his gear in it. He built a cabin, laid out the townsite and became postmaster.

Another founder of Yellow Pine was Al Hennessy, who in 1903, filed for a 160-acre homestead on Johnson Creek, part of which is now the airstrip, and received his homestead patent for the land in 1916. Mines he discovered and owned for a time were the Hermes, the Meadow Creek and the Yellow Pine. In 1952, when Hennessy was wintering at a claim on Buck Creek, he slipped on ice when getting groceries friends had dropped from a plane. He lost a foot as a result of his injuries but later came back to Yellow Pine with a wooden leg.

Archie McCoy, brother of Walter and John, the horse stealers mentioned elsewhere, brought his family to live in Yellow Pine in 1918 under the alias Bert Holland. He had several businesses, from a restaurant and freight packing to bootlegging. His children were the first in Yellow Pine and led to the opening of a school in 1920.

In 1923, the automobile road from Knox to Yellow Pine was finished, making it much easier to visit and to live there. With only the wagon road it had taken three tries to bring in a toilet without breaking it. In November, 1930 George Stonebraker started landing at the Hennessy farm to deliver mail by airplane instead of by dogsled.

Before long, people began to see the outdoor recreation potential of the area. In 1927, Clark Cox and Beulah Cox bought Alec Forstrum's homestead on Johnson Creek and began a dude ranch, which they and later his son, Lafe, and Lafe's wife, Emma, ran for many years.

Although gold was discovered at Meadow Creek, 8 miles up the East Fork of the South Fork of the Salmon from Yellow Pine, by a Mr. Baker in 1891, the area became best known for the mining of stibnite, an antimony ore, that began during World War I. Al Hennessy found gold here in 1919 and sold his claim to J.J. Oberbillig. In 1927, Oberbillig sold the mine to Fred Bradley, president of Bunker Hill. When Bradley brought in equipment in 1928, boilers, steam engines and a sawmill for the mine had to be lowered down the old Thunder Mountain wagon road by block and tackle. The next year a road was constructed from Yellow Pine to the Bradley Mine.

H.D. Bailey applied for a post office for the mine in 1930, naming it Stibnite for the antimony ore. By then, there were boarding houses and bunkhouses, shop buildings and barns at Monday Camp (the Yellow Pine Mine) and at Meadow Creek. After a 150-ton-per-day treatment plant was constructed in 1931, the Bradley Mine at Meadow Creek began producing gold and antimony and in 1936 was the largest producer of gold in the United States.

An open pit mine produced tungsten during the war to be used for the tips of shells. At the same time, the Meadow Creek underground mine produced antimony, used as an alloy, and as a lead hardener for shrapnel bullets. A 2,500-ton mill and smelter were built, and 1,500 people lived here during World War II. By 1955 Stibnite was a ghost town, and many of its houses were moved to McCall. Although mining activity continued until 1999, the sites have been reclaimed and there is little evidence of it. Stibnite has been identified as a National Historic District, but more mining is being planned.

Off to the north as you start up Monumental Summit there once were mercury mines. Bert Bartholemy and J. Pringle Smith discovered mercury deposits that produced more than $2 million during World War II. In 1941, the Hermes was the second-largest mercury mine in the country.

The town of Roosevelt grew up below the mines on Monumental Creek, which was named for the natural monument along it, seven miles below Roosevelt. By the summer of 1902, Roosevelt had 37 saloons in tents. By 1903 the post office had 7,000 people receiving mail.

To serve the mines, several pack trails reached the area: the Three Blaze Trail from Grangeville via Campbell's Ferry on the Salmon River, a trail from Council and Payette Lakes through Warrens, a trail from Wagontown north of Stanley that led up Marble Creek, a trail from Challis via Morgan Creek Summit, and a trail from Boise Basin through Bear Valley. In 1903, the Thunder Mountain Wagon Road was built, taking a still different route from near Cascade via Johnson Creek and Riordan Lake.

After yielding $350,000, the boom ended in 1907, when poorer-grade ore was found at lower depths and metal prices plunged. In 1909, a mudslide dammed Monumental Creek, turning the nearly abandoned town into Roosevelt Lake.

What you will see: A few logs from the buildings still float in the lake. At the upper end, the inlet flows into the lake across gravel between grass and willows. Gray talus on the east and a wooded ridge on the west form the sides of the lake basin. In midsummer the water is turquoise on sunny days.

The Monument rock formation

An old road used to run down the canyon to the lake from the trailhead, but it is washed out and the trail has been rerouted up on the talus for several hundred yards. On the Monumental Summit Road all of the creek crossings are bridged, but the road is steep as it begins to descend from the summit into the canyon of Monumental Creek. The view from Monumental Summit is of rugged, colorful peaks tinted rose, cinnamon, buff and gray; one is named Rainbow Peak. The canyon itself is now gray with burned trees.

From the Frank Church Wilderness boundary and the Monumental Creek trailhead (6,160 feet) 28 miles from Yellow Pine, the road continues across Monumental Creek on a bridge and up Coon Creek to the sites of the Sunnyside and Dewey Mines, giving access to the Marble Creek and Lookout Mountain Ridge trails.

Directions: From the trailhead, the trail to Roosevelt Lake first follows the old wagon road down the left (west) side of Monumental Creek through willows and talus. At about 100 yards it is washed out and the trail goes up on the rocks. It drops back to a couple of campsites along the old road in another 100 yards. Most of the rest of the way to the lake at 1.1 miles (6,069 feet) is up on the rocks with unsteady footing. The trail goes around the lake on the left side on a wooded hillside. Below the lower end of the lake at 1.4 miles, the trail fords the creek to campsites, then continues down the canyon 26.8 miles to Big Creek at Monumental Bar.

84.

The Monument

Round trip: 17.2 miles
Elevation gain: 290 feet; elevation loss (return climb): 890 feet
This section one way: 7.2 miles; Elevation gain: 240 feet; elevation loss (return climb): 790 feet
Highest point: 6,070 feet
Topographic maps: Rainbow Peak (80-foot contours), Center Mountain, Monument
Trailhead GPS: N 44 57' o.8" W 115 10' 51.6" at the Roosevelt Lake trailhead
Time: 2 days; ability: expert, due to 10 fords of Monumental Creek
Access: See Roosevelt Lake to go by trail to the lower end of Roosevelt Lake (6,069 feet) where this description begins.

What you will see: The 68-foot natural monument on Monumental Creek is a slender column of pale yellow rock studded with pink, yellow and black pebbles. A lopsided black boulder perches on top, like a chunk of licorice on a pillar of fruitcake. A baby monument 15 feet high stands next to it. The nearby eroded badlands with black boulders sitting on short, pale yellow pillars resemble a monument nursery.

On the way down Monumental Creek, the 500-foot pink cliff of Suicide Rock overlooks the canyon. At Thunder Mountain City, a few tumbledown cabins form silver shadows in the forest. The ten fords of Monumental Creek between Roosevelt

Lake and The Monument are dangerous for hikers until August in most years. After that, some will still be thigh-deep and swift, so this is not a good hike for children.

From the lower end of Roosevelt Lake (6,909 feet), the trail first fords Monumental Creek to the east just below the lake. Just before Mule Creek, the trail branches. Take the left (west) branch of the trail down a sandy bank and across to a campsite. At .5 mile, well above Monumental Creek, it passes a fenced cemetery for Roosevelt, with a metal plaque honoring the 13 people buried there.

At .7 mile, at Trap Creek, the trail returns to the west bank of Monumental Creek. A short distance up Trap Creek is an old rock house. At Suicide Rock at 2 miles, the path fords the creek to the east to avoid cliffs. Just beyond the rock, there are three more fords, two of which are not on the topographic map.

The trail climbs a fir-covered bench beside remnants of Thunder Mountain City at 3 miles. The "city" was started in 1902 by Weiser businessmen. There were five stores, a hotel and nine whisky stills.

Next the trail switchbacks down to the West Fork of Monumental Creek at 3.4 miles and fords it. At 3.5 miles is a junction with the West Fork of Monumental Creek Trail, which goes 9.5 miles to Catherine Lake and Cougar Basin.

At 4 miles, the main trail fords Monumental Creek to the immense sagebrush flat, and stone foundations of the Monumental Creek Ranch.

A little history: This ranch was started in 1913 by R.A. Wallingford. The ranch house was the old schoolhouse that had been moved down from Roosevelt on skids (logs). In the early 1920s, it was owned by Rufe and Ora Hughes and patented by them in 1928. In 1921, the Cascade News had an item about R.A. Hughes and his wife skiing 90 miles to town from their ranch. Roy Elliott became Hughes' partner and then bought the ranch from him.

In the fall of 1929, Elliott sold the ranch to Jess and Vernie Vanderpool (known by the last name of Warner) who ran it for two years. Aloha Beck McCoy, Vernie's daughter, remembered that while living on the Monumental Creek Ranch when she was a little girl, so many salmon would come up the irrigation ditches that the fields were covered with them.

When the Vanderpools couldn't pay for the place, they returned the ranch to Elliott. Gil McCoy from Yellow Pine bought it in 1933 from Elliott and lived with his family on the ranch until 1941, when he sold it to the Forest Service. He was a packer and guide and eventually became the ranger at Chamberlain. Nothing is left today of the buildings but foundations.

More directions: Beyond the site of the ranch is a campsite. At 5 miles, at Holy Terror Creek, the trail fords Monumental Creek to the west side in the deepest and swiftest water of any of the crossings.

After another sagebrush flat, the trail returns to the east side and an outfitter's campsite at 5.5 miles. After ascending a lodgepole slope, the route goes over Meadow Creek in willows at 5.9 miles. At 6.1 miles, the signed Beartrap Trail turns northeast 2 miles to Milk Lake and the Lookout Mountain Ridge Trail.

The Monumental Creek Trail returns to the west bank of Monumental Creek at 6.3 miles, at a marsh where it is easier to walk on a sandbar than on the trail. The way turns back into the canyon of Mud Creek, crosses it at 6.5 miles and climbs onto a lodgepole bench that has a campsite. Below here the canyon burned in 2000 all the way to Big Creek. After ascending through burned trees across from pale yellow and gray badlands, the route begins to descend the other side of the hill at 7.1 miles. Downhill 150 yards, a network of paths plunges to the right (east). The slope is steep and slippery, so be careful climbing down these paths to see The Monument at 7.2 miles (5,520 feet). The main trail continues down Monumental Creek 11 miles to Monumental Bar on Big Creek. Not far beyond the paths down to The Monument a landslide 125 feet long and 10 feet deep has closed the trail at present.

In the 1930s, Slim Clark located a claim about four miles down Monumental Creek from The Monument, sold shares in it, built a cabin, and brought down an old a stamp mill from another claim. In the 1960s in a dispute over the claim, Clark bled to death when he was shot by the son of one of the shareholders.

Wilbur Wiles had a ranch on Monumental Creek one mile above Big Creek, but his cabin there burned in the 2000 fires. He helped Maurice Hornocker with the famous cougar study that was described in the National Geographic in 1969. Wiles' claim was different than most claims in this wilderness because it is an opal mine. When he died in 2019, a memorial was held for him at Big Creek.

85.

Lookout Mountain Ridge

Round trip: 5.5 miles to viewpoint, 17 miles to Lookout Mountain
Elevation gain: 200 feet to viewpoint, 1,620 feet to Lookout Mountain
Elevation loss (return climb): 360 feet to viewpoint, 480 feet to Lookout Mountain
Highest point: 8,000 for viewpoint, 8,680 for Lookout Mountain
Topographic maps: Rainbow Peak , Safety Creek , Monument , Acorn Butte
Trailheads GPS: N 44 57 32.46" W 115 7' 30.9"
Time: 41/2 hours to viewpoint, 101/2 hours to two days for Lookout Mountain
Difficulty: strenuous
Access: From Cascade, drive north 1 mile on Highway 55. Turn right (east) and go 25 miles to a junction with the paved, one-lane South Fork of Salmon River Road. Turn left (north) and go 31 miles. Turn right (east) on the East Fork of South Fork of Salmon River Road and drive 14.7 miles to Yellow Pine. From Yellow Pine continue 8 miles to Stibnite and drive over Monumental Summit and down through an area burned in 2000 to the Monumental Creek trailhead 23 miles from Yellow Pine. Here turn right (south) and, avoiding side roads to mine sites, drive 4.1 miles to the Lookout Mountain Ridge trailhead.

A little history: The mining boom called Thunder Mountain happened because one day while ranching at Cabin Creek on Big Creek in 1897, Ben and Dan Caswell went looking for a lost mule; while they were searching, they discovered gold in a quartz outcrop at the base of a partly wooded hill they called Thunder Mountain.

The gold had been discovered by James Poe about 1866, but no one had wanted to mine there because of Indian problems. The Caswells and A.O. Huntley staked most

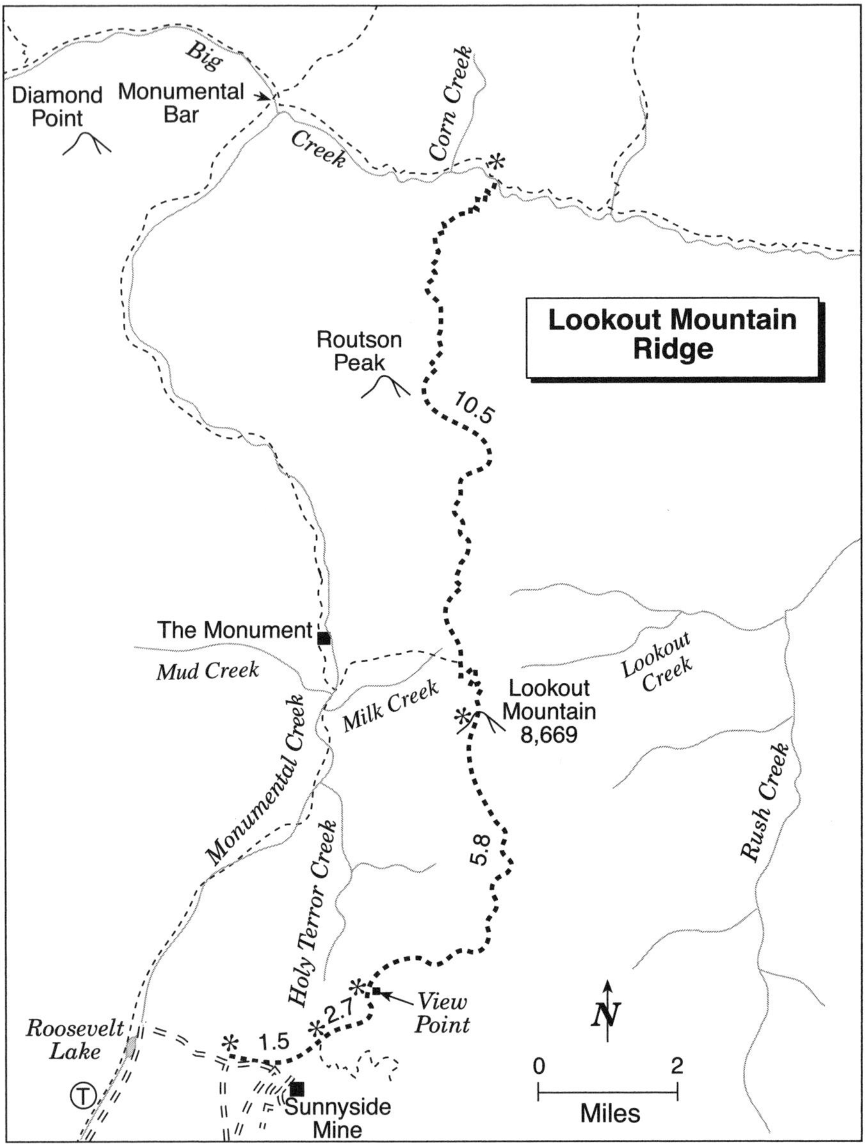

of the claims but didn't promote the discovery until 1897, when they found it was really profitable. By 1899 there were 50 other prospectors.

By 1901, the Caswells had taken out $20,000. When they sought investors, Col. W.H. Dewey from Silver City bought the largest mine, the Golden Reef, for $100,000 and started mining. That winter, newspaper accounts claiming the Caswells had found a whole mountain of gold started a rush to the area. Hundreds of miners went to Warrens to wait for the snow to melt. In February, dog teams got through with supplies, but it was May before more than a few people could reach the gold claims..

Dewey had a 10-stamp mill brought in by wagon and pack horse, with two mules carrying each of the 1,800-pound stamp stems. At each switchback, a fresh team facing the other way took over the stem. About 2,000 people arrived in 1902. From 1902 to 1906 Dewey's mine earned $50,000 a year. In 1902, the Caswells sold the Sunnyside Mine, a mine they had kept hidden from Dewey, to the Belle of Thunder Mountain Company for $125,000. A 40-stamp mill was built, but the mine didn't make a profit and was shut down in 1907.

Hiking on Lookout Mountain Ridge

What you will see: As seen from this ridge, the Frank Church Wilderness rolls on and on in an endless array of mountains in every direction, giving you an idea of its vast size. Except for the balding hill that is Lightning Peak and the wooded top of Thunder Mountain, the named peaks look insignificant. Distance shrinks 9,400-foot Two Point Mountain and its 800 feet of cliffs to the size of a rosette of icing on a cake. The trail goes up and down, following the vertebrae of the ridge.

Directions: The Payette Forest map shows a campground at the Lookout Mountain Ridge trailhead, but except for campsites and a nearby spring, there are no facilities. From the trailhead, the trail drops east down the hillside as an old jeep road, switchbacks and then passes above the spring at .2 mile. At .3 mile on a talus slope it becomes a trail. At .5 mile is the remains of the Venable Mine: a log building, an old boiler and the short cylinder of an ore crusher. Since then the Forest Service has removed many mining remnants so they may no longer be there. The trail climbs around the side of a hill, enters the Frank Church Wilderness and descends to a saddle at 1.5 miles, with a junction with an old trail to the right down Marble Creek. Both the Lookout Mountain Ridge Trail and the Marble Creek Trail are sections of the Idaho Centennial Trail but are not signed as such because that is against Forest Service policy. They have been adopted by the Selway Bitterroot Frank Church Foundation for frequent maintenance, though.

From here the Lookout Mountain Ridge Trail goes along the left side of the ridge and then the right side, where at 2.7 miles below the hilltop marked 7,922 in an open area of sagebrush and grass you can look out to the southeast and see Two Point Mountain, Norton Peak and blue peaks on the other side of the Middle Fork. The trail drops into a little saddle, then climbs along the right (south) side of the next hill,

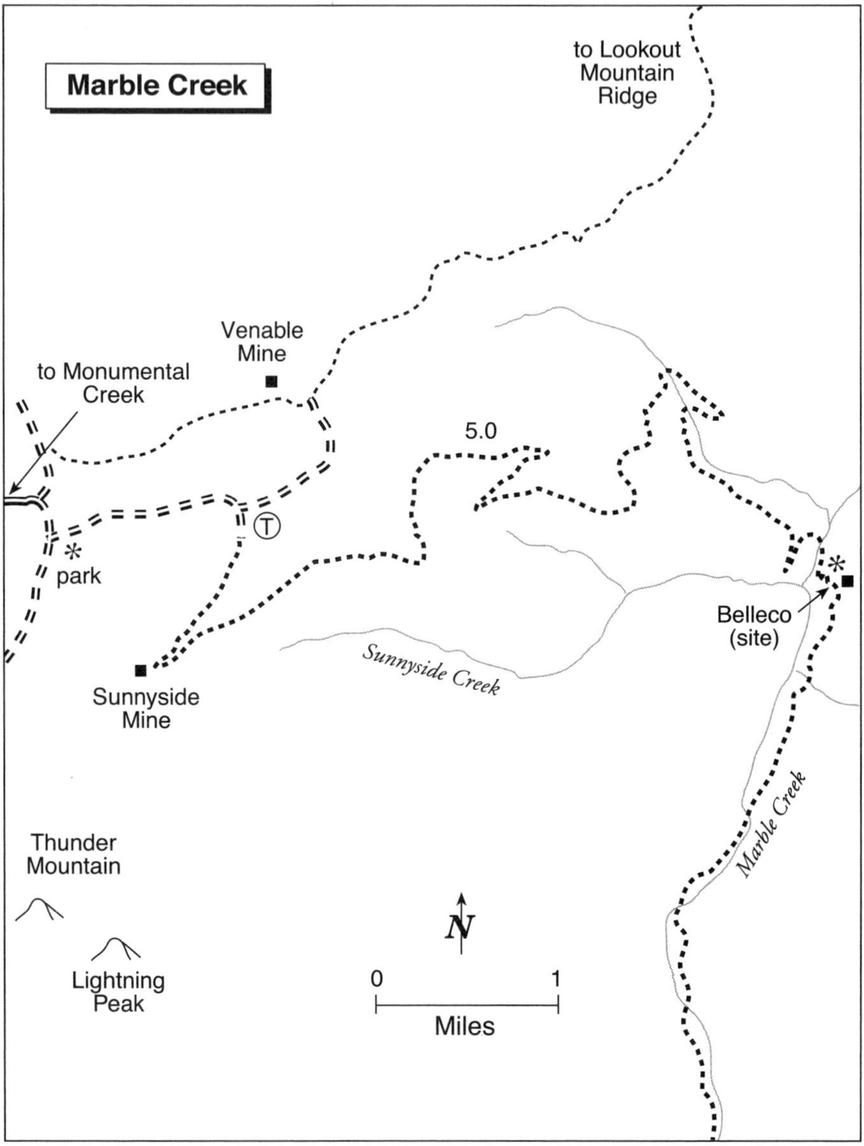

which is bare and rocky on the west end. To get a partial view north and a better view south into the canyon of Marble Creek, leave the trail here and climb this rocky slope.

From here it is still a long slog of 5.8 miles up and down the wooded hills to the summit of Lookout Mountain, which has no water and only ruins of the old lookout. From the mountain the trail continues 10.5 more miles to Big Creek, where there is no bridge.

86.

Marble Creek

Round trip: 9 miles to ruins of Belleco, 51 miles to Middle Fork

Elevation loss (return climb): 1,670 feet to the site of Belleco, 4,160 feet to Middle Fork

Highest point: 8,000 feet

Topographic maps: Rainbow Peak , Safety Creek

Trailhead GPS: N 44 57' 32,46" W 115 7' 30.9"

Time: 7 hours to Belleco, 3 to 4 days to Middle Fork; difficulty: very strenuous due to 40 fords of the creek

Access: From Cascade, drive north 1 mile on Highway 55. Turn right (east) and go 25 miles to a junction with the paved, one-lane South Fork of Salmon River Road. Turn left (north) and go 31 miles. Turn right (east) on the East Fork of South Fork of Salmon River Road and drive 14.7 miles to Yellow Pine. From Yellow Pine continue 8 miles to the site of Stibnite and then drive over Monumental Summit and down through an area burned in 2000 to the Monumental Creek trailhead 23 miles from Yellow Pine. Here turn right (south) and, avoiding side roads to mines, drive 4.1 miles to a T-intersection. To the left a spur road goes to the Lookout Mountain Ridge trailhead. Here, turn right and go about 200 yards to the signed Marble Creek trailhead. Park here and walk down a two-track past an abandoned cabin. The old road switchbacks and then becomes a trail numbered 067.

What you will see: Woods, talus, outcrops and the occasional cliff are the scenery in the 25-mile-long canyon. here are glimpses of distant peaks, such as the reddish face of twisted cliffs seen from Belleco. What is remarkable about Marble Creek is its remoteness and its wildlife. There also are elaborate rock retaining walls built by the Civilian Cinservation Corps in the 1930s. In addition, Just above the Middle Fork is a mile-long gorge with waterfalls. There are 40 fords of the creek as well as fords of side creeks. Therefore, except for the upper 4 miles, this trail is best for late summer and dry years. Seeing the old road, rotting mine timbers and the log and board ruins of Belleco gives you an idea of the difficulties miners faced in building and mining in such rugged country. A stamp mill was built in the canyon at Belleco in 1902 for the Sunnyside Mine, 1,500 feet and 2 miles above the mill. An 8,000-foot tramway brought ore down from the mine to the mill. A sawmill was constructed here as well. Campsites along Marble Creek are limited and crossing the fords requires a great deal of patience. Those hiking the Centennial Trail may find it easier to take a detour here spending two extra days hiking down the Middle Fork and up Big Creek to where the Lookout Mountain Ridge Trail fords Big Creek.

Directions: From the new trailhead it is about 1.5 miles along a former mining road to a junction on a saddle with the Lookout Mountain Ridge trail. From here the Marble Creek trail descends south along the side of the ridge, looping in and out of a gully at 1.9 miles, then switchbacking down to Marble Creek. At some of the corners are short spur roads once used by trucks or horses to wait while others passed them. Part way along the second, largest switchback you can look across the canyon of Marble Creek and see animal paths on the talus and a black nubbin, Black Pole, on top of the ridge. At 3.5 miles, the track loops back into the same gully again and crosses the stream in it. In .2 mile it crosses the stream again. At 4 miles, the track has been cut out of the rock. At a blazed tree at 4.2 miles, turn off the road onto a trail that goes downhill to the left (up the canyon.) The old road is washed out and impassable farther along. The trail cuts down the hillside, switchbacks to the right and fords Marble Creek (six feet wide) at 4.5 miles. Piles of boards between the trail and the creek mark the site of Belleco. In a grassy flat are the remains of log buildings to the left of the trail about .2 mile below the ford. Across Marble Creek and up the canyon of Sunnyside Creek are huge heaps of mine timbers.

Continuing down Marble Creek to the Middle Fork requires backpacking and much patience because of the fords and the trail's tendency to wash out. It was completely maintained by crews from the Selway Bitterroot- Frank Church Foundation in 2018 and 2019. The last 3 miles are through private property with a gate at the lower end. This little ranch was started by a Scotsman, Billy Mitchell, in 1916, who drove his cattle to market in Cascade. He sold to the Idaho Fish and Game Department in 1950.

For the last mile of the trail the creek is a cascade and the trail zigzags down beside it. The trail joins the Middle Fork Trail 25 miles from the trailhead. This junction is 32.5 miles from the beginning of the Middle Fork Trail at Boundary Creek but it is only 7 miles below the Indian Creek Guard Station on the Middle Fork. You could arrange to be picked up by one of the backcountry air services at the airstrip there. The Marble Creek Trail was the route that three of the main trails to the Thunder Mountain mines took to finish their journey. As you ford the creek again and again wearing quick-dry fleece and microfiber, imagine what it must have been like in turn-of-the century wool, leather and thick cotton, leading a pack string.

BIG CREEK AREA

87.

Missouri Ridge

Round trip: 8 miles
Elevation gain: 2,360 feet
Highest point: 8,560 feet
Topographic maps: Profile Gap, Edwardsburg
Trailhead GPS: N 45 20' 21.6" W 115 23' 0.81"
Time: 7.5 hours; Difficulty: strenuous

Access: On Highway 55, 1 mile north of Cascade, turn right (east) and drive 25 miles to a junction with the paved, one-lane South Fork of Salmon River Road. Turn left

Pinnacles from Missouri Ridge

(north) and go 31 miles to the East Fork of the South Fork of Salmon River Road. Turn right (east) and drive 14.7 miles on the improved dirt road to the turnoff for the village of Yellow Pine. Continue 4.8 more miles to the Big Creek Road. Turn left (north) on the dirt road and drive to the trailhead 9.2 miles from Yellow Pine.

What you will see: Missouri Ridge runs north to meet the mountain wall of The Pinnacles, great dark teeth that erupt from pink talus and scree. Small spires stick out of the sides of some of the teeth. East of Missouri Ridge, two small jade-green lakes float among granite benches, and below The Pinnacles, other tarns hide in trail less cirques. The hike up Missouri Ridge is on an old mining road, now a trail not open to motorized travel. The old road begins like a semicircular driveway with the trail taking off from the center of the curve.

Directions: The track passes talus and cliffs, and at .8 mile, a side trail turns south to the former Missouri Ridge Lookout. Here the south slopes of the creek burned in 1990. At 2 miles is an outfitter's cabin with a silver-gray roof. From it, the road turns southeast across the creek and makes six bends up a wooded hillside. At 2.7 miles, the grade lessens beside an intermittent stream, then turns left (north) among tiny firs and becomes steeper.

At 3.5 miles, the old road ends, but a primitive trail continues. At 3.6 miles, the trail switchbacks south, then north again with a fine view of rock towers. At 4 miles is the top of the ridge. For a view of The Pinnacles, carefully climb north 200 yards up to a rocky point (8,520 feet). For a closer view, continue along the ridge to a hill at 8,649 feet by dropping to the east 100 feet, traversing and scrambling up. To reach the two lakes below, walk south along the ridge, east along a spur and descend to the highest lake.

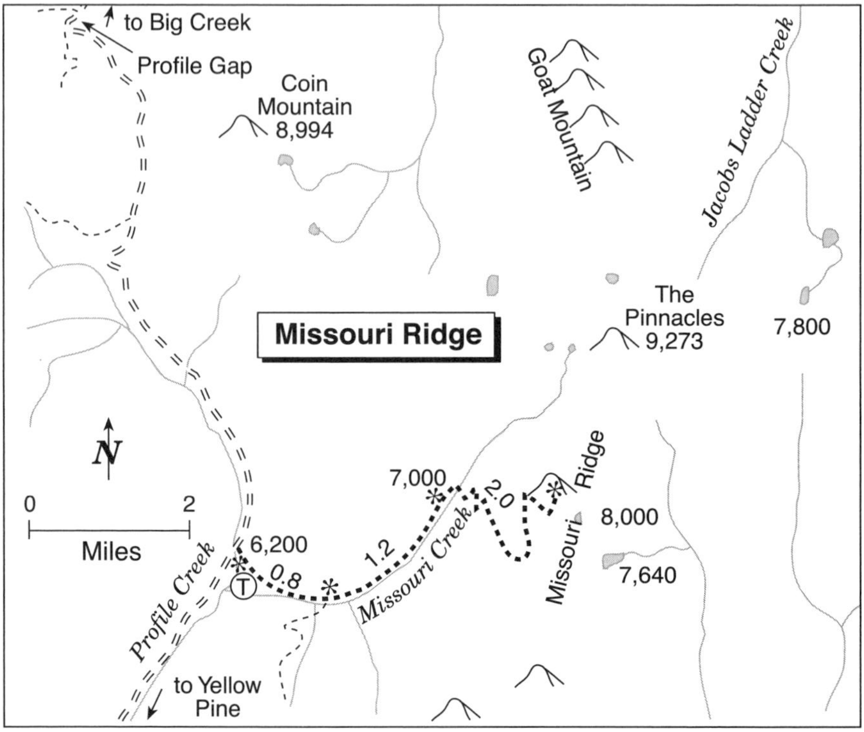

88.

Lick Lake, Cougar Basin and Bear Lake

Round trip: 15.6 miles
Elevation gain: 3,400 feet; elevation loss (return climb): 1,150 feet
Highest point: 8,713 feet
Topographic map: Edwardsburg
Trailhead GPS: N 45 06' 9.9" W 115 19' 55.2"
Time: 3 days for round trip; difficulty: strenuous

Access: On Highway 55, 1 mile north of Cascade, turn right (east) and drive 25 miles to a junction with the paved, one-lane South Fork of Salmon River Road. Turn left (north) and go 31 miles to the East Fork of the South Fork of Salmon River Road. Turn right (east) and drive 14.7 miles on the improved dirt road to the turnoff for the village of Yellow Pine. Continue 4.8 more miles to the Big Creek Road. Turn left (north) on the dirt road and drive over Profile Gap to the trailhead at 15.1 miles.

What you will see: From the top of a divide on this trail, eight ridges marching to

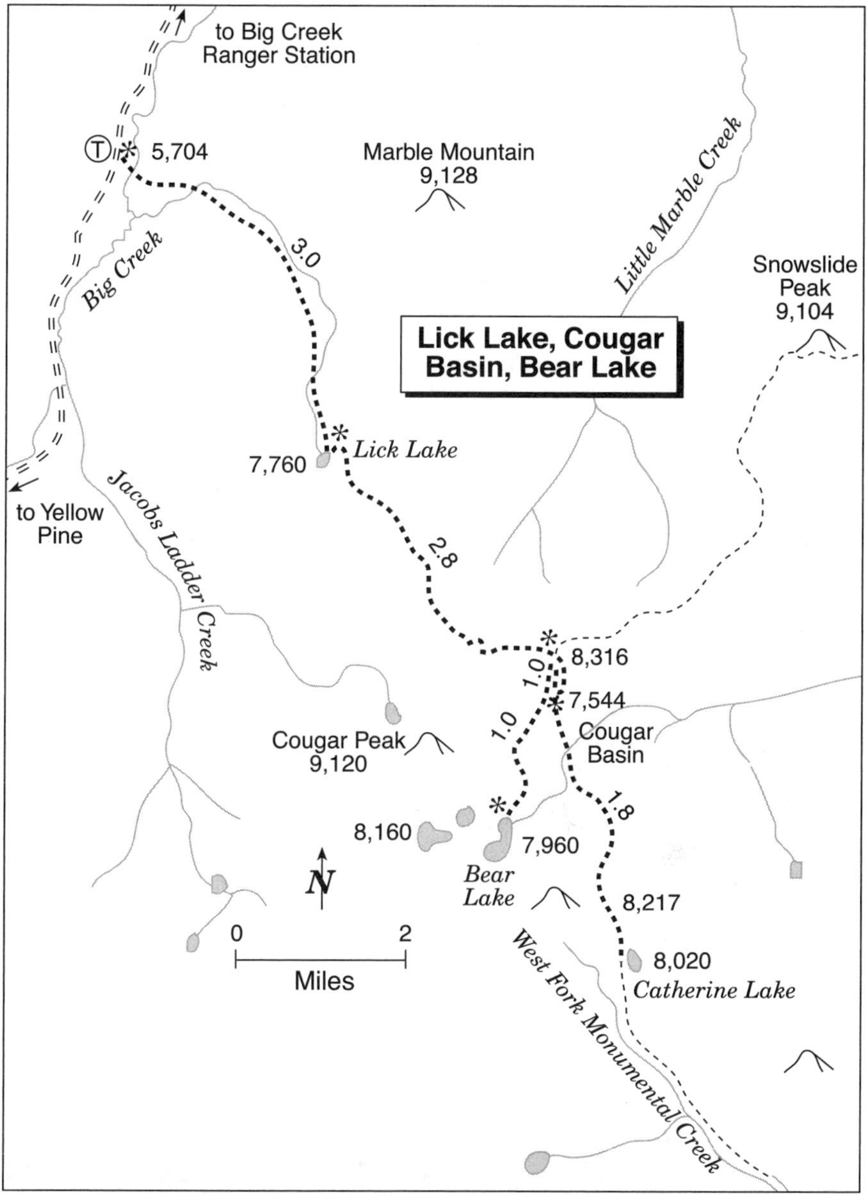

the east with 3,000-foot canyons between them, show the vast size of the Frank Church - River of No Return Wilderness. Three miles along this trail, a spur trail leads to small, green Lick Lake below the cliffs of an orange and gray dome. Two miles farther a peninsula squeezes turquoise Bear Lake into the surrounding woods below a huge cone of gray talus. The meadows of Cougar Basin are 500 feet below this lake, beneath forbidding cliffs. As you drive over the divide called Profile Gap on the way to the trailhead you are near Sam Wilson's mine. He came to mine here during the Thunder Mountain boom. "Profile Sam" saved up his highest-grade gold ore and sent it parcel post to the smelter in Tacoma, running his own post office to do this. He occupied a board and batten shack on the claim until his death in 1934, and his son Earl lived here until about 1940.

`**Directions:** The trail begins at a road bridge over Big Creek and follows the road past a cabin area, which is private property.. As a single track trail it switchbacks up through lodgepoles and alders. At 1.7 miles, on a talus slope, there is a view up the wooded canyon. At 2.2 miles, the trail goes over Lick Creek back to the east, then climbs 200 feet in .2 mile along the side of a ravine. At 3 miles, a sign points 100 yards southwest to Lick Lake (7,760 feet).

Beyond this junction, the main trail goes east up a ridge, then south to a wooded summit at 3.5 miles. After circling the head of the canyon of Little Marble Creek, the trail crosses a stream at a grassy campsite at 3.8 miles. It then zigzags up beside small waterfalls. Above them the trail goes over the stream in a flat meadow and makes one switchback across orange talus. Snow clinging in the cirque usually blocks the trail here until July 10. It reaches the 8,713-foot sandy divide at 5.2 miles.

The trail descends east along the summit ridge, then at 5.8 miles hairpins southwest and plunges off the ridge. From the hairpin, a primitive trail goes east past Snowyside Peak to meet the Big Creek Trail at 11.4 miles. The main trail switchbacks 1,200 feet down a sandy slope of whitebark pines to a junction with the Bear Lake Trail at the edge of 7,544-foot Cougar Basin at 6.8 miles.

At the junction, take the Bear Lake Trail west into the meadow. The trail is a few yards west of where it is shown on the topographic map. The other trail at the junction climbs south 1.8 miles to Catherine Lake, then descends the West Fork of Monumental Creek 7.5 miles to Monumental Creek.

After circling the meadow under Cougar Peak, the Bear Lake Trail goes southwest, crossing streams and climbing outcrops to a grassy shelf. Beyond another rise, it passes a pond and reaches the lake (7,960 feet) at 7.8 miles. The lake has campsites on a peninsula on the west side of the lake as well as beside the inlet, but there is no camping allowed within 200 feet of this lake or the nearby ones.

A path continues around the west side to the peninsula, then climbs up a stream to a small, marshy lake. From here, an unnamed upper lake as big as Bear Lake, is southwest up a dry outlet, .5 mile from the lower end of Bear Lake.

89.

Mosquito Ridge

Round trip: 17.4 miles from Smith Creek Cutoff trailhead to Mosquito Springs
Elevation gain: 3,180 feet; elevation loss (return climb):1,060 feet

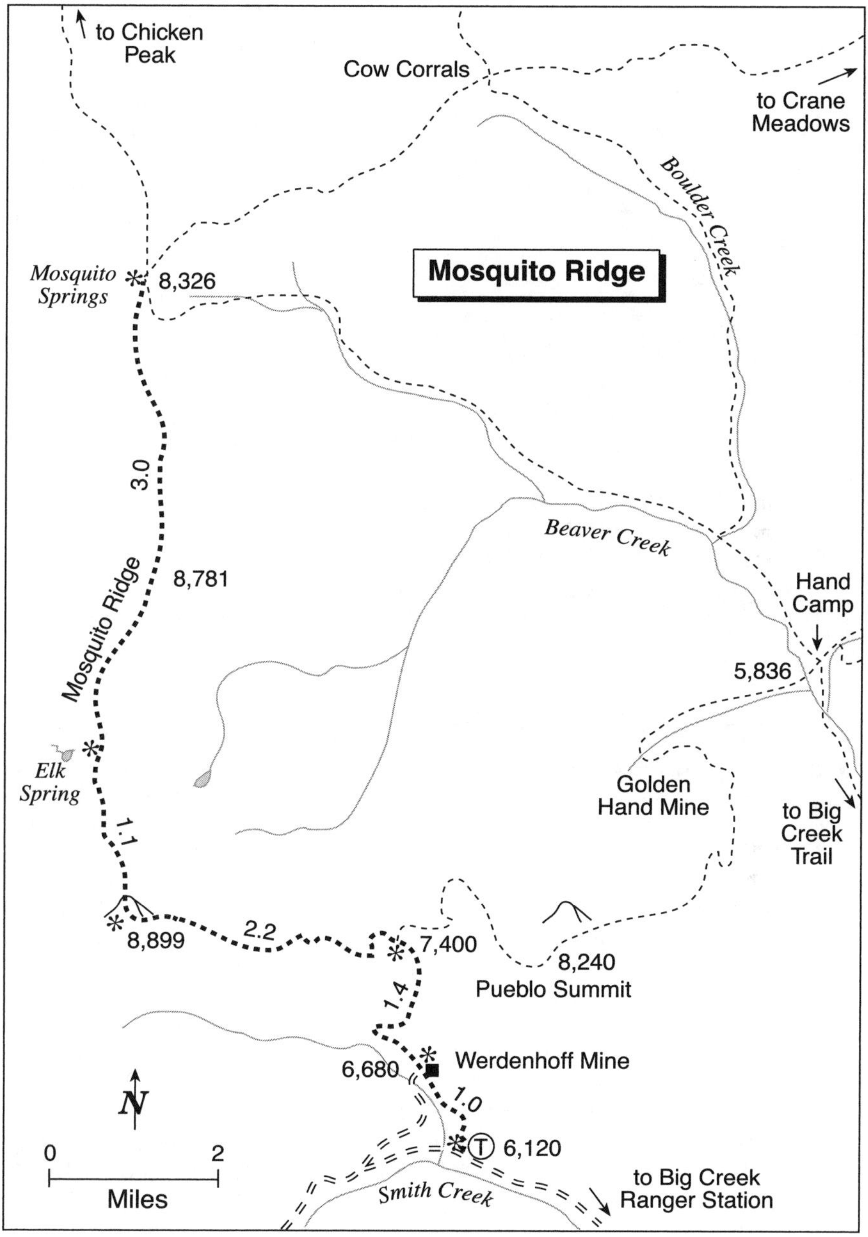

Highest point: 8,900 feet
Topographic maps: Big Creek, Wolf Fang Peak, Chicken Peak
Trailhead GPS at Smith Creek cutoff: N 45 11' 18" W 115 20' 36.2"
Time: 2 - 3 days for Mosquito Springs; difficulty: strenuous

Bear grass growing on Mosquito Ridge

Access: On Highway 55, 1 mile north of Cascade, turn right (east) and drive 25 miles to a junction with the paved, one-lane South Fork of Salmon River Road. Turn left (north) and go 31 miles to the East Fork of the South Fork of Salmon River Road. Turn right (east) and drive 14.7 miles on the improved dirt road to the turnoff for the village of Yellow Pine. Continue 4.8 more miles to the Big Creek Road. Turn left (north) on the dirt road and drive past the new trailhead for the Big Creek Trail at 25.5 miles to Smith Creek. Turn left (northwest) on the primitive road and drive 3.5 miles to the Smith Creek Cutoff Trail. (Leave passenger cars at the Big Creek trailhead and walk the 3.5 miles. Do not attempt to drive farther than the Smith Creek cutoff because of mudholes.))

A little history: On the way to the trailhead the road goes through the village of Big Creek, once a thriving mining town. Because the Big Creek Mines were farther into the mountains than many mines associated with the Frank Church Wilderness, their lodes would have had to be richer to make up for the distance from markets. The country was so rugged that when James Hand, who discovered the Golden Hand Mine, first came to Big Creek from Yellowjacket in 1889, he lost all four of his horses when they rolled off hillsides as he traveled down the Middle Fork and up Big Creek.

So, many of the miners supplemented their income by ranching, growing vegetables and trapping. In turn, most of the ranchers on Big Creek also had mining claims.

The Big Creek Mining District was started in 1883 and the nearby Alton District in 1885. Placer claims on Smith Creek were discovered in 1901. By 1902, the Cleveland Mine was shipping ore by pack train, but shipping costs took all the profit. A post office (Logan) opened in 1904, and the name was changed to Edwardsburg for William Edwards. In 1905 the state funded construction of a wagon road to Edwardsburg from Warren over Elk Summit.

Edwards was a lawyer from Georgia who came to Big Creek in 1903 during the Thunder Mountain boom. He worked the Eagle and Dixie claims on Logan Creek and Copper Camp on Big Creek. To encourage investment by wealthy friends in the east, he formed the Copper Camp Mining Company. None of Edwards' mines was successful in the long run, but he made ends meet by operating a store, ranching and trailing in cattle to butcher. His property at Big Creek is today the site of Gillihan's Lodge.

Edwards' wife, Annesley, who ran the post office, complained about the limit of 100 pounds of mail per week in summer and 50 pounds in winter for the whole settlement. Fortunately for all the residents, an automobile road was constructed from Warren over Elk Summit in 1922. Also that year a temporary ranger station was established in tents, succeeded in 1924 by log buildings. In 1934 the CCC built a road from Yellow Pine over Profile Gap and in 1935 an airstrip was constructed.

What you will see: In early summer along the trail up Mosquito Ridge, lacy white lanterns of bear grass bloom between young lodgepoles. In season, phlox, lupine, paintbrush and alpine sunflower carpet the ground under silver trunks of dead whitebark pines. From a distance, these snags with their close-together trunks resemble giant mosquitoes and next to them are clouds of real mosquitoes. To the southwest, a narrow row of rock nubbins, The Wolf Fangs, ends in a 1,000-foot dark wall. To the west sinks the blue gulf of the South Fork of the Salmon River. The Mosquito Ridge Trail is 10 miles shorter to the lakes in Chamberlain Basin than the route up Beaver and Hand creeks. It is also much more scenic. However, it doesn't open as early.

The cutoff trail climbs a grassy area, switchbacks up a wooded hillside, goes straight up and then turns left into the canyon of the North Fork of Smith Creek to rejoin the road at the Werdenhoff Mine (6,680 feet) at 1 mile. The ore of this mine was discovered in the 1880s by Pringle Smith, for whom Smith Creek is named. Smith abandoned the claim, and Charles Werdenhoff took it over in 1891. By 1903, Werdenhoff had 12 claims, several cabins and 20 men working a vein named the Octopus. In 1904, a 30-stamp mill was shipped partway to the mine, but it didn't get there until 1906, when the wagon road over Elk Summit was constructed. About 1912, John Routson, who lived on Acorn Creek, acquired the mine. It was worked by the Routsons clear into the 1950s, and they had 30 men working for them there in 1931. He was injured in 1923 in an explosion of old dynamite. After being transported over Elk Summit tied to a horse, he recovered but lost the sight of one eye. In April 1932, Noel Routson, John's son, was to take out Harold Vassar (the Big Creek Ranger at the time) and his wife, Edith, by dogsled, so she could have her baby at McCall. After the 5-mile walk in deep snow from Big Creek to the mine, Mrs. Vassar had her baby at the mine.

Directions: From the mine, take the middle of the three roads (not open to motor vehicles). It fords a branch of the North Fork of Smith Creek, angles up a ridge and switches back to the right (east) at 1.5 miles, where it curves north into the canyon of another branch of that creek. The road ascends the left (west) side of the creek to a campsite at 2.3 miles and signed trail (7,400 feet) at 2.4 miles. (The road turns sharply northeast here to Pueblo Summit and the Golden Hand Mine.)

Take the trail (west) for Mosquito Springs. Note that the only water from this point on is at Elk and Mosquito Springs. After zigzagging southeast up a spur ridge, the trail climbs the backbone of the ridge to the west. An open area of dead trees and bear grass is at 3.7 miles. Beyond this, the route levels, then turns north at 4.6 miles at a right-angle junction of two ridges at 8,899 feet.

After descending the ridge, the trail crosses a grassy, dusty area at 5.7 miles. From a cairn here, a search 200 yards to the left (west) of the trail will reveal the tiny Elk

Spring (8,440 feet).

Beyond Elk Spring, the trail descends the ridge to a level area at 6.4 miles, then climbs to a hillside meadow at 7.5 miles. Here, walk east off-trail to the crest of the ridge for an excellent view. After dropping northwest along a grassy hill, the trail descends north through woods to a junction at a flat, grassy saddle (8,320 feet) at 8.7 miles. A trail to the left at the junction goes 100 yards to an outfitter's camp and to Mosquito Springs. The Mosquito Ridge Trail continues north 10.3 miles with a 1,480-foot gain and 1,720-foot loss to a junction with a spur trail to Sheepeater Lookout. The entire ridge top burned about 1990.

Chicken Peak is a scenic side trip from Mosquito Springs with a view 6,000 feet down to the South Fork of the Salmon River. To go to Chicken Peak continue 2 miles north of Mosquito Springs on the main Mosquito Ridge Trail. It climbs along the ridge, then descends 200 feet over boulders to a saddle and circles the head of the North Fork of Porphyry Creek to a junction. From here, go north on the main trail toward Sheepeater Lookout. The other trail here, the one to the west, splits in .5 mile, one branch dropping to the South Fork and the other going northwest to Horse Heaven. The main trail north crosses a creek that begins at Chicken Spring and then switchbacks up 300 feet to the top of a ridge, 2.5 miles from Mosquito Spring. From here turn off the trail to reach the summit of Chicken Peak (8,640 feet) and the remains of the old lookout 200 yards to the west.

A little history: The trail from Horse Heaven to Chicken Peak was first built by Catley's troops in the 1879 Sheepeater War so their pack strings could get through. Their route from Rains Ranch on the South Fork up Fivemile Ridge went past Horse Heaven and Chicken Peak to Mosquito Springs, but the trail from the river to Horse Heaven no longer exists. (Material on Elk Spring to Chicken Peak contributed by Stuart Fuller.)

90.

Big Creek Trail: Big Creek to Monumental Bar

(Section 1 of Big Creek-Middle Fork through trip)

Round trip: 20.6 miles
Elevation gain: 160 feet; elevation loss (return climb): 1,030 feet
Highest point: 5,408 feet
Topographic maps: Big Creek, Bismark Mountain
Trailhead GPS: N 45 09' 14.3" W 115 18' 12.1"
Time: 3 days round trip or 2 weeks for Big Creek - Middle Fork through trip; difficulty: strenuous
Access: On Highway 55, 1 mile north of Cascade, turn right (east) and drive 25 miles

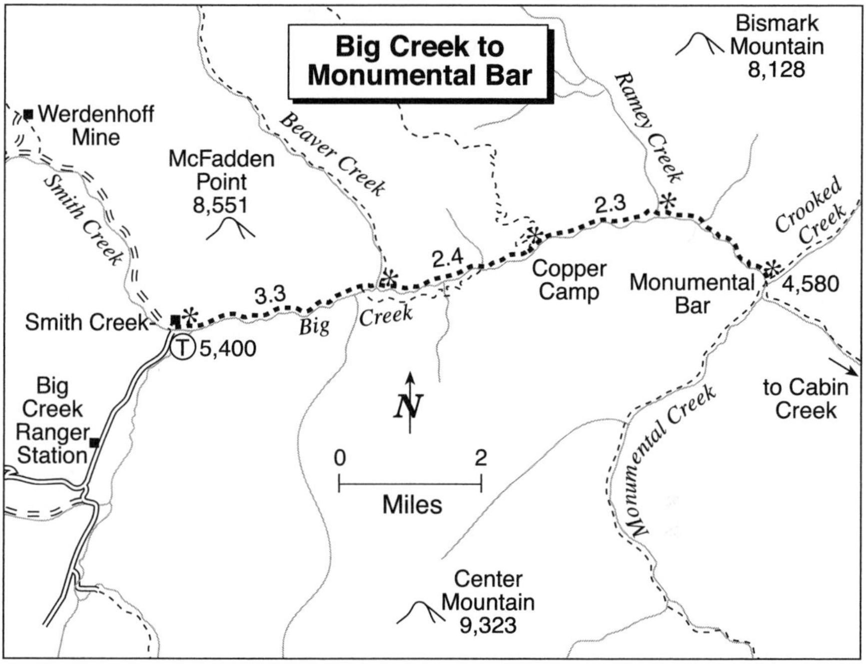

to a junction with the paved, one-lane South Fork of Salmon River Road. Turn left (north) and go 31 miles to the East Fork of the South Fork of Salmon River Road. Turn right (east) and drive 14.7 miles on the improved dirt road to the village of Yellow Pine. Continue 4.8 more miles to the Big Creek Road. Turn left (north) on the rocky dirt road and drive over Profile Gap, passing Big Creek Ranger Station, to the trailhead at 25.5 miles just above Smith Creek. Then walk down the road and across a bridge over Smith Creek to the beginning of the trail (5,400 feet), where the old road down the creek is blocked by boulders.

What you will see: South of the Big Creek airstrip, meadows and firs sweep up the canyon to Goat Mountain on the headwall, where in spring great snowbanks fill V-shaped grooves. High water in June turns Big Creek pale ice green. Later in the summer, the water slides from one emerald pool to another over amber cobblestones. A rusty boiler with a funnel-shaped top helps create a pioneer setting for the old road the trail follows for the first 10 miles. However, most of the old cabins along the trail burned in 2000 when the whole canyon from Beaver Creek to the Middle Fork burned in the Diamond/Shellrock/Point Fire.

Directions: At .2 mile, the old boiler, known locally as the "donkey steam engine," peers from shrubs near the creek. At .5 mile, the canyon become rocky with willows and alders along the creek. At .7 mile, the route climbs 100 feet above the creek beside springs and at 1.7 miles goes high above the river. Beyond Little Marble Creek at 3.1 mile, the old road crosses Big Creek, but the trail stays on the north side of the river.

At 3.3 miles, the trail bridges Beaver Creek at a junction (5,040 feet) with the

Chamberlain Trail, which goes 20.9 miles to Chamberlain Guard Station. After squeezing under cliffs, the Big Creek Trail rejoins the road and fords Copper Creek at 4.8 miles.

Some history: The mine called Copper Camp was located in 1889 by Pringle Smith and later owned by William Edwards. Edwards' son Napier, who kept the Copper Camp mine after his father died, was a little peculiar. When he came into Big Creek, he would put sourdough hotcakes rolled up in newspaper in his pocket, go to the hotel, ask for a glass of water, eat his hotcakes and sit there all afternoon without talking. He did this only between mail-order brides. Some stayed a week, but most got back on the plane and left. He did marry one who stayed two summers, but between summers she divorced him. Napier Edwards operated the mine until his death in 1974.

At the site of Copper Camp at 5.7 miles, a side road leads uphill. From it, the Ramey Ridge Trail climbs along Ramey Ridge to Upper Ramey Meadows, 14 miles from Big Creek. The ridge was named for an early packer, John Ramey. Among early settlers on this ridge were Charles Mahan (1899) William Edwards (1904) and more than a dozen others who came to mine here. Over the years, 600 claims have been made on this ridge, with total production in gold, copper and lead that only amounted to only $270,000.

Frank Lobauer had two cabins on Ramey Ridge, one to live in and one at his prospect. In 1933, his teen-age son got lost while following him from one cabin to the other and was never found, even though an air search was made. Mrs. Lobauer left the area soon after.

In December 1935, Frank Lobauer killed his neighbor and former partner, Walt Estep. At the time of the shooting, Lobauer was living at a place halfway between Cabin Creek and the Taylor Ranch. After Lobauer shot Estep, he hiked down to the Taylor Ranch and told Mrs. Taylor of the shooting. She radioed the sheriff, who asked Myron McCoy to go down there and see if Estep was dead. Myron stayed there all night and the next day until the sheriff and coroner could arrive, keeping a borrowed .45 handy. Myron said, "Lobauer asked me 'How many kids I got?' I said, 'You've got three, Frank.' He said, 'Well, two of 'em belong to that so-and-so lying out there.'"

Lobauer admitted the killing in a signed statement and was convicted of manslaughter. After he was pardoned in 1942, he came back to Big Creek in early spring, set out to walk to his claim from Copper Camp in the snow, and vanished.

At 7.5 miles, the trail along Big Creek climbs 150 feet above the creek to ford Ramey Creek at 8 miles and Little Ramey Creek at 8.9 miles. The trail passes under cliffs before reaching the pack bridge across Big Creek at Monumental Bar at 10.3 miles (4,560 feet.)

Here the old road turns left (northeast) up Crooked Creek to the Snowshoe Mine. This mine was won in 1904 in a poker game at a Roosevelt saloon by Jack and Eric Jansen (or Jensen), who were professional mining-camp gamblers. Eric also played the violin in saloons. Any time his brother faced a large pot and a skilled opponent, Eric walked around the table and signaled with his music what the opponent's cards were. They were also noted for their card tricks and jokes. They mined gold and silver at the Snowshoe for 25 years, and at one time, employed 60 people. The road down Big Creek and partway up Crooked Creek was built to give access to this mine. (It is now closed to motor vehicles at the wilderness boundary.) By 1942, when gold mines closed for the war the mine had produced $400,000. It is now owned by the Forest Service.

The Crooked Creek Trail is one end of the Cold Meadows Trail, which goes 16.3 miles to Cold Meadows. The trail to the right (southwest) up Monumental Creek climbs 11 miles to The Monument and 7 more miles to the Monumental Summit Road.

91.

Big Creek Trail: Monumental Bar to Cabin Creek

(Section 2 of the Big Creek-Middle Fork through trip)

Round trip: 45 miles
Elevation gain: 540 feet; elevation loss: 1,970 feet
This section one way: 12.2 miles; 380 feet gain, 940 feet loss
Highest point: 4,530 feet
Topographic maps: Bismark Mountain, Acorn Butte and Vinegar Hill
Trailhead GPS: N 45 9' 14.9" W 115 18' 12.1" at Big Creek trail beginning
Time: 2 weeks for entire Big Creek - Middle Fork trip; difficulty: strenuous
Access: See Big Creek Trail: Big Creek to Monumental Bar to go by trail to Monumental Bar where this description begins.

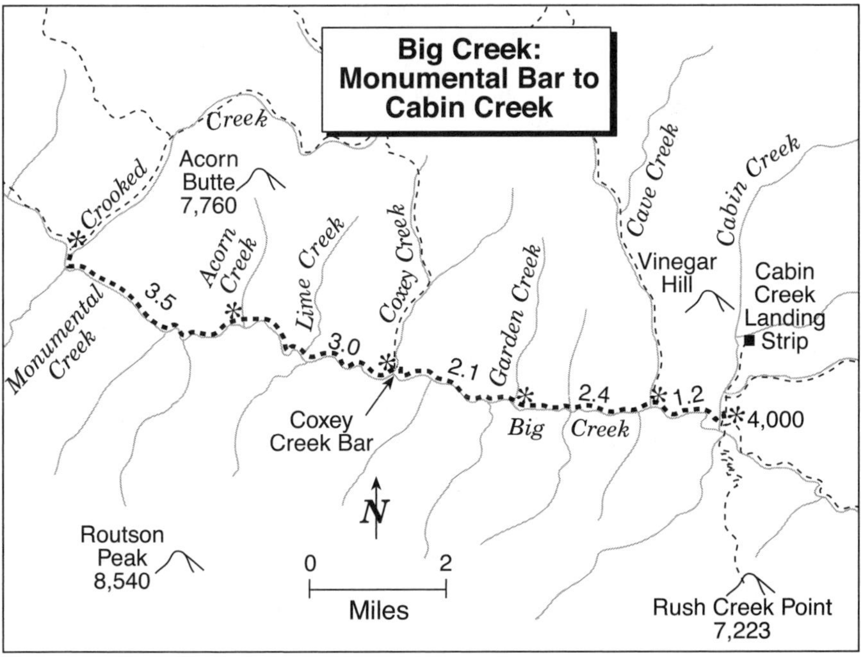

Barn at Cabin Creek Ranch

What you will see: In this section of Big Creek Canyon, dark cliffs; wide grassy bars; and towers appliqued with colorful lichens are found. At Coxey Creek, Big Creek enters jaws of rock 150 feet high on both sides, with the deep pool of Coxey Hole below. At Garden Creek, two rock towers resemble petrified warriors. The canyon along this section of trail burned in 2000.

Directions: From Monumental Bar (4,500 feet) where this description begins, the trail goes through burnt snags. At 2.5 miles is the first large bar, Mile Flat, .3 mile long. After traversing grassy slopes well above the creek, the path drops to a level area. At 3.5 miles, above a .5-mile-long bar, is a flat at Acorn Creek, site of the Moore Ranch. Part of the year, water runs in Acorn Creek, serving a couple of campsites.

Some history: Here, John Routson, his wife and six children supported the family by raising cattle, packing and working for the mines. He also had the mail route from Clover at Mile Hi Ranch on Big Creek to Warren, a 120-mile round trip. The oldest daughter, Adelia, acted as midwife when the youngest child, Bob, was born at the ranch. The Routson children made their own toys, such as miniature wagons and water wheels, but they mostly worked: gardening, chopping wood, cutting hay, boiling laundry and running a trapline. Routson bought the Acorn Creek Ranch in 1911 from Shorty Yardley, who had started ranching here about 1900. The family moved to Weiser in 1918, and after that spent summers at Acorn Creek. The Routsons sold it in 1925 to Walter Estep, who patented it in 1929 and sold it in 1932 to Phil Beal. Beal always called the ranch the Rhubarb Ranch after the rhubarb the Routsons had planted.

About 1990 I interviewed Bob Routson at his home outside Weiser. When I talked to him he was sitting on a chair the family made from old dynamite boxes when they lived at Acorn Creek. I could still see the lettering on the boxes.

After two other owners, Dewey Moore bought the property in 1947 for a big game hunting camp. He built the airstrip. Moore usually went barefoot, and his feet were so tough that once, when he was shoeing horses barefoot in the snow, he stepped on a hot piece of metal he had cut off a shoe, and smelled something burning before he felt pain.

At 4.5 miles opposite cliffs is sloping Hard Boil Bar. Here on the other side of Big Creek, the Lookout Mountain Ridge Trail descends to the creek. After crossing Lime Creek in a gulch at 5 miles, the Big Creek trail reaches Soft Boil Bar.

On the grassy slopes of usually dry Coxey Creek at 6.5 miles is a junction with the Coxey Creek Trail. This trail goes 4.5 miles to the Cold Meadows Trail above Crescent Meadows. The Big Creek Trail climbs around Coxey Hole across the face of a cliff, then returns to the edge of Big Creek at 7 miles. At 8.2 miles is an enormous grassy bar.

On a plateau north of Big Creek, between Coxey and Garden creeks, once stood the Mile Hi Ranch. It was established by Joe, Roy, and Ernest Elliott to supply the Snowshoe Mine with beef, vegetables and lumber. After Joe was taken to a mental hospital in 1926, Roy and Ernest stayed on, ran the Clover post office, and packed ore out for the miners. In 1934 Ernest died of tick fever there. Lafe and Emma Cox, owners of Cox's Ranch on Johnson Creek, then bought Mile Hi. The Coxes built a lodge in the 1940s at Mile Hi in order to guide fishing and hunting parties. Cox had an airstrip built, but it was short, hilly and dangerous. The Idaho Department of Fish and Game now owns the property. All the buildings burned in the 2000 fires.

Just beyond Garden Creek, at 8.6 miles is a large, high bar below rock towers. Garden Creek was named for Arthur "Kid" Garden. He and his wife, Viola "Auntie" received a homestead patent for a ranch here in 1913. Garden was proud of having been known in Montana as the "Yellowstone Kid," a bandit.

After creeping under a massive 400-foot cliff, the trail crosses Cave Creek at 11 miles just below a large cave. Catley and his troops are supposed to have camped here the night before they were ambushed in the Sheepeater War. From the creek crossing a trail goes 7 miles up Cave Creek to the Cold Meadows Trail.

At 11.5 miles, the trail becomes a dirt road and bisects a grassy bar that widens into an immense flood plain. At 12 miles, a faint path turns left (north) up Cabin Creek. To continue on the Big Creek Trail, stay on the main trail to a ford of Cabin Creek at 12.2 miles. Beyond the ford a side trail leads up Cabin Creek to the Cabin Creek landing strip and above it 19.3 miles to Coyote Springs.

At Cabin Creek 12.2 miles below Monumental Bar was where the discoverers of the Thunder Mountain strike, the Caswell brothers – Lou, Ben, Dan and Court – had their ranch, beginning in the late 1880s. It was the earliest agriculture in this wilderness. They raised sheep and hay, grew fruit and vegetables, trapped, hunted and prospected. After making their strike in 1902, they sold the ranch to John Conyers. Conyers built a new cabin, then sold out in 1910 to John Routson and O.M. Ables. Ables bought out Routson after a year and received the patent for the homestead in 1913. Later he acquired two adjacent parcels, one homesteaded by his sister and the other by Archie Bacon.

One day in 1920, when Ables went out to feed cattle, he was killed by a gash in his head. A bloody hay knife was found later at a nearby beaver dam. Two men staying with him were briefly suspected in his death, but the newspaper account said that Ables was gored by a bull. Four men transported his frozen body 130 miles on a sled so he could have a Masonic funeral.

In 1925, Merle (Blackie) Wallace, a former forest ranger at Cold Meadows, bought the ranch, had the airstrip constructed and ran an outfitting business called the Flying W. In 1953 Rex and Hazel Lanham bought part of the ranch for an outfitting headquarters. In 1956, Rex drove a Caterpillar bulldozer from Chamberlain to lengthen the airstrip, and built guest cabins, and a dam and Pelton wheel for electricity. Later he purchased the rest of the Cabin Creek properties. National Geographic made a film, Last of the Big Cats at Cabin Creek Ranch, with Rex doing the flying. He helped start the Outfitters and Guides License Board, and he served on it under two governors. In 1974, Lanham sold the entire ranch to the Forest Service

92.

Big Creek Trail: Cabin Creek to Big Creek Bridge

(Section 3 of Big Creek Trail - Middle Fork through trip)

Round trip: 71 miles
Elevation gain: 760 feet; elevation loss: 2,790 feet
This section, one way: 13 miles; 220 feet gain; elevation loss (return climb): 820 feet
Highest point: 4,000 feet
Topographic maps: Vinegar Hill, Mormon Mountain, Dave Lewis Peak, Puddin Mountain
Trailhead GPS: N 45 9' 14.9" W 115 18' 12.1" at beginning of Big Creel trail
Time: 2 weeks for through trip to Boundary Creek on the Middle Fork; difficulty: strenuous
Access: See Big Creek to Monumental Bar and Monumental Bar to Cabin Creek to go by trail to Cabin Creek where this description begins.

What you will see: Rock walls alternate with large bars, grassy slopes, strips of trees and burned snags in lower Big Creek Canyon. For nearly .5 mile in Big Creek Gorge, the creek thunders between pale 400-foot cliffs. At high water (14,000 cubic feet per second at the Middle Fork Lodge), the trail here will be underwater for 30 yards. Between Cabin Creek and the gorge, the trail squeezes under cliffs, then passes the green meadows of the Taylor Ranch. At Goat Creek just above the gorge, bluffs overlook a high bar split by a small creek, lined in spring by blue hyacinth and yellow Arrowleaf balsamroot. Across a ford of the creek and .5 mile up a path is Soldier Bar and the grave of Private Eagan, the soldier killed in the Sheepeater War. The canyon along this section of trail burned in 2000.

Directions: From Cabin Creek, follow the main trail, which at first is an old road along the edge of the flood plain. As the road ends in a thicket, take the trail that leads ahead to the left (northwest). Willows alternate with snags, trees, talus, grassy slopes

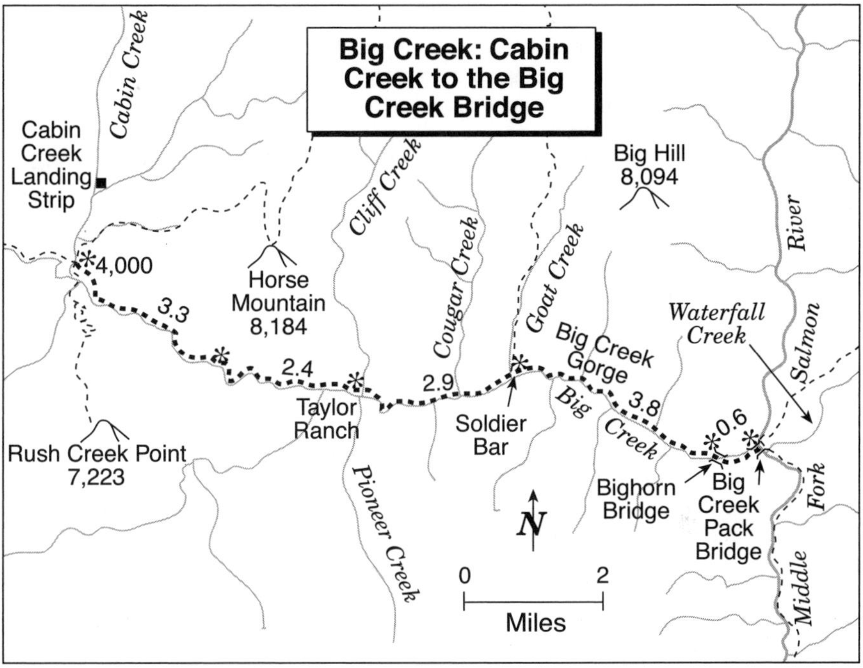

and cliffs, and a few places will be flooded at high water. At 3.3 miles, the trail is on grassy, sloping Lobauer Basin near a campsite.

In a couple of miles, on the opposite side, the long green airstrip of Taylor Ranch appears. At Cliff Creek opposite the ranch, the trail splits into foot and horse trails. The horse trail runs back up the canyon of Cliff Creek to cross it. At 5.7 miles, a steel bridge spans Big Creek from the foot trail to the ranch, which is a base for wilderness research by the University of Idaho.

A little history: About 1896, the Bull brothers settled at the site of the Taylor Ranch, then left for Thunder Mountain in 1902. John Conyers came here from Cabin Creek in 1910, built a new cabin and raised cattle and hay. After Conyers left in 1918, Cougar Dave Lewis arrived from Goat Creek. Lewis had been a Union soldier in the Civil War and a packer in the Sheepeater War, and in 1894 had returned to live on Big Creek at Goat Creek and Soldier Bar. Dave made his living first by packing supplies for the Thunder Mountain miners and later by outfitting, blacksmithing and hunting cougar for the state bounty of $15. In 1927, the year he received the patent for the ranch, he had his picture in the New York Times with his cougar dogs. In 1936, shortly before Lewis died, Jess Taylor bought the ranch that came to bear his name. Following a trip out from the ranch in the rain that year, Lewis died of pneumonia in Boise at the age of 92.

Around the time of Lewis' death, Taylor and his wife separated. Taylor left the ranch and went to Boise to become a building contractor. When he remarried in 1948, he again moved to the ranch with his new wife, Dorothy. During the first two years,

Dorothy insisted on living in a tent rather than the old log cabin, so he would build her a new house, which he did from logs he cut himself. He also leveled the airstrip with a scoop called a Fresno and a log drag, both drawn by Percheron draft horses. The Taylors operated the place as a hunting camp for 18 years and also raised hay and vegetables for their own use. When Jess reconstructed some of the trail along Big Creek for the Forest Service, Dorothy helped him assemble the bridges. When Maurice Hornocker used the ranch as a base for a five-year study of cougar with Wilbur Wiles, he made Jess see the potential of the ranch for a field station. So in 1969, Jess sold the ranch to the University of Idaho for $100,000. Hornocker's study was reported in the November 1969 National Geographic. Today the University of Idaho operates the ranch as a field station.

Beyond Cliff Creek, the main trail skirts a horse pasture, then cliffs. At a sharp bend in Big Creek, it crosses a flat grass and sagebrush bar. At Cougar Creek at 7.7 miles is a shelf where the trail branches into three. Take the right branch along the point and across the creek. Beyond here, there are campsites on a narrow, dry bar. At Goat Creek at 8.6 miles, the primitive Goat Creek Trail leads 8.2 miles north up the creek to the Coyote Springs Trail north of Black Butte. At the far end of the bar, a side trail fords Big Creek and goes .5 mile to the Soldier Bar airstrip and the grave of Private Eagan.

After squeezing past some cliffs, the main trail enters Big Creek Gorge at 9 miles. Here, the water may be waist-deep in June and requires a dangerous 300-foot detour up a slope of scree and slabs. At Burnt Creek below the gorge, a man-made cave is along the trail at 10.4 miles. This was supposed to be a tunnel but was abandoned because the rock was too crumbly and fell in when they were working on it in 1931, injuring one of the workers, Noel Routson, John Routson's son. He was transported by stretcher to Cabin Creek and rescued by air in the first instance of an airplane landing in the Big Creek area.

Two big boulders form a chute for Big Creek at Breeching Creek at 11.5 miles. At 12.4 miles, beyond a tiny campsite, the trail goes across the Bighorn Bridge to the south side of Big Creek. At 13 miles, the trail spans the Middle Fork of the Salmon River at 3,400 feet on the Big Creek Bridge, 35.5 miles from the Big Creek trailhead.

CHAMBERLAIN BASIN AREA:

93.

Chamberlain Trail: Big Creek to Ramey Ridge

Round trip: 33 miles
Elevation gain: 2,600 feet; elevation loss (return climb): 860 feet
This section one way: 12.8 miles, 2,560 feet gain, elevation loss (return climb): 80

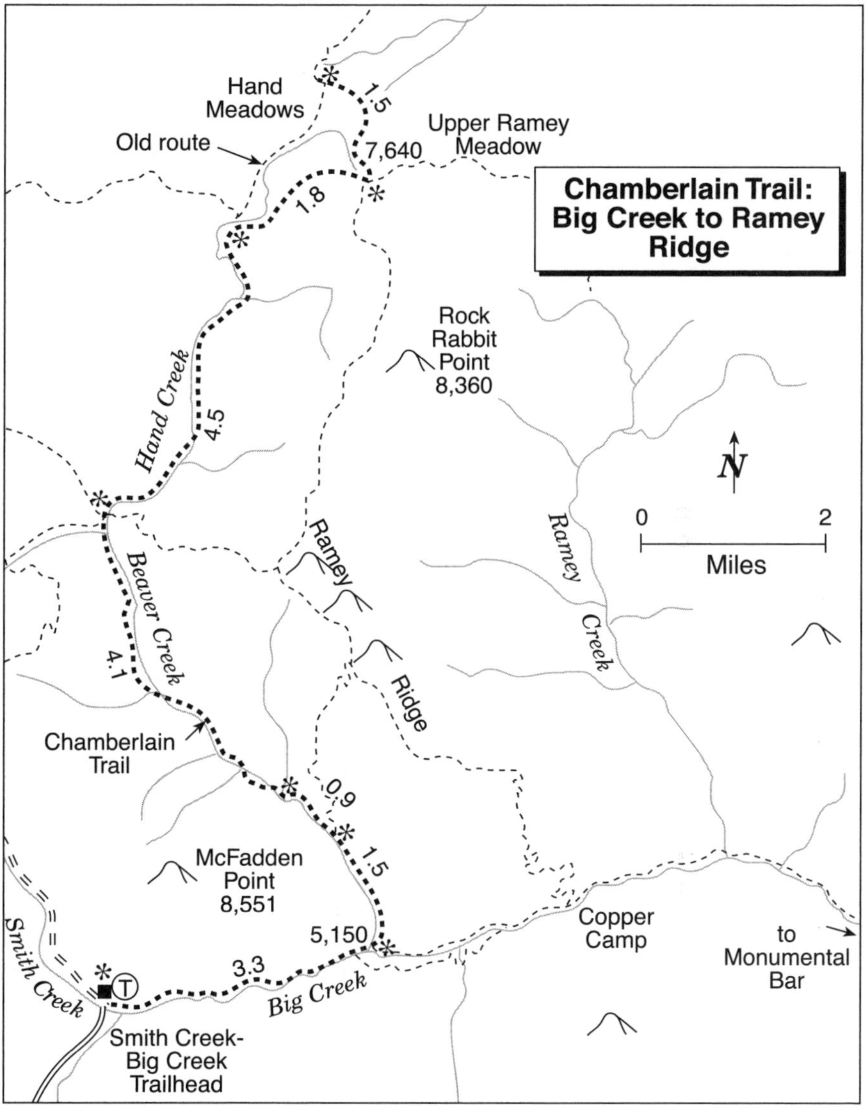

feet

Highest point: 7,520 feet

Topographic maps: Big Creek, Mosquito Peak, Bismark Mountain

Trailhead GPS: N 45 9' 14.9" W 115 18' 12.1" at beginning of Big Creek trail

Time: 3 days; difficulty: strenuous

Access: See Big Creek Trail: Big Creek to Monumental Bar to go by trail to the junction of the Big Creek and Chamberlain trails, where this description begins.

What you will see: This trail follows forested and snag-filled canyons to marshy meadows where the tea-colored curves of tiny Hand Creek swirl below low, wooded hills. The trail is accompanied by flowering shrubs and wildflowers. Higher up, the lime-green leaves and tiny, red berries of grouse whortleberry brighten the matchsticks of dead lodgepoles.

Directions: This hike description begins where the Chamberlain Trail up Beaver Creek turns north off the Big Creek Trail 3.3 miles from the trailhead. The trail first runs through forest burned in 2000 and then forest burned in 1986.

From this junction (5,040 feet), the Chamberlain Trail follows the east side of Beaver Creek. After going through talus and shrubs near the creek, the path climbs above the creek to a junction at 1.5 miles with the Estep Trail, which climbs 4 miles to the Ramey Ridge Trail.

From the Estep junction, the Chamberlain trail winds in and out of dry gullies and across talus to Mulligan Creek at 2.4 miles. Beyond the creek, a campsite sits on a high grassy flat. After passing under cliffs, the route crosses Beaver Creek to the west side at 2.8 miles.

There are three timber bridges over Beaver Creek along here, but their locations vary from the creek crossings shown on the topographic map. Beyond the first crossing of the creek, the trail climbs a steep wooded hillside, fords two small side streams and at 3.5 miles returns to the east side of the creek near a campsite.

Beyond a talus slope, the trail crosses the creek again to the west side at a narrow flat at 4.2 miles. At 4.3 miles, the trail crosses Clark Creek, then climbs 200 feet opposite short cliffs. At 6.2 miles, the track drops to the confluence of Beaver Creek and Hand Creek. Here it fords Beaver Creek to the east side.

A little history: James Hand worked the first claim in the Big Creek District, at the confluence of these creeks, where he built the cabins of Hand Camp in 1893. On Coin Creek, Hand discovered the Golden Hand Mine, where he put in three shafts, a steam-powered stamp mill, a bunkhouse and cabins and mined for 50 years.

The trail winds away from the creek to a junction and the site of Hand Camp (5,836 feet) at 6.5 miles. From this junction a trail leads west 4.7 miles past the Golden Hand Mine to the road and wilderness boundary at Pueblo Summit. Straight ahead, a primitive trail in poor shape after the first mile follows Beaver Creek for 7 miles to the Mosquito Ridge Trail south of Mosquito Springs. Take the Chamberlain Trail to the right (northeast) up Hand Creek.

At 200 yards is a junction with the Ramey Cutoff Trail (also called Mahan Trail) that climbs 3 miles to the Ramey Ridge Trail. At 7.2 miles, the Chamberlain Trail goes across an unnamed creek, then crosses Hand Creek at 8 miles and ascends a hillside well above the creek. At 9 miles is a helmet-shaped outcrop on the opposite canyon wall, and at 10 miles the route returns to the creek across from 200-foot cliffs.

After crossing a side creek beyond the cliffs, the path continues up Hand Creek. At a campsite at the head of a meadow at 10.9 miles, the trail leaps the creek. At 11 miles, .2 mile before a trail turns west to go 4.3 miles through Crane Meadows to Cow Corrals, the trail turns east. It no longer goes to Hand Meadows as shown on the topographic map and described in the first edition of the book. Instead it joins the Ramey Ridge Trail at the Ramey Meadows junction on Ramey Ridge in a four-way intersection at 12.8 miles. Here the Ramey Ridge Trail becomes the Chamberlain Trail and circles Hand Meadows well to the east.

94.

Chamberlain Trail: Ramey Ridge to Chamberlain Guard Station

Round trip: 50 miles
Elevation gain: 2,760 feet; elevation loss (return climb): 2,890 feet
This section one way: 8.5 miles; elevation loss (return climb): 2,030 feet
Highest point: 7,680 feet
Topographic maps: Mosquito Peak, Lodgepole Creek, Meadow of Doubt
Trailhead GPS: N 45 9' 14.9" W 115 18' 12.1" at beginning of Big Creek trail
Time: 6 days; difficulty: strenuous
Access: See Big Creek Trail: Big Creek to Monumental Bar and Chamberlain Trail: Big Creek to Ramey Ridge to go by trail to the Ramey Ridge - Ramey Meadows junction, where this description begins.

What you will see: From the Ramey Ridge-Ramey Meadows junction, the trail descends more than 2,000 feet through lodgepoles, Douglas firs and burnt snags to the vast meadows surrounding the Chamberlain Guard Station. The meadows are enclosed by dark green and feathery gray hills. In season, pale green elk thistle, blue littleflower penstemon and golden shrubby cinquefoil grow here. Although the landing field may hold several planes, elk and deer use the trails in Chamberlain Basin far more often than humans bad stock do.

Directions: From Ramey Ridge, the Chamberlain Trail first circles the east side of Hand Meadows at a distance from it to a junction with the old trail south to Hand Meadows at 1.5 miles. From this junction, which may no longer be noticeable, the main trail curves around the head of a ravine down to a stream. This stream is the last water source until Chamberlain Creek near the landing field. Then the trail climbs a hill to its high point at 2.5 miles, where the mountains behind Cold Meadows stand out blue in the distance. It then drops to a four-way junction at 3.5 miles. Here, the primitive Lodgepole Meadows Trail goes east 7 miles to the Cold Meadows Trail near Lodgepole Point. The Three Blaze Trail goes left (west) 3.5 miles through Moose Jaw Meadows to the Smokehouse ruins, but from there to the Fish Lake Trail is no longer maintained.

From this junction, the Chamberlain Trail descends the ridge and at 4.5 miles makes a long switchback. Soon Little Lodgepole Creek, a water source, is within 200 yards of the trail. At 6.2 miles, the route drops over the end of the ridge.

The trail levels at 8.2 miles beside a wooded knoll, and at 8.5 miles, a trail from Chamberlain to Cold Meadows (22.2 miles) turns east. (This route to Cold Meadows avoids the ford and marsh shown on the topographic map at the Hotzel Ranch.) Just beyond the junction, the Chamberlain Trail plunges into a willow marsh, then bridges Chamberlain Creek. The path climbs a low rise to the landing strip and campsites at

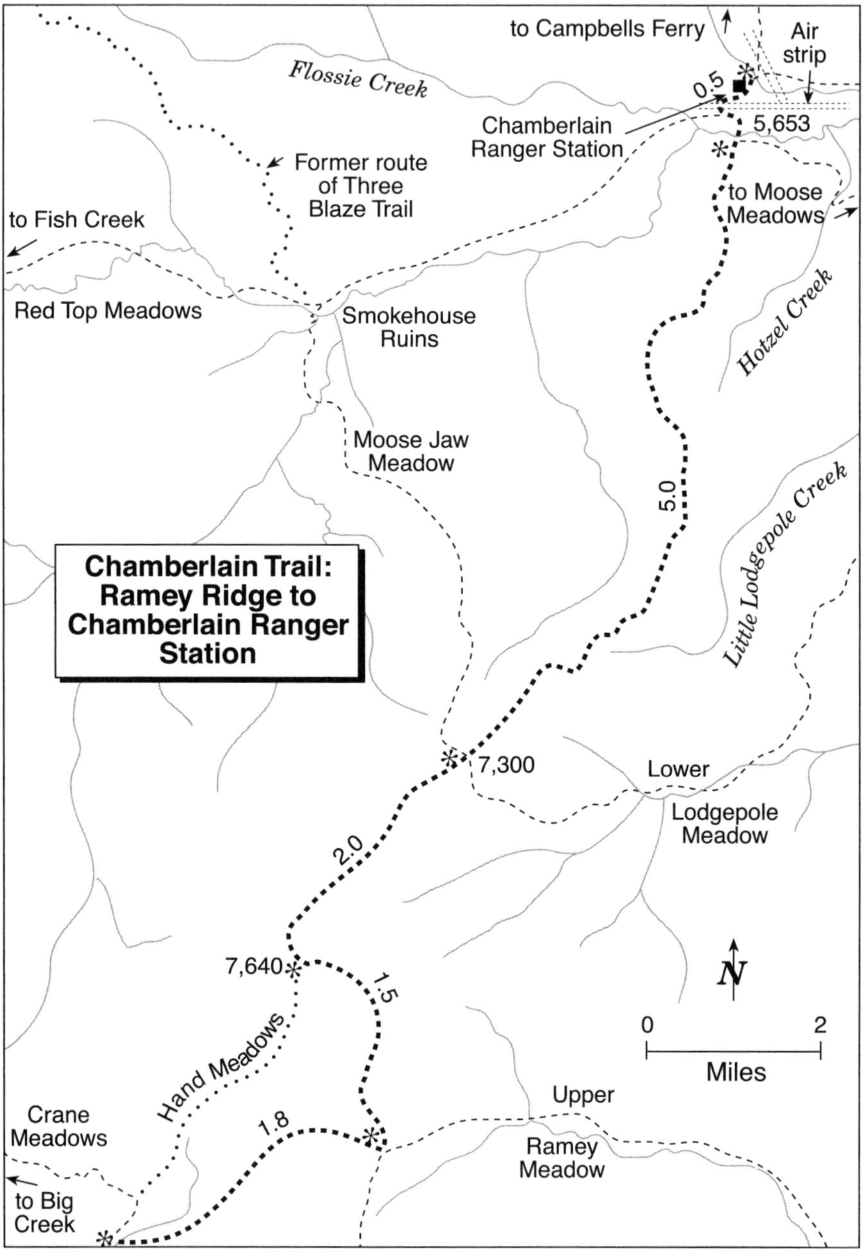

8.7 miles.

To reach the guard station, take the left (west) path when the trail reaches a T-shaped intersection at the top of the hill. Go through the gate at the campground onto the landing field and, while watching for planes, walk along the field to the guard station at 9 miles. At the T, the path to the right leads to additional developed campsites. Another large campsite is across the airstrip from the guard station. The trail past that campsite to the Hotzel Ranch leads to the Chamberlain Creek Trail, which runs 18.5 miles down to the Salmon River.

A little history: This guard station and airstrip are the center of what is called Chamberlain Basin. The basin is about 600 square miles of rolling forest and meadows located between the Middle and South Forks of the Salmon River and north of Big Creek. It was named for John Chamberlain, a trapper who was the first to settle here in 1885.

The first Europeans to see Chamberlain Basin were trappers from the Rocky Mountain Fur Company who are said to have trapped beaver on Chamberlain Creek in the winter of 1831. During the gold rushes of the 1850s and 1870s, miners exploring the Chamberlain Basin found several placer deposits.

Early settlers in the Chamberlain area were W.A. Stonebraker in 1908, August Hotzel in 1915, and George Stonebraker in 1916. Others settling nearby were Erb and Jess Root on Whimstick Creek at the site of the Root Ranch in 1893, Ralph Davis at Moose Meadows in 1918 and R.A. Wallingford on McCall a Creek in 1915.

Chamberlain Basin was part of the Payette National Forest when it was established in 1905, and in 1906 a log ranger station was built there by the first Chamberlain ranger, David Laing. Homesteaders here provided beef for the Thunder Mountain miners, but when the miners left, cattle raising was no longer profitable.

The present log buildings for the Chamberlain Guard Station were constructed in 1939, the landing field in 1940 and the northwest runway in 1954. To build this runway, a Caterpillar bulldozer was brought in overland.

95.

Flossie Lake

Round trip: 12 miles from Chamberlain (add 50 miles to go to and from Chamberlain by trail.)

Elevation gain: 1,450 feet; elevation loss (return climb): 80 feet

Highest point: 7,026 feet

Topographic maps: Lodgepole Creek, Meadow of Doubt, Sheepeater Mountain

Trailhead GPS: at Chamberlain Guard Station N 45 22' 30.8" W 115 11' 56.3"

Time: 8.5 hours from Chamberlain plus 6 days to go to and from Chamberlain; difficulty: strenuous

Access: See Big Creek Trail: Big Creek to Monumental Bar and Chamberlain Trail: Big Creek to Ramey Ridge and Ramey Ridge to Chamberlain Guard Station to go by trail (or air) to Chamberlain Guard Station, where this description begins.

What you will see: In late afternoon, above dark green Flossie Lake the sun shines through lime-green aspens below a 300-foot gray cliff. Below, ridges of burned trees, brush and granite boulders enclose the other sides of the oval lake. Near the inlet, a grassy point thrusts into the water. Around the lake and along the trail in July, yellow false lupine colors open areas. This hike description begins at Chamberlain Guard Station, which can be reached by 25 miles of trail from the Big Creek trailhead. The whole area from Chamberlain to Flossie Lake burned in 2000.

Directions: From Chamberlain, 200 yards north of the guard station, cross the landing field to the east side and take a primitive road north. On a sandy hill at .5 mile, turn left (west) uphill on a trail, 200 yards before a signed junction. From here, the Chamberlain Trail continues 23 miles down to Campbells Ferry on the Salmon River. Turn west at the junction onto the Flossie Lake Trail, which runs along Ranch Creek.

At 1.2 miles, an unsigned path from the Stonebraker Ranch meets the trail at a meadow. At 1.8 miles, the main trail crosses a branch of Ranch Creek. Beyond another meadow, it goes west across two more branches of the creek at 2.5 miles. After zigzagging up a lodgepole ridge, at 3 miles the path levels and at 4 miles you can look out to the north. The next definite landmark is a lily pond or marsh at 5.5 miles. After circling the north side of the pond, the trail cuts through burned spruces and subalpine firs above a field of boulders to the lake (7,026 feet) at 6 miles. Most of the lakeshore is too steep for camping.

96.

Fish Lake From Flossie Lake

Loop trip: 20.5 miles from Chamberlain by way of Flossie Lake and returning down Chamberlain Creek. (Add 50 miles round trip to go to and from Chamberlain from Big Creek.)

Elevation gain: 2,280 feet; elevation loss (return climb): 810 feet

This section one way: 5.3 miles, 830 feet gain; elevation loss (return climb): 730 feet

Highest point: 7,856 feet

Topographic map: Sheepeater Mountain

Reached from Chamberlain Guard station:

Time: 3 - 4 days; difficulty: strenuous

Access: See Big Creek Trail: Big Creek to Monumental Bar and Chamberlain Trail: Big Creek to Ramey Ridge and Ramey Ridge to Chamberlain Guard Station to go by trail to Chamberlain Guard Station, then by trail to Flossie Lake, where this description begins.

What you will see: At Fish Lake, two streams meander through a wildflower meadow over honey-colored sand. A grayed backdrop of partly burned ridges contrasts with the brilliant greens of the marsh and the cobalt blue of the half-mile-long lake.

A little history: Part of the route from Flossie Lake to Fish Lake is on the historic Three Blaze Trail. It was constructed by miners in the Thunder Mountain gold rush.

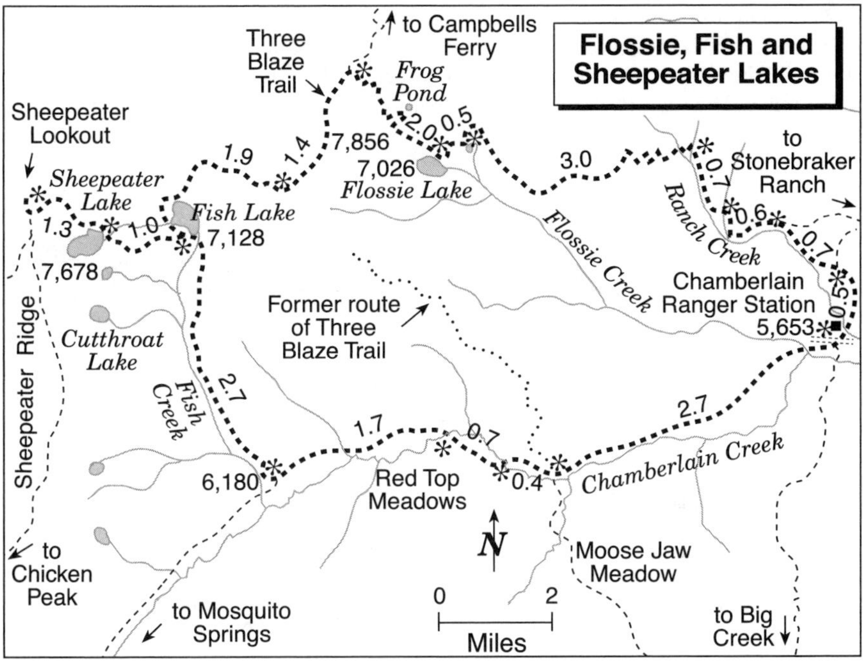

This trail was built in 1900 when miners, packers and businessmen contributed $3,000 to pay William Campbell, Bill Stonebraker, Harry Donahue and August Hotzel to construct a trail from Campbell's Ferry on the Salmon River through Chamberlain Basin to the Thunder Mountain mines. As counted by Jim Moore, who lived at the ferry, 1,800 men used this trail from 1900 to 1902. To keep the large number of tenderfeet using it from getting lost, it was marked with distinctive blazes of three squares in a column. Most of it is still in use today, but few, if any of the unique blazes remain, since most of the area along the trail burned in the Flossie/Three Bears Fire of 2000.

Above Flossie Lake (7,026 feet), the trail zigzags up the canyon of the inlet. At .7 mile, it turns left (west) past a pond known as Frog Pond, and at 1 mile circles left of a small meadow. The trail hairpins up a 200-foot ridge to a view of ridges and snow-covered peaks. At 2 miles, the trail intersects the Three Blaze Trail. From here, the Three Blaze Trail goes north and south. To the north it follows Highline Ridge, then descends to Wet Meadows at 5.3 miles.

Take the Three Blaze Trail south along the top of Highline Ridge to a junction at 3.4 miles with the Fish Lake Trail (also called the Flossie Cutoff). The Three Blaze Trail used to continue southeast 4.5 miles to cabin ruins called the Smokehouse, but this section is no longer maintained.

Take the Fish Lake Trail to the right (west) down the side of a ridge, which curves south at 4.2 miles, where it passes paths that go to Upper Trout Creek meadows. After descending toward Fish Lake, the trail turns west at 4.6 miles and circles the lake well above it, crossing several streams, including two large ones at 4.8 miles. Beyond these, a path drops to campsites near the lakeshore at 7,128 feet.

The main trail continues around the lake to a junction with the trail to Sheepeater Lake at 5.3 miles. Just east of this junction, another path leads to campsites at the shore. At the junction, the left (east) trail descends Fish Creek to Chamberlain Creek at 2.7 miles. The right (west) branch climbs 1 mile to Sheepeater Lake (7,678 feet).

97.

Sheepeater Lake and Lookout From Chamberlain Guard Station

Round trip: 22 miles from Chamberlain Guard Station (add 50 miles for reaching Chamberlain.)

Elevation gain: 2,950 feet; elevation loss (return climb): 120 feet

Highest point: 8,486 feet

Topographic maps: Lodgepole Creek, Mosquito Peak, Sheepeater Mountain

Trailhead GPS at Chamberlain Guard Station: N 45 33' 30.8" W 115 11' 56.4"

Time: 2 to 3 days plus 6 days for round trip to Chamberlain; difficulty: strenuous

Access: See Big Creek Trail: Big Creek to Monumental Bar and Chamberlain Trail: Big Creek to Ramey Ridge and Ramey Ridge to Chamberlain Guard Station to go by trail (or air) to Chamberlain, where this description begins.

What you will see: Above blue-green Sheepeater Lake, a row of cliffs sweeps to the talus cap of Sheepeater Mountain, where the lookout perches on orange rocks. Beargrass growing along the rocky ridge resembles splashes of green paint. As seen from the summit, the once-dark green rug of wooded hills is now patched with the silver, black and rust of burned trees. To the northwest is the dark blue and gray abyss of the Main Salmon River. Below, the bright blue platters of Sheepeater and Fish lakes brighten the somber landscape.

This route is 2 miles shorter than the one by way of Flossie Lake but not as scenic. Except for Red Top Meadows, which burned in 1990, the whole area from Chamberlain to Sheepeater Lake burned in 2000 in the Flossie/Three Bears Fire.

Directions: From the landing field at Chamberlain, take a trail west along the south side of the strip. Turn left (southwest) toward Red Top Meadows and cross Flossie Creek .5 mile from the guard station. After leading through forest and bogs, the trail circles a steep hill at 2 miles. At 3.2 miles, it crosses the Three Blaze Trail at the Smokehouse ruins. The "Smokehouse" was one of two way stations on the Three Blaze Trail. The other was called Shake Cabin, and it was near Wet Meadows.

At 3.6 miles, where the trail fords the creek, you will probably want to find a footlog. The route returns to the north side of the creek in a marsh at 4.3 miles. It crosses a side steam near two campsites at 5.3 miles, then edges the north side of Red Top Meadows.

A 6 miles is a junction with a trail north up Fish Creek. The trail along Chamberlain

Footlog on trail from Chamberlain Guard Station to Sheepeater Lake

Creek continues southwest along the creek and its south fork 10.3 miles to Mosquito Springs. Take the trail to the north, which zigzags up the canyon wall into the canyon of Fish Creek. At 8.5 miles, it turns west, crosses Fish Creek on logs, and passes a path to the shore of Fish Lake. At 8.7 miles is the Fish Lake - Sheepeater Lake junction. Near here, several paths reach the edge of Fish Lake.

To reach Sheepeater Lake, take the west branch of the trail up a wooded hillside. At 9.4 miles, a blazed trail leads left (south) to a small unnamed lake at 7,560 feet. From here, you can go south .5 mile cross-country to Cutthroat Lake.

After crossing the outlet at 9.6 miles, the trail reaches 7,678-foot Sheepeater Lake at 9.7 miles. Camping is uncomfortable because of beargrass.

Above the north side of Sheepeater Lake, the trail to the lookout follows a ridge of granite benches west, then cuts southwest above cliffs to a junction at 1 mile with the trail south along Sheepeater Ridge to Chicken Peak. To reach Sheepeater Lookout, take the other trail at the junction north .3 mile to the lookout (8,486 feet).

From the junction, the trail south to Chicken Peak climbs 8.5 miles along Sheepeater Ridge. About .2 mile south of the junction, a primitive, little-used trail that goes partway to Lemhi Point turns off to the west. Near this junction James Hand located the gold of the Sheepeater Claim in 1932. When H.G. Weber relocated the claim in 1949, he discovered silver, lead and zinc as well.

98.

Chamberlain Guard Station to Moose Meadows

Round trip: 19 miles from Chamberlain (add 50 miles round trip to go to and from Chamberlain)

Elevation gain: 1,640 feet; elevation loss (return climb): 1,300 feet

Highest point: 6,774 feet

Topographic maps: Lodgepole Creek, Wapiti Creek

Trailhead GPS at Chamberlain: N 45 22' 30.8" W 115 11' 56.4"

Time: 2 days from Chamberlain; 8 days from Big Creek; difficulty: strenuous

Access: See Big Creek Trail: Big Creek to Monumental Bar and Chamberlain Trail: Big Creek to Ramey Ridge and Ramey Ridge to Chamberlain Guard Station or arrange to be flown to Chamberlain Guard Station, where this description begins.

What you will see: Below wooded ridges, yellow-flowered shrubby cinquefoil brightens the green expanse of Moose Meadows around a large island of trees. In the meadows, McCalla and Moose Jaw creeks flow over golden sand and lacy water plants. This description begins at the bridge over Chamberlain Creek south of the ranger station, which can be reached by 24.5 miles of trail from the Big Creek trailhead. The whole area from Chamberlain to Moose Meadows burned in 2000.

Directions: On the south side of the bridge .5 mile south of the guard station, turn east onto a trail toward Cold Meadows. (Another trail goes east from the ranger station past the Hotzel Ranch and across a marsh to the Cold Meadows Trail, but it has no bridge over Chamberlain Creek.)

From the bridge, the trail enters woods, crosses a narrow meadow at 1 mile, skirts a hill and turns south up Hotzel Creek. After crossing this creek at 1.4 mile, it goes north, then at 1.6 miles, turns east over a hill to cross an unnamed creek and join the trail from the Hotzel Ranch at 2 miles.

Turn right (south) here on the main trail, cross the creek and climb to a saddle at 2.7 miles. The trail drops into the canyon of Little Lodgepole Creek and crosses it at 4.3 miles and Lodgepole Creek at 4.8 miles amid a splash of red paintbrush. (The primitive Lodgepole Meadow Trail turns southwest just after Little Lodgepole Creek to go 7 miles to the Chamberlain Trail above Lower Lodgepole Meadow.

After zigzagging 900 feet up a ridge to a saddle at 6.3 miles, the trail follows McCalla Ridge. At 7.6 miles is a sign for water to the south at the upper end of Pole Creek. Moose Meadows Point (6,774 feet) with its outcrops, is at 8.2 miles. The trail zigzags downhill, climbs onto a second small ridge, drops again to a sagebrush knoll with a view of Moose Meadows (6,000 feet) and at 9.5 miles reaches a junction in the meadows.

From this junction the McCalla Creek Trail goes southwest for 4 miles to Haypress Meadows. The trail going north descends 11.7 miles along McCalla Creek to the Chamberlain Creek Trail near the Salmon River. From the junction take the trail straight ahead (southeast), which crosses Moose Jaw Creek and goes out into Moose Meadows, where its path tends to disappear.

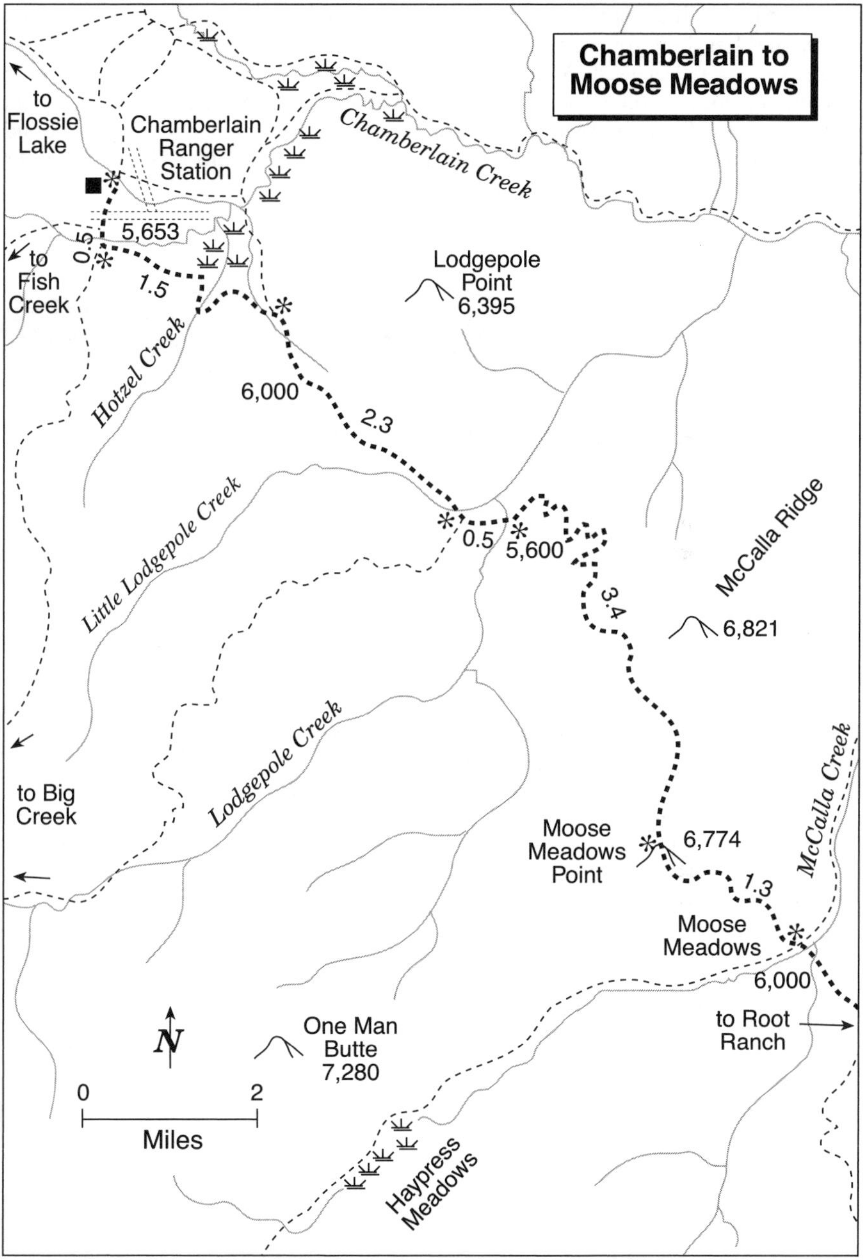

A little history: Down McCalla Creek about six miles used to stand the McCoy cabin, built by Walter McCoy and his brother Sam about 1905 as a homestead cabin. Sometime in the 1920s, after Sam moved to the Salmon River, Walter obtained a duplicate key to the Chamberlain Ranger Station and for about five years wintered on supplies left there for early spring use by rangers. To stop this, the rangers left no supplies in the fall of 1928. When McCoy came to the station, he left an angry note demanding "his" supplies and stole tents and other items. After he found the note, Ranger Dan LeVan hunted McCoy for three days by airplane. When McCoy was found he came along peacefully, but kept complaining that the "Pitchfork Gang" was after him and was committed to the asylum in Orofino.

99.

Moose Meadows to Cold Meadows

Round trip: 44.6 miles from Chamberlain (add 50 miles to go to and from Chamberlain)

Elevation gain: 4,620 feet; elevation loss (return climb): 3,360 feet

This section: 12.8 miles one way, 2,980 feet gain; elevation loss (return climb): 2,060 feet

Highest point: 7,480 feet

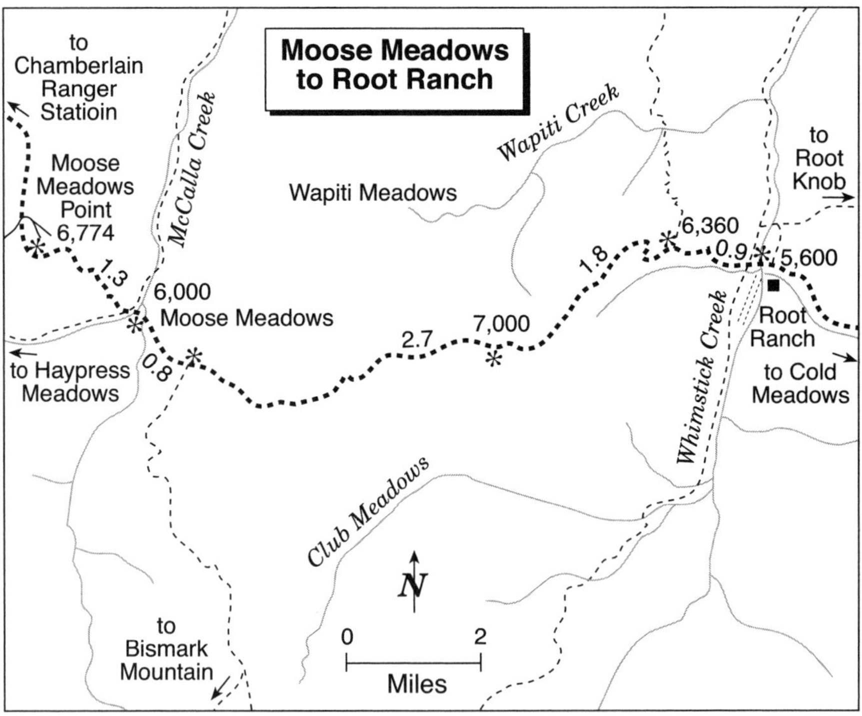

Topographic maps: Wapiti Creek, Cold Meadows
Reached from Chamberlain Guard Station:

Time: 4 days from Chamberlain plus 6 days to go to and from Chamberlain; difficulty: strenuous

Access: See Big Creek Trail: Big Creek to Monumental Bar, Chamberlain Trail: Big Creek to Ramey Ridge and Ramey Ridge to Chamberlain Guard Station, and Chamberlain Guard Station to Moose Meadows to go by trail to Moose Meadows, where this description begins.

Whimstick Creek below Root Ranch (photo by Stuart Fuller)

What you will see: In July, blue littleflower penstemon and yellow cinquefoil dapple the green in 2.5-mile-long Cold Meadows. Marking the landing strip is a fluorescent orange windsock, and the old log guard station hides in the trees at the edge of the meadows. Halfway between Moose and Cold meadows, the log buildings of the Root Ranch flank the west side of a long, narrow meadow and landing strip. Bordering the east side of this meadow is sparkling Whimstick Creek, named in 1912 for its large number of willows, which made good water-witching sticks. From Moose Meadows to the Root Ranch, the trail goes through forest burned in 2000; from there to Cold Meadows is a 1988 burn.

A little history: After settling on Whimstick Creek in 1893 with his father Erb, Jesse Root received a patent for the homestead in 1919. After he drowned in the Salmon River in 1935, movie actor Wallace Beery acquired the ranch in 1938. He had the airstrip constructed and let the Forest Service use it for fire control. However, he didn't pay the taxes on it, and Raleigh Campbell of the Circle C Ranch in New Meadows bought it for the $417 due. After two other owners, Howard Elkins and Ruth Vernon, the Flying B Ranch Company acquired it.

The airstrip at Cold Meadows was established in 1933, and the Forest Service built seven buildings there of peeled lodgepole pine logs beginning in 1913.

Directions: This description begins at Moose Meadows, which can be reached by a 9.5 mile trail from Chamberlain airstrip. In Moose Meadows (6,000 feet), there is often no tread where the trail crosses the meadows. The route goes southeast, crossing McCalla Creek, then skirts the meadow on the left. Near the south end of the meadow is a campsite on a wooded knoll that resembles an island of trees. There are no other campsites until the Root Ranch due to steep ground along the creeks and no water in

Cold Meadows

the level areas. At .5 mile, the trail heads up a branch of McCalla Creek and at .8 mile passes the primitive Bismark Mountain Trail, which goes south 12.2 miles to Big Creek. A second section of Moose Meadows with a beaver pond is at 1.5 miles. The path climbs the creek to a 7,000-foot ridge at 3.5 miles. From clearings there are glimpses of furrowed mountains beyond Cold Meadows. At 5.3 miles is a junction with a four-mile primitive trail north to Wapiti Creek.

The main trail descends a branch of Whimstick Creek to a four-way junction near the Root Ranch (5,600 feet) at 6.2 miles. From here, a trail goes south 7.7 miles to Club Meadows, Silver Creek and Crescent Meadows. A trail to the north leads 4.9 miles down Whimstick Creek to the McCalla Creek Trail. The best campsite at the Root Ranch is at the edge of an east branch of the meadow, .5 mile north of the ranch.

To go on to Cold Meadows, cross the landing strip to the east side on the trail. On the far side, the trail splits. A trail to the north goes 2.3 miles to the Dismal Ridge Trail on the side of Root Knob. Take the trail going east up a branch of Whimstick Creek. It curves away from the creek and then back to it in sagebrush at 7 miles. After turning left (north) below scattered rocks at 8 miles, it ascends an intermittent stream. Then it climbs a ridge above the creek's canyon.

At 9.1 miles is a junction with the Dismal Ridge Trail, also called the Dismal-Starvation Trail, which goes 4.5 miles to the Grass Mountain Trail on Dismal Creek. Keep on the Cold Meadows Trail, which climbs to a ridge top (7,240 feet) at 9.5 miles and then to a saddle. The East Fork of Whimstick Creek and Dismal Creek provide nearby water. Beyond a high point of 7,470 feet at 11 miles, the trail descends the ridge to 6,960-foot Cold Meadows at 12 miles.

The main trail goes south along the meadows to a junction at 12.8 miles. Here, the Cold Meadows Trail continues 16.3 miles south up Cottonwood Creek and down Crooked Creek to Big Creek at Monumental Bar. Another trail from Cold Meadows goes from this junction 13.2 miles past the Cold Meadows Guard Station to Runaway

Ridge and the Disappointment Trail at Hungry Creek.

When fire overran Cold Meadows in 1988, the forest technicians at the guard station had to be rescued by helicopter, but a wind shift kept the station from burning. A horse party that had camped in the meadows escaped by abandoning their gear and riding away bareback. Between the junction and the guard station, the Cottonwood Creek Trail turns southeast to Middle and Lower meadows, giving access to Black Lake, 10.7 miles from Cold Meadows.

100.

Cold Meadows to Black Lake

Round trip: 21.4 miles from Cold Meadows (plus 58 miles to go to and from Cold Meadows from Big Creek via Crooked Creek, the shortest route)

Elevation gain: 1,060 feet; elevation loss (return climb): 1,200 feet

Highest point: 6,882 feet

Topographic maps: Cold Meadows, Cottonwood Butte

Trailhead GPS at Cold Meadows: N 45 17' 8.6" W 114 36' 32.4"

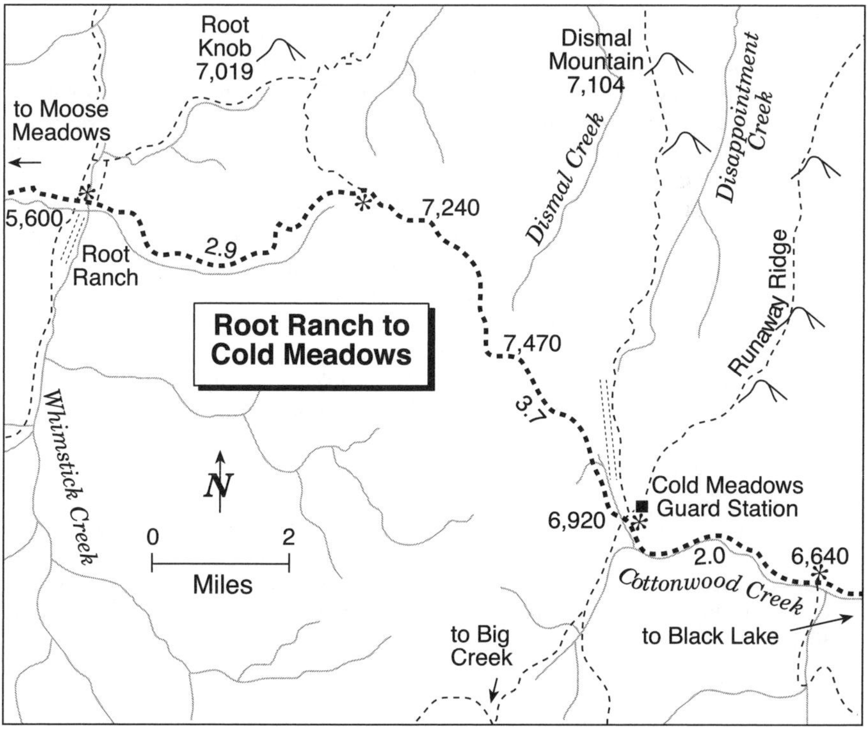

Time: 2 to 3 days plus 10 days to go to and from Cold Meadows by trail; difficulty: strenuous

Access: Go by air to Cold Meadows or see Big Creek Trail: Big Creek to Monumental Bar to go by trail to Cold Meadows, where this description begins.

What you will see: A 1,500-foot bluff of dark gray ledges shadows the east side of Black Lake. From the trail above the 3/4-mile-long lake, the water appears brownish-green, but from the shore, it is dull blue. Any wind starts a circular parade of floating logs. Along the trail, Middle Meadows and Lower Meadows are so large that haze blues the ridges surrounding them. Most of the way to Black Lake the trail goes through recent burns.

Directions: Black Lake can also be reached in 28.5 miles by using the Stoddard and Cottonwood Butte trails.

The trail, signed Cottonwood Creek, leads south from the Cold Meadows guard station past a turnoff for Runaway Ridge. At .4 mile, it turns left (east) along Cottonwood Creek. When the meadows end at .5 mile, snags, willows and grassy flats begin. At .7 mile, the trail goes across the creek and back again on logs. At 2 miles is a junction with the Coyote Spring Trail, which goes 20.3 miles south over Black Butte to Big Creek at Cabin Creek, passing Coyote Spring at 6 miles.

The trail to Black Lake crosses a side creek at 2.7 miles and the upper end of Middle Meadows at 3 miles. It edges the left (west) side of the meadows, through boggy places. At each of three arms of the meadow, an early-season path detours up the arm to avoid a bog and access a campsite.

At 4.5 miles, the trail fords Cottonwood Creek to the east side, then climbs 2,250 feet over a saddle and down to cross Farrow Creek at 5.3 miles. At 5.7 miles, it descends into Lower Meadow (6,320 feet), then fords both Farrow Creek and Cottonwood Creek at 6 miles. The route follows posts north-northeast across the meadow. At the edge of the meadow, keep right as a dead-end trail turns left. At 6.2 miles, where the Black Lake Trail goes right (southeast), the Cottonwood Creek Trail continues north 3 miles to the Runaway Ridge Trail at Hungry Creek Point.

Continue on the Black Lake Trail, which fords a side stream at 6.3 miles, then passes a turnoff to the right (southeast) at 6.4 miles to Farrow Mountain. The Farrow Mountain Trail goes 9 miles over the side of Farrow Mountain to Coyote Spring near Papoose Lake. Keep straight ahead on the main trail on the left (northwest) side of Cottonwood Creek along a boulder field. After fording the creek to the east side at 6.7 miles, the trail wades back again at 7 miles. At 7.3 miles is a campsite on a grassy flat. The trail ascends past outcrops, then at 8 miles returns to the creek in a mud hole. At 8.1 miles, it crosses Cottonwood Creek to the east side one last time.

From here the trail goes under a rock gargoyle and up a side stream, which it crosses at 8.3 miles. Then it zigzags up a lodgepole hillside. On a level part of the ridge is a four-way intersection; keep straight ahead here. (The side trails here are not on any maps.) The main trail curves gradually to the right at the edge of a lodgepole thicket and at 9.7 miles (7,120 feet) looks down on Black Lake. It descends rocks above the lake to the south shore at 10.7 miles (6,438 feet). Large campsites are in the forest 200 to 300 yards south, up the inlet.

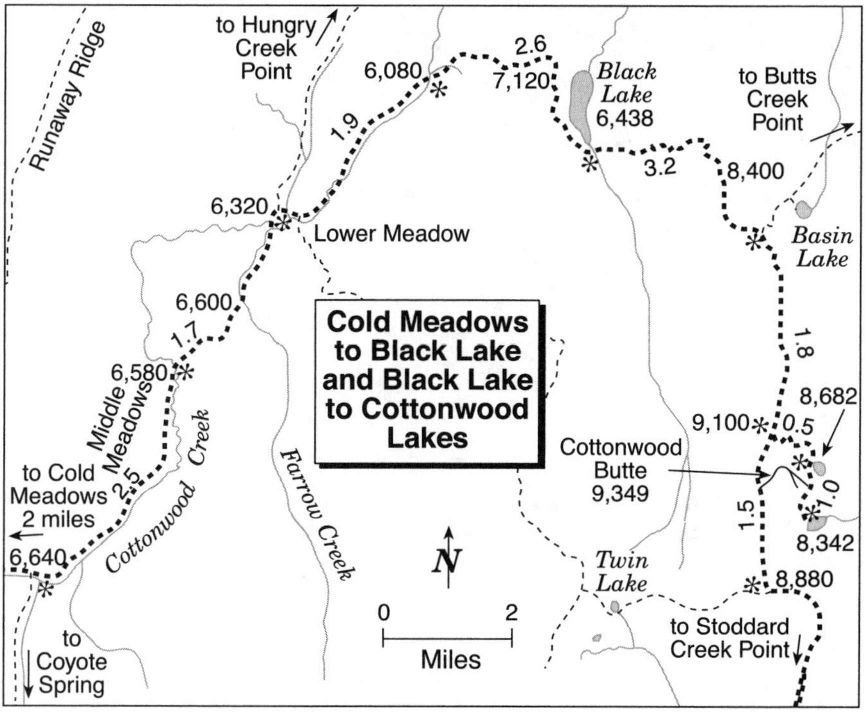

101.

Black Lake to Cottonwood Lakes

Round trip: 34.4 miles from Cold Meadows (add 58 miles to go to and from Cold Meadows from Big Creek via Crooked Creek, the shortest route)

Elevation gain: 4,040 feet; elevation loss (return climb): 2,280 feet

This section one way: 6.5 miles, 2,980 feet gain; elevation loss (return climb): 1,080 feet

Highest point: 9,120 feet

Topographic map: Cottonwood Butte Reached from Cold Meadows

Time: 7 hours for this section, one way; difficulty: strenuous

Access: See Cold Meadows to Black Lake to go by trail to Black Lake where this description begins

What you will see: East of Cottonwood Butte, an inlet ribbons through alpine wildflowers and beside knobby whitebark pines into an unnamed lake. White talus and gray ledges slope from its shallow green water to the gentle top of the butte. Southeast of the butte below a row of crumbled cliffs, the dark green water of Cottonwood Lake mirrors green-black woods.

Trail at Aparejo Point along the Middle Fork of the Salmon River during high water (see Middle Fork Salmon River: Flying B to Loon Creek)

Directions: From Black Lake (6,438 feet) where this description begins, the trail runs south along the inlet 300 yards, then begins zigzagging up into lodgepoles, rocks and a grassy area. At 1 mile, it climbs a spur, then at 2.2 miles, turns southeast along a furrow on the side of the ridge and goes up to the top of it. After dropping to a notch at 2.5 miles with a view of the Salmon River Canyon, it climbs to 8,400 feet. At 2.8 miles, the trail curves east down the end of the ridge with a view of Basin Lake, which divides forest from a boulder field. At a saddle at 3.2 miles, a good trail leads .5 mile down to Basin Lake (7,688 feet) to the northeast and continues 10.5 miles down to the Salmon River near Horse Creek.

To reach the Cottonwood Lakes, take the main trail south from the saddle up a ridge. At 4 miles, it levels on an open slope of white talus at 8,960 feet with a view of Black Lake below.

An unmarked junction with an informal trail to both Cottonwood Lakes is below a notch at 5 miles. Turn left (east) here and zigzag 300 feet down to the upper lake (8,682 feet) at 5.5 miles.

To reach the lower lake, marked Cottonwood Lake on the topographic map, follow a path from the west end of the upper lake. It climbs above the lake over a 200-foot ridge (8,680 feet) at 6 miles. Then it winds 500 feet down to the lower lake (8,342 feet) at 6.5 miles.

APPENDIX

NOTES ON SELECTED OTHER TRAILS AND ROUTES

In the hike descriptions, as side trails are passed, information is given about them in the text. With such a large number of trails and a huge area to cover, inaccuracies are difficult to eliminate. Some of the trails have never been logged (measured with a wheel on the ground). Some of the existing logs are inaccurate because it is difficult for those doing the calculations to keep from substituting the mileposts for the distances between them. Information on trails not covered in detail that are listed below has been provided by district rangers and forest technicians.

SALMON - CHALLIS NATIONAL FOREST: MIDDLE FORK RANGER DISTRICT

SEAFOAM AREA

BERNARD CREEK – Access: Beaver Creek - Loon Creek Road. From that road to Duffield Creek Trail .5 mile east of Sheep Mountain Road. 5 miles, elevation loss (return climb): 1,240 feet. **Topographic maps:** Pinyon Peak, Greyhound Mountain.

HARDSCRABBLE – Access: From primitive, private Greyhound Mine Road near Josephus Lake. From Greyhound Mine over Greyhound Mountain, down Hardscrabble Creek to Rapid River. Rough trail, 9 miles, 560 feet gain, elevation loss (return climb) 4,020 feet. **Topographic maps:** Soldier Creek, Greyhound Mountain, Little Soldier Mountain.

LITTLE SOLDIER LOOKOUT – Access: Sheep Mountain or Rapid River Road. From junction with Lake Creek Trail to Little Soldier Lookout. 1 mile, 800 feet gain. **Topographic map:** Little Soldier Mountain.

MUSKEG CREEK – Access: Josephus Lake Campground near Seafoam and Soldier Basin Trail. From Soldier Basin Trail 3 miles west of Cutthroat Lake east to the Cutthroat Lake Trail and then down Muskeg Creek to the Soldier Creek Trail about 5 miles above the Middle Fork. Rough trail. 11.5 miles, elevation loss (return climb): 1,600 feet. **Topographic map:** Soldier Creek.

SHEEP MOUNTAIN RIDGE TRAIL – 2.5 miles southeast of Little Soldier Mountain to Middle Fork Lodge. 5 miles, elevation loss (return climb): 3,200 feet. **Topographic map:** Little Soldier Mountain.

SOLDIER RIDGE – Access: Greyhound Mine Road near Seafoam. From Greyhound Mine to Middle Fork. No bridge over Middle Fork. 7 miles, 320 feet gain, elevation loss (return climb): 3,440 feet. **Topographic map:** Soldier Creek.

WEST FORK THOMAS CREEK – Access: Sheep Mountain Ridge Trail from Sheep Mountain. From Sheep Mountain Ridge Trail 2.5 mile southeast of Little Soldier Mountain to Middle Fork Lodge. 5 miles, elevation loss (return climb): 3,200

Sheepeater Hot Springs; see Middle Fork Salmon River: Boundary Creek to Artillery Creek

feet. **Topographic map:** Little Soldier Mountain.

LANDMARK AREA

BIG BALDY LOOKOUT – Access: Big Baldy Ridge trail from Burntlog Road or Pistol Creek Trail. A spur trail from the Big Baldy Ridge Trail to lookout. Primitive, steep, rocky. 1 mile, 640 feet gain. **Topographic map:** Big Baldy

KIWAH – Access: Meadow Creek Lookout Road. From Mule Hill to Kiwah Meadow on Indian Creek. Also known as Mule Hill Trail. Very steep, rough. 4 miles, elevation loss (return climb) 2,200 feet. **Topographic map:** Big Chief Creek.

LOON CREEK AREA

BLUE LAKE – Access: Beaver Creek - Loon Creek Road. From that road over ridge and down to Blue Lake and below it to Little Loon Creek. Lake has no outlet. Fair condition. 5.5 miles, 1,080 feet gain, elevation loss (return climb): 2,120 feet. **Topographic maps:** Pinyon Peak, Sliderock Ridge.

CASTLE FORK – Access: Indian Springs Road. From Loon Creek Point Trail 1 mile north of Indian Springs to Little Loon Creek Trail. Leads to Little Loon Creek. 5 miles, elevation loss (return climb): 2,040 feet. **Topographic maps:** Falconberry Peak, Sliderock Ridge.

CHINA LAKES – Access: Loon Creek Road. Trailhead shown on an old Challis forest maps is just a small campground, not a developed trailhead, but people do hike a non-system trail and then go cross-country from it to China Lakes. 4 miles, 2,000 feet. **Topographic maps:** Casto, Mount Jordan.

COUGAR CREEK – Access: Indian Springs Road. From Loon Creek Point Trail 3.5 miles northwest of Indian Springs to the east side of the Middle Fork Trail at Cougar Creek Ranch. 7 miles, elevation loss (return climb): 3,520 feet. **Topographic maps:** Falconberry Peak, Sliderock Ridge.

LITTLE LOON CREEK – Access: Indian Springs Road and Castle Fork Trail. From Sheep Mountain Ridge Trail to Middle Fork. 16 miles, elevation loss (return climb): 4,360 feet. **Topographic maps:** Sliderock Ridge, Pinyon Peak.

SLEEPING DEER AREA

BRIDGE CREEK RIDGE – Access: Sleeping Deer Road at 36-mile point. From that road to Warm Spring Creek near confluence with Loon Creek. Steep, but has switchbacks. Hard to find in brush. No water. Lightly used. 9.6 miles, 1,400 feet gain, elevation loss (return climb): 5,360 feet. **Topographic maps:** Sheldon Peak, Rock Creek.

COVE CREEK – Access: Sleeping Deer Road. From Macarte Ridge Trail to Grouse Creek Trail near Middle Fork. 3 miles, no gain, elevation loss (return climb): 4,460 feet. **Topographic maps:** Sleeping Deer, Ramey Hill.

KERR CREEK – Access: Sleeping Deer and Parker Mountain (four-wheel drive) roads. From Parker Mountain Road at Parker Mountain to Warm Spring Creek 4 miles above Showerbath Hot Springs. Mining traffic. Steep. 1.5 miles, elevation loss (return climb): 1,480 feet. **Topographic map:** Challis Creek Lakes.

FLUME CREEK - SOUTH FORK CAMAS CREEK TRAIL – Access: Meyers Cove. From 2.5-mile point of West Fork Camas Creek Trail to Liberty Creek Ridge Trail, then continues to South Fork Camas Creek. Dead-ends in hunters' camp near Liberty Creek Ridge Trail. Turnoff for Liberty Creek Ridge is .2 mile farther. Creek and bog crossings. West Fork Camas Creek to Liberty Ridge Trail: 5.3 miles, 3,680 feet gain. Liberty Ridge to South Fork Camas: 4.7 miles, 160 feet gain, elevation loss (return climb): 2,860 feet loss. **Topographic maps:** Meyers Cove, Sheldon Peak.

FLY CREEK TRAIL – Access: Sleeping Deer Road. From that road east of Fly Creek Point to South Fork Camas Creek Trail. Steep, but switchbacks. Erosion problems. Trail hard to find at trailhead. Campsites near creek crossing. 5.1 miles. 400 feet gain, elevation loss (return climb): 2,520 feet. **Topographic maps:** Sheldon Peak, White Goat Mountain

HOT CREEK – Access: Sleeping Deer Road. From Sleeping Deer Road to Warm Spring Creek Trail. Access to hot springs near junction with Warm Spring Trail. Primitive. 5.1 miles, 520 feet gain, elevation loss (return climb): 3,720 feet. **Topographic maps:** Rock Creek, Sheldon Peak.

LIBERTY CREEK RIDGE – Access: Sleeping Deer Road at 40-mile point. From Sleeping Deer Road to Flume Creek - South Fork Camas Creek Trail. Gives rough cross-country access to Liberty Lakes near trailhead. Steep, few switchbacks, narrow tread. Difficult to follow, treacherous footing. Water only at Flume Creek Trail junction, so no campsites. 7 miles, 2,240 feet gain, elevation loss (return climb): 2,320 feet. **Topographic maps:** Rock Creek, Sleeping Deer, Meyers Cove.

SOUTH FORK CAMAS CREEK TRAIL – Access: Sleeping Deer Road at 37.2-

mile point and .5-mile spur road. Closed at the Sleeping Deer end by fire that burned campground and covered trail with downed timber. Ran from former South Fork Transfer Camp to Camas-Eddy Creek Trail on Camas Creek. Overgrown, wet and swampy. Many fords. Gentle grade. Few campsites. 9.3 miles, elevation loss (return climb): 2,680 feet. **Topographic maps:** Rock Creek, Twin Peaks, Sheldon Peak

WOODTICK CUTOFF – Access: Sleeping Deer Road. From Martin Mountain Trail down to Woodtick Creek. Steep, not on topographic map. Rockslides and washouts. Rough but passable; open rocky country. Watch for wildlife. 2 miles, elevation loss (return climb): 4,200 feet. **Topographic maps:** Sleeping Deer Mountain, Aparejo Point.

NORTH FORK DISTRICT

BIGHORN CRAGS AREA

BIG DEER CREEK – Access: Bighorn Crags or Panther Creek roads. From Panther Creek to Bighorn Crags Road just east of junction with Yellowjacket Road. Primitive, poor condition, little or no maintenance. Not recommended for stock. 17 miles, 3,970 feet elevation gain. **Topographic maps:** Blackbird Mountain, Gant Mountain, Gant Ridge.

MIDDLE FORK PEAK CUTOFF – Access: Middle Fork Peak Road and spur road to campground. From campground to Camas Creek - Hoodoo Meadows Trail. Poor condition, lightly used. 1 mile, 600 feet gain. **Topographic map:** Aparejo Point.

SOUTH FORK WATERFALL CREEK – Access: Bighorn Crags and Waterfall Trails from Crags Campground. From Waterfall Trail south to dead end .1 mile west of Plateau Lake. 6.5 miles, 1,630 feet gain, elevation loss (return climb): 280 feet. Lightly used. **Topographic map:** Puddin Mountain

YELLOWJACKET – Access: road to Yellowjacket. From Yellowjacket Road 2.3 miles northwest of Yellowjacket up Yellowjacket Creek to Yellowjacket Lake Road at Frog Meadows. 9 miles, 1,590 feet gain. **Topographic maps:** Blackbird Mountain, Hoodoo Meadows.

WARM SPRING – Access: Middle Fork Peak Road and Camas Creek - Hoodoo Meadows Trail at Middle Fork Peak to Middle Fork at the northern of the two Warm Spring creeks. Coincides with Camas Creek - Hoodoo Meadows Trail for upper 2.5 miles. 7.3 miles, 80 feet gain, elevation loss (return climb): 5,360 feet. **Topographic map:** Aparejo Point.

PANTHER CREEK AREA

BIRCH CREEK – Access: Panther Creek Road. From Panther Creek Road to Gant Mountain via Squaw Camp Creek. Blocked by private property. Mostly outside of Frank Church Wilderness. Primitive; within area burned in 2000 fires. 10 miles, 4,670 feet gain. **Topographic maps:** Pine Creek Rapids, Gant Mountain

Ruffneck Peak sets a dramatic backdrop to nearby lakes (see Langer, Island and Ruffneck Lakes).

Old hotel at Yellowjacket (see Lake Creek Lakes from Middle Fork Peak)

NORTH FORK AREA

BUTTS POINT – Access: Cottonwood Butte Trail or from Corn Creek Campground by boat to Cunningham Bar. From Cottonwood Butte Trail 1.5 miles southwest of Butts Creek Point to Salmon River. 5.9 miles, 40 feet gain, elevation loss (return climb): 5,190 feet. **Topographic maps:** Cottonwood Butte, Butts Creek Point.

HORSE CREEK PASS AREA

SKUNK CAMP – Access: Long Tom Ridge and Corn Lake Roads. From Corn Lake over Skunk Camp (a hill) to Horse Creek at Colt Creek. No shade and only one spring. Partly primitive. 8.2 miles, 720 feet gain, elevation loss (return climb): 5,160 feet. **Topographic maps:** Horse Creek Butte, Square Top.

BITTERROOT NATIONAL FOREST - WEST FORK DISTRICT

ELKHORN MOUNTAIN – Access: Shoup - Elk City or Eakin Ridge trails. From Eakin Ridge Trail 1 mile north of Eakin Spring to site of Elkhorn Lookout. 3 miles,

240 feet gain, elevation loss (return climb): 160 feet loss. **Topographic maps:** Waugh Mountain , Devils Teeth Rapids.

ELKHORN SPRING – Access: Shoup - Elk City or Eakin Ridge Trail. From Elkhorn Mountain Trail .3 mile southeast of lookout to spring. .5 mile, elevation loss (return climb): 240 feet. **Topographic maps**: Devils Teeth Rapids , Waugh Mountain.

GOLD PAN CROSS COUNTRY – Access: Nez Perce Trail Road. From Kim Creek Saddle to Hells Half Acre-Salmon Mountain Trail at head of Langdon Gulch. Access to Gold Pan and Elk Track lakes in early summer before road over Salmon Mountain is open. Poor condition. 4 miles, 1,120 feet gain, elevation loss (return climb): 160 feet. **Topographic map:** Magruder Mountain.

GRASS LUNCH TRAIL – Access: Hells Half Acre Road. From Hells Half Acre - Salmon Mountain Trail to Grass Ridge Trail at head of Lunch Creek, then southeast to Grass Ridge Trail 1 mile west of Hells Half Acre Lookout. 3.8 miles, 1,720 feet gain, elevation loss (return climb): 40 feet. **Topographic map:** Beaver Jack Mountain.

HELLS HALF ACRE MOUNTAIN – Access: Hells Half Acre Road. From that road at head of Vance Creek along ridge between Lazy and Storm creeks to Divide Trail. 4 miles, 880 feet gain, elevation loss (return climb): 1,360 feet. **Topographic map:** Nez Perce Peak.

KIM CREEK – Access: Nez Perce Trail Road at Magruder Guard Station. From guard station it fords the Selway to the west side and goes around Haystack Mountain to Kim Creek Saddle. 6 miles, 2,200 feet gain, elevation loss (return climb): 400 feet. **Topographic maps:** Beaver Jack Mountain, Magruder Mountain.

LANGDON POINT – Access: Hells Half Acre Road and Hells Half Acre - Salmon Mountain Trail. From that trail west of Upper Crossing, south over Langdon Point to Goat Ridge Trail. 4 miles, 1,280 feet gain, elevation loss (return climb): 1,080 feet. **Topographic maps:** Beaver Jack Mountain, Wood Hump.

SABE CREEK – Access: Nez Perce Trail Road. From Horse Heaven Saddle on that road to Dennis Creek Trail at Hamilton Creek in canyon of Sabe Creek. Joins no trails on the Nez Perce Forest because the Ring Creek Trail stops short of Sabe Creek. No trail down Sabe Creek to Salmon River. Lightly used, poor condition. 7 miles, elevation loss (return climb): 2,740 feet. **Topographic maps:** Sabe Mountain , Dennis Mountain.

STORM CREEK – Access: Nez Perce Trail Road and Divide Trail. From Divide Trail at Two Buck Spring southwest to Wood Hump Trail 1.5 miles southeast of Wood Hump. 10 miles, 1,000 feet gain, elevation loss (return climb): 4,680 feet. **Topographic maps:** Blue Joint, Wood Hump.

STORM RIDGE – Access: Hells Half Acre Mountain Trail. From Hells Half Acre Mountain Trail 1.3 mile southeast of Hells Half Acre Road, over Devils Point, along Storm Creek Ridge and down to Storm Creek Trail at Storm Creek Flat. 9.7 miles, 880 feet gain, elevation loss (return climb): 3,160 feet. Nez Perce Peak, Blue Joint, Wood Hump.

SURPRISE CREEK – Access: Selway River or Wood Hump Trails. From Wood Hump Trail 1.5 miles southeast of Wood Hump to Selway River Trail at Stripe Creek. 6 miles, elevation loss (return climb): 800 feet. **Topographic map:** Wood Hump.

NEZ PERCE-CLEARWATER NATIONAL FOREST - RED RIVER DISTRICT

BARGAMIN CREEK – Access: Nez Perce Trail Road. From Poet Creek Campground to mouth of Bargamin Creek on the Salmon River. Area below about 6,000 feet was burned in the 2000 fires. Passes through rockslides below mouth of Cache Creek. Two fords necessary at upper end, which are hazardous before mid-July. Scenic deep canyon. Several possible day hikes on side trails. Plenty of water. 6 miles, 480 feet gain, elevation loss (return climb): 2,880 feet. **Topographic maps:** Spread Creek Point, Sheep Hill , Hida Point.

LEMHI – Access: Road to Robinson Dike Mine. From that mine to Salmon River. Good tread, easily followed, but listed as primitive trail. Steep last 3 miles, very little water. 8 miles, 800 feet gain, elevation loss (return climb): 4,380 feet. **Topographic map:** Dixie.

RABBIT POINT – Access: Rhett Creek Trail and Dixie. From Churchill Trail to Rhett Creek Trail near lookout site on Rabbit Point. Ridge trail with no major elevation change. Edge of river breaks, but no real view. Little water. 6 miles, 1,040 feet gain, elevation loss (return climb): 360 feet. **Topographic map:** Dixie.

RHETT CREEK – Access: Road to Comstock Mine. From old Comstock barn to Salmon River near Jim Moore Place. Passes within 1 mile of Rabbit Point Lookout site. Confusing junction with Rabbit Point Trail. Views of Salmon River. 11 miles, 1,060 feet gain, elevation loss (return climb): 4,280 feet. **Topographic maps:** Whitewater Ranch, Dixie.

PAYETTE NATIONAL FOREST - KRASSEL DISTRICT

SOUTH FORK OF SALMON RIVER AREA

HORSE HEAVEN – Access: By detour foot trail around the Mackay Bar property and jeep trail not open to public motorized use up South Fork of Salmon River to Badley Bridge. The South Fork Trail is not maintained beyond that point to 5 miles below the South Fork Ranch, so access is poor from the South Fork Ranch also. From just north of Badley Bridge 2.4 miles south of Mackay Bar to Horse Heaven and along Horse Heaven Ridge to junction with Chicken Peak Trail .4 mile below Chicken Spring, and then to Mosquito Springs. Climbs cheat grass hills in more than 100 switchbacks to ridge above Station Creek. Beautiful view. 14 miles, 6,680 feet gain, elevation loss (return climb): 560 feet. Climbs 5,120 feet in first 6.5 miles. **Topographic maps:** Chicken Peak, Mackay Bar

THUNDER MOUNTAIN AREA

BIG CHIEF – Access: Meadow Creek Lookout Road. From that road near the

CCC workers transplanting beaver in the Salmon National Forest

lookout down Big Chief Creek to Indian Creek Trail. Very rough, much downed timber. Access to hot spring. 5.3 miles, elevation loss (return climb): 2,080 feet. **Topographic map:** Big Chief Creek

CANYON CREEK – Access: Marble Creek and Norton Lake trails. From Marble Creek at 6-mile point, up Canyon Creek to Norton Lake Trail near Ramey Hill. Rugged, closed during high water. 4.5 miles, 2,450 feet gain. **Topographic map:** Norton Ridge.

GRAYS PEAK – Access: Indian Creek Guard Station. From Indian Creek Trail 1 mile up from Middle Fork to Grays Peak. Steep. 7.9 miles, 4,040 feet gain. **Topographic map:** Pungo Mountain

RAMEY HILL – Access: White Creek and Middle Fork Trails. From White Creek Trail near Norton Ridge to Ramey Hill. Very steep. 2.2 miles, 740 feet gain, elevation loss (return climb): 240 feet. **Topographic maps:** Ramey Hill, Norton Ridge.

TELEPHONE CREEK – Access: Monumental Creek Trail. From Lookout Mountain Ridge Trail down Telephone Creek to the Rush Creek Trail at Shellrock Creek. Primitive, lightly used., choked by brush and downed timber 4.4 miles, no gain, elevation loss: 2,480 feet. **Topographic maps:** The Monument , Safety Creek , Shellrock Peak.

BIG CREEK AREA

RUSH CREEK POINT – Access: Cabin Creek Airstrip. From Big Creek Trail .6

Pack train leaving Chamberlain with all the parts for a lookout

mile west of Cabin Creek south over a ford to Rush Creek Point. Lookout is on the National Register of Historic Lookouts. 4.7 miles, 3,000 feet gain. **Topographic maps:** Vinegar Hill, Mormon Mountain.

CHAMBERLAIN AREA

ARCTIC POINT – Access: Chamberlain Guard Station. From Chamberlain to Arctic Point. Lookout. Burned in 2000. Access to Hot Springs Meadow. 11.4 miles, 2,280 feet gain, elevation loss (return climb): 680 feet. **Topographic maps:** Meadow of Doubt, Arctic Point

DEER CREEK CUTOFF – Access: Chamberlain Guard Station or Whitewater Ranch. From Chamberlain Creek Trail at Chamberlain northeast to Stonebraker Ranch, then northwest to Arctic Point Trail south of Hot Springs Meadow. 13 miles, 2,440 feet gain, elevation loss (return climb): 1,080 feet. **Topographic maps:** Meadow of Doubt, Arctic Point.

DISAPPOINTMENT – Access: Cold Meadows Guard Station. From Grass Mountain to Runaway Ridge Trail at Hungry Creek and then down Disappointment Creek to Main Salmon River across from Lantz Bar. The Forest Service has considered building a bridge across the Salmon River here, but it probably won't happen. Disappointment Creek was once the route of a Nez Perce Trail that allowed the Indians to go south around the unnavigable section of the Salmon River from Wa-toss-pa (Mackay) Bar to the mouth of this creek, which was first called Anita Creek. 6.8 miles, no gain, elevation loss (return climb): 2,960 feet. **Topographic map:** Devils Teeth Rapids

COLD MOUNTAIN RIDGE – Access: Cold Meadows Guard Station or Cabin Creek airstrips. From Coxey Creek Trail junction at Caswell Crossing east along Cold Mountain Ridge to Coyote Springs Trail 1.5 miles west of Coyote Springs. 8.4 miles, 4,190 feet gain, elevation loss (return climb): 1,160 feet. **Topographic maps:** Vinegar Hill, Papoose Peak.

GUIDE TO HIKES

Some trails fit into more than one category; for example, a moderate hike could have some cross-country travel and would be listed under both categories.

EASY

Up to 7 miles and up to 1,000 feet elevation gain in the round trip, no cross-country travel

Golden Trout Lake: only a mile but steep and slippery
Helldiver Lake
Lookout Mountain Ridge to viewpoint
Lost Lake (non-system trail)
Pinyon Lake (scary access road)
Reynolds Lake (bad access road)
Rock Lakes (long, rocky access)
Roosevelt Lake
Sleeping Deer Lookout

MODERATE

7 to 10 miles round trip: 1000 - 2000 feet elevation gain, no cross-country travel

Cache Creek Lakes
Collie Lake (non-system trail)
Cougar Point
Jim Moore Place
Langer, Island and Ruffneck lakes (cross-country to Ruffneck Lake)
Marble Creek down to site of Belleco
Marsh Creek to Big Hole
Pioneer Creek to Tango Creek
Soldier Lakes
Vanity Lakes (non-system trail)

HIKES WITH CROSS-COUNTRY TRAVEL

Bernard Lake
Boston Mountain Lake
Buck, Doe, Fawn, Echo, Twin Cove and Turquoise Lakes
Finger Lakes
Honeymoon Lake
Lake Creek Lakes (Middle Fork Peak)
Lost Lake
Mount Mills and Hasbrouck lakes
Mystery Lake
Ruffneck Lake

Boyle children on skis.

Upper Cache Creek Lakes
Upper Vanity Lakes

EXPERT ABILITY

Because of route-finding problems, treacherous footing, dangerous fords, high summer temperatures or lack of water

Bernard Lake
Big Baldy Ridge (no water)
Buck, Doe, Fawn, Echo, Twin Cove and Turquoise Lakes
Buckskin Bill's Museum
Dome Mountain to Goat Lake
East Fork Mayfield Creek
Fish Lake (Loon Creek)- unsigned, trail has disappeared
Garden Creek – finding the new beginning, the ford and trail beyond it challenging
Lake Creek Lakes (Middle Fork Peak)
Marble Creek (many fords of creek, new beginning of trail at upper end))
Missouri Ridge
Mystery Lake
Sagebrush Lookout (scarce water, and springs have rattlesnakes))
Showerbath Hot Springs – water often high in Warm Springs Creek
The Monument (10 fords of creek)
Wilson Creek from Hoodoo Meadows- viewpoint to end of trail; at hot spring-trailhead hard to find, access road difficult

DANGEROUS OR IMPASSABLE AT HIGH WATER

Bear Valley Creek
Big Creek Trail: Cabin Creek to Big Creek Bridge
Buckskin Bill's
Camas Creek
Clear Creek
Dagger Falls to Marsh Creek
East Fork Mayfield Creek
Garden Creek
Horse Creek to Cayuse Creek
Loon Creek to Horseshoe Lake
Marble Creek
Middle Fork Trail: Big Creek to Flying B, Flying B to Loon Creek, Boundary Creek to Artillery Creek, Marsh Creek to Dagger Falls
Rapid River
Selway River
South Fork of Salmon River
The Monument

LOOP TRIPS

There are very few possibilities. Most long trips must either be through trips with a car shuttle, which is sometimes impractical because of driving distance, or trips that return the same way. Some airstrips, such as Chamberlain and Cold Meadows, give opportunities for loop trips. Loop trips from airstrips along the Middle Fork can be made but have elevation gains of up to 5,000 feet in 8 or 10 miles to get out of the canyon.

OPENING DATES

MAY (BUT NOT JUNE BECAUSE OF HIGH WATER):
Big Creek and Middle Fork trails by air only
Camas Creek
Lower Garden Creek
Lower Clear Creek
Salmon River Trail at Corn Creek

OPEN JUNE 1:
Jim Moore Place

OPEN JULY 1:
Bernard Lake
Buckskin Bill's
Cayuse Creek
Marsh Creek to Big Hole

Mountain Meadow and Camptender Trail
Roosevelt Lake
South Fork Salmon River
Sulphur Creek

OPEN AUGUST 1 OR LATER:
The Monument
Grouse Lake
Showerbath Hot Springs
Cache Creek Lakes
Swet Lake Pond and Swet Lake
Rock Lakes
Waugh Mountain and Lake
Sleeping Deer Lookout
Lake Creek Lakes from Middle Fork Peak
W. Fork Camas Creek Lakes
Bear Point and Sheep Hill
Salmon Mountain Lookout
(Trails not mentioned usually open about the middle of July.)

ACCESS ROADS OPENING DATES:

May 15: Meyers Cove

June 1: Nez Perce Pass, Whitewater Ranch, Morgan Creek Summit

June 15: Boundary Creek, Hettinger Ranch, Knapp/Asher Creek

July 1: Snowshoe Cabin, Loon Creek, Reynolds Lake, Nez Perce Trail Road to 14-Mile Tree, Monumental Summit, Profile Gap, Vanity Summit, Horse Creek Hot Springs, Mackay Bar

July 15: Crags Campground, Middle Fork Peak, Josephus Lake, Nez Perce Trail Road to Kim Creek Saddle, Mosquito Ridge, Beaver Creek - Loon Creek, Lookout Mountain Ridge, Indian Springs

July 30: Nez Perce Trail Road to Dry Saddle and Salmon Mountain, Sleeping Deer Road

ACCESS ROADS CLOSING DATES:

October 1: Dry Saddle and Salmon Mountain, Sleeping Deer Road beyond Twin Peaks

October 15: Boundary Creek, Snowshoe Cabin, 14-mile Tree, Beaver Creek - Loon Creek, Middle Fork Peak, Crags Campground, Indian Springs

November 1: Kim Creek Saddle, Loon Creek, Hettinger Ranch, Lookout Mountain Ridge, Vanity Summit, Horse Creek Hot Springs.

November 15: Monumental Summit, Profile Gap, Mackay Bar

December 1: Whitewater Ranch, Nez Perce Pass, Meyers Cove

ROAD ROUGHNESS

HIGH-CLEARANCE ROADS:

Roads suitable only for high-wheelbase vehicles, but four-wheel drive not needed;

primitive surfaces, but have culverts and bridges over major creeks. (The Forest Service calls these roads "high clearance.")

Big Mallard Creek (Whitewater Ranch)
Burntlog
Crags Campground: 4-wheel drive for last 3 miles
Gattin Ranch
Hettinger Ranch
Josephus Lake: beyond Vanity Summit
Little West Fork Morgan Creek
Lookout Mountain Ridge
Mackay Bar (recommended four-wheel drive low last 5 miles)
Monumental Summit
Nez Perce Trail Road between Salmon Mountain and 14-Mile Tree
Profile Gap (sedans might make it)
Rapid River
Sleeping Deer : 4 wheel drive may be needed
Smith Creek Cutoff : mud holes require 4-wheel drive

ROADS SUITABLE ONLY FOR FOUR-WHEEL DRIVE

Artillery Dome
Beaver Creek - Loon Creek
Hoodoo Meadows
Indian Springs
Middle Fork Peak
Parker Mountain (off the Sleeping Deer Road)
Reynolds Lake
Seafoam Creek to the lakes (walking recommended)
Snowshoe Cabin site
Yellowjacket Lake

Roads not listed are suitable for passenger cars with standard shifts but might have occasional rocks, ruts, potholes, mud holes, or downed trees (carry a saw) and can be very slippery in wet weather.

HIKE DESCRIPTIONS CONTAINING HISTORICAL INFORMATION

BEAR VALLEY: Bear Valley Creek
BIG CREEK MINES: Mosquito Ridge
BIG CREEK RANCHES: sections of the Big Creek Trail
BITTERROOT VALLEY: Horse Creek Trail
CHAMBERLAIN BASIN: Chamberlain Trail: Ramey Ridge to Chamberlain
COBALT AND LEESBURG: Clear Creek Trail
CUSTER AND BONANZA: Crimson Lake
DEADWOOD: Sulphur Creek
DIXIE: Buckskin Bill's
ELK CITY: Boston Mountain

FORNEY AND YELLOWJACKET: Lake Creek Lakes from Middle Fork Peak
LOON CREEK AND OROGRANDE: Loon Creek Hot Springs, Pinyon Lake
MAGRUDER MURDER: Salmon Mountain
MEYERS COVE: Camas Creek
MIDDLE FORK RANCHES AND BOATING: sections of the Middle Fork Trail
MONUMENTAL CREEK RANCHES: The Monument
NEZ PERCE TRAIL: Divide Trail
PARKER TRAIL: Base Camp to Swet Lake Pond
PISTOL CREEK MINES: Big Baldy Ridge Trail
SALMON RIVER BOATING AND SETTLERS: Salmon River Trail to Lantz Bar, Buckskin Bill's, Salmon River Trail: Whitewater Ranch to Jim Moore Place
SEAFOAM: Langer, Island and Ruffneck lakes; Soldier Lakes
SHEEPEATER WAR: Indians of Central Idaho in the Introduction
SHOUP: Salmon River Trail to Lantz Bar
THREE BLAZE TRAIL: Fish Lake from Flossie Lake
THUNDER MOUNTAIN: Lookout Mountain Ridge
WARRENS AND SOUTH FORK RANCHES: South Fork Salmon River Trail
YELLOW PINE, STIBNITE AND ROOSEVELT: Roosevelt Lake

SOURCES OF MORE INFORMATION

BITTERROOT NATIONAL FOREST
1801 N. 1st St.
Hamilton, MT 59840
406-363-7100

WEST FORK RANGER DISTRICT
6735 West Fork Road
Darby, MT 59829
406-821-3269

NEZ PERCE-CLEARWATER NATIONAL FOREST
903 3rd. St.
Kamiah, Id. 83526
208-935-2513

RED RIVER RANGER DISTRICT (ELK CITY RANGER STATION)
200 American River Road
Elk City, ID 83525
208-842-2245

PAYETTE NATIONAL FOREST
500 N. Mission St.
McCall, ID 83638
208-634-0700

KRASSEL RANGER DISTRICT

500 N. Mission St.
McCall, ID 83638
208-634-0600

SALMON-CHALLIS NATIONAL FOREST
50 Highway 93 South
Salmon, ID 83467
208-756-5000

MIDDLE FORK RANGER DISTRICT
311 North Highway 75
Challis, ID 83226
208-879-4101

CHALLIS-YANKEE FORK RANGER DISTRICT
311 N Highway 75
Challis, ID 83226
208-879-4100

NORTH FORK RANGER DISTRICT
11 Casey Road
North Fork, ID 83466
208-865-2700

IDAHO DEPARTMENT OF AERONAUTICS
IDAHO TRANSPORTATION DEPARTMENT
3483 Rickenbacker St.
Boise, ID 83705
208-334-8775

IDAHO DEPARTMENT OF FISH AND GAME
600 South Walnut
Boise, ID 83702
208-334-3700

IDAHO HISTORICAL SOCIETY
610 Julia Davis Drive
Boise, ID 83702
208-334-2682

U.S. GEOLOGICAL SURVEY
www..usgs.gov (for maps)

U.S. FOREST SERVICE
www.fs.fed.us under "forests by name" and Region 4 for Payette and Salmon-Challis Forests; Region 1 for Bitterroot and Nez Perce-Clearwater

SELWAY– BITTERROOT- FRANK CHURCH FOUNDATION

www.selwaybitterroot.org
P.O. Box 1886
Boise, ID 83701
208-871-1906

NATIONAL WEATHER SERVICE
www noaa.gov
Idaho office: 3905 Vista
Boise, ID 83705
208-334-9860

Leave No Trace Inc.
www.lnt.org

SUGGESTED READING

Akenson, Jim and Holly. *7003 Days in the Frank Church Wilderness*. Caldwell, Idaho, Caxton Press 2006

Bailey, Robert G. *River of No Return*. Lewiston, Idaho: Bailey-Blake Printing Co., 1935.

Beatty, Jeanne Kellar. *Lookout Wife*. New York: Random House, 1953.

Brown, William Carey. *The Sheepeater Indian Campaign, 1879*. Boise: Idaho Historical Society, 1972.

Carrey, Johnny and Conley, Cort. *River of No Return*. Cambridge, Idaho: Backeddy Books, 1978.

Carrey, Johnny and Conley, Cort. *The Middle Fork: A Guide, third edition*. Cambridge, Idaho. Backeddy Books. 1992.

Cox, Chana B. *A River Went Out of Eden*. Lagunitas, California, Lexikos 1992.

Elsensohn, Sister M. Alfreda. *Pioneer Days in Idaho County, Vol. 1*. Caldwell, Idaho.: Caxton Printers, 1947.

Gibbs, Rafe. *Beckoning the Bold*. Moscow, Idaho: The University Press of Idaho, 1976.

Holm, Richard. *Bound For the Backcountry: A History of Idaho's Remote Airstrips*. McCall, Idaho: Cold Mountain Press 2012

Jordan, Grace. *The King's Pines of Idaho*. Portland, Oregon: Metropolitan Press, 1961.

Josephy, Alvin. *The Nez Perce Indians and the Opening of the Northwest*. Lincoln, Nebraska and London: University of Nebraska Press, 1965.

Minskoff, G. Wayne. *Cabin Creek Chronicle*. Pocatello, Idaho. Streamside Scribe Press, 2019.

Parke, Adelia Routson. *Memoirs of an Old Timer*. Weiser, Idaho: Signal - American Printers, 1955.

Parker, Aaron; Shearer, George; Brown, Col. W.C., and Carrey, John. *Sheepeater Indian Campaign (Chamberlain Basin Country)*. Grangeville, Idaho: Idaho Country Free Press, 1968.

Parker, The Rev. Samuel. *Parker's Exploring Tour Beyond the Rocky Mountains*.

Minneapolis: Ross & Haines, 1967, reprinted from the 1838 edition.

Peek, Pat Cary. *One Winter in the Wilderness*. Moscow, Idaho: University of Idaho Press 1998

Peek, Pat Cary. *Cougar Dave, Mountain Man of Idaho*. Moscow, Idaho. Ninebark Publications 2004

Peterson, Harold. *The Last of the Mountain Men*. Cambridge, Idaho: Backeddy Books, (1983 (reprint of 1969 book).

Preston, Peter. *An Outline of the Cultural History of the Frank Church Wilderness Administered By the Payette National Forest*. Ogden, Utah: USDA Forest Service, Intermountain Region, 2001.

Ross, Alexander. *The Fur Hunters of the Far West*. Kenneth A. Spaulding, ed., Norman, Oklahoma: University of Oklahoma Press, 1956.

Shoup, George. *A History of Lemhi County*. Boise, ID: Idaho State Library, 1969.

Tims, Doug. *Merciless Eden: A River of No Return Wilderness Homestead*. Boise, ID Ferry Media 2013.

Wells, Merle. *Gold Camps and Silver Cities*. Moscow, Idaho: Idaho Bureau of Mines and Geology, Bulletin 22, Second Edition, 1983.

Wells, Merle et al. *Idaho, An Illustrated History*. Boise, Idaho: Idaho Historical Society, 1976.

Wisner, Frances Zaunmiller. *My Mountains: Where the River Still Runs Downhill*. Grangeville, Idaho: Idaho County Free Press, 1987.

Yarber, Esther. *Land of the Yankee Fork*. Denver, Colorado: Sage Books, 1963.

Yarber, Esther and McGown, Edna. *Stanley - Sawtooth Country*. Salt Lake City, Utah: Publishers Press, 1976.

ACKNOWLEDGEMENTS

I would like to thank all those who helped me with all three editions of this book, especially my youngest son, Stuart. He was was a companion on more than half the hikes. In addition, my oldest son, Doug, who together with Stuart endured the 15-day Big Creek - Middle Fork hike at high water, also, my husband, Wayne, who accompanied me on several of the hikes I added to the second edition. I would also like to thank my other children, Leslie, Neal and Hilary, who accompanied me on some of the original hikes as well as the many friends who either hiked with me or generously provided lodging or transportation.

Rangers of the Bitterroot, Salmon-Challis, Nez Perce-Clearwater and Payette forests provided trail information and edited the completed hike descriptions for the first two editions. Some of the people who provided information for the various editions were Laurie Matthews, Jim Upchurch, Ken Wotring, George Matejko, Nick Hazelbaker, Laurie Doman, Cindy Haggas, Leonard Lake, Josh Page, Kathy Seaberg, Linda Pterian, Nancy Russell, Larry Kingsbury Clem Pope, Geoff Fast, and Joshua Simpson. In addition, I would like to thank the late Lafe Cox for providing information no one else had. I especially want to thank the family of the late Bethine Church for her writing and updating a foreword and for the photo of her husband; Jerry Painter for maps; Matt TeNgaio for book design and layout; Ryan Magryta for fulfilling book orders and the USDA Forest service for the following photos: Boyle Children on skis, the CCC transplanting beaver, horses carrying parts for a lookout, and the Yellowjacket Hotel. I would especially like to thank Sally Ferguson, Executive director of the Selway-Bitterroot – Frank Church Foundation, for writing a special foreword for this edition.

ABOUT THE AUTHOR

Margaret Fuller was born and raised in Palo Alto, California. While growing up, she hiked in the Tahoe, Muir Trail and Mount Lassen areas. In 1956, she received her B.A. in biology from Stanford University, where she was active in the Alpine Club. She has lived in Idaho since 1957, in Boise and Caldwell first and in Weiser since 1985.

Margaret and her husband, Wayne, a retired district judge, have five grown children and seven grandchildren. She has written four other hiking guidebooks, three books of natural history, and a book on the history of Idaho ski areas, present and historical. The hiking guidebooks are Trails of the Sawtooth and Boulder-White Cloud Mountains (now in its 6th edition); Trails of Western Idaho; The Weiser River Trail: Idaho's Longest Rail Trail and with co-author Jerry Painter, Trails of Eastern Idaho. The natural history books are Mountains: A Natural History and Hiking Guide; Forest Fires, An Introduction to Wildland Fire Behavior, Management, Firefighting, and Prevention; and with co-author Betty Derig, Wild Berries of the West. The history book is Ski the Great Potato: Idaho Ski Areas, Past and Present, written with co-authors Jerry Painter

Margaret Fuller with arrowleaf balsamroot behind her house in Weiser

and her son, Doug Fuller. In her research for the hiking guidebooks she has hiked more than 6,000 miles on Idaho trails.

In 1982, she received the Writer of the Year Award from the Idaho Writers League. In 1990, the Idaho Centennial Commission designated her first three trail guides as Centennial books. In 1991 she received the Achievement Award from the Idaho Trails Council. In 1992, Forest Fires won first place in the Northwest Outdoor Writers Association annual contest, and Library Journal mentioned it as "one of the best sci-tech books of 1991." In 1997, she was elected to membership in the Society of Woman Geographers, an international organization honoring women who have traveled widely, engaged in research in a field related to geography, and produced or published in permanent form a record of their work. In 1998, the Silver Sage Girl Scout Council gave her the Woman of Today and Tomorrow award for the outdoors. In 2010 she received the Pat and Keith Axline Awards for environmental Activism from the Idaho Conservation League. In 2012 Backpacker Magazine honored her as one if its heroes. In 2014 Ski the Great Potato received the Skade Award from the International Skiing History Association.

Margaret has taught backpacking and mountain ecology in workshops and community education courses and given more than 250 slide and PowerPoint shows about Idaho mountains to community, church and school groups.